INSTRUMENTATION

Stuart E. Smith

STUDY GUIDE SERIES for EASA examinations

British Library Cataloguing in Publication Data
A catalogue record for this book is pending from the British Library

First published in the United Kingdom by Cranfield Aviation Training School Limited. 2002

Further volumes in this series are:

Aircraft General Knowledge: Airframes / Systems / Powerplant / Electrics / Emergency Equipment
Aviation Law & Air Traffic Procedures
Flight Planning & Monitoring
General Navigation
Human Performance & Limitations
Mass & Balance
Meteorology
Operational Procedures
Performance
Principles of Flight
Radio Navigation
VFR & IFR Communications

Series editor: Dr. Stuart E. Smith

CRANFIELD AVIATION TRAINING SCHOOL LTD. PART FCL 1 FTO N° 276
CATS INNOVATION CENTRE, LUTON, Bedfordshire LU2 8DL U.K. **www.catsaviation.com**

Subject	022 - AIRCRAFT GENERAL KNOWLEDGE – INSTRUMENTATION	*Aeroplane*		*Helicopter*			*IR*
Syllabus reference	**Syllabus details and Learning Objectives**	ATPL	CPL	ATPL/IR	ATPL	CPL	
022 00 00 00	**AIRCRAFT GENERAL KNOWLEDGE – INSTRUMENTATION**						
022 01 00 00	**SENSORS AND INSTRUMENTS**						
022 01 01 00	**Characteristics and General Definitions, Ergonomy, Signal transmission and Indicators.**						
Statement	*In these Learning Objectives an instrument (or instrument system) is considered to consist of the following composing parts: sensor, processor and indicator/actuator. The composing parts are not necesssarily in one housing/casing!*						
	Except where specified, the content of this topic refers to all aircraft systems and not only to the engine. For example, pressure gauges must be described not only for the engine oil system but also for other aircraft systems such as the IDG, the hydraulic system, the pneumatic system including the flight instruments.						
022 01 01 01	Characteristics and General Definitions						
LO	measuring range. sensitivity/resolution. accuracy: relative- and absolute error, systematic- and random error, tolerance. reliability: Failure rate, MTBF, MTBO. Instrument error.						
022 01 01 02	Ergonomy						
LO	Location: • Basic-6/Basic-T, instrument panels. • Avionics bay (E&E bay). Readability: • Eye reference point, parralax, analogue vs digital indicators, circular vs straight scales, linear vs logarithmic scales. Inside-out/outside-in presentation. Coloured arcs: • Green: normal operating (range). • Yellow/amber: caution (range). • Red: (warning). Colour standardisation: • white: status. • Blue: temporary situation. • green: normal, safe. • yellow/amber: caution. • Red: warning. JAR colour code rules JAR-25.						
022 01 01 03	Signal transmission						
LO	Mechanical, pneumatical, hydraulical. Electr(on)ical: • Torque synchro system, synchro-servo system. Digital: • ARINC-429, ARINC-629.						
022 01 01 04	Indicators						
LO	Mechanical: • Gears, levers, rods, axes, pointers etc. Electrical: • Moving coil meter, Ratiometer, Synchro's, Servo driven indicators. Electronical: • 7-segment display, 5x7 display, CRT, LCD.						
022 01 02 00	**Pressure measurement**						
022 01 02 01	Different types, design, operation, characteristics, accuracy						

Subject	022 - AIRCRAFT GENERAL KNOWLEDGE – INSTRUMENTATION	*Aeroplane*		*Helicopter*			*IR*
Syllabus reference	**Syllabus details and Learning Objectives**	ATPL	CPL	ATPL/IR	ATPL	CPL	
LO	General (definition, purpose & application) • P = F/A. • Units: inches Mercury (in or "Hg), hecto Pascal (hPa), pounds per square inch (psi), bar, units. • Interrelation between units. • Aircraft (system) and Engine condition- and performance monitoring and control. • Temperature compensation. • Absolute pressure sensor (aneroid), differential pressure sensor. • Low, medium and/or high pressures. • Aircraft (system) pressures: pitot, static, cabin, bleed-air, anti-ice, hydraulic and instrument air. • Engine pressures: MAP, EPR, oil and fuel. Sensors (construction, operating principle, characteristics & error behavior): • Diaphragm, Capsule: deflection, corrugations, stack, elasticity (hysteresis and lag). • Bellows: deflection. • Bourdon tube: deflection. • Quartz crystal: change in electrical resistance (piezo-resistive).	x	x	x	x	x	
022 01 02 02	Manifold Absolute Pressure (MAP)						
LO	General (definition, purpose & application): • Manifold absolute pressure is the absolute pressure in the inlet manifold of a piston engine. • Measure MAP to monitor engine performance. • State MAP is an absolute pressure measurement. Design (construction, operation & characteristics): • MAP supplied capsule or belows that measures against aneroid, ventilated instrument casing, mechanical processing, mechanical indication. Indication & Control: • Mechanicallly driven analogue display calibrated in inches Mercury ("Hg). Error behavior & Cross checks: • Shows QFE when on ground and engines out. • Relation between MAP and engine power: fuel flow and rpm. • Relation between MAP and altitude. • Relation between MAP and turbo-boosted piston engines.						
022 01 02 03	Engine Pressure Ratio (EPR)						

Subject	022 - AIRCRAFT GENERAL KNOWLEDGE – INSTRUMENTATION	*Aeroplane*		*Helicopter*			*IR*
Syllabus reference	Syllabus details and Learning Objectives	ATPL	CPL	ATPL/IR	ATPL	CPL	
LO	General (definition, purpose & application): • Engine Pressure Ratio (EPR) is the ratio between the outlet pressure and the inlet pressure of a jet-engine. • Distinct between the EPR of a fan-jet and the EPR of a straight jet. • Measure EPR for engine performance monitoring and engine control. • Applied in aeroplanes with a gasturbine engine that is EPR controlled. Design (construction, operation & characteristics): • The engine outlet pressure is admitted to a differential pressure sensor which is surrounded by engine inlet pressure. The output of the differential pressure sensor is divided by the output of an absolute pressure sensor that measures engine outlet pressure: (Pt7 – Pt2)/Pt2. • State engine inlet pressure can be measured at the compressor inlet or by the Pitot tube. • State engine outlet pressure can be measured halfway the turbine section, behind the turbine section or behind the fan. • State construction with capsules and (electro)mechanical processor. • State construction with solid state sensors and digital processor (FADEC). • Moving coil meter, servo-driven indicator or electronic display. Indication & Control: • Digital and/or analogue display calibrated in units starting at '1'. • Mention the use of the adjustable EPR setting pointer. Error behavior & Cross checks: • Shows '1' when engine is off.						
022 01 02 04	Oil pressure						
LO	General (definition, purpose & application): • Measure oil pressure for engine condition monitoring. Design (construction, operation & characteristics): • State construction with bourdon tube and (electro)mechanical processor. • State construction with solid state sensor and digital processor (FADEC). • State construction with pressure switch (diaphragm operated electric contact). • Moving coil meter, servo-driven indicator or electronic display. Indication & Control: • Digital and/or analogue display calibrated in psi. • Electronic engine display system. • Low oil pressure alert. Error behavior & Cross checks: • Low oil pressure may be caused by low oil quantity, failure of oil pump or oil leak. • Low oil pressure may cause damage to engine. • During engine start increasing oil pressure has to be monitored.						
022 01 02 05	Fuel pressure						

Subject	022 - AIRCRAFT GENERAL KNOWLEDGE – INSTRUMENTATION	*Aeroplane*		*Helicopter*			*IR*
Syllabus reference	Syllabus details and Learning Objectives	ATPL	CPL	ATPL/IR	ATPL	CPL	
LO	General (definition, purpose & application): • Measure fuel pressure to monitor fuel pump. Design (construction, operation & characteristics): • State construction with bourdon tube and (electro)mechanical processor. • State construction with solid state sensor and digital processor (FADEC). • Moving coil meter, servo-driven indicator or electronic display • State construction with pressure switch (diaphragm operated electric contact). Indication & Control: • (Electro)mechanicallly driven, analogue pointer that shows engine fuel pressure on a vertical or circular scale with green, yellow and red band and graduated in psi. • Electronic engine display system. • Low fuel pressure alert. Error behavior & Cross checks: • Low fuel pressure may be caused by low fuel quantity, failure of fuel pump failure or fuel leak. • Low fuel pressure may cause engine flame out.						
022 01 03 00	**Temperature measurement**						
022 01 03 01	Different types, design, operation, characteristics, accuracy	x	x	x	x	x	
LO	General (definition, purpose & application): • Temperature change causes alteration of energy state. • Units: Degrees Celsius, degrees Fahrenheit, Kelvin and units. • Interrelation between units. • Aircraft (system) and Engine condition- and performance monitoring and control. • Aircraft (system) temperatures: compartment, component, OAT, SAT, TAT and tank. • Engine temperatures: CHT, Carburetor, EGT, ITT, TIT, TGT, fuel and oil. Sensors (construction, operating principle, characteristics & error behavior): • Vapor-pressure thermometer: relation between temperature and pressure for a fixed Volume. • Bi-metallic thermometer: expansion/contraction, spiral wound or contact. • Thermistor/Semiconductor: change of electrical resistance (NTC/PTC). • Thermocouple: thermo-electric effect (Seebeck effect) causes a potential difference (voltage), cold junction compensation. • Infrared sensor: heat radiation.						
022 01 03 02	Cylinder Head Temperature (CHT)	x	x	x	x	x	
LO	General (definition, purpose & application): • Cylinder head temperature is the temperature of the cylinder head of a piston engine. • Measure and show the CHT for engine condition monitoring. • Application in air-cooled piston-engine driven aircraft. • Usually measured at one (hottest) cylinder: cylinder that receives the least cooling. Design (construction, operation & characteristics): • Thermocouple sensor on hottest cylinder. • Electrical processing. • Moving coil meter type indicator. Indication & Control: • (Electro)mechanicallly driven, analogue pointer that shows CHT along scale graduated in degrees C or F. Error behavior & Cross checks: • Do not use engine power when CHT is too low. • Too high CHT may be an indication of engine cooling problems. • Too high CHT may cause mechanical damage to engine. • Relation between power and CHT.						

Subject	022 - AIRCRAFT GENERAL KNOWLEDGE – INSTRUMENTATION	*Aeroplane*		*Helicopter*			*IR*
Syllabus reference	**Syllabus details and Learning Objectives**	ATPL	CPL	ATPL/IR	ATPL	CPL	
022 01 03 03	Exhaust Gas Temperature (EGT) piston engine						
LO	General (definition, purpose & application): • EGT is the temperature of the gases that leave the exhaust of a piston or gasturbine engine. • Measure and show the EGT for engine condition monitoring. • To allow fuel/air mixture control in order to safe fuel flow. • Application in piston engine driven aircraft. Design (construction, operation & characteristics): • Thermocouple in exhaust. • Electrical processing. • Moving coil meter type indicator. Indication & Control: • (Electro)mechanicallly driven, analogue pointer that shows EGT on scale graduated in markings with a maximum EGT marking in the form of an asterisk. • Control via the mixture lever. Error behavior & Cross checks: • State the relation between fuel/air mixture and EGT. • State the relation between power and EGT						
022 01 03 04	Carburetor temperature						
LO	General (definition, purpose & application): • Carburetor temperature is the temperature of the carburetor of a piston engine. • Measure and show whether the carburetor tenmperature is in the icing range or not. • To allow the pilot to select the carburetor heating on when the carburetor temperature is in the icing range. • Application in piston engine driven aircraft with a carburetor. Design (construction, operation & characteristics): • Thermistor on carberetor. • Electrical processing. • Moving coil meter type indicator. Indication & Control: • Analogue display calibrated in degrees C or F. • Control via carburetor heating switch/lever. Error behavior & Cross checks: • State the consequence of carburetor ice.						
022 01 03 05	Gas temperatures (EGT, ITT, TIT and TGT) gasturbine engine						

Subject	022 - AIRCRAFT GENERAL KNOWLEDGE – INSTRUMENTATION	*Aeroplane*		*Helicopter*			*IR*
Syllabus reference	**Syllabus details and Learning Objectives**	ATPL	CPL	ATPL/IR	ATPL	CPL	
LO	General (definition, purpose & application): • EGT is the exhaust gas temperature: the temperature of the gases at the exhaust of piston and gasturbine engine. • ITT is the inter-turbine temperature: the temperature of the gases between the HP and LP turbine. • TIT is the turbine inlet temperature: the temperature of the gases that enter the turbine. • TGT is the total gas temperature: the total temperature of the gases that leave the engine. • EGT, ITT, TIT or TGT is a measure for engine condition monitoring and control. Design (construction, operation & characteristics): • Ring of parallel thermocouples, electr(on)ical processing, moving coil meter or servo driven indicator. • Infrared sensor, digital processing and electronic display. Indication & Control: • Digital and/or analogue display with scale calibrated in degrees Celsius. • Maximum EGT pointer (trailing pointer). • Overheat alert. Error behavior & Cross checks: • A too high EGT may cause mechanical damage to the engine . • State the relation between egine power and EGT. • State some engines are limited by EGT pressure may cause damage to engine.						
022 01 03 06	Fuel temperature						
LO	Definition, purpose & application: • Temperature of fuel in the tank and/or in the fuel line. • To allow detection of possible icing. • Wing type fuel tanks of aeroplanes that fly in the upper parts of the troposphere. Design, construction, operation, characteristics: • Thermistors, electr(on)ical processing, moving coil meter, ratiometer or alert light. Indication, control: • Discrete or analogue display with scale graduated in degrees C or F. • Discrete low fuel temperature alert. Error behavior, accuracy, cross checks: • Low fuel temperature may cause any water to freeze which in turn may cause fuel starvation. • Prolonged flights at high altitudes may cause low fuel temperatures.						
022 01 03 07	Oil temperature						
LO	Definition, Purpose & Application: • Temperature of the oil in the oil tank. • Engine (oil system) condition monitoring. • All engine driven aircraft. Construction, operation, characteristics: • Thermistor, electr(on)ical processing and -indicator. • Bi-metallic switch, electrical processing, discrete alert. Indication & Control: • Analogue display calibrated in degrees C. • High oil temperature alert. Error behavior, accuracy & cross checks: • High oil temperature may be caused by failure of the oil cooling system. • Low oil temperature will decrease performance of oil cooling and lubrication system. • In many engine use is made of a fuel cooled oil cooler. Fuel is heated by cooling engine oil. A failure of the oil cooler affects the fuel heater.						

Subject	022 - AIRCRAFT GENERAL KNOWLEDGE – INSTRUMENTATION	*Aeroplane*		*Helicopter*			*IR*
Syllabus reference	Syllabus details and Learning Objectives	ATPL	CPL	ATPL/IR	ATPL	CPL	
022 01 04 00	**Quantity measurement**						
022 01 04 01	Different types, design, operation, characteristics, accuracy						
LO	General (Definition, Purpose & Application): • Quantity measurement based on measurement of level (height). • Level converted into volume units (small aeroplanes) or mass units (large aeroplanes). • Volume is height times surface area (V = h.A). • Mass is volume times density (m = ρ.V). • Units: Liter (l), Gallon (gal), kilogram (kg), pound (lb) and units. (quart, pint) • Interrelation between units. • Determination of operational status of aircraft. • Liquid level depends on temperature, aircraft attitude and on accelerations. • Aircraft system quantities: fuel (individual and total), hydraulic and water. • Engine system quantities: engine oil, IDG oil, water/methanol system. Sensors (Construction, operating principle, characteristics & error behavior): • Inspection window: visual. • D(r)ipstick: measurement of height/level with help of cohesion forces. • Float: float operated potentiometer or reed switches. • Capacitor: change of electrical capacity (C = □.A/d). • Ultrasonic probe: measurement of frequency.						
022 01 04 02	Fuel quantity indicating system	x	x	x	x	x	
LO	General (definition, purpose & application): • Fuel quantity is the amount of fuel in the tanks of the aircraft. • Fuel quantity for aircraft performance monitoring. • Since volume depends on temperature, mass is a better parameter for amount of energy. Design (construction, operation & characteristics): • D(r)ipsticks: Several sticks per tank, access, calibration in volume units, mass units or just units. • Float: One float per tank, electrical processing, moving coil meter/ratiometer. • Capacitors: Several capacitors per tank, reference capacitor, temperature compensation, densitometer, electronic processing, servo-driven indicator. • Ultrasonic probes: Several probes per tank, electronic processing, electronic indication. Indication & Control: • Digital and/or analogue display of individual and/or total fuel quantity calibrated in liters, gallons, pounds or kilograms. • Total fuel quantity is also transferred to the FMS. Error behavior & Cross checks: • Consequence of water in the tank. • Consequence of different fuel densities (stratification) + solution (mixers) • Effect of aircraft attitude changes + solution (baffle plates). • Effect of aircraft accelerations. • Initial fuel quantity minus FMS calculated fuel burn should reflect total fuel quantity.						
022 01 04 03	Engine oil quantity						

Subject	022 - AIRCRAFT GENERAL KNOWLEDGE – INSTRUMENTATION	*Aeroplane*		*Helicopter*			*IR*
Syllabus reference	**Syllabus details and Learning Objectives**	ATPL	CPL	ATPL/IR	ATPL	CPL	
LO	General (definition, purpose & application): • Measure oil quantity for engine condition monitoring. • Measure of oil cooling and lubrication system Design (construction, operation & characteristics): • Dipstick + visual inspection. • Float and reed switches and electr(on)ical processor and electr(on)ical indicator. Indication & Control: • Digital and/or analogue display calibrated in units, liters, gallons, quarts or pints. Error behavior & Cross checks: • Low oil quantity may cause engine cooling and lubrication problems and subsequent engine damage. • Low oil quantity may be caused by oil leak or high oil consumption of engine. • Oil quantity has to be checked before engine start.						
022 01 05 00	**Flow measurement**						
022 01 05 01	Different types, design, operation, characteristics, accuracy						
LO	General (definition, purpose & application): • a.k.a. consumption gauge. • Flow measurement based on differentiating a quantity over time. • Flow expressed in volume units (small aeroplanes) or mass units (large aeroplanes). • Units: liters per hour (l/h), gallons per hour (gal/h), kilograms per hour (kg/h) and pounds per hour (lb/h). • Interrelation between units. • Measurement of fuel flow per engine for engine condition and performance monitoring. • Calculation of total fuel used for aircraft performance calculation. Sensors (construction, operating principle, characteristics & error behavior): • Venturi: pressure differential (Bernoulli), volume flow measurement. • Dynamic vane: P = F/A, volume flow measurement. • Turbine: induction of EMF, volume flow measurement, with temperature compensation mass flow measurement. • Rotor torque: rotating impeller, measurement of angular momentum, mass flow measurement. • Stator torque: stationary impeller, measurement of angular momentum, mass flow measurement. • Motorless: measurement of angular momentum, mass flow measurement.						
022 01 05 02	Fuel flow	x	x	x	x	x	

Subject	022 - AIRCRAFT GENERAL KNOWLEDGE – INSTRUMENTATION	*Aeroplane*		*Helicopter*			*IR*
Syllabus reference	**Syllabus details and Learning Objectives**	ATPL	CPL	ATPL/IR	ATPL	CPL	
LO	Definition, Purpose & Application: • Definition: Fuel flow is change of fuel quantity over time . • Purpose: Measurement of fuel flow per engine for engine condition and performance monitoring. • Application: in piston- and gasturbine engines driven aircraft. Design (construction, operation, characteristics): • Volume units: o Venturi: mechanical processor- and indicator. o Dynamic vane: (electro)mechanical processor- and indicator. o Turbine: electrical processor- and indicator. • Mass units: o Rotor torque: electr(on)ical processor- and indicator. o Stator torque: electr(on)ical processor- and indicator. o Motorless: electr(on)ical processor and indicator. Indication & Control: • Digital and/or analogue display calibrated in fuel units per hour. Error behavior & Cross checks: • Fuel flow integrated over time results in fuel used. • Fuel used used in FMS to determine aircraft weight. • Cross check fuel flow with total fuel quantity and with FMS calculation.						
022 01 06 00	**Position measurement**						
022 01 06 01	Different types, design, operation, characteristics, accuracy						
	General (Definition, Purpose & Application): • Discrete position sensors and analogue position sensors. • Angular and linear displacement sensors • Units: degrees, millimeters or centimeters. • Measurement of position of aircraft- and engine systems for indication and control. • Aircraft and engine system position: doors, landing gear, flight controls, hydraulic and pneumatic valves, instrument, inlet guide vanes, thrust reverser. • Instrumentation: position of capsules, bellows, bordon tubes, shafts etc. • Effect of voltage, resistance, frequency, vibration, corrosion etc. Sensors (Construction, Operating principle, Characteristics & Error behavior): • Micro-switch: discrete position sensor; electric contact; fatique, corrosion, wear, arcing. • Proximity sensor: discrete position sensor; determination of impedance (Z). • Potentiometer: analogue position sensor for linear and angular displacements; changing electrical resistance, wear. • E-I pick-off: analogue position sensor for very small linear and angular displacements; inductive pick-off. • LVDT: analogue position sensor for small linear displacements; inductive pick-off. • RVDT: analogue position sensor for angular displacements; inductive pick-off. • Synchro: analogue position sensor for angular displacements; inductive pick-off.						
022 01 06 02	Discrete position sensors	x	x	x	x	x	

Subject	022 - AIRCRAFT GENERAL KNOWLEDGE – INSTRUMENTATION	*Aeroplane*		*Helicopter*			*IR*
Syllabus reference	**Syllabus details and Learning Objectives**	ATPL	CPL	ATPL/IR	ATPL	CPL	
LO	Definition, Purpose & Application: • A discrete position sensor is a sensor used to pick-up only one discrete postion of a component. • Indication and control. • Pushbuttons, rotary switches, limit switches etc. Design (construction, operation, characteristics): • Micro switch: electrical processing and indication. • Proximity sensor: electronic processing and indication. Indication & Control: • Alert light/message. Error behavior & Cross checks: • Wrong adjustment causes false alerts.						
022 01 06 03	Analogue position sensors						
LO	Definition, Purpose & Application: • An analogue sensor is a sensor used to pick up each position of a component ithin a given mesuring range. • Indication and control. • Measurement of position of: rotary selector knobs, mechanical pressure sensors, actuators, gyroscopes, flight control surfaces. Construction, Operation & Characteristics: • Potmeter, electrical processing and indication. • E-I, electr(on)ical processing • LVDT/RVDT, electr(on)ical processing, indication and control. • RVDT, electr(on)ical processing, indication and control. • Synchro, electrical processing, indication and control. Indication & Control: • Analoge display calibrated in degrees. • Control of instrument systems. Error behavior & Cross checks: • Wrong adjustment. • Cross checks with help of visual indicators.						
022 01 07 00	**Torque measurement**						
022 01 07 01	Different types, design, operation, characteristics, accuracy						
	General (Definition, Purpose & Application): • Define torque (T): two equal but opposite forces each acting on a different part of the same component. • A.k.a. twist or expressed as a forceless turning moment. • Units: Nm, foot-punds (ft lbs), braked mean effective pressure (psi), percentage of maximum torque (%). • To determine the output torque of a turboprop engine for indication and control. • Torque is a measure for engine power (P = T x rpm). • Too high torque causes engine and propeller damage. • Relation between torque, blade angle and rpm. • Engine torque: turboprops only Sensors (Construction, Operating principle, Characteristics & Error behavior): • Planetary gear system: measurement of oil pressure necessary to keep planetary gear system in position. • Electronic system: two inductive pick-offs measure twist in torsion shaft.						
022 01 07 02	Engine and or propellor torque system	x	x	x	x	x	

Subject	022 - AIRCRAFT GENERAL KNOWLEDGE – INSTRUMENTATION	*Aeroplane*		*Helicopter*			*IR*
Syllabus reference	**Syllabus details and Learning Objectives**	ATPL	CPL	ATPL/IR	ATPL	CPL	
LO	Definition, Purpose & Application: • Measure oil pressure for engine condition monitoring. Construction, operation & characteristics: • Planetary gear system, hydromechanical processor and indicator. • Two gear-wheels with inductive pick-ups, electronic processing and indication. Indication & Control: • Digital and/or analogue display calibrated in psi, Nm or %. Error behavior & Cross checks: • Consequences of oil leak						
022 01 08 00	**Angular speed measurement (Tachometer)**						
022 01 08 01	Different types, design, operation, characteristics, accuracy						
LO	General (Definition, Purpose & Application): • Measurement of angular shaft speed. • Units: revolutions per minute (rpm) for piston engines and percentage of maximum rated speed (%) for gasturbine engines. • Engine condition- and performance monitoring and control. Sensors (Construction, Operating principle, Characteristics & Error behavior): • Mechanical tachometers: o Centrifugal tachometer: springloaded fly-weights. o Eddy-current tachometer: induction of eddy currents set-up in a sprinloaded cup. • Electrical tachometer: o DC-tachometer: measurement of DC voltage. o AC-tachometer: measurement of induced single-phase AC voltage. o Rotary-current tachometer: frequency based measurement of induced three-phase AC voltage. • Electronic tachometer: o Tachoprobe: frequency based measurement of induced AC voltage.						
022 01 08 02	Tachometer piston engines	x	x	x	x	x	
LO	General (definition, purpose & application): • Tachometer must show the engine rpm. Operating principle & Construction: • Centrifugal tachometer, mechanical processing and indication, possible connection with hour meter • Eddy-current tachometer, mechanical processing and indication. • DC-tachometer, electrical processing and indication. • AC-tachometer, electrical processing and indication. Indication & Control: • Analog display calibrated in rpm. • Red arc: area in which continuous operation may cause vibration and must be avoided Error behavior & Cross checks: • Maximum cable length between sensor and processor 2 m. • Effect of electrical line resistance.						
022 01 08 03	Tachometer gasturbine engine	x	x	x	x	x	

Subject	**022 - AIRCRAFT GENERAL KNOWLEDGE – INSTRUMENTATION**	*Aeroplane*		*Helicopter*			*IR*
Syllabus reference	**Syllabus details and Learning Objectives**	ATPL	CPL	ATPL/IR	ATPL	CPL	
LO	General (definition, purpose & application): • Tachometers for gasturbine engines must be able to measure rotational speeds up to several ten-thousands rpm. • For each shaft there is one tachometer. Design (construction & operation) • Rotary-current tachometer, electrical processing and electromechanical indication with eddy-current head. • Tachoprobe, electronical processing and indication, frequency converter, DC amplifier, servo-driven indicator or eletronic display. Indication & Control: • Depending on type: digital- and analog display calibrated in % of the maximum rated rpm. • Indications in fan rpm, rotor rpm, propellor rpm or just n1, n2 and (sometimes) n3 • Trailing pointer which can be reset by crew. Error behavior & Cross checks: • Usually different shaft speeds measured, check for interrelation.						
022 01 08 04	Synchroscope						
LO	General (definition, purpose & application): • Sysnchroscopes are used to manually or automaticaly synchronise propellers. • Synchronised propellers produce less noise and vibration. • Applied in multi-engined propeller driven aeroplanes. General (construction & operation): • A rotary-current tachometer on each engine supplies its signals to synchroscope • Synchroscope consists of three-phase stator and three-phase rotor • When rotating stator field en rotor field have the same speed, rotor does not turn. • Rotor connects to indicator. Indication & Control: • Analogue pictorial display. • Possibility to automatically control synchronisation. Error behavior & Cross checks: • Use synchroscope in comparison with rpm indicators. • Nearly synchronised propellers will cause an audible beat frequency.						
022 01 09 00	**Vibration monitoring**	x	x	x	x	x	
022 01 09 01	Different types, design, operation, characteristics, accuracy						
LO	General (Definition, Purpose & Application): • Change in amplitude at a relative high frequency. • Vibration may cause mechanical damage to components. • Engine condition and trend monitoring. Sensors (Construction, Operating principle, Characteristics & Error behavior): • Inductive pick-off: EMF by induction, magnetic proof-mass suspended in coil. • Quartz crystal: F=m.a, generation of AC-voltage when subjected to vibration (piezo-electricity).						
022 01 09 02	Inductive pick-off	x	x	x	x	x	

Subject	022 - AIRCRAFT GENERAL KNOWLEDGE – INSTRUMENTATION	*Aeroplane*		*Helicopter*			*IR*
Syllabus reference	**Syllabus details and Learning Objectives**	ATPL	CPL	ATPL/IR	ATPL	CPL	
LO	General (definitions, purposes, applications) • To measure engine radial shaft vibration for engine condition and trend monitoring • Engine radial shaft vibration: Turbofan en turbojet engines • State that on turbofan/jet engines vibration sensors may be located on all shafts (N1, N2, etc) • State usually two perpendicular sensors per shaft • Continuous indication of vibration level of all engines • Vibrating frequency depends on rpm, • Calibration in amplitude, speed or in units • Procedure when too high vibration. • Vibration may be caused by mechanical damage or wear						
LO	Operating principle & Construction: • Inductive pick up: AC output, filtering, integration, amplification, electrical indication. • Quartz crystal: AC output, filtering, integration, amplification, electronic indication. Indication & Control: • Separate indicator or part of electronic engine display system. • Digital and/or analogue display calibrated in milli-inches, milli-inches per second (mils) or in units. • In case of too much vibration > alert. • Registartion in ACMS or FDR datalink Error behavior & Cross checks: • Reducing engine power usually helps to reduce the vibration level.						
022 01 10 00	**Time measurement**						
022 01 10 01	Different types, design, operation, characteristics, accuracy						
	General (definition, purpose & application): • Definition of time: ongoing process divided in units that allow counting • Purpose: to structure life, organise things • Application: worldwide, industryFlight deck: time: local, UTC, stopwatch, flight time, elapsed time, timed turns, engine operating hours. Sensors (Construction, Operating principle, Characeristics & Error behavior): • Wounded spiral spring that slowly unwinds in time. • DC supplied quartz crystal with internal battery that supplies AC pulses in time • Wounded spring tends to leave its strenght in time • wrong insertion of time.						
022 01 10 02	Clock	x	x	x	x	x	

Subject	022 - AIRCRAFT GENERAL KNOWLEDGE – INSTRUMENTATION	*Aeroplane*		*Helicopter*			*IR*
Syllabus reference	**Syllabus details and Learning Objectives**	ATPL	CPL	ATPL/IR	ATPL	CPL	
LO	Definition, Purpose & Application: • Show different times: UTC. Operating principle & Construction: • Spiral spring: mechanical processing and indication (gears, levers, pointers) • Quartz chrystal: electronic processing and indication (counter, amplifier, indication). Indication & Control: • Digital and/or analogue display calibrated in hours, minutes and (tenth of) seconds. • Winding knob. • Setting knobs. • FT, ET button. • Stopwatch/timer function: start-stop-reset. • Flight time based on airspeed or ground/flight switch. Error behavior & Cross checks: • Not wounded. • Internal back-up battery empty. • Crosscheck with FMS or GPS time. • Wrong insertion of time.						
022 01 10 03	Engine hour meter	x	x	x	x	x	
LO	Definition, Purpose & Application: • Instrument that counts engine operating time. • Used to administrate engine hours. • Applied in aircraft with piston engines. Operating principle & Construction: • Quartz crystal, electronic processing and indication (pulse counter). Indication & Control: • Separate or integrated in rpm indicator, digital display calbrated in hours and tenth of hours. • Controlled via oil pressure, rpm and sometimes via airspeed switch. Error behavior & Cross checks: • Cross check with time written down in logbook.						
022 02 00 00	**MEASUREMENT OF AIR DATA PARAMETERS**						
LO	Study the ICAO Standard Atmosphere with regard to relationship between altitude and pressure, temperature and density in the troposhere and in the stratosphere. Understand interrelation between pressure, temperature and density. Give the values for pressure, temperature and density at MSL in the ISA.						
022 02 01 00	**Pitot-static system**						
022 02 01 01	General: definitions, purpose, applications, operating principle	x	x	x	x	x	X
LO	Define total pressure (pitot pressure) and static pressure. A pitot-static system is a system that measures and supplies both total pressure and static pressure to the related aircraft instruments and -systems. The pitot-static system must measure the total pressure and the static pressure. State that in larger aeroplanes more than one pitot-static system is installed. Pitot-static system uses of a pitot tube to stop the airflow in order to measure total pressure and uses static sources to measure the pressure of the undisturbed airflow in order to measure static pressure.						
022 02 01 02	Design, different types, construction, operation	x	x	x	x	x	X

Subject	022 - AIRCRAFT GENERAL KNOWLEDGE – INSTRUMENTATION	*Aeroplane*		*Helicopter*			*IR*
Syllabus reference	**Syllabus details and Learning Objectives**	ATPL	CPL	ATPL/IR	ATPL	CPL	
	Pitot tube: • Outside boundary layer, head and mast, location on aircarft, opening parallel to airflow, stagnation wall, water drain, head & mast, electrical heating elements, low speed and high speed design, effect of heater and water drain on sensed pressure. Static source: • opening perpendicular to airflow, electrical heating elements, location on aircraft. Pitot/static probe (pressure head): • Combined pitot tube and static source(s), loaction on aircraft. Pipelines: • Water traps, static balancing. • State that in modern aircraft the pipelines are replaced by electrial wires because of the use of electronical pressure transducers with built-in fault correction and A/D conversion directly connected to the pitot and/or static sources. Pitot-static system small, unpressurised aeroplane: • Pitot tube, two interconnected static sources to compensate for side slip, pipelines, water traps, alternate static source and selector valve in cabin. Pitot-static system of a large, pressurised aeroplane: • Pitot tube or pitot/static probe, two interconnected static ports to compensate for side slip, pipelines, water trap.						
022 02 01 03	Indication & Control	x	x	x	x	x	X
LO	Pitot /static source heater on/off plus alert. Alternate static source selector valve (unpressurised aircraft).						
022 02 01 04	Error behavior, accuracy, cross-checks						
LO	State the effects of a malfunction of the pitot tube and/or static source heating elements. Cross check heater operation with standby magnetic compass reading or Amp-meter. State the effect of blocked pitot tubes and/or static ports. State the effect of a leakage of the pitot and/or static lines in both a pressurised and non-pressurised aircraft. Explain when the alternate static source is required. State that when alternate static source is used the sensed cabin presuure is usually lower than static pressure. Explain static source error (static pressure error) plus possible corrections (AFM). Mention parameters that affect static source error.						
022 02 02 00	**Air temperature measurement: Aeroplane**						
022 02 02 01	General: definitions, purpose, application.	x	x				
LO	State the different definitions and their relationship: OAT, TAT, SAT, Recovery factor, ram rise. State that air temperature is needed for aircraft and engine performance calculations, anti-ice control, calculation of TAS.						
022 02 02 02	Designs, different types, principle of operation	x	x				
LO	Small aeroplanes • OAT indicator: bi-metallic type sensor with mechanical processing and indication or thermistor type sensor with electrical processing and indication Large aeroplanes: • TAT probe: aspirated, non-aspirated, thermistor, heater, operation, ram rise, recovery factor, electronical processing in ADC, separate or integrated combined TAT/SAT indicator. Design: Sensor, processor, indicator.						
022 02 02 03	Display and control	x	x				

Subject	**022 - AIRCRAFT GENERAL KNOWLEDGE – INSTRUMENTATION**	*Aeroplane*		*Helicopter*			*IR*
Syllabus reference	**Syllabus details and Learning Objectives**	ATPL	CPL	ATPL/IR	ATPL	CPL	
LO	Separate OAT indicator: digital and/or analogue display calibrated in degrees C and/or F. Separate or integrated in EFIS, digital TAT/SAT dispaly calibrated in degrees C.						
022 02 02 04	Error behavior, accuracy & Cross checks						
LO	Mention possible countermeasures against influence of direct sunlight, M/airspeed, boundary layer, recovery factor. State accuracy of separate OAT indicator and of combined TAT/SAT indicator.						
022 02 03 00	**Air temperature measurement: Helicopter**			x	x	x	
022 02 03 01	General: definitions, purpose, applications & operating principle			x	x	x	
LO	State the different definitions and their relationship: OAT, TAT, SAT, Recovery factor, ram rise. State that air temperature is needed for helicopter and engine performance calculations, anti-ice control, calculation of TAS.						
LO	Understand that in addition to the normal outside air temperature gauge the latest helicopters have additional sensors for FADEC and Air Data Unit.			x	x	x	
022 02 03 02	Design: different types, construction & operation			x	x	x	
LO	Small helicopters • OAT indicator: bi-metallic type sensor with mechanical processing and indication or thermistor type sensor with electrical processing and indication Large helicopters: • TAT probe: aspirated, non-aspirated, thermistor, heater, operation, ram rise, recovery factor, electronical processing in ADC, separate or integrated combined TAT/SAT indicator. Design: Sensor, processor, indicator.						
022 02 03 03	Display and control						
LO	Separate OAT indicator: digital and/or analogue display calibrated in degrees C and/or F. Separate or integrated in EFIS, digital TAT/SAT dispaly calibrated in degrees C.						
022 02 03 04	Error behavior, accuracy, cross-checks						
LO	Mention possible countermeasures against influence of direct sunlight, M/airspeed, boundary layer, recovery factor. State accuracy of separate OAT indicator and of combined TAT/SAT indicator.						
022 02 04 00	**Angle of attack measurement**	x	x	x			
022 02 04 01	General: definitions, purpose, applications, principle of operation						
LO	Angle between undisturbed airflow and main wing chord. State purpose: indication and control Mention applications: ADS, SWS, GPWS.						
022 02 04 02	Designs: different types, construction & operation						
LO	Small aeroplanes: Whistle: system that responds to pressure difference between upper part and lower part of wing. Flapper switch: heated springloaded electric contact in leading edge of wing. Large aeroplanes: Vane: heated symmetrical triangular shaped vane that aligns itself with the airflow. null-seeking probe: double slotted probe with a differential pressure sensor and an electric motor.						
022 02 04 03	Display & control						
LO	Separate AoA indicator: analogue display calibrated in degrees. AoA indicator integrated in EFIS: digital and/or analogue display calibrated in degrees.						
022 02 04 04	Error behavior , accuracy, cross checks						
LO	Two installed systems allow for cross check. Understand relation between weight, speed and angle-of-attack						
022 02 05 00	**Pressure Altimeter**						

Subject	**022 - AIRCRAFT GENERAL KNOWLEDGE – INSTRUMENTATION**	*Aeroplane*		*Helicopter*			*IR*
Syllabus reference	**Syllabus details and Learning Objectives**	ATPL	CPL	ATPL/IR	ATPL	CPL	
022 02 05 01	General: definitions, purpose, applications, principle of operation	x	x	x	x	x	X
LO	State the definitions of the different barometric references: QNH, QFE and STD (1013.25 hPA), height, indicated altitude, true altitude, pressure altitude and density altitude. Principle of operation: pressure measurement acc ISA. Electric pick-off of pressure altitude for ATC-transponder (encoding altimeter).						
022 02 05 02	Designs: different types, construction, operation	x	x	x	x	x	X
LO	Sensitive pressure altimeter: • Stack of temperature compensated aneroid capsules, compensation for non-linear pressure-altitude relation, mechanical processing and indication, subscale + knob . Servo-driven altimeter: • Stack of temperature compensated aneroid apsules, compensation for non linearity, E-I pickoff, mechanical processing and indication, electric pick-off for ATC transponder and FDR, vibrator, subscale + knob.						
022 02 05 03	Display & control	x	x	x	x	x	X
LO	Separate altimeter, linear scale, analogue and digital presentation, pointer system, low altitude warning flag, vibrator failure flag, use of subscale + knob, location of subscale knob, range of subscale, calibration of subscale in in HG and/or hPa, calibration of altitude scale in ft.						
022 02 05 04	Error behavior, solutions, accuracy, cross checks	x	x	x	x	x	X
LO	Explain the instrument errors that affect the altimeter: • Mechanical friction, solution vibrator. • Lag in indication during rapid descents. • Decreasing sensitivity at increasing altitudes. List the atmospheric errors that affect the altimeter: • Deviations from ISA > P and T > P: subscale setting (procedures) and T: no compensation other than bij calculation > nav comp > or rule of thumb State the effects of errors of the pitot-static system that affect the altimeter during straight and level flight and during climb and descent. State advantages of servo-driven altimter over mechanical pressure altimeter State the tolerances at MSL of the different altimeters in use: 30,000 ft range: 60 ft at MSL, 50,000 ft range: 80 ft at MSL servo driven altimeters: 30 ft at MSL. State that in RVSM airspace pressure altimeters must have a smaller tolerance. Cross-check possibility with second altimeter, standby altimeter and radio altimeter.						
022 02 06 00	**Vertical Speed Indicator (VSI)**						
022 02 06 01	General: definitions, purpose, applications, principle of operation	x	x	x	x	x	X
LO	State the purpose of the VSI is to sense, process and indicate the aeroplane's vertical speed. The vertical speed is defined as the change in altitude per unit of time. The VSI measures the change in static pressure per unit of time according to ISA. Explain how VSI compensates for non-linear pressure-altitude relation in ISA.						
022 02 06 02	Design: different types, construction, operation	x	x	x	x	x	X
LO	Capsule-type VSI: Differential pressure capsule, temperature compensated orifice (calibrated leak), blade spring to allow logaritmic scale, adjuster screw. Capsule type Instantaneous VSI (IVSI) : Same as VSI plus springloaded pistion in cylinder acting as a vertical accelerometer.						
022 02 06 03	Indication and control						
LO	Separate analogue indicator, calibrated in feet per minute (ft/min or fpm), logarithmic scale, one pointer, zero when horizontal.						

Subject	022 - AIRCRAFT GENERAL KNOWLEDGE – INSTRUMENTATION	*Aeroplane*		*Helicopter*			*IR*
Syllabus reference	**Syllabus details and Learning Objectives**	ATPL	CPL	ATPL/IR	ATPL	CPL	
022 02 06 04	Error behavior, solutions, accuracy, cross checks						
LO	Explain the instrument errors that affect the VSI: • Slow response (time lag) of the VSI of up to several seconds. • State the purpose of the zero adjustment screw. List the atmospheric errors that affect the VSI. State the effects of errors of the pitot-static system that affect the VSI during straight and level flight and during climb and descent. State the maximum permissible tolerance of the VSI as ± 30 fpm for the first 500 fpm then 5% of indicated. Describe the behaviour of the IVSI during turns. State the effect of turbulence on the IVSI indication. Cross-check with second VSI, changing altitude on altimeter or on radio altimeter. State the generally accepted method and consequences of restoring blocked static ports by breaking the glass of the VSI in non-pressurised aircraft only.						
022 02 07 00	**Airspeed Indicator**						
022 02 07 01	General: definitions, purpose, application, principle of operation	x	x	x	x	x	X
LO	Define: Equivalent Air Speed (EAS), Indicated Air Speed (IAS) and Calibrated Air Speed (CAS). Compare values of IAS and CAS and required corrections between the speeds. Operating principle based on measurement of dynamic pressure (q) in the case of non-compressible airflows and impact pressure (q_C) in the case of compressible airflows based on difference between total pressure and static pressure (P_T - P_S). Airspeed indicator shows speed of aeroplane relative to the surrounding air for performance monitoring and control. Calibration in knots. Describe relationship between IAS and CAS, during climb and descent in the troposphere and in the stratosphere. Define v_{S0}, v_{S1}, v_{FE}, v_{NO}, v_{NE}, v_{LO}, v_{LE}, v_{YSE}, v_{MO} and M_{MO}.						
022 02 07 02	Design: different types, construction & operation.	x	x	x	x	x	X
LO	Distinguish between airspeed indicators for small aeroplanes and large aeroplanes. IAS meter: • Differential pressure capsule, blade spring, mechanical processing and indication. CAS meter: • Differential pressure capsule, blade spring, mechanical processing and indication. Maximum airspeed pointer: • Integral with airspeed indicator, aneroid capsule, mechanical processing and indication, barberpole.						
022 02 07 03	Indication & control	x	x	x	x	x	X
LO	Small aeroplanes: • Analogue circular linear or logarithmic scale calibrated in kts. • Explain the colour codings of the airspeed indicator. • Assign the following speeds to the colour codings: V_{SO}, V_{S1}, V_{FE}, V_{NO}, V_{NE}, v_{YSE}. Large aeroplanes: • Analogue circular linear or logarithmic scale calibrated in kts. • Maximum speed indicator (V_{MO}/M_{MO} pointer or barberpole). • Adjustable speed bugs. • Speed selector with indicator to allow the setting of a reference speed for indication and control.						
022 02 07 04	Error behavior, solutions, accuracy, cross-checks						

Subject	022 - AIRCRAFT GENERAL KNOWLEDGE – INSTRUMENTATION	*Aeroplane*		*Helicopter*			*IR*
Syllabus reference	**Syllabus details and Learning Objectives**	ATPL	CPL	ATPL/IR	ATPL	CPL	
LO	List the instrument errors that affect the airspeed indcator. List the atmospheric errors that affect the airspeed indicator. State the effects of errors of the pitot-static system that affect the airspeed indicator during straight and level flight and during climb and descent. Cross-check airspeed with pitch and power. Cross-check airspeed with TAS, Mach number and groundspeed.						
022 02 08 00	**Machmeter**						
022 02 08 01	General: definition, purpose, application & operating principle	x	x				
LO	Mach number is the true airspeed of the aeroplane in relation to the local speed of sound (M = TAS/a). Since the local speed of sound depends on temperature, the Mach number is also temperature dependent. The Mach number is used because of its relation with compressibiliy effects to take place. The measurement of the Machmeter is based on the ratio between airspeed and altitude: $M \sim (P_T - P_S)/P_S$. Describe relationship between IAS, CAS, and M during climb and descent in the troposphere and in the stratosphere.						
022 02 08 02	Design: different types, construction & operation	x					
LO	Mach meter: • Total pressure and static pressure, differential pressure capsule, blade spring, aneroid capsule, mechanical processing and indication. Mach-airspeed indicator: • Total pressure and static pressure, differential pressure capsule, blade spring, aneroid capsule, mechanical processing and indication. • State the operating principle of the V_{MO}/M_{MO} pointer in the Mach-airspeed indicator.	x					
022 02 08 03	Indication & control	x					
LO	Digital and/or analogue display calibrated in units of Mach number.						
022 02 08 04	Error behavior, accuracy & cross-checks						
LO	List the instrument errors that affect the Machmeter. List the atmospheric errors that affect the airspeed indicator. State the effects of errors of the pitot-static system that affect the Machmter during straight and level flight and during climb and descent. Cross-check M with airspeed and TAS. State the accuracy of the Machmeter.						
022 02 09 00	**True Air Speed**						
022 02 09 01	General: definition, purpose, application, operating principle						
LO	The TAS meter determines the true airspeed by correcting the Mach number for the local speed of sound (TAS = M.a). State the relation between true airspeed, wind and groundspeed. Describe relationship between IAS, CAS, TAS and M during climb and descent in the troposphere and in the stratosphere.						
022 02 09 02	Design: different types, construction, operation						
LO	TAS meter: • Differential pressure capsule, blade spring, aneroid capsule, temperature capsule, mechanical processing and indication. Combined CAS/TAS indicator: • Airspeed indicator with subscale + knob that allows for setting of pressure altitude versus temperature to allow reading of TAS.						
022 02 09 03	Indication & control						
LO	Digital and/or analogue dispaly calibrated in knots. Understand the use of the subscale knob in case of the combined CAS/TAS indicator						
022 02 09 04	Error behavior, solutions, accuracy, cross-checks						

Subject	022 - AIRCRAFT GENERAL KNOWLEDGE – INSTRUMENTATION	*Aeroplane*		*Helicopter*			*IR*
Syllabus reference	**Syllabus details and Learning Objectives**	ATPL	CPL	ATPL/IR	ATPL	CPL	
LO	List the instrument errors that affect the TAS meter. List the atmospheric errors that affect the TAS meter. State the effects of errors of the pitot-static system that affect the TAS meter during straight and level flight and during climb and descent. Cross-check TAS with airspeed and Mach number (at 25,000 ft. TAS ≈ 600.M). State the accuracy of the TAS meter.						
022 02 10 00	**Air Data Computer**						
022 02 10 01	General: definitions, purpose, applications, operating principle	x		x	x		
LO	Computer that holds several modules to process air data parameters for monitoring and control. The ADC uses a limited number of inputs to calculate a large number of outputs. Describe the inputs and outputs of the ADC: • Input modules: o total pressure, static pressure, temperature and angle of attack, barometric reference, power supply. • Processing modules: o Static Source Error Correction (SSEC), monitor (BITE). • Output modules: o Pressure altitude, altitude, vertical speed, airspeed, Mach number, V_{MO}/M_{MO}, overspeed, true airspeed, SAT, TAT and corrected angle of attack.						
022 02 10 02	Design: different types, construction, operation	x		x	x		
LO	Central Air Data Computer (CADC): • Analogue, electromechanical computer with several modules to calculate analogue output parameters that are sent to servo-driven indicators and to other systems. Digital Air Data Computer (DADC): • Digital computer with several modules to calculate digital output parameters that are sent to EFIS and to other systems. • Two types exist: type with built-in pressure transducers and with external pressure transducers. Air Data Inertial Reference Unit (ADIRU): • DADC and Inertial Reference Unit • DADC part is digital computer with several modules to calculate output parameters.						
022 02 10 03	Indication, control						
LO	State that ADC outputs are sent to servo-driven indicators or EFIS, ATC transponder, autoflight system, EGPWS, INS/IRS, FMS. Overspeed warning. Use of barometric reference knob.						
022 02 10 04	Error behavior, solutions, accuracy & cross checks						
LO	Internal monitor (BITE) to detect ADC failure Test switch that drives outputs to predetermined value. Describe the effect of loss of one or more input/output signal of the ADC to the pilot's instrument indication. Cross-check with standby air data instruments.						
022 03 00 00	**MAGNETISM – DIRECT READING COMPASS AND FLUX VALVE**						
	Formulas are not required for this topic. It is expected that students already have a basic understanding of magnetism, such as: • Definition and properties of a magnet. • Hard iron and soft iron. • Make distinction between permanent magnetism and electro-magnetism. • Relation between magnetic flux, magnetic density, magnetic field strength and permeability.						
022 03 01 00	**Earth magnetic field**	x	x	x	x	x	X

Subject	022 - AIRCRAFT GENERAL KNOWLEDGE – INSTRUMENTATION	*Aeroplane*		*Helicopter*			*IR*
Syllabus reference	**Syllabus details and Learning Objectives**	ATPL	CPL	ATPL/IR	ATPL	CPL	
LO	(Change of) Location and meaning of Magnetic North Pole and Magnetic South Pole. Resolution of the earth's total magnetic field (T) into a vertical component (V) and a horizontal component (H). Define the dip angle (inclination). Define the term variation. State that variation depends on location on earth and changes with time. Define isogonals. Define the magnetic equator. Area of uncertainty around the magnetic poles.						
022 03 02 00	**Aircraft magnetic field**						
LO	Explain and distinguish between hard iron and soft iron magnetism on aircraft. State that aircraft magnetic field can be resolved in three vectors (P, Q and R) along the three aircraft axes (X, Y and Z). Distinguish between permanent magnetic field and temporary magnetic fields. Explain deviation as the influence of the aircraft magnetic field on the magnetic compass. Mention the change of deviation with change of latitude and with change in aircraft's heading. State the importance of keeping magnetic materials clear of the compass. State that the compass swing procedure is used to minimise the deviation. State the situations requiring a compass swing. State that residual deviation is plotted on a deviation correction card or curve mounted on the flight deck.						
022 03 03 00	**Direct reading magnetic compass**						
LO	General: definitions, purpose, application, operating principle • Direct Reading Magnetic Compass (DRMC) often called standby compass. • Measure and show direction of horizontal component of earth's magnetic field. • Internal magnets are free to align themselves with horizontal component of earth's magnetic field. • Normally used as a standby magnetic compass. Design: different types, construction, operation • E-type compass only: o Pendulous suspended magnets, fluid filled bowl, looking glass with lubber line, diaphragm, illumination, magnetic deviation compensation device (adjustable N-S and E-W magnets) Indication, control: • Analogue display with scale graduated every 5 degrees and letters at the cardinal headings N, E, S and W. Error behavior, accuracy, cross-checks: • Describe and interpret the effects of the turning and acceleration errors. • Describe and interpret the effect of the deviation. • Describe and interpret the effect of the aircraft attitude on the compass reading (attitude error) • Interpret the deviation correction card or -curve. • State the maximum permissible values for deviation. • State the possible effect of illumination on the compass reading. • Cross check with heading indicator. • Identify the geographical areas where the magnetic compass is unreliable.	x	x	x	x	x	X
022 03 04 00	**Flux valve**						
022 03 04 01	General: definitions, purpose, location, application, operating principle	x	x	x	x	x	X

Subject	**022 - AIRCRAFT GENERAL KNOWLEDGE – INSTRUMENTATION**	*Aeroplane*		*Helicopter*			*IR*
Syllabus reference	**Syllabus details and Learning Objectives**	ATPL	CPL	ATPL/IR	ATPL	CPL	
LO	Wherever flux valve is stated one can also read flux gate! The flux valve is an electromagnetic field sensor. The flux valve is located as far as possible from disturbing magnetic fields, preferably in the tip of the wing or vertical stabiliser. The flux valve must measure the direction of horizontal component of earth's magnetic field. Operation based on measurement of the direction of the earth magnetic field that saturates electromagnetic fields set up in the flux valve.						
022 03 04 02	Design: different types, construction, components, operation						
LO	Pendulous suspended electromagnetic field sensor, 25-30 degrees in freedom in pitch and roll, no freedom around vertical axis, fluid filled bowl, electromagnetic deviation compensation device.						
022 03 04 03	Indication, control						
LO	No indicator; flux valve output is used to stabilise the gyromagnetic compass or to supply some inertial navigation systems with Magnetic Heading (MH).						
022 03 04 04	Error behavior, accuracy, cross-checks						
LO	Describe and interpret the effects of the turning and acceleration errors. Describe and interpret the effect of the deviation. Describe and interpret the effect of the aircraft attitude on the flux valve (attitude error). State that because of the electromagnetic deviation correction, the flux valve output does not need a deviation correction card or –curve. Identify the geographical areas where the flux valve is unreliable.						
022 04 00 00	**GYROSCOPIC INSTRUMENTS**						
022 04 01 00	**Gyroscope: basic principles**						
022 04 01 01	General: definition, purpose, application, operating principle	x	x	x	x	x	X
LO	Define a gyroscope and its components (fast spinning mass (rotor/disc/wheel) around a spinaxis) Explain the power supply: ▪ Pneumatically with a regulated differential pressure of ≈ 5 " Hg caused by a mechanically or electrically driven vacuum or pressure pump. ▪ Electrically wheras the gyro is the rotor of a DC or AC electric motor. ▪ Compare both types of power supply with respect to rpm and altitude behavior. Explain the following gyroscopic properties: ▪ Rigidity, using the first gyro law $H = I.\square_G$ ▪ Precession, using the second gyro law $\square_P = T/H$. ▪ Drift (wander and topple), distinguish between real drift and apparent drift. o Apparent drift: distinguish between earth rate and travel rate (transport wander). Explain the relationship between rigidity and precession. Explain how rigidity and precession can be increased/decreased.						
022 04 01 02	Design: different types, construction, operation						

Subject	022 - AIRCRAFT GENERAL KNOWLEDGE – INSTRUMENTATION	*Aeroplane*		*Helicopter*			*IR*
Syllabus reference	**Syllabus details and Learning Objectives**	ATPL	CPL	ATPL/IR	ATPL	CPL	
LO	Explain a free (space) gyro and an earth gyro. Explain the suspension of a gyro in one or two gimbals. Define a Single Degrees of Dreedom gyro (SDF) (a gyro with only one gimbal and one sensitive (measuring) axis that makes use of precession. Define a Two Degrees of Freedom gyro (TDF) (a gyro with two perpendicuar gimbals and two sensitive measuring axes that makes use of rigidity). Note: By convention the degrees of freedom of a gyroscope does not include its spin axis! Explain a vertical gyro and a horizontal gyro. Explain the construction and operating principle of a rate gyro (SDF gyro with spring attached to gimbal that is used to measure an angular rate □). Explain the construction and operating principle of rate integrating gyro (SDF gyro in casing which is surrounded by temperature controlled fluid that is used to measure an angular displacement θ). Explain the construction and operating principle of a Ring Laser Gyrsocope (RLG). Explain the construction and operating principle of a Fibre Optic Gyroscope (FOG). Compare the conventional gyroscope with the RLG and the FOG.						
022 04 01 03	Operational use: indication, control						
LO	State the monitoring options for gyro instruments: ▪ Electrically driven gyroscopes: flag warning. ▪ Pneumatically driven gyroscopes: air pressure indicator. State that pneumatically driven gyroscopes have an alternate power supply that is manually selected.						
022 04 01 04	Error behavior: accuracy, cross checks	x	x	x	x	x	X
LO	Describe gimbal lock plus solutions (mechanical stops, extra gimbal). Describe gimbal flip. Describe the effects of gyro drift. Describe cross-coupling. Describe the effect of a defective power supply on the gyro instruments. Describe how a defective power supply can be detected: ▪ Electrically driven gyroscopes: flag warning. ▪ Pneumatically driven gyroscopes: air pressure indicator. Explain the reasons for using different types of gyro power supply on an aircraft.	x	x	x	x	x	X
022 04 02 00	**Rate of Turn indicator**						
022 04 02 01	General: definition, purpose, application, operating principle	x	x	x	x	x	X
	A.k.a. turn and bank indicator or turn and balance indicator. Purpose is to show the angular speed around the local vertical axis when flying a coordinated (balanced) turn. Define a rate-one turn and a two-minute turn. Operating principle based on the precession of rate gyroscope when performing a turn. Pneumatic or electric power supply. Explain the relation between bank angle, rate one turn and true airspeed. Slipball shows coordinated (balanced) flight.						
022 04 02 02	Design: different types, construction, operation						

Subject	022 - AIRCRAFT GENERAL KNOWLEDGE – INSTRUMENTATION	*Aeroplane*		*Helicopter*			*IR*
Syllabus reference	**Syllabus details and Learning Objectives**	ATPL	CPL	ATPL/IR	ATPL	CPL	
LO	Rate of turn indicator: ▪ SDF horizontal rate gyro, spinaxis aligned with lateral axis of aircraft, gimbal aligned with longitudinal axis of aircraft, forward rotating gyro, reversing mechanism, damper and pointer. Turn co-ordinator: ▪ SDF horizontal rate gyro, spinaxis aligned with lateral axis of aircraft, rearward tilted gimbal, forward rotating gyro, reversing mechanism, damper and pointer symbol. Slipball: ▪ Curved concave glass tube filled with a damping fluid and a ball. ▪ Distinguish between slip and skid. Compare the rate of turn indicator with the turn co-ordinator with respect to the direction of the sensitive axis.						
022 04 02 03	Operational use: indication, control						
LO	Rate of turn indicator: ▪ Display with vertical pointer, left and right marking and slipball. Turn co-ordinator: ▪ Display with aeroplane symbol and slipball Interpret the indication of the rate of turn indicator and the turn co-ordinator during a co-ordinated turn and during non co-ordinated turns. Explain how to correct slip and skid in order to achieve co-ordinated flying.						
022 04 02 04	Error behavior: accuracy, cross checks						
LO	State the indication during a failure of the power supply (instrument air indicator or flag warning) State the behavior of the instrument in the event of a failure. State the instrument only shows corect for one TAS. State the instrument only shows correct when flying co-ordinated. Cross-check possibility with the stopwatch and heading indicator.						
022 04 03 00	**Attitude indicator**						
022 04 03 01	General: definition, purpose, application, operating principle	x	x	x	x	x	X
	A.k.a artificial horizon or Attitude Director Indicator (ADI). The attitude indcator shows both pitch attitude and roll attitude. Pneumatic or electric power supply. The attitude indicator makes use of TDF vertical gyro that is (kept) erected with help of an erection mechanism. Describe the prupose of the erection system (compensate for drift (topple)). Describe the principle of operation of the erection mechanism (makes use of gravity and precession). State different types of erection mechanism (pendulous vanes, ball erection system, electric system with liquid level switches and torque motors). State the erection speed of an artificial horizon (2-4 °/s)						
022 04 03 02	Design: different types, construction, operation						
LO	Mechanical attitude indicator: • Sensor, processor and indicator in one housing in cockpit • TDF vertical gyro, mechanical or pneumatical erection system, inner horizontal gimbal and outer vertical gimbal aligned with the longitudinal axis of the aircraft, pitch reversing mechanism, attitude scale, skypointer. Remote horizon: • Sensor in remote vertical gyro unit. • TDF vertical gyro, electrical erection system, inner horizontal gimbal and outer vertical gimbal aligned with the longitudinal axis of the aircraft, electrical transmission with synchros to indicator. • Servo-driven attitude sphere in Attitude Director Indicator (ADI).						
022 04 03 03	Operational use: indication, control						

Subject	022 - AIRCRAFT GENERAL KNOWLEDGE – INSTRUMENTATION	*Aeroplane*		*Helicopter*			*IR*
Syllabus reference	**Syllabus details and Learning Objectives**	ATPL	CPL	ATPL/IR	ATPL	CPL	
LO	Attitude display: • Aircraft symbol. • Pitch scale: markings every 2.5 degrees. • Roll scale: markings from 10, 20, 30, 45 and 60 degrees. • Explain the purpose of the test function in the remote horizon system. • State the purpose of the adjuster knob for the aircraft symbol and the purpose of the knob for fast erection. • State the function of the caging mechanism. Describe the monitoring indications (instrument air indicator or flag warning).						
022 04 03 04	Error behavior: accuracy, cross checks						
LO	State the disadvantage of the erection system (sensitive to horizontal accelerations). Describe the effect of longitudinal and lateral accelerations (take-off and turns). Explain how compensations for turn and acceleration errors are achieved in both pneumatically and electrically driven horizons (counterweight, PECO and RECO switches). Explain the behaviour of the artificial horizon in the event of a gyro failure (low air pressure, flag warning , decreased rigidity). Decsribe the behavior during a looping (gimbal lock and gimbal flip). Cross-check with rate of turn indicator.						
022 04 04 00	**Directional gyroscope**						
022 04 04 01	General: definition, purpose, application, location, operating principle	x	x	x	x	x	X
	A.k.a heading indicator or gyrocompass. The Directional Gyro (DG) shows the heading of the aircraft. State the power supply (pneumatic or electric). The directional gyro makes use of TDF horizontal gyro that must be manually kept aligned in a N-S direction. State the need for an erection system (compensate for drift). Distinguish between drift around the vertical axis and the horizontal axis. Describe the methods to solve for drift around the vertical axis (latitude nut, electrical system with liquid level switches and torque motor) Describe the methods to solve for drift around the horizontal axis (wedge, electrical system with liquid level switches and torque motor). State the erection speed of the directional gyro (2-4 °/s).						
022 04 04 02	Design: different types, construction, components, operation						
LO	Ring-type DG: • Sensor, processor and indicator in one housing in cockpit • TDF horizontal gyro, erection system, inner horizontal gimbal and outer vertical gimbal aligned with the vertical axis of the aircraft, erection system, horizontal ring-type heading scale. Card-type DG: • Sensor, processor and indicator in one housing in cockpit • TDF horizontal gyro, erection system, inner horizontal gimbal and outer vertical gimbal aligned with the vertical axis of the aircraft, erection system, vertical card-type heading scale.						
022 04 04 03	Operational use: indication, control						
LO	Heading display: • Aircraft symbol. • Heading scale: markings every 5 degrees. • State the purpose of the adjuster knob for the compass card. • State the function of the caging mechanism. Describe the monitoring indications (instrument air indicator or flag warning).						
022 04 04 04	Error behavior: accuracy, cross checks						

Subject	022 - AIRCRAFT GENERAL KNOWLEDGE – INSTRUMENTATION	*Aeroplane*		*Helicopter*			*IR*
Syllabus reference	**Syllabus details and Learning Objectives**	ATPL	CPL	ATPL/IR	ATPL	CPL	
LO	Compare the indications of a directional gyro and a magnetic compass during a turn and acceleration, and compare the accuracy of the indications over a lengthy period. Describe the behaviour of the instrument in the event of a gyro failure. (decreased rigidity) Define gimbal error and explain the effects (during pitch and roll manoeuevrs at headings other than N, E, S and W the DG will rotate around its vertical axis and show a false heading). Explain the necessity and time interval to re-set the DG against the magnetic compass. Describe the adjustment procedure (in unacellerated level flight). Calculate apparent drift of an uncompensated directional gyro (no real drift or travel rate (transport wander) at a given earth position.						
022 04 05 00	**Slaved gyrocompass**						
022 04 05 01	General: definition, purpose, application, operating principle	x	x	x	x	x	X
LO	A.k.a gyrosyn compass or remote reading magnetic compass (RRMC). State the purpose of the slaved gyro compass (show gyro-stabilised magnetic heading). Explain the principles of operation of the slaved gyro compass Describe in general terms the signal flow. Using a block diagram, explain the operation of a remote compass system Comparator that compares magnetic heading from flux valve with heading from DG						
022 04 05 02	Design: different types, construction, components, operation						
LO	Gyromagnetic compas: • Remote earth magnetic field sensor (flux valve). • Integral Directional Gyro, TDF horizontal gyro, electrical erection system, inner horizontal gimbal and outer vertical gimbal aligned with the longitudinal axis of the aircraft, card type indicator. • Differential synchro-servo system with torquer on horizontal gimbal. Remote heading reference unit: • Remote earth magnetic field sensor (flux valve). • Remote TDF horizontal gyro, electrical erection system, inner horizontal gimbal and outer vertical gimbal aligned with the longitudinal axis of the aircraft, electrical transmission with synchros to indicator. • Differential synchro-servo system with torquer on horizontal gimbal. • Servo-driven compass card in Horizontal Situation Indicator (HSI).						
022 04 05 03	Operational use: indication, control						
LO	Heading display: • Aircraft symbol. • Heading scale: markings every 5 degrees. Integral or separate compass control unit: • Fast slave knob. • Slaving indicator. • Free-slaved switch. Describe the different modes of operation. Describe the monitoring indications (instrument air indicator or flag warning).						
022 04 05 04	Error behavior: accuracy, cross checks						
LO	Describe the behaviour of the instrument in the event of a gyro failure (decreased rigidity). Describe the behavior of the instrument when the flux valve input is disconnected (behave like a DG). Cross-check with direct reading magnetic compass.						
022 05 00 00	**INERTIAL NAVIGATION AND REFERENCE SYSTEMS**						
022 05 01 00	**Gyro-stabilised inertial platform**						
022 05 01 01	General: definition, purpose, application, operating principle	x		x			

Subject	022 - AIRCRAFT GENERAL KNOWLEDGE – INSTRUMENTATION	*Aeroplane*		*Helicopter*			*IR*
Syllabus reference	**Syllabus details and Learning Objectives**	ATPL	CPL	ATPL/IR	ATPL	CPL	
LO	Autonomous navigation system. Outputs: navigation parameters (position, track, ground speed, drift angle, wind and attitude (pitch, roll and heading). Large transport aeroplanes. 1, 2 or 3 system installed. Double integration of accelerations in 3D space. State that a gyrostabilised inertial platform also holds a lateral flight plan computer that allowed for the programming of up to ten waypoints.						
022 05 01 02	Design: different types, components, construction, operation	x		x			
LO	North seeking system, Azimuth free (Azimuth wander) system Describe the platform stabilisation with help of three rate integrating gyroscopes or two TDF gyroscopes, a resolver, a computer and platform servomotors. Describe the attitude measurement function with help of three synchros. Describe the navigation with help of three accelerometers, accelerometer corrections and a computer. Describe the platform alignment: phases, gyros started, gimbals perpendicular, insertion of present position, auto detection of latitude, application of apparent drift corrections, alignment time.						
022 05 01 03	Operational use: indication, control, outputs						
LO	MSU: rotary switch (OFF-SBY-ALGN-ATT) and annunciators (ALGN, BAT). CDU: displays, function knobs, operating modes, operational use and flight plan function. ADI (pitch and roll) and HSI (heading or track). Autoflight systems, GPWS.						
022 05 01 04	Error behavior: accuracy, cross checks						
LO	Schuler oscillation, platform drift, accelerometer error. Corrections for following accelerations: centripetal, Corioli and gravity. Baro-inertial altitude and baro-inertial vertical speed.						
022 05 02 00	**Strapped-down inertial platform**						
022 05 02 01	General: definition, purpose, application, operating principle	x		x			
LO	Autonomous navigation system. Outputs: navigation parameters (position, track, ground speed, drift angle, wind and attitude (pitch, roll and heading). Large transport aeroplanes. 1, 2 or 3 system installed. Double integration of accelerations in 3D space.						
022 05 02 02	Design: different types, components, construction, operation	x		x			
LO	Inertial Reference System (IRS), Attitude Heading Reference System (AHRS) Describe the platform stabilisation with help of three ringlaser gyroscopes or three fibre optic gyros and computer. Describe the attitude measurement function with help of the computer. Describe the navigation with help of three accelerometers, accelerometer corrections and a computer. Describe the platform alignment: phases, insertion of present position, auto detection of latitude, application of apparent drift corrections, alignment time.						
022 05 02 03	Operational use: indication, control						
LO	MSU: rotary switch (OFF-ALGN-ATT) and annunciators (ALGN, BAT). CDU: displays, function knobs, operating modes, operational use. EADI (pitch and roll) and EHSI (heading, track, wind, ground speed, drift).						
022 05 02 04	Error behavior: accuracy, cross checks						
LO	Schuler oscillation, platform drift, accelerometer error. Corrections for following accelerations: centripetal, Corioli and gravity. Barometric corrections for vertical accelerometer measurement.						
022 06 00 00	**AEROPLANE: AUTOMATIC FLIGHT CONTROL SYSTEMS**						
	No MCQ's will refer to operational, type related values/limits (eg speed, distance and angle of interception in the LOC mode or V/S in the ALT mode).						

Subject	**022 - AIRCRAFT GENERAL KNOWLEDGE – INSTRUMENTATION**	*Aeroplane*		*Helicopter*			*IR*
Syllabus reference	**Syllabus details and Learning Objectives**	ATPL	CPL	ATPL/IR	ATPL	CPL	
022 06 01 00	**General**						
022 06 01 01	Control system theory	x	x				
LO	Static stability and dynamic stability. Blockdiagrams. Symbols. Open loop and closed loop. Feed-back and feed-forward. Servo loop, inner loop, outer loop. PID-controller.						
022 06 01 02	Sensor systems						
LO	State that the FD and/or AP can receive information from the following instrument systems: • Vertical gyro (pitch, roll), • Inertial navigation reference system: aircraft attitude and rate signals (pitch, roll, and heading), acceleration; • Gyromagnetic compass system: magnetic heading; • Navigation receivers: VOR, LOC, G/S, MLS and GPS deviation signals, DME distance and MB info; • Flight management system: TKE, XTK, DSTK; • Air data computer: altitude, vertical speed, speed, Mach number, angle of attack; • Radio altimeter: height.						
022 06 01 03	FD and/or AP modes						

LO	Distinguish between basic modes and upper modes:
	• Basic pitch mode pitch hold (non-integrated concept) and V/S HOLD (integrated concept)
	• Basic roll mode WINGS LEVEL (non-integrated concept) and HDG HOLD (integrated concept)
	Distinguish between roll (lateral) modes, pitch modes and comon modes:
	• Describe the arming, capture and tracking criteria of the following roll modes of the FD and/or AP:
	  • Wings level or Turn knob (hold & select),
	  • Heading (hold & select),
	  • VOR/LOC/Back beam,
	  • LNAV (NAV).
	• Describe the arming, capture and tracking criteria of the following pitch modes of the FD and/or AP:
	  • Pitch attitude (hold, select),
	  • Vertical speed (hold, select),
	  • VNAV (Profile),
	  • (Flight) Level change,
	  • Altitude (hold & select),
	  • IAS or Mach (hold, select),
	  • GS MAN, GS AUTO.
	• Describe the arming, capture and tracking criteria of the following common modes of the FD and/or AP:
	  • Approach (LAND, ILS, MLS, GPS).
	  • Take-Off/Go around.						

022 06 02 00	**Flight Director**						
022 06 02 01	General: definition, purpose, application, operating principle	x	x				
LO	State that the FD gives pitch and roll steering commands in order to increase the stability and to fly the aircraft along a specified path or attitude. State that the FD pitch and roll steering signals are sent to the FD indicator and to the AP. Name the following components of a flight director: computer, control panel, flight Mode Annunciator (FMA), FD command indicator (crossbars/V-bar). Closed loop control						

Subject	022 - AIRCRAFT GENERAL KNOWLEDGE – INSTRUMENTATION	*Aeroplane*		*Helicopter*			*IR*
Syllabus reference	**Syllabus details and Learning Objectives**	ATPL	CPL	ATPL/IR	ATPL	CPL	
022 06 02 02	Design: different types, components, construction, operation	x	x				
LO	State that the flight director computer has a pitch channel and a roll channel. State that the commands of the flight director are given in such a way that structural limits of the aircraft for pitch and bank attitude will not be exceeded Name the task of the gain program in the approach mode as being to reduce the command bar deflections during approach based on marker beacons, radio altitude or DME distance. State the task of the beam sensors as being to switch from an armed (standby) condition to a capture (acquire or intercept) condition in radio mode (VOR, LOC, G/S) when reaching a certain threshold value. State that the effects of disturbances such as cross winds and changes in centre of gravity, landing gear position, flaps, slats and (spoilers) speed brakes can be compensated for with the flight director. State that in the flight director computer, actual values are compared with reference values and displayed as control commands.						
022 06 02 03	Operational use: indication, control, outputs						
LO	The FD modes are selected from the FD and/or AP control panel. State that per channel (pitch/roll) only one mode at a time active can be active. State that the FD switch on the control panel enables the FD. State that the control commands of the flight director are displayed as pitch and roll commands, located in the (Electronic) Attitude Director Indicator (ADI) or Primary Flight Display (PFD). List that the mode annunciation can be given either by electromechanical devices, annunciator lights or as an electronic indication on the Primary Flight Display of the EFIS system. Describe the indications on the Flight Mode Panel (FMP) with respect to the FD: use of colours, symbols, armed (standby), capture (acquire or intercept) and active (track or hold) modes. Name that the flight director indication on the ADI or PFD can be given as two rectangular cross bars or as a V-shaped command bar. Describe the operation of the FD modes in the following flight phases: take-off, climb, cruise, descent, approach, land, go-around.						
022 06 02 04	Error behavior: accuracy, cross checks						
LO	State that the flight director monitors: power supply, input signals, computer and display. State and interpret the following monitoring options: warning flag, bar removal, annunciator.						
022 06 03 00	**Automatic Pilot**						
022 06 03 01	General: definition, purpose, application, operating principle	x	x				
LO	State that the autopilot gives elevator, aileron and rudder steering signals to fly the aircraft along a specified path or at a specified attitude. An AP channel is a closed loop control system that controls one aircraft axis (pitch, roll, yaw). State that an AP computer consists of one or more channels. Non-integrated concept: one computer per channel (pitch, roll and yaw computer). Integrated concept: FD and AP channels in one computer (APFD computer with pitch, roll and yaw channel). Name the following component units of an autopilot: sensor, computer, control panel, autopilot actuator, Flight Mode Annunciator Describe a three channel AP using a simplified block diagram consisting of sensor inputs, actuators, computer, control panel and indicators. State the AP compares actual values with reference values and passes control commands to the AP actuators. State the JAR-OPS requirement the installation of an AP: (single pilot IFR or at night: AP at least heading hold and altitude hold.						
022 06 03 02	Design: different types, components, construction, operation	x	x				

Subject	022 - AIRCRAFT GENERAL KNOWLEDGE – INSTRUMENTATION	*Aeroplane*		*Helicopter*			*IR*
Syllabus reference	**Syllabus details and Learning Objectives**	ATPL	CPL	ATPL/IR	ATPL	CPL	
LO	Describe AP gain programming with respect to the servo-, inner- and outer loop. Describe and distinguish between AP pitch-, roll- and common (mixed) modes. AP actuators: • Types: electric, hydraulic, pneumatic, • Components: clutch, motor, position sensor, rate sensor, • Describe series and/or parallel control together with applications. State that when engaging the AP, the clutches are engaged. AP engaged in Command (CMD) or in Control Wheel Steering (CWS). State that when AP engaged in CMD, the AP is supplied by the FD pitch and roll commands. State that when AP engaged in CWS, the AP is supplied by force transducers on control column and on control wheel. State CWS creates pitch rate and roll rate signals. State the relation between the AP pitch computer/channel and the roll computer/channel with respect to lift compensation during turns ($1/\cos\varphi$). State the relation between the AP roll computer/channel and the YD computer/channel with respect to turn coordination. State the relation between the AP pitch computer/channel and the auto pitch trim computer/channel with respect to automatic pitch trim. Automatic synchronisation when disengaged or mode not selected. Describe how to handle a non self-synchronising AP before engagement using AP trim indicators. Describe the Fly By Wire (FBW) system.						
022 06 03 03	Operational use: indication, control	x	x				
LO	Describe the controls and indications of the FMP with respect to AP (dis)engagement in CMD or in CWS. Describe the indications on the FMP with respect to the APuse of colours, symbols, armed (standby), capture (acquire or intercept) and active (track or hold) modes. AP normally (dis)engaged from FMP. Quick release buttons on either control wheel. AP annunciations on FMP. Aural and visual warning on AP disengagement. Describe the AP operation of the FD pitch and roll modes during the following flight the phases: take-off, climb, cruise, descent, approach, land, go-around. State that an AP can only be selected in CMD when in flight.						
022 06 03 04	Error behavior: accuracy, limits, cross checks						
LO	Decsribe the relation between the AP with the automatic pitch trim system. No take-off use of AP in CMD. Describe the AP monitor function together with the automatic cut-out in case of a failure. Describe the engage interlock system. Torque limiter on AP servo's to prevent hard-overrides and slow-overrides. State the AP override requirement: must always be possible to override the AP. State that a fail safe autopilot automatically disengages whenever a failure occurs. State the AP pitch (+20° and -10°) and roll (35°) limits. Bank angle limiter (manual/automatic). State that the AP is programmed to prevent overload of the control surfaces and structure.						
022 06 04 00	**Automatic landing**						
	A basic knowledge of the minima for the low visibility take-off and landing procedures can be given to the students. No MCQ will refer to such a knowledge.						

Subject	022 - AIRCRAFT GENERAL KNOWLEDGE – INSTRUMENTATION	*Aeroplane*		*Helicopter*			*IR*
Syllabus reference	**Syllabus details and Learning Objectives**	ATPL	CPL	ATPL/IR	ATPL	CPL	
LO	Ref. JAR-AWO. Study the fail passive and fail operational (fail active) concept. Describe the following AP categories: CAT 1, CAT 2 and CAT 3A, -B and –C. State the minimum requirements for making an autoland. Explain a typical autoland sequence with respect to the APFD pitch channel, roll channel, yaw channel and the autothrottle. APFD pitch channel: glideslope > flare > touchdown > nose lowering mode > roll-out > manual disengage. APFD roll channel: localiser > touchdown > roll-out > manual disengage. APFD yaw channel: align (decrab) > roll-out > manual disengage. Autothrottle: speed > retard > automatic disengage upon touchdown. Decsribe the role of the pitch trim system during an autoland. Describe the use, the operation and the indication of the autoflight system during an autoland. State that the approach/land mode is a common mode, which requires localiser and glide slope reference signals. State that during an approach/autoland and go-around more than one autopilot can be used. State the importance of equalisation when more AP computers operate simultaneously. Name the task of the gain programming in the approach/land mode. State the role of the radio altimeter during an autoland. State that below a certain radio altitude the autoland can only be interrupted when disenganing the AP or selecting go-around. Describe the consequence of an AP failure during an autoland.						
022 07 00 00	**HELICOPTER: AUTOMATIC FLIGHT CONTROL SYSTEMS**						
022 07 01 00	**General principles**						
022 07 01 01	Stabilisation			x	x	x	
LO	Understand the simularities and differences between SAS and AFCS the latter can actually fly the helicopter to perform certain functions selected by the pilot. Some AFCS's just have altitude and heading hold whilst others, include a vertical speed or IAS hold mode, where a constant rate of climb/decent or IAS is maintained by the AFCS. Understand the importance of not engaging the AFCS until after take-off and to dis-engage before landing.						
022 07 01 02	Reduction of pilot work load			x	x	x	
LO	Appreciate how effective the AFCS is in reducing pilot work load by improving basic aircraft control harmony and decreasing disturbances.						
022 07 01 03	Enhancement of helicopter capability			x	x	x	
LO	Understand how the AFCS improves helicopter flight safety with the following: • increases the capability for search and rescue • flight by sole reference to instruments • under slung load operations white out conditions in snow covered landscapes and lack of visual cues on approach to land						
022 07 01 04	Failures			x	x	x	
LO	Understand the various redundancies and independent systems that are built into the AFCS's.			x	x	x	
LO	Appreciate that the pilot can override the system in the event of a failure.			x	x	x	
LO	Understand a series actuator 'hard over' which equals aircraft attitude runaway.			x	x	x	
LO	Understand the consequences of a saturation of the series actuators.			x	x	x	
022 07 02 00	**Components – Operation**						
022 07 02 01	Basic sensors			x	x	x	
LO	Understand the basic sensors in the system and their functions			x	x	x	

Subject	022 - AIRCRAFT GENERAL KNOWLEDGE – INSTRUMENTATION	*Aeroplane*		*Helicopter*			*IR*
Syllabus reference	**Syllabus details and Learning Objectives**	ATPL	CPL	ATPL/IR	ATPL	CPL	
LO	Understand that the number of sensors will be dependant on how many couples modes are in the system			x	x	x	
022 07 02 02	Specific sensors			x	x	x	
LO	Understand the function of the micro switches and stain gauges in the system which sense pilot input to prevent excessive feed back forces from the system			x	x	x	
022 07 02 03	Actuators: - parallel and series, spring box and clutches, trim system			x	x	x	
LO	Understand the principles of operation of the series and parallel actuators, spring box clutches and the auto trim system.			x	x	x	
022 07 02 04	Pilot/System interface						
LO	Describe the typical layout of the AFCS control panel.			x	x	x	
LO	Understand the system indications and warnings.			x	x	x	
022 07 02 05	Operation						
LO	Understand the functions of the redundant sensors simplex and duplex channels (single/dual channel)			x	x	x	
022 07 03 00	**Stability Augmentation System (SAS)**						
022 07 03 01	General principles and operation - Rate damping - Short term attitude hold - Effect on Static stability - Effect on Dynamic stability - Aerodynamic Cross coupling - Effect on Manoeuvrability - Control response - Engagement/disengagement - Authority			x	x	x	
LO	Understand and describe the general working principles and primary use of SAS by damping pitch, roll and yaw motions caused by gusts			x	x	x	
LO	Describe the simplest SAS with forced trim system, which uses magetic clutch and springs to hold cyclic control in the position where it was last released.			x	x	x	
LO	Understand the interaction of trim with SAS/SCAS/ASS stability system.			x	x	x	
LO	Appreciate that the system can be overridden by the pilot and individual channels deselected.			x	x	x	
LO	Understand that the system should be turned off in severe turbulence or when extreme flight attitudes are reached.			x	x	x	
LO	Understand the safety design features built into some SAS's to limit the authority of the actuators to 10% to 20% of full control throw, to allow the pilot to override if actuators demand an unsafe control input.			x	x	x	
LO	Understand how cross coupling produces an adverse affect roll to yaw coupling, when the helicopter is subject to gusts.			x	x	x	
LO	Have an understanding of collective to pitch coupling, side slip to pitch coupling and inter axis coupling.			x	x	x	
022 07 04 00	**Autopilot – Automatic Stability Equipment**						
022 07 04 01	General principles - Long term attitude hold - Fly through - Changing the reference (beep trim, trim release)			x	x	x	
LO	Understand the general principles related to: - Long term attitude hold - Fly through - Changing the reference (beep trim, trim release)			x	x	x	
022 07 04 02	Basic mode (three axis/four axis) - AFCS operation on cyclic axis (pitch/roll), yaw axis, collective (fourth axis)			x	x	x	

Subject	022 - AIRCRAFT GENERAL KNOWLEDGE – INSTRUMENTATION	*Aeroplane*		*Helicopter*			*IR*
Syllabus reference	**Syllabus details and Learning Objectives**	ATPL	CPL	ATPL/IR	ATPL	CPL	
LO	Understand the AFCS operation on cyclic axis (pitch/roll), yaw axis, collective (fourth axis).			x	x	x	
022 07 04 03	Automatic guidance/modes of AFCS: - Altitude hold - Airspeed hold - Heading hold - V/S hold - Navigation coupling - VOR/ILS coupling - SAR modes, Automatic transition to hover			x	x	x	
LO	Understand the function of the attitude hold system in an AFCS.			x	x	x	
LO	Understand the function of the heading hold system in an AFCS.			x	x	x	
LO	Understand the function of the vertical speed hold system in an AFCS.			x	x	x	
LO	Understand the function of the navigation coupling system in an AFCS.			x	x	x	
LO	Understand the function of the VOR/ILS coupling system in an AFCS.			x	x	x	
LO	Understand the function of the SAR mode (Automatic transition to hover) in an AFCS.			x	x	x	
022 07 04 04	Flight director - Monitoring - Guidance			x	x	x	
LO	LOs TO BE DEFINED						
LO	Understand that some helicopters have the addition of a collective setting bar indication on the Flight Director.			x	x	x	
022 07 05 00	**Fly by wire – Enhanced Control laws**						
022 07 05 01	General principles and operations: - multiplex system - fail safe system - limitations			x	x	x	
LO	Appreciate the principles of the current civil helicopter developments and the current military helicopter use of 'fly by wire' control systems: - multiplex system - fail safe system - limitations			x	x	x	
LO	Understand the fly by wire system literally replaces phsical control of the aircraft with an electrical interface.			x	x	x	
LO	Understand the pilot inputs go through an electronic interface to operate actuators at each control surface.			x	x	x	
LO	Understand that actuators initially were hydraulic, but in recent years are fully electronic actuators.			x	x	x	
LO	Understand that the autopilot is now part of the electronic controller.			x	x	x	
LO	Understand that hydraulic circuits are similar except that mechanical servo valves are replaced by electronically controlled servo valves.			x	x	x	
LO	Understand that fly by wire systems are triply or quaderuply redundant, they have 3 or 4 computers in parallel and as many wires to each contrl surface			x	x	x	
LO	Appreciate the software can prevent pilots exceeding the flight envelope.			x	x	x	
LO	Understand limitations in regard to electromagnetic control interference.			x	x	x	
LO	Appreciate future developments are moving towards fly by optics which transfer data at higher speeds. The wires cables are replaced with fibre optic cables. Advantages include immunity to electromagnetic control interference.			x	x	x	
022 07 05 02	Rate command attitude hold (RCAH)			x	x	x	
LO	Understand the functions of RCAH systems in helicopters.			x	x	x	
022 07 05 03	Attitude command attitude hold (ACAH)						
LO	Understand the functions of ACAH systems in helicopters.			x	x	x	
022 08 00 00	**TRIMS – YAW DAMPER – FLIGHT ENVELOPE PROTECTION**						

Subject	022 - AIRCRAFT GENERAL KNOWLEDGE – INSTRUMENTATION	*Aeroplane*		*Helicopter*			*IR*
Syllabus reference	**Syllabus details and Learning Objectives**	ATPL	CPL	ATPL/IR	ATPL	CPL	
	Aerodynamic notions may be used to introduce the following paragraphs but no MCQs will refer to aerodynamic.						
022 08 01 00	**Trims**						
LO	The purpose is to neutralise the elevator control forces necessary to maintain a desired pitch attitude. Elevator control forces are trimmed away by adjusting the angle of incidence of the horizontal stabilizer or elevator trim tab. Name the following possible tasks of the pitch trim system: automatic pitch trim, manual electric pitch trim, Mach trim. Describe the interaction between the autopilot and the pitch trim system. Explain the pitch trim system using a simplified block diagram: input signals, computer, control panel, stabiliser trim indicator and actuator. Inputs: elevator position, Mach number, manual electric pitch trim switches. State that the pitch trim computer compares reference signals with actual signals and passes control commands to the pitch trim actuator. State the task of the airspeed input (gain programming). Pitch trim actuator: parallel actuator that controls the horizontal stabiliser or the elevator trim tab. Pitch trim engage switch. Two in series connected manual electric pitch trim switches on either control wheel. Stabiliser trim indicator: function of green band and CoG range. Out-of-trim alert light. State the consequence of a pitch trim system failure. State the alert when there is a excessive pitch trim command.						
022 08 02 00	**Yaw damper**						
LO	Name the following possible tasks of the yaw damper: Dutch roll damping, N-1 compensation, turn coordination. Describe the interaction between the autopilot and the YD. Explain the yaw damper using a simplified block diagram: input signals, computer, control panel, YD indicator, YD servo. Inputs: yaw rate (rate gyro), engine out (N-1) and roll or lateral acceleration (turn coordination). State that the yaw damper computer compares reference signals with yaw rate and passes control commands to the yaw damper servo of the rudder State task of airspeed input (gain programming). Yaw damper servo: series actuator that adds/subtracts the YD input to/from the rudder deflection controlled by the autopilot or rudder pedals. Control and indication: YD switch, YD indicator that shows YD input to rudder and YD failure light. State that during a stall warning the YD is disabled. State the consequence of a yaw damper failure.						
022 08 03 00	**Flight envelope protection**						
LO	Describe flight envelope protection as a protection against: extreme attitudes, exceeding the aircraft ceiling, too low speeds, too high speeds, too high angle-of-attacks, high positive and negative G-forces. State and explain the following input data: AoA, speed/Mach number, altitude, attitude, acceleration. State and explain the following output data: flight director commands, flight control surface (rate) limit signals, autothrottle system, speed limits on EFIS speed tape.						
022 09 00 00	**AUTOTHROTTLE – AUTOMATIC THRUST CONTROL SYSTEM**						
022 09 01 00	**Autothrottle**						

Subject	**022 - AIRCRAFT GENERAL KNOWLEDGE – INSTRUMENTATION**	*Aeroplane*		*Helicopter*			*IR*
Syllabus reference	**Syllabus details and Learning Objectives**	ATPL	CPL	ATPL/IR	ATPL	CPL	
LO	State that the auto-throttle computer compares actual values with reference values and passes control commands to the servomotors of the throttles. Explain the engagement of the autothrottle from the FMP and the disengagement from the disconnect buttons on the throttles. State the use, location and operation of the TO/GA button on the throttles. State the autothrottle system operates in the thrust mode or in the speed mode. Monitoring: FMP, EFIS, ERP/MCDU, local light. Explain the fast/slow indicator on the ADI. Describe the use of the auto-throttle system during flight: take-off, climb, cruise, descent, holding, approach and land. Describe the autothrottle system using a simplified block diagram: inputs/outputs, computer, control panel, indications. Automatic or manual mode selections via the thrust rating function. State that there is a rate feedback in order to control throttle speed. Explain the clamp mode. Explain the thrust latch mode (alpha floor). Explain the windshear escape mode. Explain the retard mode. Distinguish between an approach autothrottle system and a full-flight regime autothrottle system. State the role of the PMC in the autothrottle system.						
022 09 02 00	**Automatic thrust control**						
LO	State parameters that affect required (target) power calculation and maximum (limit) power calculation: ambient conditions, engine rating selection, selected performance mode and selected speed/Mach number. Name and explain the following engine ratings including time limits: Take-Off (TO), Go-Around (GA), Max. Continuous Thrust (MCT), Climb (CL), Cruise (CRZ), Flexible Take Off (FLX TO). Distinguish between thrust command system (N1, EPR or TRQ) and speed command system (speed or Mach number). Automatic and manual thrust and/or speed/Mach selections. Thrust ratings selected from the engine rating panel (separate or integral with FMS CDU) Describe the autothrust system using a simplified block diagram: inputs/outputs, computer, control panel, indications. Speed/Mach selected from FMP or through the FMS CDU. Describe the engine rating function using a simplified blockdiagram showing engine rating computer based on comparison of set values versus measured values. Control and indications on engine rating panel (separate or integral with FMS CDU), Flight Mode Annunciator List the outputs of the power computation system: target and limit values for N1, EPR or TRQ, auto thrust system, engine rating panel, F/S indicator. List the inputs for a thrust rating (limit) computer: bleed valve position, engine rating selection, altitude, Mach number, airspeed, TAT and actual N1/EPR/TRQ. Describe the use of the power computing system during flight: take-off, climb, cruise, descent, holding, approach and land. Monitoring via N1, EPR or TRQ indicators, FMA and engine rating panel. State the role of the FADEC in the autothrottle system. Make a comparison between autothrottle and automatic thrust control system.						
022 10 00 00	**COMMUNICATION SYSTEMS**						
022 10 01 00	**Radio transmitters/receivers**	x		x			
	State components of radio equipment: control panel, transmitter/receiver, transmisison lines, antennas. Radio transmitter/receiver: oscillators (LC-circuit, quartz crystal, magnetron), modulator/demodulator, amplifiers, filters, beat frequency oscillator (BFO).						
022 10 02 00	**VHF and HF Communication (VHF-COM and HF-COM)**	x		x			

Subject	022 - AIRCRAFT GENERAL KNOWLEDGE – INSTRUMENTATION	*Aeroplane*		*Helicopter*			*IR*
Syllabus reference	**Syllabus details and Learning Objectives**	ATPL	CPL	ATPL/IR	ATPL	CPL	
LO	VHF: • Frequency band: 118 – 137 MHz. • Channel separation: 8.33 kHz. • Control panel: standby-active frequency display, channel selector, squelch, volume control. HF: • Frequency band: 3 –30 MHz. • Channel separation 100 kHz. • HF sensitivity switch. • Explain SSB and DSB. • State HF civil is USB, HF military is LSB. • AM = DSB, USB = SSB. • Control panel: standby-active frequency display, channel selector, squelch, volume control.						
022 10 03 00	**Satellite comunication (SAT-COM)**	x					
LO	Global coverage multi channel system through ground earth stations via orbiting satelites. Voice and data communication. Duplex voice and data communication to (pre)selected adresses (telephone numbers). Components: satellite data unit and MCDU.						
022 10 04 00	**ARINC Communication, Adressing and Reporting System (ACARS)**	x					
	Two-way digital communication between aircraft and ground data networks (uplink and downlink). Manual and automatic downlink. Makes use of VHF-COM, HF-COM or SAT-COM radio's. Radio's must be set from VOICE to DATA. Components: ACARS management unit and MCDU. Messages: flight log, meteo reports, free text messages, time base. Overview of organisations using the datalink transmission: ATSU/DCDU, the ATN program and its network.						
022 10 05 00	**Future Air Navigation System (FANS)**	x					

LO	Definition, Purpose & Application:
	• FANS covering Communications, Navigation, and Surveillance (CNS) + Air Traffic Management (ATM)
	• Air Traffic Control (ATC) and Airline Operational Control (AOC)
	• Use of:
	  • ARINC Communication, Adressing and Reporting System (ACARS)
	  • Satellite Communication (SATCOM)
	  • Global Postioning System (GPS)
	  • Global Navigation Satellite System (GNSS)
	  • Aeronautical Telecommunications Network (ATN)
	  • Free flight concept
	  • Automatic Dependent Surveillance type B (ADS-B)
	  • Controller Pilot Data Link Communications (CPDLC)
	  • VHF Data Link (VDL) modes 1, 2, 3 and 4
	  • VHF Digital Radio (VDR)
	Operation, construction, indication, control, error behavior & cross checks
	• ACARS, SATCOM and VDR
	Multi-function Control and Display Unit (MCDU)						

022 10 06 00	**SELCAL/CALSEL**	x					
LO	Selective calling and Calling a selective station. HF and VHF. Ground stations desiring communication with the aircraf can use SELCAL. Aircraft desiring communication with a ground station can use CALSEL. Audio and visual alert on incoming call.						

Subject	022 - AIRCRAFT GENERAL KNOWLEDGE – INSTRUMENTATION	*Aeroplane*		*Helicopter*			*IR*
Syllabus reference	**Syllabus details and Learning Objectives**	ATPL	CPL	ATPL/IR	ATPL	CPL	
022 10 07 00	**Interphone**	x		x			
	Flight interphone: communication between flight crew members and with ground personnel near the nose wheel. Service interphone: communication between maintenance personnel at various locations around aircraft. Cabin interphone: comunication between flight deck and flight attendant stations Call system: informs flight crew that communication is desired from the ground or from the cabin.						
022 10 08 00	**Passenger adress system**	x					
	Alows cabin annoncements to be made from the flight deck or from the flight attendant stations. When making a PA announcements all other conversations are overridden.						
022 11 00 00	**FLIGHT MANAGEMENT SYSTEM (FMS)**						
022 11 01 00	**Flight Management Computer (FMC)**						
022 11 00 01	General: definition, purpose, application, operating principle	x		x	x		
LO	Goals, design, operation : Functions and modes of operation will be studied but the systems used by the F.M.S. (the systems and the input/ouput components) will be just listed. They are studied according to the syllabus in the relevant topic. As no standard of FMS can be defined, the ability for each manufacturer to define a specific system for each customer will be highlighted : the FMS is not related to an aeroplane but to a customer. - inputs, data computation and functions, outputs and display units. position computations (multi-sensors), flight management, definition of the cost index, lateral/vertical navigation and guidance, interfaces with AFCS and auto thrust/auto throttle systems : presentation of the three types of links with AFCS : targets, steer through and hybrid. fuel computations, radio tuning (Comm, Nav), datalink (AOC/ATC) control and display, EFIS, CMU.						
022 11 00 02	Different types, components, construction, operation						
LO	Types: Flight Management System (VNAV + LNAV) and Navigation Management System (LNAV only). Input- and output modules, microprocessor and databases. Input modules: MCDU, IRS, ADS, Radio receivers (GPS, VHF-NAV). Databases: aircraft database, engine database and navigation data base. Navigation database 28 days validity. Contents of Navigation database. State the different operating modes of an FMS. Cost index vs minimum time, minimum fuel and economy mode. Strategic, tactical and situational modes. Multi sensors: FMC position calculated out of inertial and/or radio position. Computations based on measured data (use of sensors): ETA (Estimated Time of Arrival), TTG (Total Time to Go), RTA (Requested Time of Arrival). Computations based on stored information (data base): fuel computations, VNAV path predictions, wind models. Operational limits of an FMS : accuracy of the data, reliability, Identify the parameters that relate to the vertical flight profile: speed/M, altitude, path (open loop (air mass referenced) and closed loop (earth referenced). Identify the parameters that relate to the lateral flightplan: desired track, track, track angle error, cross track distance. Automatic tuning of radiobeacons based on Figure of Merit and Lines of Position (LOP). Navigation accuracy and approach capability. Interface with Automatic Flight System: • LNAV/NAV outputs to autoflight system aileron channel. VNAV/PROF outputs to autoflight system elevator channel and thrust control system.						
022 11 00 03	Indication and control						

Subject	022 - AIRCRAFT GENERAL KNOWLEDGE – INSTRUMENTATION	*Aeroplane*		*Helicopter*			*IR*
Syllabus reference	**Syllabus details and Learning Objectives**	ATPL	CPL	ATPL/IR	ATPL	CPL	

LO	*General overview, examples will be given for information only, but no MCQ will refer to a specific system!*
	Multifunction Control- and Display Unit:
	• Display unit:
	  • Title field, scratch pad, left and right columns consisting of 6 lines.
	  • Line Select Keys (LSK).
	  • Symbols: dashes, brackets, small and large fonts.
	  • Scroll buttons and previous and next page buttons.
	• Keyboard:
	  • Function & Mode keys, Alphanumeric keyboard, Annunciators.
	  • Cursor Control Device and interactive display units (touchscreen).
	• General FMS alert.						

022 11 00 04	Error behavior: accuracy, cross checks						
LO	Degraded modes of operation: Inertial only, Radio only or back up navigation, use of raw data (Dead Reckoning (DR). RAIM function for RNAV procedures. Fuel: independance between FMS computations and fuel system totalizer. Examples with non standard configurations: One engine out, landing gear down, flaps down, increases of consumption due to a CDL item, use of anti-ice systems, etc. Explain the differences between dual mode and independent mode.						
022 11 02 00	**Operational use of the FMS**						
LO	Multifunction Control and Display Unit (MCDU) as interface with FMS. Understand/explain menu structure: index page, subpages. Explain the use of the function- and mode buttons. Use of execute button Use of alphanumeric keyboard. Make distinction between computations based on measured data (use of sensors) versus computations based on database information Computed data/information displayed: checking and confirmation with LSK. Use of (M)CDU to create and modify a lateral and vertical flight plan: use of keyboard commands, interpret display and annunciations. Interface with Flight Mode Panel: LNAV/NAV mode and/or VNAV/PROF mode, relation with altitude select function, Speed/M window blanked when FMS in control. Interface with EFIS: EADI (PFD): FD & FMA, EHSI (ND): Map mode & Plan mode (colors, symbols). Cross check possibility of stored flight plan with help of EFIS Plan mode. Check for discontinuities. Possible consequences of wrong navigation database. Consequences of selection and insertion of wrong waypoint (with same name but different location). State the importance of situational awareness by interpretation of other navigation sources/methods.						
022 12 00 00	**ALERTING SYSTEMS, PROXIMITY SYSTEMS**						
022 12 01 00	**Alerts**						
LO	Refer to AMJ 25.1322 Alerting systems, with respect to use of colours: red, amber, green, blue, white. State other kinds of warning indications: warning flag, bar removal, pointer mask, aural warnings (bell, buzzer etc.), removal of information, drawing a red cross on cathode ray tube or liquid crystal display, vibration (stick shaker for stall warning).						
022 12 02 00	**Flight Warning system**						
022 12 02 01	Definition, Purpose & Application	x		x	x	x	

Subject	022 - AIRCRAFT GENERAL KNOWLEDGE – INSTRUMENTATION	*Aeroplane*		*Helicopter*			*IR*
Syllabus reference	**Syllabus details and Learning Objectives**	ATPL	CPL	ATPL/IR	ATPL	CPL	
LO	State that the FWC is a dual channel computer. State that the FWC monitors the operational status of aircraft systems and gives a visual and aural alert in case of a system failure. State that the FWC uses 12 flight phases for the inhibiting function which are detected automatically by the FWC using several input signals from other aircraft systems. State that the FWC generates standard attention getting sounds (attensons) or chimes. State that the FWC generates aural alerts for specific situations: autopilot disconnect, overspeed, excessive pitch trim and altitude alert. State that the FWS makes use of an annunciator panel for back-up purposes. Describe the operation of the Master Caution Light and Master Warning Light. Define the ARINC classifications of level 0, 1, 2 and 3 alerts. Standardisation of coloured visual and aural alerts. State that a FWC single channel failure does not cause system degradation. State that a FWC dual channel failure causes visual alerts only to be presented on the annunciator panel.						
022 12 03 00	**Stall warning & protection**						
022 12 03 01	Definition, Purpose & Application	x	x				
LO	Define a stalled wing and state the consequences. State the stall warning system is used to give a prestall warning when exceeding the critical angle of attack. State how the stall warning is given. State the JAR-25 requirements regarding a stall warning system in an operational environment.						
022 12 03 02	Construction & Operation						
LO	Describe the stall warning system of a small aeroplane, consisting of a flapper switch and warning horn or a whistle. Describe the operation of the stall warning system with help of a simplified blockdiagram which at least includes: inputs, computer, outputs. Inputs: AoA, wing configuration, aeroplane weight, ground inhibit, ground test Describe the need for an altitude compensation too prevent a slow response at high altitudes. Outputs: stick shaker, flight warning system, EFIS, stick pusher, autopilot disconnect. Describe the operation, construction and location of the stickshaker. State some aeroplanes have a stickpusher as a stall recovery system. State that the stickpusher has a disconnect facility.						
022 12 03 03	Control & Indication						
LO	An impending stall is indicated by both visual and aural means. EFIS equipped aeroplanes have a marking on the pitch scale of the attitude indicator and along the speed tape that must prevent a too high angle of attack or a too low speed. Test switch.						
022 12 03 04	Error behavior & Cross checks						
LO	Understand the relation between AoA, airspeed and attitude.						
022 12 04 00	**V_{MO}/M_{MO} warning**						
LO	State the consequences of exceeding V_{MO}/M_{MO}. State that the overspeed warning system warns the pilot aurally that airspeed is above maximum allowable speed v_{MO} or maximum allowable mach number M_{MO}. Name that the warning is typically an interrupted sound (clacker) made by the FWC. State that the FWC receives the V_{MO}/M_{MO} directly from the ADC. State the use of the test button. State that the maximum allowable speed is shown on the Mach/airspeed indicator.						

Subject	022 - AIRCRAFT GENERAL KNOWLEDGE – INSTRUMENTATION	*Aeroplane*		*Helicopter*			*IR*
Syllabus reference	**Syllabus details and Learning Objectives**	ATPL	CPL	ATPL/IR	ATPL	CPL	
022 12 05 00	**Take-off warning**						
LO	State the consequence of taking-off with an aeroplane not being in the correct take-off configuration. State visual and aural alert when throttles are advanced on ground and aircraft is not in correct take-off configuration. Mention monitored parameters.						
022 12 06 00	**Altitude alert system**						
LO	State visual and aural alert when aircraft acquires or deviates from a pre-selected baro altitude. State altitude alert is not given when in approach configuration. State altitude alert system independent from AP. State the JAR-OPS requirements regarding the altitude alert system.						
022 12 07 00	**Radio-altimeter**						
LO	Measures height. Based on measurement of radio frequency difference. Low range radio altimeter only. 2,500 ft. FMCW. Accuracy. SHF > 4200 - 4300 MHz > 4250 MHz, 100 MHz sweep. Components: Tx antenna, Rx antenna and transceiver. Illustrate and interpret different types of indication. R/A indicator: circular scale, straight scale and EFIS. Outputs: R/A indicator, EGPWS, Autoflight. Decision height visual and aural alert. Aircraft Installation delay. Cross checks.						
022 12 08 00	**Ground proximity warning systems**						
LO	EGPWS, GPWS, GCAS, TAWS and differences. Purpose. Operating range. Difference between GPWS and EGPWS. Warning modes. Warning mode modulation. Inputs and outputs. Simple blockdiagram. Control and indication. JAR-OPS requirements. Test.						
022 12 09 00	**Airborne Collision Avoidance System (ACAS/TCAS)**						

Subject	022 - AIRCRAFT GENERAL KNOWLEDGE – INSTRUMENTATION	*Aeroplane*		*Helicopter*			*IR*
Syllabus reference	**Syllabus details and Learning Objectives**	ATPL	CPL	ATPL/IR	ATPL	CPL	
LO	Definition, Purpose & Application • ICAO > JAR-25 > ACAS • TCAS II version 7 to prevent mid-air collisions Operation & Construction • Resolution Advisory (RA), Traffic Avisoriy (TA), Proximity traffic and Non-threat traffic • Corrective and preventive RA's: pitch channel only • Coordination link • Components: TCAS computer, top and bottom antenna, control panel, Mode-S transponder • Capacity, range • Quadrantal scan with directional antennas • Interrogation of transponders • Calculation of time to closest point of approach out of : altiutde, altitude rate, relative bearing, distance, relative speed • Inhibits at low altitude Indication & Control • Outputs: visual and aural alerts, indicators, symbols Error behavior & (Cross) checks • Test function • Explain that the pilot must not interpret the horizontal track of an intruder on the display						
022 12 10 00	**Rotor/engine overspeed alert system**						
022 12 10 01	Design, operation, displays, alarms			x	x	x	
LO	Understand the basic design principles, displays and warning/alarm systems fitted to different helicopters						
022 12 11 00	**Laser obstacle detector**						
022 12 11 01	Design, operation, displays, limitations			x	x	x	
LO	(NOTE WAITING FOR INFORMATION REGARDING THIS SUBJECT)						
022 13 00 00	**INTEGRATED INSTRUMENTS – ELECTRONIC DISPLAYS**						
022 13 01 00	**Display Units**						
022 13 01 01	Cathode Ray Tube (CRT): • Construction, principle of operation • Monochrome and full colour CRT • Stroke writing and raster writing Liquid Crystal Display: • Construction, principle of operation • Normal LCD and Active Matrix LCD Compare CRT with LCD with respect to: • Viewing angle, power consumption, weight, temperature, cooling requirement, glare, radiation, backlighting, missing pixels. Give examples: EFIS, EICAS/ECAM/MFDS, MCDU	x	x	x	x	x	x
022 13 02 00	**Integrated Instrument System (IIS)**						
022 13 02 01	IIS predecessor of EFIS. Electromechanical ADI and HSI. Inputs/outputs.	x	x	x	x	x	x
022 13 03 00	**Electronic Flight Instrument System (EFIS)**						

Subject	022 - AIRCRAFT GENERAL KNOWLEDGE – INSTRUMENTATION	*Aeroplane*		*Helicopter*			*IR*
Syllabus reference	**Syllabus details and Learning Objectives**	ATPL	CPL	ATPL/IR	ATPL	CPL	
LO	List and describe the function of each of the EFIS system components: • Computer: symbol generator unit or display management computer • Display units: EADI or PFD and EHSI or ND • Control panel switches: brightness control, mode selection, range selection, display options • (Remote) light sensor on glarehield for automatic brightness control. PFD/ND: flight instruments and flight mode annunciator. ND/EHSI: (radio)navigation information. Source select buttons. List inputs, describe outputs. Information displayed. JAR-25 color coding Brightness control: brightness switch, remote light sensor, integral light sensor. DU failure: indication, DU transfer, composite display. Failure of electronics unit Failure of one or more sources/inputs. Simple block diagram of a typical aircraft installation. Compare EFIS with IIS.	x		x	x		
022 13 04 00	**Systems and procedures displays (EICAS, ECAM, MFDU)**						
LO	Purpose: common display system of engine and system parameters and alerts. State that FWS makes use of EICAS/ECAM for display of alerts. Components: computer(s), display units, control panel (switches: brightness control, system pages, Cancel and recall). List inputs; describe outputs. DU: warning or primary display and system or secondary display. DU failure: indication, DU transfer or composite display. Selection of pages: manual or automatic. Simple block diagram of a typical aircraft installation.	x	x	x	x	x	x
022 13 05 00	**Head Up Display (HUD)**						
LO	Different presentation types: projection or generation. Purpose: enhance safety during Take-off or CAT 3 approaches under low visibility conditions. Displayed parameters. System requirements: collimator, contact analogue presentation, eye reference position.	x	x				
022 13 06 00	**Engine First Limit Indicator**						
022 13 06 01	Design, operation, indications and displays						
LO	Understand the principles of design, operation and compare the different indications and displays available in the industry.			x	x	x	
LO	Understand what will be displayed on the screen, when in the limited screen composite mode.			x	x	x	
LO	Understand how the engine first limit indicator system is now being integrated into some flight management systems.			x	x	x	
022 13 07 00	**Night vision goggles**						
022 13 07 01	Design, operation, displays, limitations			x	x	x	
LO	Understand the function of night vision goggles and the basic design concepts, each eye tube intensifies the available light source more than 3000 times.			x	x	x	
LO	Understand the limitations of NVGs • minimum 2 minilux level needed for effective use • lack of depth perception (two dimensional image) • limited field of view • need to reduce bank angles to avoid risk of spatial disorientation • fatigue of neck muscles with prolonged use, due to extra weight on helmet			x	x	x	
LO	Understand the importance of proper training before using in flight and the NAA's regulations governing the use of NVGs.			x	x	x	

Subject	022 - AIRCRAFT GENERAL KNOWLEDGE – INSTRUMENTATION	*Aeroplane*		*Helicopter*			*IR*
Syllabus reference	**Syllabus details and Learning Objectives**	ATPL	CPL	ATPL/IR	ATPL	CPL	
LO	Understand the importance of logging battery usage and changing batteries at correct intervals.			x	x	x	
LO	Understand the danger of mis-handling of Lithium bateries (used on some NVGs).			x	x	x	
LO	Appreciate the high cost of conversion (panel lights) of the aircraft prior to NVG use			x	x	x	
022 14 00 00	**MAINTENANCE, MONITORING AND RECORDING SYSTEMS**						
	No JAR-OPS knowledge will be tested in these MCQs						
022 14 01 00	**Cockpit Voice Recorder (CVR)**						
LO	State the JAR-25 requirements concerning the CVR. To register all voice conversation from the pilot stations on a shock-, fire- and water resistant medium in order to facilitate accident or incident investigation. State that the voice recorder is designed to record: direct conversation between crew members and all aural warnings in the cockpit, communications received and transmitted by radio, intercom conversations between crew members, announcements transmitted via the passenger address system. Record on endless magnetic tape with a 30 minute capcity or in solid state memory with a capacity of 2 hours. Components: Area microphone, Crashproof four track recorder located in the aft section of the aircraft near the pressure bulkhead, underwater locater beacon working with ultrasonic waves. Start on ground with at least one fuel lever open, stop whenboth fuel levers closed. State that many aircraft have a switch to start recording already before the fuel lever is set to open. State the possibility to erase the recording with the erase button and only when on ground and the parking brake set.	x		x	x	x	
022 14 02 00	**Flight Data Recorder (FDR)**						
LO	State the JAR-25 requirements concerning the installation of a FDR. State the recording of mandatory system related parameters. Early type FDR is analogue scratch foil (metal) recorders with a maximum capaity of 400 hours. Modern digital FDR is a solid state design recorder with a capacity of 25 hours. Name the following components of a flight data recorder: shock-, temperature- and fire-proof recording unit, underwater locater beacon working with ultrasonic waves. State that the flight recorder obtains its operating voltage from the emergency power supply. State that the flight recorder operates as soon as electric power is on and a fuel lever is open. State that the scratch foil recorder has a control panel in the cockpit that allowed the tape to be marked prior to each flight with help of thumbwheels. State that in modern aircraft the FMS is used to mark the recording medium prior to each flight. Mention the function of the event button. State that the FDR is monitored and in case of malfunction an alert is given to the pilot.	x		x	x	x	
022 14 03 00	**Combination recorder**	x					
LO	State that a combination recorder is a recorder that records all parameters that are required by a CVR and by a FDR.						
022 14 04 00	**Maintenance and Monitoring systems**						

Subject	022 - AIRCRAFT GENERAL KNOWLEDGE – INSTRUMENTATION	*Aeroplane*		*Helicopter*			*IR*
Syllabus reference	**Syllabus details and Learning Objectives**	ATPL	CPL	ATPL/IR	ATPL	CPL	
LO	Aircraft Integrated Data System (AIDS) and Aircraft Condition Monitor System (ACMS). Components: Flight Data acquisition unit (FDAU), Central computer, CDU (separate or integral with MCDU), Airborne printer, Flight maintenance recorder or Quick Access Recorder (QAR). State that AIDS incorporates the FDR and the QAR including devices for system control, input and presentation of data . State that the FDR and the QAR records inputs from ADC, compass system, engine instruments, navigation receiver, COM receiver, flight controls positions, aircraft configuration, g-forces etc. State that data from the flight maintenance recorder can be printed out for purposes of maintenance. State that aircraft relevant data can be transmitted from the aircraft integrated data system system in certain intervals to ground for an engine trend monitoring. State that the following information is entered into a flight maintenance recorder: day, month, flight number, take-off weight.	x	x	x	x	x	
022 14 05 00	**Weight and Balance system**						
LO	Function. Determines aircraft gross weight and center of gravity. Gear mounted sensors. Control and indication via MCDU.						
022 15 00 00	**DIGITAL CIRCUITS AND COMPUTERS**						
022 15 01 00	**Digital techniques**						
LO	Mention the difference between analogue and digital technique. Explain and convert the following number systems: decimal, binary. Mention the following number systems: decimal, binary, octal, hexadecimal. Mention the difference between positive logic and negative logic Mention the use of the following binary codes: BCD, 2 out of 5 (MOON), GRAY, ASCII. Describe the difference between a BIT and a BYTE. Explain the difference between kiloBytes, MegaBytes, GigaBytes and TeraBytes.	x		x	x		
022 15 02 00	**Digital circuits**	x		x	x		
LO	Explain the following logic gates together with their symbols: INVERTER (NOT), (N)AND, (EX)(N)OR. Using RDL-technique, explain a logic '0' and a logic '1'. Describe an Integrated Circuit (IC). Mention the applications of IC's: logic circuits, micro-processor, memories, converters, etc. Describe the Analog-to-Digital Converter with respect to the sampling process and the quantification process. Describe the multiplexer and demultiplexer. Describe the ARINC-429 Digital Information Transfer System (DITS). Describe the difference between the ARINC-429 and ARINC-629 data bus with respect to speed, capacity, number of wires. Describe the following memories: ROM, PROM, EPROM, EEPROM. Describe the following properties of a memory: RAM, Sequential Access, Read/Write. Explain that memory capacity is expressed in BYTES.						
022 15 03 00	**Architecture of a computer**						

Subject	022 - AIRCRAFT GENERAL KNOWLEDGE – INSTRUMENTATION	*Aeroplane*		*Helicopter*			*IR*
Syllabus reference	**Syllabus details and Learning Objectives**	ATPL	CPL	ATPL/IR	ATPL	CPL	
LO	Definition: A computer is a machine that makes use of a stored programm to processes data. Application: Aircraft and engine systems (autoflight systems, air data systems, warning systems etc. Name the difference between an analogue computer and a digital computer. Define a microcomputer. Describe the basic operating philosophy of the micrcocomputer with help of Von Neumann (fetch, decode, execute). Describe the peripheral equipment: sensors, keyboard, display units etc. Name the consisting parts of a microcomputer in terms of I/O modules, microprocessor (central processor unit or CPU) and memories. Describe the I/O modules. Explain the function of the CPU. Define the instruction set of a CPU. Name the components of the CPU and their functions as being: control unit, Arithmetic and Logic Unit (ALU) and registers. Mention the following registers and state their function: Instruction-register, Program-counter, Accumulator. Describe the following buses with their purpose which are used for the communication between the different components: control-bus, adress-bus, data-bus. Distinguish between background memory and internal memory.	x		x	x		
022 15 04 00	**Software**	x		x	x		
LO	Describe the term 'software'. Mention the difference between software and hardware. Define the term 'operating system'. Explain the difference between machine-code, assembler and compiler.						

CHAPTER 1
Air Data Instruments

1.1 Introduction

Air data systems (also known as manometric systems) sense the total pressure created by an aircraft as it moves through the air and the static pressure in the atmosphere surrounding it. This is done by sensors which are connected directly to mechanical type instruments or indirectly via an air data computer to electro-mechanical or servo type instruments. The measured data is presented on these instruments in terms of speed, altitude and rate of change of altitude.

1.2 Pitot and Static Systems

Pitot and static systems allow air data to be measured by sensing total (pitot) pressure and static pressure and transmitting this information to the air data system. The pressures are sensed by probes located in the airstream and these probes may be a combined pitot-static tube or a separate pitot tube and static vent(s). In a basic air data system the probes are connected via pipelines (with integrated drains) to the 3 primary air data instruments (i.e. airspeed indicator, altimeter and vertical speed indicator).

1.2.1 Pitot Probe

A pitot probe measures total (stagnation) pressure. This pressure is distributed to the airspeed indicator

A typical pitot probe consists of an open ended tube or probe attached to the aircraft in such a manner that it is clear of local disturbances (propeller or jet-wash and aerofoil flow), with its open end pointing forward directly into the airflow. To ensure the pitot tube receives (as far as is possible) an uninterrupted laminar flow of air, the most common locations for mounting the pitot tube on slower aircraft is on the fuselage side near the nose, wing tips or the tip of the fin. For supersonic aircraft the pitot tube is usually mounted on a long probe attached to the aircraft's nose. Most aircraft of moderate or larger size have at least two pitot tubes.

The stagnation (pitot) pressure is sensed at the open end of the probe and transmitted via the pressure tube to the appropriate instrument in the system. The heater element provides protection against icing.

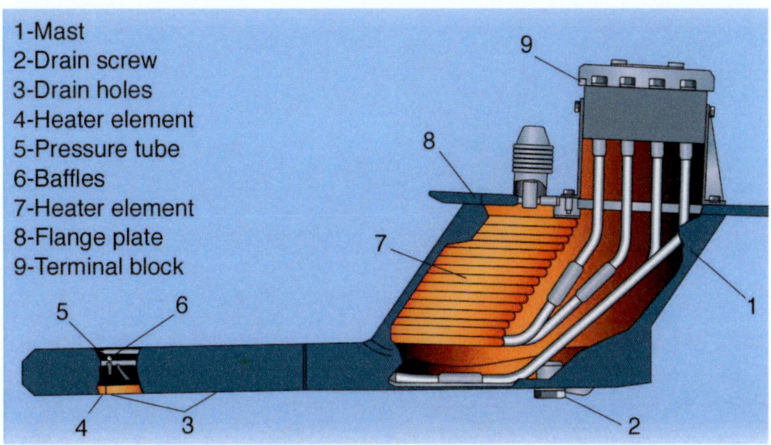

Figure 1.1 Pitot probe

1.2.2 Pitot-Static Probe

In some instances the static source may be co-located with the pitot tube in what is known as a "pitot-static pressure head" or simply a "pressure head". The pitot tube, which is open at the forward end, is mounted concentrically within an outer static tube, the forward end of which is closed. Static pressure is admitted to the pressure head through ports or holes cut into the static casing. The different pressures are fed to the flight instruments via separate, seamless and corrosion-resistant metal pipelines. The figure below shows an example of a simple pressure head. An electric heating element is connected to the aircraft supply to prevent ice forming inside the pressure head and hence obstructing the airflow.

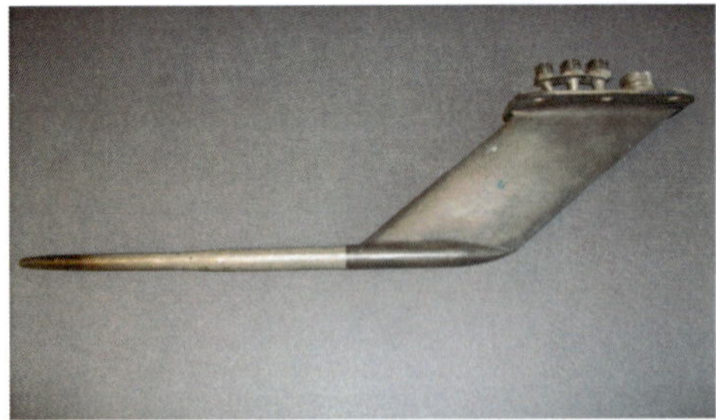

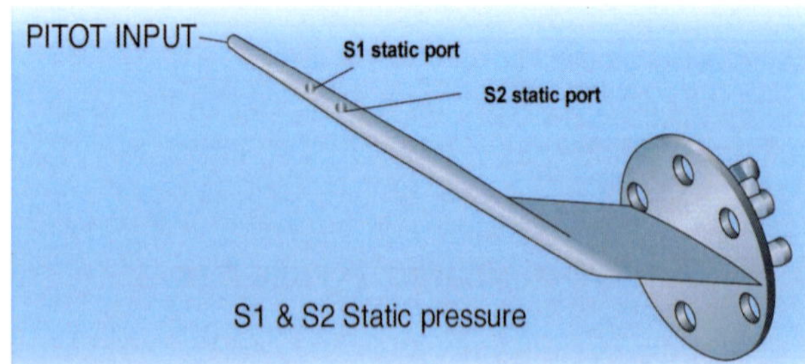

Figure 1.2 Pitot-static probe

1.2.3 Static Vent

The static vent measures the static (atmospheric) pressure surrounding the aircraft; it is distributed to the airspeed indicator, the altimeter and the vertical speed indicator

The ambient pressure of the air mass surrounding the aircraft, or static_pressure, is obtained via a static source. The static source or static vent (see figure below) is placed in the most advantageous position on the airframe, where the air surrounding the aircraft is least disturbed by the aircraft's forward movement. Aeroplanes, other than the very simple single engine type, have two static vents, one on each side of the fuselage. These are fed into a common static feed line. The purpose of this is to even out differences of pressure that may be caused by sideways motion of the static vent such as will occur during a yaw or sideslip. This is known as static balancing. Moderate or large aircraft will normally have a minimum of two static systems each fed by a pair of balanced static vents. The manufacturer, during prototype development, determines the precise location of static vents.

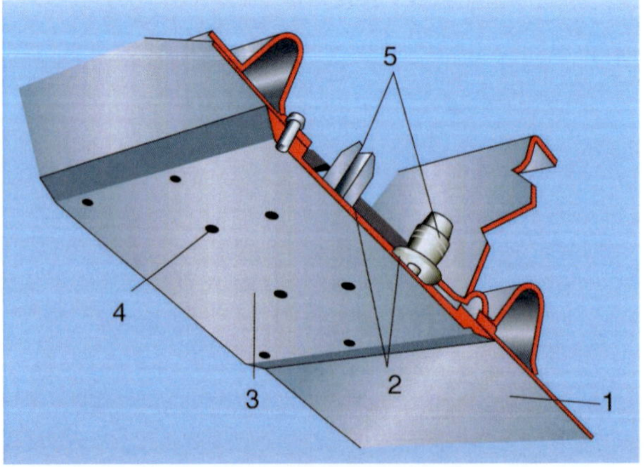

Figure 1.3 Static vent

1.2.3.1 Static Pressure Error

Static pressure error is the amount by which the local static pressure at a point in the flow field differs from the free stream static pressure. It is due to the fact that the probes designed to measure pressure actually disturb the airflow they are measuring and the airflow around the aircraft itself is disturbed by the attitude of the aircraft. These factors have greatest effect on the static pressure sensing section of the system.

The static pressure error is also referred to as the position or pressure error and affects the readings of the airspeed indicator and the altimeter; however, it does not affect the vertical speed indicator readings.

Pressure (Position) error can vary with speed, angle of attack and configuration. Consequently, deployment of flaps or turbulence encounters can cause fluctuations in measured pressure.

1.2.4 Malfunctions

Any blockage or a break of the total pressure or static pressure lines will cause the air data instruments to give inaccurate readings. Depending on the circumstances, the instruments may over read, under read or give no reading at all. This topic will be discussed further when examining the individual instruments in greater detail.

1.2.5 Alternate Static Source

If failure of the primary pitot/static pressure source should occur, for example icing up of a probe due to a failed heater circuit, errors will be introduced in the indications of those instruments and other areas dependent on such pressure.

As a safeguard against failure, a standby system may be installed in some aircraft, whereby static pressure and/or pitot pressure from alternate sources can be selected and connected into the primary system. The changeover is executed by means of selector valves located in the pitot and static lines. These are located on the flight deck, within easy reach of the flight crew. The layout shown in Figure 1.4 illustrates a method using an alternate static source only (normal position shown). It should be noted however, that some aircraft are designed with alternate sources for both pitot and static pressures.

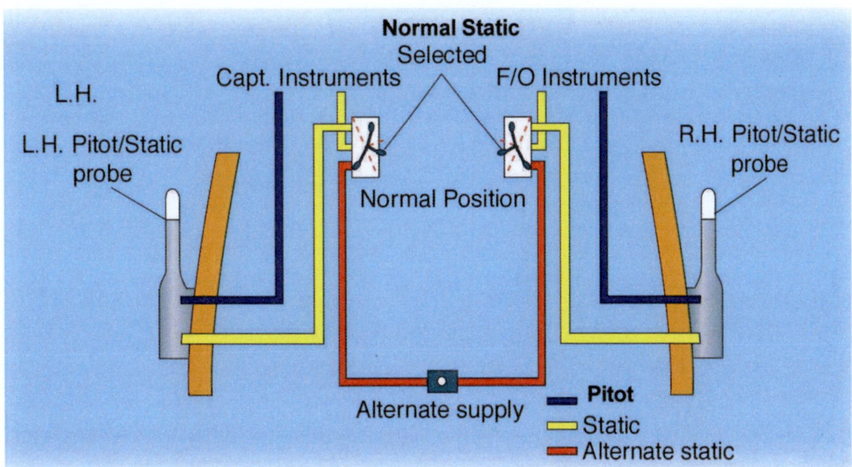

Figure 1.4 Alternate Static Source - Normal Position

Alternate static source use will almost always result in a different profile of pressure error. The sensed static pressure will usually be lower than it should be since the optimum position for the vent is that least affected by the venturi effect and, logically, this is chosen to be the position of the primary static source. The most probable effect on the airspeed indicator would be for it to over-read. When the alternate pressure system is used, correction values may be obtained from the Flight Manual.

1.3 Altimeter

The gaseous envelope, which surrounds the Earth, is divided into several concentric layers extending outwards from the Earth's surface. The lowest layer, the one in which we live, is termed the troposphere and it extends to an average height of about 36 090' whilst the outer layer is called the exosphere, and is located some hundreds of kilometres out in space. Throughout the layers, the atmosphere undergoes a gradual transition from its characteristics at sea level to those at the fringes of deep space.

1.3.1 Pressure Variation

The atmosphere is held in contact with the Earth by the force of gravity, the effect of which decreases with increasing distance from the Earth's surface. Atmospheric pressure, therefore, decreases steadily with height until, at tropopause height, the pressure has fallen to about one quarter of its sea level value. The steady fall in atmospheric pressure as altitude increases has a controlling effect on air density, which changes in direct proportion to changes in air pressure.

1.3.2 Temperature Variation

Another factor affecting the atmosphere is its temperature structure. Air in contact with the Earth is heated and rises. As the air rises, pressure falls allowing it to expand and drop in temperature with height up to the tropopause. Beyond the tropopause, the temperature at first remains constant before varying again with height, finally increasing to a maximum of 2 000°C at approximately 200 km.

1.3.3 International Standard Atmosphere (ISA) Factor

In order to obtain indications of altitude, air speed and rate of altitude change, the relationship between the pressure, temperature, density and altitude must be known. Relative to altitude, the value of the three variables would be difficult to continuously measure and compensate for. A standard atmosphere in which the value of pressure, temperature and density vary at a prescribed rate (with altitude) is therefore accepted and used internationally as a reference and a datum to which air data instruments are calibrated. The following table gives the pressures and temperatures at significant levels in the International Standard Atmosphere.

Altitude	Press. (hPa)	Temp. °C
0	1013.2	+15
3000	908.1	+9
6000	812.0	+3
10000	696.8	-4
14000	595.2	-12.7
18000	506.0	-20.7
21000	446.5	-26.6

Altitude	Press. (hPa)	Temp. °C
24000	392.7	-32.5
27000	344.3	-38.5
30000	300.9	-44.4
33000	262.0	-50.4
36000	227.3	-56.2
39000	196.8	-56.5
43000	162.4	-56.5

Note that sea level pressure is assumed to be 1013.2 hPa, sea level temperature of +15°C and temperature reduces at 1.98°C per 1000' from sea level up to a height of 36 090'.

1.3.4 Sensitive Altimeter

The altimeter is an instrument that is designed to measure static pressure and, using the conditions of the standard atmosphere, convert that pressure into a value of altitude. For example if the pressure measured is 506 hPa the altitude that the altimeter is calibrated to indicate is 18 000'.

1.3.5 Construction

The sensitive altimeter has a minimum of two aneroid capsules. This provides for a more accurate measurement of pressure and also provides more power to drive the mechanical linkage. The capsules are stacked together with one face fastened down, permitting movement due to pressure changes at the other end. The movement of the capsules in response to change in height (pressure) is transmitted via a suitable mechanical linkage to three pointers that display (against a graduated instrument scale) the aircraft height.

The whole assembly is encased in a container, which is fed with static pressure, but is otherwise completely airtight. Within the mechanical linkage a bi-metallic insert is fitted to compensate for temperature changes that could affect the movement. As the aircraft climbs and air pressure falls, the capsules expand; similarly, as the aircraft descends, static pressure increases and the capsules contract.

Since it is necessary to allow for different values of mean sea level pressure and to allow the altimeter to be used for indicating height above the aerodrome, the pilot must be provided with a means of adjusting the level at which the altimeter indicates zero'. Fitting a barometric subscale mechanism does this. This adjusts the mechanical linkage and operates a set of digital counters, or calibrated dial. This displays in a window in the face of the altimeter the datum pressure setting above which the instrument is now displaying altitude. The desired setting is made using the knurled knob at the bottom of the instrument.

In order to obtain a linear altitude scale from the non-linear pressure/altitude relationship a conversion is carried out within the altimeter mechanism by use of the pressure-deflection characteristics of the capsules and a variable magnification lever and gear system.

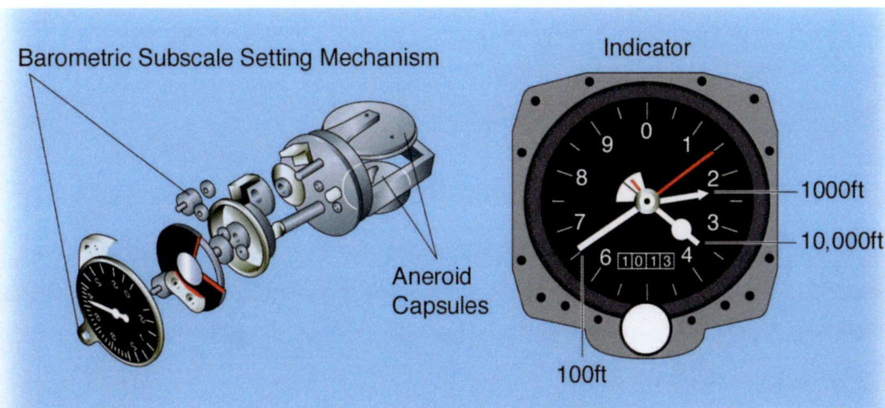

Figure 1.5 Pressure Altimeter

1.3.6 Height Displays

A number of different types of pressure altimeter are manufactured; however, the majority differ in detail of height band covered, accuracy of instrument and method of displaying altitude. Types of display vary from multi-needle to needle plus digital counters, with accuracy varying from ± 100' at 0' to ± 1 000' at 35 000' in early models, to ± 35' at 0' to ± 600' at 60 000' in later models. A selection of typical displays are shown below; included is an instrument face showing a sector flag, barber pole display or low altitude warning sector. The sector flag, which has stripes in black and white, appears in a window when the height is 16 000' or lower, giving the pilot clear warning of approaching low altitudes in rapid descents.

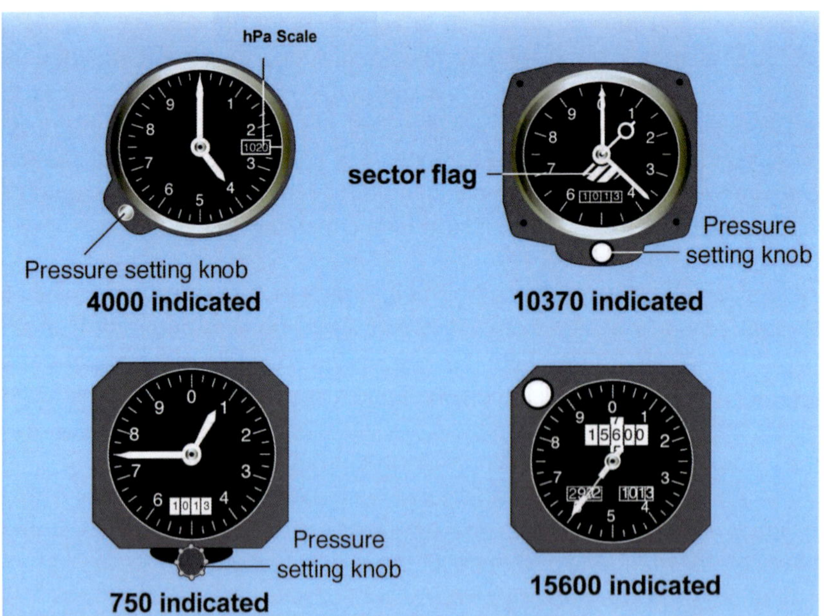

Figure 1.6 Altimeter Types

1.3.7 Vibrator Assembly and Power Supply Indication

Modern altimeters are fitted with a vibrator assembly. The induced vibration in the mechanism reduces the initial opposition to motion of the moving parts and reduces frictional lag in the system

The electrical supply also energises a warning flag solenoid in the digitiser circuit code converter. In the event of a power supply failure, the solenoid is de-energised and allows a power failure warning flag to appear in an aperture in the dial; at the same time the code converter will revert to a recognised fail-safe position of “All Zeros”.

1.3.8 Datum Sub-scale Settings

The setting of altimeters to datum barometric pressures is part of flight operating procedures and is essential for maintaining adequate separation between aircraft and terrain clearance during take-off and landing. Titles for the settings have been adopted universally and form part of the ICAO “Q” code of communication. The code consists of three-letter groups, each having “Q” as the first letter. Those normally used in relation to altimeter settings are:

QFE The pressure prevailing at an airfield, the setting of which on the altimeter subscale will cause the altimeter to read zero on landing and take-off.

QNE Setting the standard pressure setting of 1013.25 hPa causes the altimeter to indicate the pressure altitude in the standard atmosphere.

QNH Setting the pressure scale to make the altimeter read airfield elevation on landing and take-off.

The subscale settings may be given in hPa or inches of Mercury (in Hg) with a conversion between the two being carried out as follows:

$$1013.25 \text{ hPa} = 29.92 \text{ in Hg}$$

$$1 \text{ in Hg} = \frac{1013.25}{29.92} = 33.9 \text{ hPa}$$

1.3.8.1 Definitions

Height – the vertical distance of a level, point or object considered as a point measured from a specified datum

Indicated altitude – altitude read from the altimeter when it is correctly adjusted to the local altimeter setting

True altitude – actual height of an object above mean sea level

Pressure altitude – altitude displayed on the altimeter when the sub-scale is set to 1013.25 hPa

Density altitude – pressure altitude corrected for non-standard temperature, it is used to determine aeroplane performance. Density altitude is equal to pressure altitude when standard temperature conditions exist.

1.3.9 Servo Altimeter

Servo-assisted altimeters use the same basic principles as sensitive altimeters, whereby pressure changes are measured using the expansion and contraction of evacuated capsules. Height is indicated by a digital counter system and a single pointer.

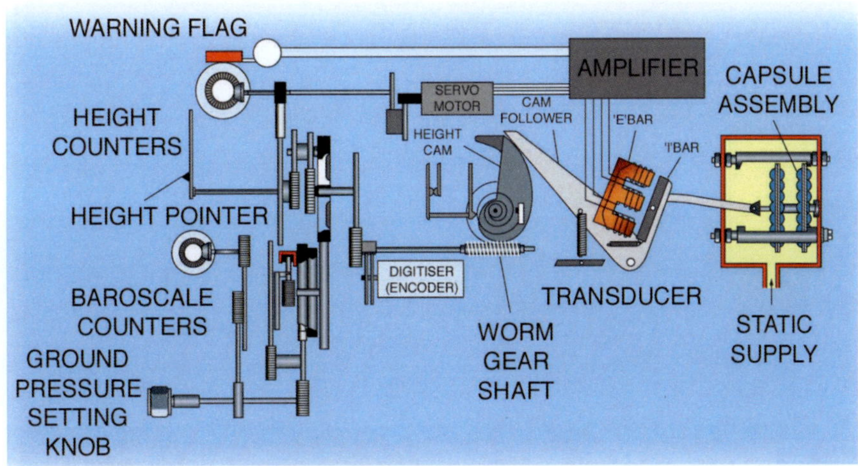

Figure 1.7 Servo Altimeter

1.3.9.1 Principle of Operation

The mechanism of a typical servo-altimeter is shown schematically in Figure 1.7, from which it can be seen that the pressure sensing capsules are coupled mechanically to an electrical E and I pick-off assembly. Movement of the aneroid capsules is transmitted through a linkage to the "I" bar of the E and I inductive pick-up. The amplitude of the AC voltage output from the secondary windings depends on the degree of deflection of the "I" bar, which is a function of pressure change. Polarity of the output signal will depend on whether the capsules expand or contract. The output signal is amplified and used to drive a motor whose speed and direction of rotation will depend on the amplitude and phase of the signal. The motor drives the gear train, which rotates the height digital counters and the pointer. The motor also drives, through gearing, a cam that imparts an angular movement to a cam follower. The "E" bar of the inductive pick-off is attached to the follower. Sense of movement is such that the "E" bar is driven until it reaches a position where the air gaps between "E" and "I" bars are again equal, thus completing the servo-loop. The system is very sensitive to small changes in pressure and through the motor assembly provides adequate torque to drive the indicating system.

1.3.9.2 Datum Pressure Setting

The datum pressure setting knob is linked to the cam via a gear train and worm shaft, as shown in Figure 1.7. Rotation of the knob causes the worm shaft to slide forwards or backwards and thus rotate the cam. Angular movement of the cam alters the relationship between the "E" and "I" bars, resulting in an electrical output which causes rotation of the counters and drives the inductive pick-off back to its neutral position. The hPa sub-scale displays the value of the datum pressure set.

1.3.9.3 Advantages

Servo-altimeters have the following advantages over conventional altimeters:

1. At high altitude very little pressure change takes place for a given change of altitude, with the result that capsule movement is considerably less than for the same change of altitude at lower levels. This factor reduces the efficiency of ordinary altimeters at high levels, whereas the servomechanism will pick up a capsule movement as small as 0.0002 inches per thousand feet.
2. Power transmission gives greater accuracy.
3. There is practically no time lag between arrival of new pressure in the instrument and positioning of counters.
4. Being an electrical system, correction for pressure error could be made and an altitude-alerting device may be incorporated.
5. Although conventional altimeters now employ digital presentation, it is generally more common with servo-altimeters. The digital presentation reduces the possibility of misreading.
6. A pointer is still available on the servo-altimeter for use at low level in assessing rate of change of height.

The appearance of a typical indicator including alerting unit is shown below.

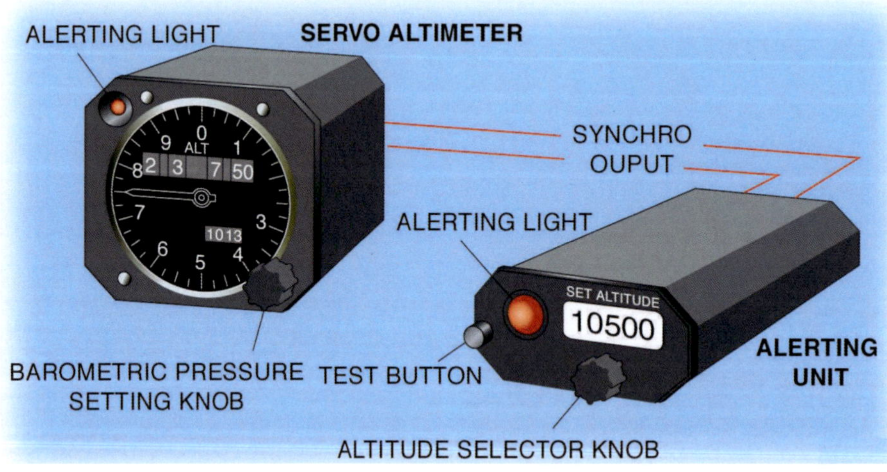

Figure 1.8 Indicator and alerting Unit

1.3.10 Errors

1.3.10.1 Instrument Error

Since capsule movements must be greatly magnified, it is impossible to ignore the effect of small irregularities in the mechanism. Certain manufacturers' tolerances have to be accepted, and errors generally increase with height.

1.3.10.2 Pressure Error

Pressure error arises because the true external static pressure is not accurately transmitted to the instrument. A false static pressure arises because of disturbed airflow in the vicinity of the pressure head or static vent. Pressure error is negligible at low altitude and speeds; the error becomes significant as speed increases. Correction for pressure error takes the form of a correction to be applied to indicated height and must be determined by calibration. Air data computers are designed to compensate for pressure error.

1.3.10.3 Time Lag Error

Because the response of the capsule and linkage is not instantaneous, the altimeter needle lags whenever height is changed. Subsequent over-indication during descent could be dangerous and should be allowed for in rapid descents. Time lag is virtually eliminated in the servo-assisted altimeter.

1.3.10.4 Barometric Error

Barometric error occurs when the actual datum level pressure differs from that to which the subscale has been set. Figure 1.9 illustrates the effect for a subscale set to 1000 hPa. A subscale error of 1 hPa is equivalent to an indicated altitude error of 27'. Since the QNH has reduced to 980 hPa this represents a height change of approximately 540'. The subscale datum must now be at a point that is effectively 540' below sea level and this is the level from which the altimeter is measuring.

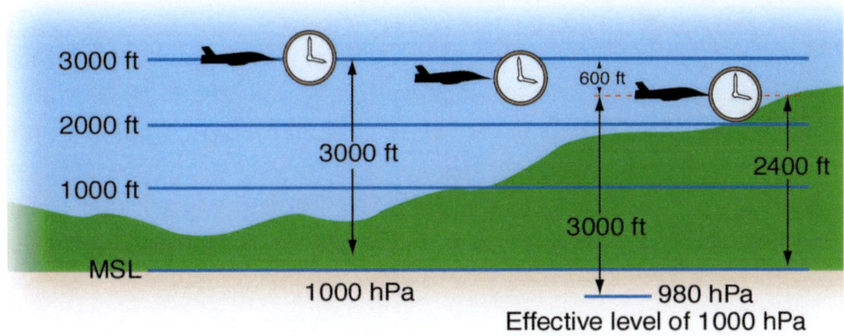

Figure 1.9 Barometric Error

1.3.10.5 Orographic Error

Differences from standard may occur when air is forced to rise/descend over hills or mountains. Low pressure tends to occur in the lee of mountains with high pressure on the windward side. Additionally, vertical movement of air can result in change of temperature from ISA, inducing further errors in altimeter readings.

1.3.10.6 Temperature Error

Temperature error arises whenever mean atmospheric conditions below the aeroplane differ from the standard atmosphere. If the actual temperature lapse rate differs from the assumed one, then indicated height will be incorrect. In general, if the air below the aeroplane is warmer than standard, the air will be less dense and the aircraft will be higher than indicated. If colder than standard, the air will be more dense and the aeroplane will be lower than standard. Figure 1.10 illustrates the effect when flying from a warm atmosphere through a standard and then to a cold atmosphere. It assumes no change in surface pressure or subscale setting. Correct height may be obtained from that indicated by use of the navigation computer. For 'rule of thumb' work, a temperature difference of 10°C, from standard, will cause an error of approximately 4% of indicated height.

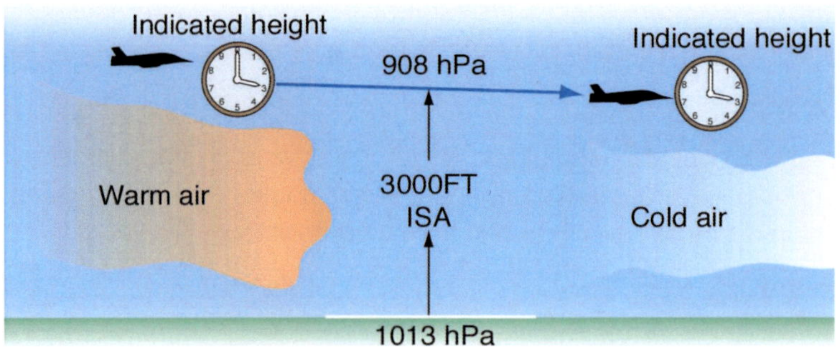

Figure 1.10 Temperature Error

1.3.11 Blockages

Should the static tube or vents become blocked, the pressure within the instrument case will remain constant and the altimeter will continue to indicate the height of the aircraft when the blockage occurred

In unpressurised aircraft, an alternative source inside the fuselage is available. However, the static pressure inside an aircraft differs from that external to the fuselage, being influenced by blowers, ventilation, etc, so that a different correction for pressure error is necessary: this is normally given in the aircraft manual.

1.4 Airspeed Indicator (ASI)

1.4.1 Introduction

Knowledge of the speed at which an aircraft is travelling through the air, i.e. the airspeed, is essential to the pilot, both for the safe and efficient handling of the aircraft and as a basic input to the navigation calculations. An aircraft stationary on the ground is subject to normal atmospheric or static pressure, which acts equally on all parts of the aircraft structure. In flight the aircraft experiences an additional pressure on its leading surfaces, due to a build up of the air through which the aircraft is travelling. This additional pressure, due to the aircraft's motion, is known as dynamic pressure and is dependent upon the forward motion of the aircraft and the density of the air, according to the following formula:

$$P_t = p + \tfrac{1}{2}\rho V^2$$

Where P_t = total pressure (also known as pitot pressure or stagnation pressure)
p = static pressure
ρ = air density
V = velocity of aircraft (true airspeed)

Re-arranging the formula, the difference between the pitot and static pressures is equal to $\tfrac{1}{2}\rho V^2$ (dynamic pressure).

The airspeed indicator measures the difference between total pressure and static pressure and provides a display indication graduated in units of speed (e.g. KT, kph)

1.4.2 Principle of Operation

In the ASI, a capsule acting as the pressure sensitive element is mounted in an airtight case, as shown in Figure 1.11. Pitot pressure is fed into the capsule and static pressure is fed to the interior of the case which, when the aircraft is in motion, thus contains the lower pressure. A pressure difference will cause the capsule to open out with movement proportional to pressure differential across the capsule skin (pitot - static).

A mechanical link is used to transfer the capsule movement to a pointer moving around a dial. It should be noted that although the expansion of the capsule is proportional to V^2 the scale of the instrument is ASI linear; the instrument is therefore square-law compensated.

A bi-metallic strip is incorporated in the mechanical linkage to compensate for expansion/contraction of the linkage due to temperature variation

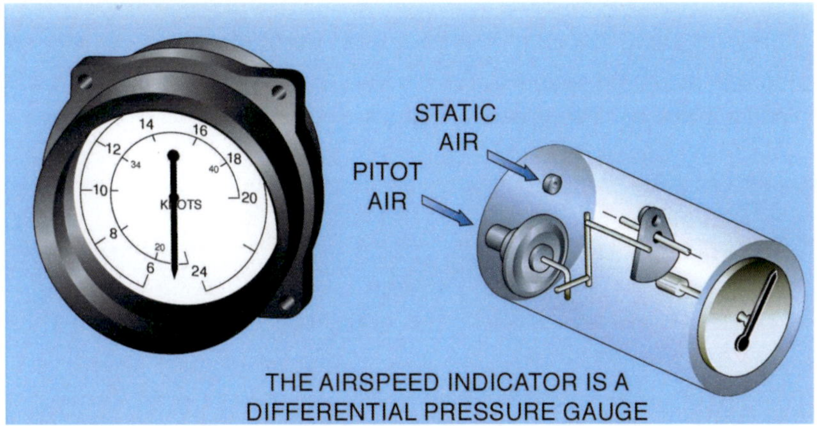

Figure 1.11 Airspeed indicator

In a sensitive ASI, which reacts to smaller pressure changes, a stack of two or more interlinked capsules are connected to the pointers by an extended gear train. This arrangement provides indications of smaller changes in airspeed.

1.4.3 Calibration

Since dynamic pressure varies with air speed and air density, and since density varies with temperature and pressure, standard datum values are used in the calibration of air speed indicators. This negates the need for complicated sensors to correct for variations in atmospheric conditions.

The datum values used are the sea level values of pressure and temperature in the International Standard Atmosphere

1.4.4 Speed Indications

1.4.4.1 Definitions

The following definitions are based on *JAR 1 –Definitions*.

Indicated Air Speed (IAS) - the speed of an aircraft as shown on its pitot static airspeed indicator calibrated to reflect standard atmosphere adiabatic compressible flow at sea level uncorrected for airspeed system errors.

Calibrated Air Speed (CAS) – the indicated airspeed of an aircraft, corrected for position and instrument error. Calibrated airspeed is equal to true airspeed in standard atmosphere at sea level.

Equivalent Air Speed (EAS) - the calibrated airspeed of an aircraft corrected for adiabatic compressible flow for the particular altitude. Equivalent airspeed is equal to calibrated airspeed in standard atmosphere at sea level.

True Air Speed (TAS) - the airspeed of an aircraft relative to undisturbed air. True airspeed is equal to equivalent airspeed compensated for density. The equivalent airspeed is multiplied by $(\rho_0/\rho)^{1/2}$. Where ρ_0 = density at sea level in ISA conditions and ρ = density at particular altitude.

V_{S0} – the stall speed or the minimum steady flight speed in the landing configuration
V_{S1} – the stall speed or the minimum steady flight speed obtained in a specified configuration
V_{FE} – maximum flap extended speed
V_{NO} – maximum structural cruising speed
V_{NE} – never-exceed speed
V_{LO} – maximum landing gear operating speed
V_{LE} – maximum landing gear extended speed
V_{YSE} – the single-engine best rate of climb speed

The dials of some light aircraft ASIs are colour coded, as illustrated below, as follows:

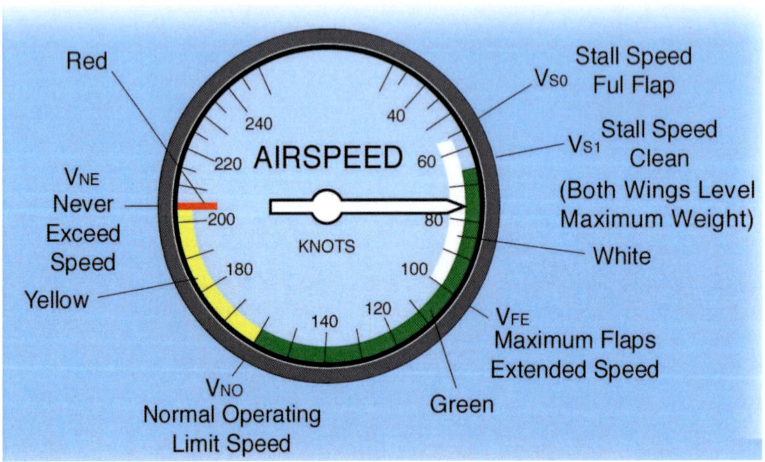

Figure 1.12 Airspeed indicator markings

- White arc – extends from V_{SO} (stall full flap) to V_{FE} (maximum speed with flaps extended) and marks the flap operating range of speeds
- Green arc – from V_{S1} (stall clean) to V_{NO} (normal operating speed). This is the normal operating range of speeds.
- Yellow – from V_{NO} to V_{NE} (never exceed speed). This denotes the 'use with caution' range. It should not be used in conditions other than smooth air,
- A red radial line marks V_{NE}.
- A blue radial line marks V_{YSE}.

Some ASIs have adjustable bugs that can be used to set a "target" speed, e.g. threshold speed.

The relationship between the various air speeds may be summarised as follows:

IAS = Air Speed Indicator Reading (ASIR)
CAS = IAS + Pressure Error Correction + Instrument Error Correction
EAS = CAS + Compressibility Error Correction
TAS = EAS + Density Error Correction

In practice, the corrections are combined to give:
ASIR + Instrument Error Correction + Pressure Error Correction = CAS
CAS + Compressibility Error Correction + Density Error Correction = TAS

1.4.5 Errors

The dial of the ASI is calibrated to a formula which assumes constant air density (standard mean sea level) and no instrument defects. Any departure from these conditions, or disturbance in the pitot or static pressures being applied to the instrument, will result in a difference between the indicated and true air speed. There are four sources of error:

1.4.5.1 Instrument Error

Instrument error is caused by manufacturers' permitted tolerances in construction of the instrument. The error is determined during calibration.

1.4.5.2 Pressure Error

Pressure error arises from movement of the air around the aircraft. This causes disturbances in the static pressure. Pressure error is tabulated in the aeroplane's flight manual.

1.4.5.3 Compressibility Error

The calibration formula for most airspeed indicators does not contain any compensation for the fact that the air is compressible. At low speeds this is insignificant but at high speeds (above 300 KT) this factor becomes important. This is especially so at high altitudes where the less dense air is easily compressed. Compressibility causes an in increase in the measured value of dynamic pressure, which causes the ASI to over-read. Thus, compressibility varies with speed and altitude. The error and correction can be compensated on some mechanical navigation computers but is tabulated against altitude, temperature and CAS in the handbooks of others.

1.4.5.4 Density Error

Dynamic pressure varies with air speed and density of the air. In calibration, standard mean sea level pressure is used; thus, for any other condition of air density, the ASI will be in error. As altitude increases, density decreases and indicated air speed (IAS) and thus equivalent air speed (EAS) will become progressively lower than true air speed (TAS). In practice, a correction for density is made using the navigation computer to convert CAS to TAS accounting for altitude and outside air temperature.

1.4.6 Faults

1.4.6.1 *Blockages*

Blockage of the pitot tube, possibly by ice, means the ASI will not react to changes of speed in level flight. However, the capsule will behave as a barometer or altimeter capsule, reacting to changes in static pressure, giving an indication of increase in speed if the aircraft climbs, and decrease in speed if it descends. If the static line is blocked, the ASI will over-read at lower altitudes and under-read at higher altitudes than that at which the line became blocked.

1.4.6.2 Leaks

A leak in the pitot system will cause the ASI to under-read, whilst a leak in the static line will cause the ASI to over-read in an unpressurised fuselage (cabin pressure usually lower than static) and under-read in a pressurised aircraft (cabin pressure higher than static).

1.5 Mach Meter

During flight, aircraft emit pressure disturbances (sound waves) which radiate in all directions at the speed of sound. As the airspeed of an aircraft increases, the aircraft gets progressively closer to the waves ahead of it until, at the speed of sound, the pressure waves combine into a shock wave attached to the aircraft. The effect of the shock wave is to greatly increase the drag forces attached to the aircraft and to significantly alter the stability and control characteristics. It is therefore very important for a pilot to know how close to the speed of sound his aircraft is. This is indicated by a Machmeter (Figure 1.13), an instrument that measures the ratio of the aircraft's speed to the local speed of sound and displays it as a Mach number (MN).

$$MN = \frac{TAS}{LSS}$$

where TAS = true airspeed and LSS = local speed of sound

The local speed of sound is given by the formula:

$$LSS = 38.94\sqrt{T}$$

where T is absolute temperature (measured in degrees Kelvin, °K = °C + 273), therefore as temperature decreases (e.g. an increase in altitude), the local speed of sound decreases and for a given true airspeed, Mach number increases.

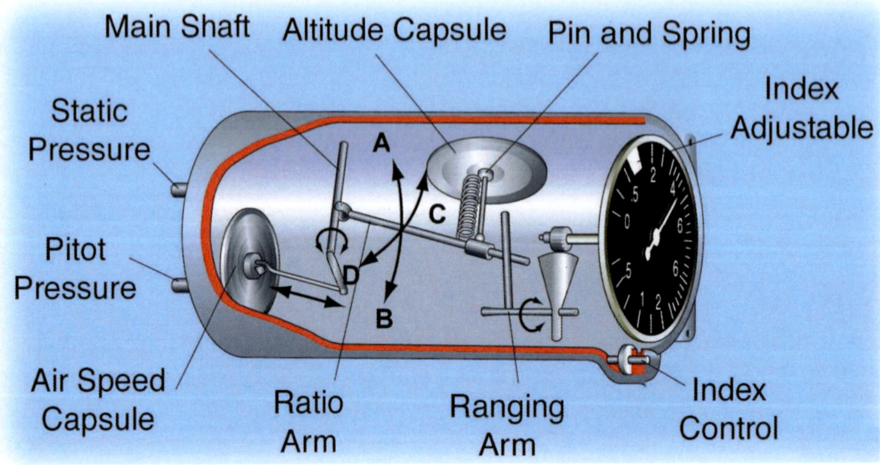

Figure 1.13 Machmeter

1.5.1 Critical Mach Number (M_{crit})

The speed of an aircraft is defined in terms of the speed of the free stream airflow; in practice the speed of the local airflow at any point around the structure varies considerably and the local airflow may reach the speed of sound when the free stream speed is much lower.

The free stream speed at which any element of the local airflow reaches the speed of sound – resulting in local shockwaves forming on the structure – is defined as the Critical Mach Number (M_{crit})

Unless specifically designed for the purpose, an aircraft should not be flown beyond M_{crit} and the value of M_{crit} is highlighted by an index mark on the face of the Machmeter. In commercial operations, it is common practice to set a lower limit known as the Maximum Operating Mach number (M_{MO}).

1.5.2 Principle of Operation

The TAS is a function of the dynamic pressure and the local density. Dynamic pressure is the difference between pitot (P_t) and static (p) pressures i.e. $P_t - p$. The local speed of sound (LSS) is a function of temperature and from basic gas physics temperature is a function of static pressure (p) and density.

As density is the common factor in both functions, it will be seen that

$$MN = \frac{TAS}{LSS} \propto \frac{P_t - p}{p}$$

The Machmeter is designed to measure the ratio of pitot excess pressure (the difference between pitot and static) and static pressure. A typical Machmeter is shown in Figure 1.13. It consists of a sealed case containing two capsule assemblies and the necessary mechanical linkages. The interior of one capsule unit, the air speed capsule, is connected to the pitot pressure pipeline, while the interior of the instrument case is fed with static pressure. The second capsule unit, is an aneroid capsule, which responds to static pressure changes. The air speed capsule measures the difference between pitot and static pressure and expands or contracts in response to air speed changes. Movement of the capsule is transferred by the air speed link to the main shaft, causing it to rotate and move a pivoted ratio arm in the direction A-B, see Figure 1.13.

The altitude (aneroid) capsule expands or contracts, responding to changes in altitude. Movement of the capsule is transferred to the ratio arm via a spring and pin, causing it to move in the direction C-D.

The position of the ratio arm depends, therefore, upon both pitot excess and static pressure, movement of the ratio arm controls the ranging arm which, through linkage and gearing, turns the pointer, thus displaying Mach number corresponding to the ratio of pitot excess pressure and static pressure. An increase in altitude and/or air speed results in higher Mach number. Critical Mach number is indicated by a specially shaped lubber mark located over the Machmeter dial. It is adjustable so that critical Mach number for the particular type of aircraft may be displayed.

1.5.3 Errors

As Mach number is a function of the ratio of pitot excess pressure to static pressure, only those errors in the measurement of this ratio will affect the Machmeter. Variations in air temperature and density from standard mean sea level values will have no effect in the measurement of Mach number. There are only two such errors:

1.5.3.1 Instrument Errors

Like all instruments, Mach meters are subject to tolerances in manufacture. They are, however, small.

1.5.3.2 Pressure Errors

These are small at the altitudes and speed ranges at which we use this instrument.

1.5.3.3 Blockages

A blocked static line will affect the instrument indications in all circumstances where there is a change in the outside static pressure. For example, if the aircraft is descending with a blocked static line, the Mach meter will over read. In this case, the altitude capsule will not contract (i.e. the instrument thinks it is higher than it actually is) and the airspeed capsule will expand too much (against a lower static pressure than what the aircraft is experiencing). The overall effect is therefore for the instrument to over read.

1.5.4 Tolerance

Accuracy is within ± 0.01Mach at normal operating range but decreases to ± 0.02 Mach at the limits of that range.

1.5.5 Serviceability Checks

The instrument should read zero with the aeroplane stationary. In flight, a rough check of IAS/TAS against Mach number may be made using your computer. For example, near sea level an IAS of 330 KT should give an indication of M 0.5.

1.6 Mach/Airspeed Indicator

The Mach Airspeed Indicator (M/ASI) is designed to combine the functions of both the airspeed indicator and the Machmeter into a single instrument; as the Machmeter contains an airspeed capsule it is a relatively simple matter to incorporate the IAS output from the capsule into the display.

1.6.1 Display

To improve clarity, digital readouts are provided for MN and IAS as well as a conventional pointer for IAS.

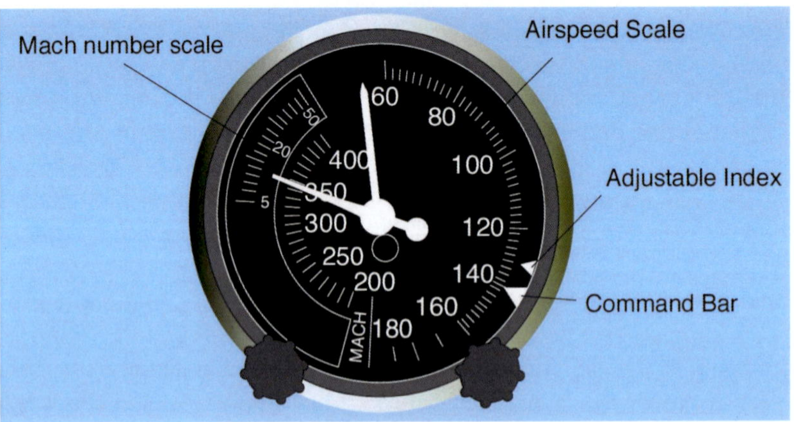

Figure 1.14 Mach/IAS Indicator

1.6.2 V_{MO}/M_{MO} Pointer

A special feature of the M/ASI is the V_{MO} Pointer, also known as the Barber's Pole, because it is striped red and white. At low altitudes, the V_{MO} Pointer retains a fixed position, which indicates the maximum operating IAS permitted. As altitude increases, V_{MO} corresponds to an increasing MN until M_{NO} is reached, at which point the V_{MO} Pointer reading progressively reduces to reflect the overriding MN limit. Movement of the V_{MO} Pointer can be mechanical but modern practice is to drive the M/ASI display from an Air Data Computer (ADC).

1.6.3 Driven Cursor

The Driven cursor can be adjusted, either by the flight crew or automatically by the aircraft's systems, to indicate target speeds for particular phases of flight.

1.6.4 Bugs

Bugs are fixed indexes set prior to flight to indicate important speeds such as V_1, V_2, V_R etc.

1.6.5 Linkages

The M/ASI is often linked to the auto-throttle/flight management systems to provide two way feedback. Further links to visual and audio warning devices may be incorporated.

1.6.6 Errors

The MASI suffers from the same errors as the ASI and Machmeter

1.7 Vertical Speed Indicator (VSI)

1.7.1 Introduction

A VSI is a sensitive differential pressure gauge. It records the rate of change of atmospheric pressure in terms of rate of climb or descent when an aircraft departs from level flight.

1.7.2 Principle

The principle employed is that of measuring the difference of pressure between two chambers, one of which is enclosed within the other, as shown below. The static pressure of the atmosphere is communicated directly to the inner chamber (i.e. a capsule) and through a calibrated bleed (metering unit) to the outer chamber (i.e. the instrument case). When pressure changes, as in a climb or descent, the lag between capsule and outer chamber results in a pressure differential across the metering unit, which is a measure of the aircraft's rate of climb or descent. Movement of the capsule is transmitted via mechanical linkage to a pointer moving against a calibrated dial on the face of the instrument.

Static pressure is fed to the vertical speed indicator

Figure 1.15 Vertical speed indicator

In the calibration of the VSI, the indications are arranged in a logarithmic scale. This allows the scale in the range 0 to 1000 fpm to be more easily interpreted while, at the same time, allowing smaller changes in vertical speed to be registered at that range. This makes it easier to achieve a given flight profile. The metering unit of the VSI is required to provide a pressure differential across the capsule case for any given rate of climb or descent while compensating for variations in temperature and pressure of the atmosphere with changes of altitude. The compensation is achieved by incorporating in the metering unit both an orifice and a capillary, whose sizes are chosen so that indicator readings remain correct over a wide range of temperature and altitude conditions.

1.7.3 Errors

1.7.3.1 Instrument Error

This is due to manufacturers' tolerances. However, in service the instrument pointer can be re-adjusted to the zero position using a screw adjustment.

1.7.3.2 Lag Error

When an aircraft is suddenly made to climb or descend, a delay of a few seconds occurs before the pointer settles at the actual rate of climb or descent, due to time required for the pressure difference to develop.

1.7.3.3 Pressure Error

If the static port is subjected to a changing pressure error (e.g. lowering flaps, initiation of climb or descent) the VSI may briefly indicate incorrectly. However, there will be no such error in a prolonged climb or descent as the instrument measures a differential pressure and not its magnitude.

1.7.3.4 Manoeuvre Induced Error

Errors induced by manoeuvres or flight in turbulence can cause any pressure instrument to misread for up to 3 s at low altitudes and up to 10 s at high altitudes. The times for the VSI may be even longer. Thus, during any manoeuvre involving change of attitude, absolute reliance must not be placed on the VSI. Pitching causes the greatest error.

1.7.4 Faults

1.7.4.1 Blockage

Blockage of the static line renders the instrument completely unserviceable, the pointer registering zero whatever the aircraft's vertical speed.

1.7.4.2 Breakage of Static Line

A breakage or leakage of the static pressure supply line will cause the static pressure value to change as the breakage occurs. E.g. if the breakage occurs in a pressurised section of the aeroplane the VSI will initially show a high rate of descent then stabilise to a zero indication. The instrument will respond to cabin height changes thereafter.

1.7.5 Instantaneous Vertical Speed Indicator (IVSI)

The IVSI consists of the same basic elements as a conventional VSI, but in addition employs an accelerometer unit which is designed to create a more rapid differential pressure effect; specifically, at the initiation of climb or descent. The accelerometer comprises two small cylinders or dashpots (Figure 1.16), containing pistons held in balance by springs and their own mass. The cylinders are connected in the capillary tube system leading to the capsule and are thus open to the static pressure source. When a change in vertical motion is initiated, the force that results from the vertical acceleration displaces the pistons. This creates an immediate pressure change inside the capsule and an instantaneous movement of the indicator pointer. The accelerometer output decays after a few seconds, but by this time the change in actual static pressure is effective. Errors are generally the same as those affecting the conventional VSI, but lag and manoeuvre error are virtually eliminated. It should be noted however, that the dashpots are not vertically stabilised and errors are produced during turns. At bank angles greater than 40° the IVSI is unreliable.

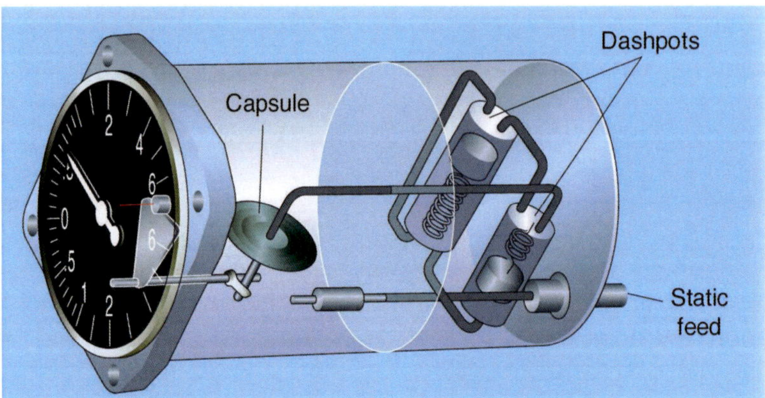

Figure 1.16 Instantaneous vertical speed indicator

1.8 Air Data Computer

1.8.1 Introduction

By now it must be apparent that the air pressures on which the operation of many of the primary flight instruments depends are transmitted from the pitot/static probes through a system of pipelines before reaching the sensors in the instruments. As aircraft become larger, the "pipe work" becomes ever longer, heavier and more complex. This results in two major effects:

- the viscosity of the air causes lag errors that increase with length of supply pipe
- the increasing length increases the risk of breakage/leakage.

To overcome this and to create other benefits, most modern transport aircraft utilise units known as Air Data Computers (ADC). Pressures are transmitted to the ADC unit which converts the data into electrical signals and transmits it them through cables/data busses to the relevant indicators and systems. An ADC may be analogue or digital.

The analogue ADC is made up of the following modules (see Figure 1.17):

1. Altitude module
2. CAS module
3. Mach module
4. TAS module
5. Vertical speed module

It is possible to integrate circuits with these modules to correct for pressure error, barometric pressure changes and compressibility. Additionally, true airspeed may be calculated from an air temperature input

The outputs of the ADC are altitude, vertical speed, CAS, Mach number, static air temperature, TAS plus outputs to various systems such as the flight director, automatic flight control system.

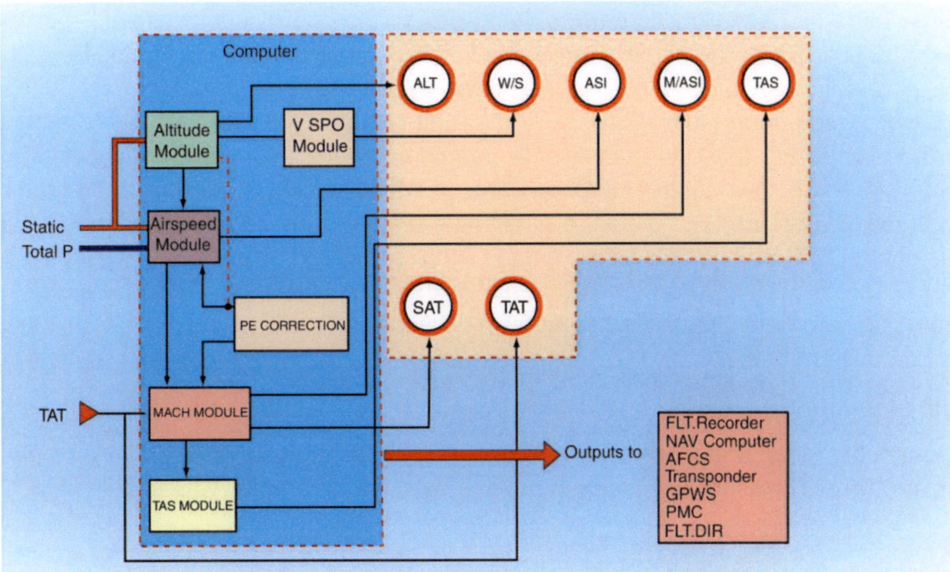

Figure 1.17 ADC Block Schematic Diagram

Note that some modern systems may also measure angle of attack and sideslip angle.

1.8.2 Principle of Operation

Pressure sensing is accomplished by two pressure transducers, one sensing static pressure in the altitude module and the other sensing both pitot and static pressures within the computed air speed (CAS) module. The Mach speed module and true air speed (TAS) module are pure signal generating devices, which are supplied with air speed and altitude data from the respective modules. Static air temperature data required for computing TAS is sensed by a temperature probe and is routed to the TAS module through the Mach speed module.

An example of a pitot-static pressure transducer utilising an "E/I" bar type of inductive pick-off unit is shown below. The transducer operates on what is termed the force-balancing principle and comprises two capsules, the interior of one being connected to pitot pressure source, while the other is connected to static pressure source.

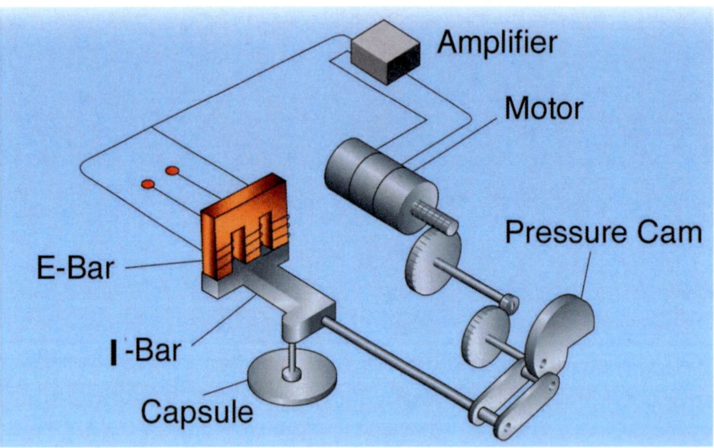

Figure 1.18 Pressure transducer

When a change in air speed takes place, the capsules respond to the corresponding change in differential pressure and the force produced deflects the pivoted beam, thereby displacing the "I" bar relative to the outer limbs of the "E" bar. Thus the air gaps are varied to cause out of balance signals to be induced in the outer limb coils of the "E" bar. Signals are amplified and applied to a servomotor which, via a mechanical linkage, moves the pivoted beam and hence the "I" bar unit. When a constant speed (balanced situation) is reached no further signals are fed to the amplifier and the servomotor and output shaft cease to rotate. With the output shaft connected to a control (CX) synchro, in which power is applied to the rotor, its angular position can be measured in terms of pressure differential (P_t - p). This can then be transmitted in terms of air speed to the control (CT) transformer stator located in the computed air speed (CAS) indicator.

In the digital air data computer, piezoelectric pressure transducers converted data to a digital format for transmission to various systems.

1.8.2.1 System Monitoring

A warning logic circuit is incorporated into each module of the ADC and activates if its associated data signal is lost. Annunciator lights corresponding to each module are located on the ADC and illuminate in the event of failure.

The pilot's instrument indicators are also provided with monitoring circuits which come into operation in the event of a loss of power or data signal from the ADC. These are usually flags which obscure some part of the display counter (e.g. on airspeed indicators the flag obscures the digital counter display).

1.8.3 Temperature Measurement

Static Air Temperature (SAT) – temperature of the air under static conditions

Total Air Temperature (TAT) – temperature measured when air is brought to rest adiabatically

Air temperature is one of the basic parameters used to establish data vital to the performance monitoring of modern aircraft; it is, therefore, necessary to have a means of in-flight measurement. The temperature of greatest use is that of air under pure static conditions at the various flight levels. Regrettably, the measurement of Static Air Temperature (SAT) by direct means is not possible for all types of aircraft, because measurement can be affected by adiabatic compression of air resulting from increased air speed. In general, the boundary layer of air at the outside surface of aircraft flying below M 0.2 is very close to SAT. At higher Mach numbers the boundary layer can be slowed down or stopped relative to the aircraft. This produces adiabatic compression and will raise the air temperature well above SAT. This increase above SAT is commonly referred to as "RAM rise", and the temperature indicated under such conditions is known as the total outside air temperature (TAT).

TAT = SAT + RAM rise

The RAM rise is always pre-calculated and is tabulated or graphed as a function of Mach number in the operations or flight manual for each type of aircraft. The proportion of RAM rise measured is dependent on the ability of the sensor to sense (or recover) the temperature rise. The sensitivity is expressed as a percentage and termed recovery factor. If, for example, a sensor has a recovery factor of 0.80, it will measure SAT + 80% of the RAM rise. Various types of air temperature sensors are in service, the particular type depending on whether SAT or TAT is required and the normal operating speed of the host aircraft.

1.8.3.1 Direct Reading Thermometer

The simplest type, indicating only SAT, is a direct reading thermometer, which operates on the principle of expansion and contraction of a bi-metallic element when subjected to temperature changes. As the temperature changes, the helix will expand or contract, winding or unwinding as it does so, and causing the pointer to rotate against a scale. The thermometer is secured in the aircraft, passing through in the fuselage or canopy with the sensitive element projecting into the airflow.

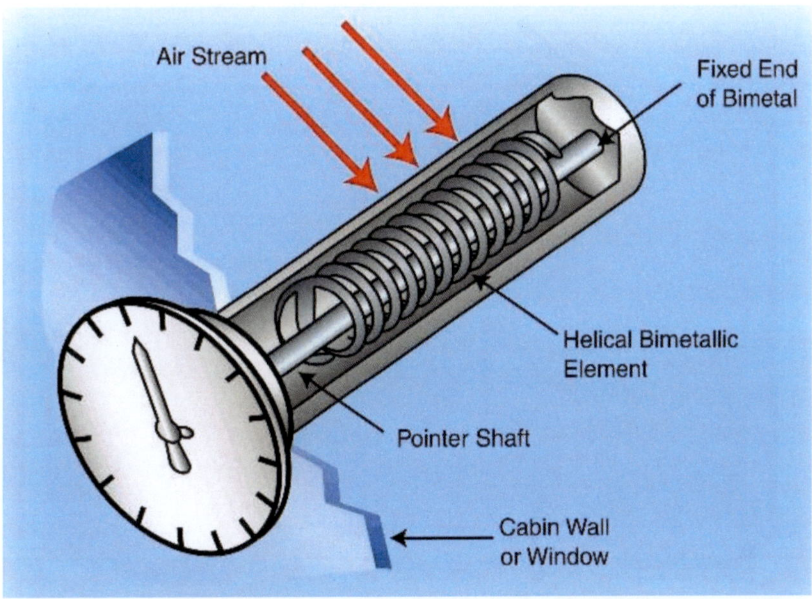

Figure 1.19 Direct Reading Thermometer

1.8.3.2 Wheatstone Bridge

The resistance of an electrical conductor is dependent on temperature, the effect of which is to change the dimension of the conductor by thermal expansion and the resistance offered to current flow. The first effect is comparatively small, the main effect is obtained from change of resistance.

The most common method of employing the temperature/resistance technique is the Wheatstone Bridge thermometer, as shown in Figure 1.20. Changes in of resistance of the resistor R4 can be measured and displayed as a change in temperature.

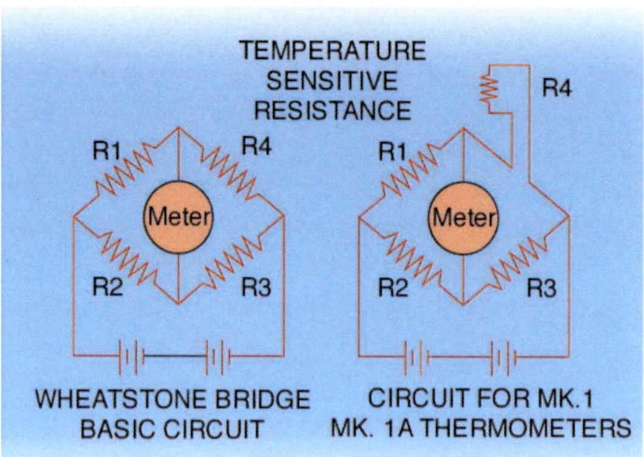

Figure 1.20 Wheatstone bridge

1.8.3.3 Total Air Temperature Probe

For aircraft operating at high Mach numbers, it is customary to sense and measure the maximum temperature rise possible; this is called the Total Air Temperature (TAT) and is found when air is brought to rest (or nearly so) without addition or removal of heat. For this purpose, probes of the type shown in Figure 1.21 were introduced and may be found on a number of modern transport-type aircraft. They have several advantages over the flush bulb type, notably virtually zero time lag, a high recovery factor of approximately 1. The probe is normally connected to a flight deck indicator and to a Mach number Mode 1 of the air data computer.

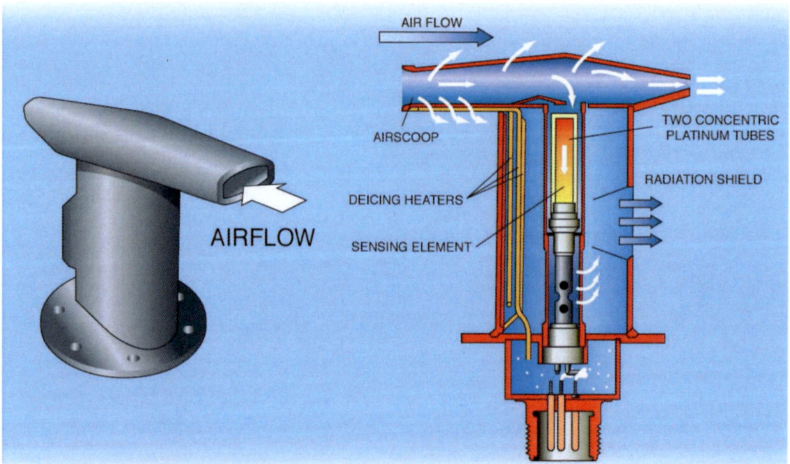

Figure 1.21 Total Temperature Thermometer (Rosemount Probe)

1.8.3.3.1 Construction

An air intake mounted on top of a small streamlined strut is secured to the aircraft skin at a predetermined location around the nose, free from any boundary layer activity. In flight, air pressure within the probe is higher than outside, and air flows through the probe, as shown in the diagram. Separation of water droplets from the air is achieved by causing the flow of air to turn through 90° before passing around the sensing element. Bleed holes in the casing permit boundary layer air to be drawn off by pressure differential across the casing. A pure platinum wire resistance is used, sealed within two concentric platinum tubes. A heating element is mounted on the probe to prevent ice formation. Although the heater does have an effect on indicated temperature readings, the effect is very small, typical values being 0.9°C at M 0.1 and 0.15°C at M 1.0.

Self-Assessment Test 1

1. Air density is a function of:
A) Air pressure
B) Air temperature and air pressure
C) Air temperature
D) None of these

2. Dynamic pressure is sometimes referred to as:
A) q
B) S
C) L
D) D

3. Kinetic energy and dynamic pressure are the same; the formula is:
A) V^2S
B) VS
C) $½\rho V^2$
D) $½\rho V^2S$

4. A pitot tube measures:
A) Static pressure and the tube is located close to the engine air intakes
B) Static pressure and the tube is located in a position of undisturbed airflow
C) Dynamic pressure ands the tube is located close to the junction of major components
D) Total pressure and is located in a position of undisturbed airflow

5. Static pressure (p) is sensed by:
A) Static vents and these are located, as far as possible, in an area of undisturbed flow
B) Pitot vents located in the free airstream
C) A temperature compensated bulb located in the free airstream
D) Static vents and these are located near to areas of turbulent flow to provide maximum mixing affect

6. A pitot/static head:
A) Measures pitot and static pressure and is located near to the junction of major aircraft components
B) Measures pitot and static pressure and is located in an area of least disturbed airflow
C) Is located in a supercharger outlet casing and measures dynamic and static pressure
D) Is concerned with the measurement of pitot and static pressure in unusual areas of turbulence

7. Static vents are:
A) Located on only one side of the aircraft
B) Located on both sides of the aircraft and are independent
C) Located on both sides of the aircraft and are cross-coupled, system by system, to minimize side-slip errors
D) Only located in the pressurised zone of the aircraft to provide indication of cabin height

8. Where the difference in the values of two pressures is measured, it is usual to utilize:
A) A pressurised capsule and case pressure
B) An aneroid capsule and bi-metallic strip
C) Static vents and an evacuated capsule
D) An aneroid capsule and internal case pressure

9. With reference to air temperature:
A) SAT is the true outside temperature of the air and the ram rise is the total outside air temperature
B) TAT is the true outside air temperature and SAT is the temperature corrected for ram rise
C) TAT is the total air temperature and SAT is the corrected or true outside air temperature
D) RAT is the temperature due to ram rise and TAT is the corrected outside air temperature

10. Assuming a recovery factor of 0.8
A) 80% of the total outside air temperature will be corrected
B) 80% of the SAT will be corrected
C) 80% of the ram rise will not be included into the final TAT
D) 80% of the ram rise will be corrected by the probe and added to the SAT to give an approximate TAT

11. It is assumed that the recovery factor of a Rosemount probe is:
A) 2
B) 1
C) 0.8
D) 0.9

12. An altimeter basic calibration factors are:
A) 1013.25 mb/hPa; 15°C; 1225 g/cu metre
B) 1013.25 mb/hPa; 1225 g/cu metre only
C) 1013.25 mb/hPa only
D) 15°C only

13. With the aircraft on the ground and:
A) QFE set, the altimeter will indicate airfield elevation
B) QFE set, the altimeter will indicate pressure altitude
C) QNE set, the altimeter will indicate airfield height
D) QNH set, the altimeter will indicate airfield elevation

14. In ISA conditions the tropopause:
A) Is at Sea level
B) Is at 35 000'
C) Is at 36 090'
D) Follows the contours of the nearest cumulonimbus cloud formation

15. In a sensitive altimeter a minimum of two capsule stacks ensures that:
A) Sufficient power is available to drive the linkage
B) Sufficient power is used to drive the linkage and to provide greater instrument accuracy
C) The power required to drive the mechanism is sufficient to balance the effects of pitot pressure
D) Restricted static pressure is calibrated against normal static pressure

16. The errors inherent in a simple and sensitive altimeter are as follows:
A) Instrument, scale, pitot lag, time lag, barometric, temperature, hysteresis
B) Instrument, pressure, time lag, hysteresis, barometric, temperature, orographic
C) Temperature and barometric only
D) Hysteresis only

17. Assume an aircraft is flying in an area of high barometric pressure where the regional pressure setting (RPS) is 1000 hPa. It now transits into an area where the RPS is 960 mb but the altimeter sub-scale is maintained at 1000 mb (assume 1 hPa = 30'). The aircraft will now be flying:
A) 1 200' lower
B) 1 200' higher
C) 120' lower
D) 120' higher

18. An evacuated capsule has differing elastic properties throughout its operating range. This is known as:
A) Elastic limited error
B) Yield point error
C) Pressure error
D) Hysteresis loss

19. In a cold air mass:
A) Density is lower than in a warm air mass and the altimeter will underread
B) Density is higher than in a warm air mass and the altimeter will underread
C) Density is higher than in a warm air mass and the altimeter will overread
D) Density is lower than in a warm air mass and the altimeter will overread

20. Altimeter pressure error is caused by:
A) Manufacturing tolerances
B) The effect of airflow over a static vent
C) The lack of instantaneous response to pressure change, by the capsule
D) Long wave effect caused by pitot interference

21. In a servo altimeter, the:
A) 'I' bar is positioned by the capsule stack which, in turn, alters the magnetic field in the limbs of the 'E' bar. The resulting flux change is amplified and drives a servo motor which positions the height pointers and/or drum
B) The 'E' bar is positioned by the capsule stack which, in turn, alters the magnetic field around the 'I' bar. The output is amplified and drives a servo motor which positions the height pointers and/or drum
C) Capsule stack operates the height pointers and/or drum directly
D) The 'I' bar is positioned by the capsule stack which, in turn, drives the height pointers and/or drum via the height cam

22. If a static vent system becomes blocked the altimeter will continue to:
A) Read the height at the time of the failure
B) Read the height at the time of the failure but will indicate correctly when the aircraft descends through the failure height
C) Read the height at the time of failure until the aircraft climbs above the failure height
D) Read the height at the time of the failure until such times as the integral cleaning system operates

23. Pitot pressure comprises:
A) Dynamic pressure only
B) Static pressure only
C) Dynamic pressure plus static pressure
D) Dynamic pressure plus static pressure minus static pressure

24. In an ASI:
A) Pitot pressure is connected to the case and static pressure is connected to the inside of the capsules
B) Static pressure is connected to the case and pitot pressure is connected to the inside of the capsules
C) Restricted static is connected to the case and pitot pressure is connected to the capsule stack
D) Pitot pressure is connected to the case and restricted static is connected to the capsule stack

25. ASI errors are:
A) Density and compressibility, hysteresis and pressure error losses
B) Instrument, pressure, compressibility and density
C) Density, TAS and height
D) Height, pressure, relative density and IAS

26. An ASI measures:
A) True air speed
B) Calibrated air speed
C) Equivalent air speed
D) Indicated air speed

27. Compressibility error correction is added to:
A) CAS to produce EAS
B) IAS to produce CAS
C) TAS to produce EAS
D) EAS to produce TAS

28. Density error correction is added to:
A) IAS to produce EAS
B) CAS to produce EAS
C) EAS to produce IAS
D) EAS to produce TAS

29. If the IAS reading at 40 000' is 250 KT, the TAS will be approximately:
A) 250 KT
B) 300 KT
C) 500 KT
D) 400 KT

30. Pressure errors are influenced in the main by:
A) Angle of attack and IAS
B) Angle of attack, IAS, configuration and sideslip
C) Angle of attack, IAS, configuration, sideslip and cabin height
D) Angle of attack and configuration

31. A blocked pitot tube will result in:
A) An decrease in IAS as the aircraft climbs
B) An increase in IAS as the aircraft descends
C) An increase in IAS as the aircraft climbs
D) An increase in altimeter reading as the aircraft descends

32. If a static line becomes blocked:
A) The ASI will overread at a higher altitude and underread at a lower altitude than that at which the blockage occurred
B) The ASI will overread at a lower altitude and underread at a higher altitude than that at which the blockage occurred
C) The ASI pointers will become fixed at the time of the failure
D) The ASI will be at a maximum at the time of the blockage

33. The principle of operation of a VSI is based on the measurement of a:
A) Difference in pressure across a controlled static air bleed to the instrument case and static pressure supplied to a capsule
B) Difference in pressure across the instrument case
C) Difference in pressure across the static supply
D) Difference in pressure between that at sea level and that at the height of the aircraft

34. The errors in the VSI are due to:
A) Temperature and pressure differences
B) Density changes
C) Pressure, instrument, manoeuvre and lag errors
D) Those of the same type as the altimeter

35. In an IVSI:
A) Lag error is reduced by the effect of a pitot bleed
B) An integral accelerometer reduces the effects of lag error
C) A reduction or increase in static pressure is arranged to match the rate of climb or descent and so reduce lag error
D) Lag error is negated by the effects of a much more responsive linkage and a multi-leaved capsule stack

36. A blocked static line will cause the VSI to:
A) Indicate a rapid descent
B) Indicate a rapid climb
C) Remain at zero indication regardless of the aircraft flight path
D) Indicate zero at the height at which the failure occurred and normal operation outside this height

37. If a static line to a VSI breaks, the indication will be as follows:
A) In a pressurised aircraft (aircraft height above cabin height) the VSI will indicate a rapid descent and stabilize at zero when pressures are equalized. When the aircraft descends and depressurises for landing, the indication will be near normal
B) In an unpressurised aircraft the VSI will become totally inoperative
C) In a pressurised aircraft the VSI will remain totally inoperative regardless of the aircraft flight path and pressurization settings
D) There are no specific failure modes

38. The speed of sound is dependent upon:
A) Air pressure and temperature
B) Air temperature
C) Air pressure
D) Humidity

39. Assuming the air temperature to be minus 10°C, the absolute temperature will be:
A) 283° K
B) 293° K
C) 263° K
D) -10° K

40. Assuming the absolute temperature to be 293° K, the temperature in °C will be:
A) + 20°C
B) + 30°C
C) + 273°C
D) - 20 K

41. Assuming the air temperature to be +20°C, the local speed of sound will be:
A) 621 KT
B) 669 KT
C) 610 KT
D) 609 KT

42. If the local speed of sound is 577 KT, what is the temperature in °C:
A) - 65°C
B) - 75°C
C) - 45°C
D) - 55°C

43. If the TAS is 480 KT and the local speed of sound is 570 KT, the Mach No is:
A) 0.82
B) 0.81
C) 0.86
D) 0.84

44. If the Mach No is 0.88 and the local speed of sound is 565 KT, the TAS is:
A) 497 KT
B) 487 KT
C) 477 KT
D) 507 KT

45. M_{CRIT} is defined as the speed at which:
A) The airflow over the wing first becomes sonic with respect to the freestream airflow speed
B) The airflow over any part of the aircraft structure becomes sonic with respect to the freestream airflow speed
C) Mach cone effects impose control limitations
D) The lower limit of the aircraft flight envelope that can be demonstrated

46. In terms of pitot (P) and static (S) pressure, Mach number is a function of:
A) $\frac{P - S}{S}$
B) $\frac{P + S}{S}$
C) P X S
D) P – S

47. In simple terms, a machmeter measures the ratio of:
A) The local speed of sound to the speed of the aircraft
B) The local speed of sound to the IAS
C) The aircraft speed (TAS) to the local speed of sound
D) None of the above

48. Name the components of the Machmeter shown below:
A) A: Ratio arm, B: Ranging arm; C: Altitude capsule; D: Static pressure capsule; E: Pitot pressure; F: Altitude capsule
B) A: Ranging arm; B: Ratio arm; C: Air speed capsule; D: Pitot pressure; E: Static pressure; F: Altitude capsule
C) A: Ranging arm; B: Ratio arm; C: Altitude capsule; D: Pitot pressure; E: Static pressure; F: Air speed capsule
D) A: Ratio arm; B: Ranging arm; C: Altitude capsule; D: Static pressure; E: Pitot pressure; F: Airspeed capsule

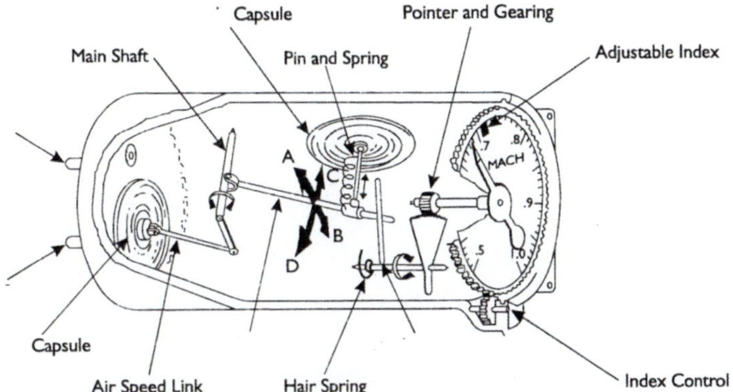

49. In a Machmeter:
A) An airspeed capsule is supplied with pitot pressure, an altitude capsule responds to case internal pressure and the case is connected to static pressure
B) An altitude capsule is connected to pitot pressure, an airspeed capsule is connected to static pressure and the case is connected to a mixture of pitot and static pressure
C) Both capsules are connected to static pressure and the case is connected to pitot pressure
D) Both capsules are connected to pitot pressure and the case is connected to static pressure

50. A Machmeter has the following errors:
A) Instruments and compressibility
B) Density and pressure
C) Instrument and pressure
D) Instrument, pressure, compressibility and density

51. The positioning of the airspeed link in the Machmeter is dependent upon:
A) Pitot pressure connected to the capsule and static pressure in the case
B) Static pressure in the airspeed capsule and pitot pressure in the case
C) Potit pressure connected to the airspeed case and static pressure in the altitude capsule
D) Pitot pressure connected to the airspeed capsule and atmospheric pressure connected to the altitude capsule

52. The V_{MO} pointer located on a Mach/IAS indicator:
A) Is usually coloured black and white and indicates the limiting Mach No
B) Is usually coloured black and indicates the rough airspeed and Mach Number
C) When set to the SPS, indicates the maximum airspeed obtainable
D) Is striped red and white and indicates the maximum operating IAS permitted. At the relevant altitudes it will indicate the Mach/IAS equivalent limiting speeds

53. The basic inputs required by an ADC are:
A) Pitot pressure and static pressure
B) Pitot pressure and air temperature
C) Pitot pressure, static pressure and air temperature
D) Static pressure and air temperature

54. A piezo-electric transducer:
A) Produces an electrical signal output when subject to mechanical deformation
B) Is a transformer which reacts to electrical control signals
C) Is a rotary transformer which produces a variable output dependent upon the magnitude of the signal input
D) Produces an electrical signal output when rotated at synchronous speed

55. The main modules in an ADC are:
A) Altitude and CAS module
B) CAS and PE module
C) Mach, PE and altitude modules
D) Altitudes, CAS, Mach and TAS modules

Self-Assessment Test 1 Answers

1	B
2	A
3	C
4	D
5	A
6	B
7	C
8	A
9	C
10	D
11	B
12	A
13	D
14	C
15	B
16	B
17	A
18	D
19	C
20	B
21	A
22	A
23	C
24	B
25	B
26	D
27	A
28	D
29	C
30	B

31	C
32	B
33	A
34	C
35	B
36	C
37	A
38	B
39	C
40	A
41	B
42	D
43	D
44	A
45	B
46	A
47	C
48	B
49	A
50	C
51	A
52	D
53	C
54	A
55	D

CHAPTER 2
Gyroscopic Instruments

2.1 Gyro Fundamentals

A gyroscope may be defined as any wheel that spins on its axis, e.g. the wheel of a car or an aircraft propeller. As a result of the spinning motion, the wheel acquires two properties: rigidity in space and precession.

2.1.1 Rigidity

Rigidity is the reluctance of a gyro to change the direction of its spin axis

$$\text{Rigidity} \propto \frac{I\omega}{F}$$

Where I = moment of inertia of the spinning body
ω = angular velocity (a measure of how fast the wheel is spinning)
F = the external force acting on the body

The moment of inertia is defined as the mass of a body times the square of the distance at which the mass acts (i.e. radius) from the centre of rotation. For a body such as a wheel, the mass of individual segments of the wheel are considered separately and summed to give a moment of inertia (Σmass x radius^2).
It will be seen from above that increasing mass, angular velocity or radius will make a spinning body more rigid whilst increasing the external force will have an adverse effect on the rigidity.

2.1.2 Precession

If a force is applied to a spinning wheel it does not act at the point of application but acts at a point which is 90°removed from it in the direction of rotation. This tendency to move is called precession

$$\text{Precession} \propto \frac{F}{I\omega}$$

2.1.3 Types of Gyros

Gyroscopes may be classified in a number of ways, but in these notes they are classified by the degrees of freedom permitted of each type. The degrees of freedom and method of control will be discussed more fully as each instrument is reviewed.

2.1.3.1 Free (Space) Gyros

A gyroscope having freedom to rotate around 3 axes is called a free gyro. The gyroscope below is a free gyro. The gyro is mounted in two concentrically pivoted rings, called the inner and outer gimbal rings. In the example shown, there are two horizontal axes and one vertical axis. The gyro has the ability to spin about the x-axis, tilt about the y-axis and veer about the z-axis. There is no means of external control over a space gyro, a feature that distinguishes it from a tied or Earth gyro.

The Free (Space) gyro is said to have 2 degrees of freedom (i.e. the number of gimbal rings = number of degrees of freedom)

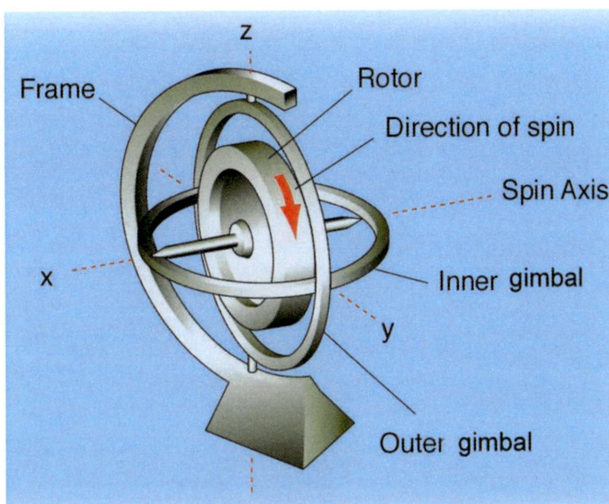

Figure 2.1 Free space gyro

2.1.3.2 Tied (Displacement) Gyros

This is a free gyro that has a means of external control. Being essentially a free gyro, a tied gyro has freedom to rotate around 3 axes. However, an uncontrolled free gyro would be of no practical use in an instrument where the gyro is required to be set to and maintain a certain direction, so the tied gyro has its freedom to rotate reduced or controlled by application of an external force.

2.1.3.3 Earth Gyro

This is a displacement gyro in which the controlling force is the Earth's gravity.

2.1.3.4 Rate Gyro

This is a gyro having freedom to rotate around only 1 axis in addition to the spin axis. The axis of freedom being 90° removed from the axis of rotation. It is utilised to measure rate of turn around the third axis and employs restraining springs.

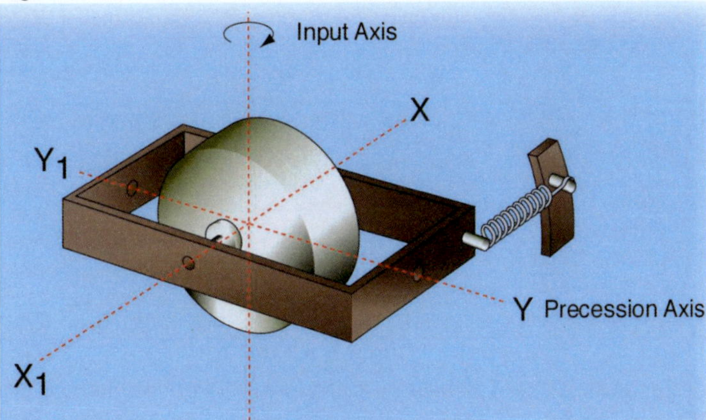

Figure 2.2 Gyro axis

2.1.3.5 Rate Integrating Gyro

An integrating gyroscope is a single degree of freedom gyro, using viscous restraint to damp the precession rotation about the output axis. The integrating gyro is similar to the rate gyro, except restraining springs are omitted and the only factor opposing gimbal rotation about the output axis is the viscosity of a fluid. The gyro's main function is to detect turning about the input axis by precessing about its output axis. The integrating gyro was designed for use on inertial navigation stable platforms.

2.1.3.6 Ring Laser Gyro

Unlike a conventional mechanical gyro, changes and rate of changes in aircraft attitude are sensed by measuring the frequencies of 2 contra-rotating beams of light within the triangular shaped laser ring. Three ring laser gyros (RLG) are perpendicular to each other and measure movement about all 3 axes. When the aircraft changes attitude, the changes in light beam frequency are detected and used in the same way as the output from conventional gyros.

2.1.3.6.1 Advantages and Disadvantages of a RLG

Advantages	Disadvantages
High reliability Very low 'g' sensitivity No run-up or warm up time Digital output High accuracy Low power requirement Low life-cycle	High capital cost

2.1.4 Gyroscopic Applications

For use in aeroplanes, gyros are required to establish 2 datums for measuring motion around the three axes. Vertical spin axis gyros are used to detect pitch and roll attitude and horizontal spin axis gyros are used to detect changes in yaw.

The basic gyro properties are used as follows:

- Rigidity provides a stabilised reference which is not affected by the movement of the body which supports the gyro
- Precession controls the effect of real and apparent drift

2.1.5 Gyro Wander, Drift and Topple

Wander is defined as any deviation of the gyro axis from its set direction, it is a combination of drift and topple and may be real or apparent. Real wander is a physical deviation of the gyro axis from a fixed direction in space, apparent wander is caused by the Earth's rotation.

Gyro drift – any deviation of the gyro axis from its set direction in the horizontal plane. Drift may be sub-divided into real drift and apparent drift.

Gyro topple (tilt) – any movement of the gyro axis in the vertical plane.

2.1.5.1 Real drift

Real drift is any physical deviation of a gyro axis from a fixed direction in the horizontal plane

It may be caused by imperfections in the gyro mechanism (e.g. friction, shifting of the centre of gravity of the gyro), turbulence, etc. These imperfections cause unwanted precession and as they are more or less random they cannot be corrected for.

2.1.5.2 Apparent Drift

Apparent drift is the apparent deviation of a gyro axis due to the rotation of the Earth

The gyro axis does not physically drift but to an observer it appears to have changed direction; this is because the gyro maintains it direction with reference to a fixed point in space whilst the observer is rotating with the Earth (or moving over the rotating Earth).

2.1.5.3 Variation of drift and topple with latitude

Consider a horizontal axis gyro at the North Pole as shown below. The Earth is being viewed from space and rotates anti-clockwise at a rate of 15° per h.

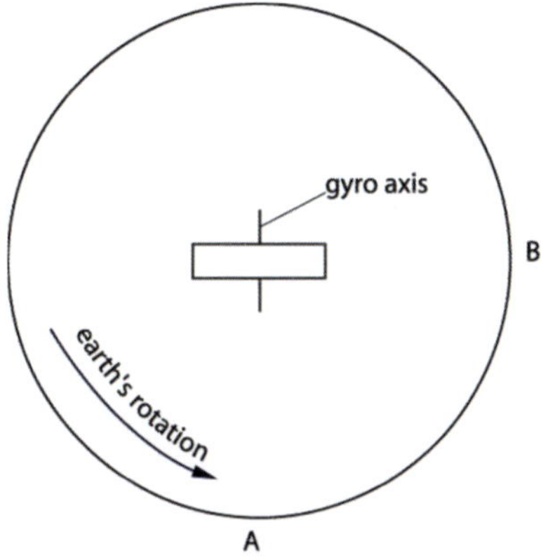

Figure 2.3

An observer at A is initially aligned with the spin axis of the gyro, in 6 h time the observer will be in position B which is 6 x 15 = 90° removed from A. Due to its rigidity the gyro axis remains fixed in space and to the observer it will appear as if the gyro has rotated clockwise through 90°. There is no apparent movement of the gyro in the vertical plane (i.e. no topple). There is maximum drift and no topple at the pole(s).

Assume a horizontal axis gyro placed at the equator with its spin axis aligned with the equator (i.e. in a east-west direction) at position A in the figure below.

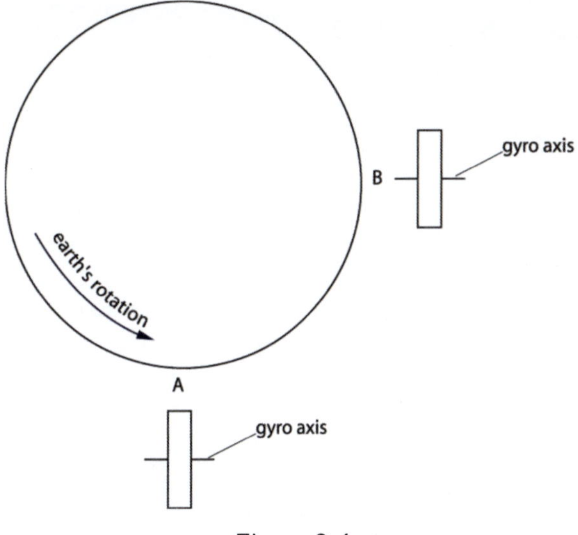

Figure 2.4

In 6 h time (at B) the gyro will appear to have toppled through 90° but as the axis has not moved in the horizontal plane there is no apparent drift. There is maximum topple and no drift at the equator.

Now consider a vertical axis gyro at the North Pole as shown in the figure below (side-on view). The Earth rotates beneath the axis of the gyro and there is no drift or topple.

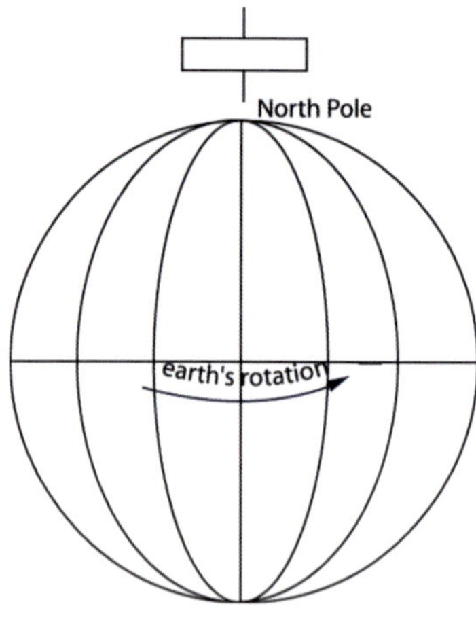

Figure 2.5

Finally, consider a vertical axis gyro at the equator as shown in the figure below. As an observer, moves from A to B with the Earth's rotation the gyro will appear to topple through 90° and there is no apparent drift. There is maximum topple and no drift.

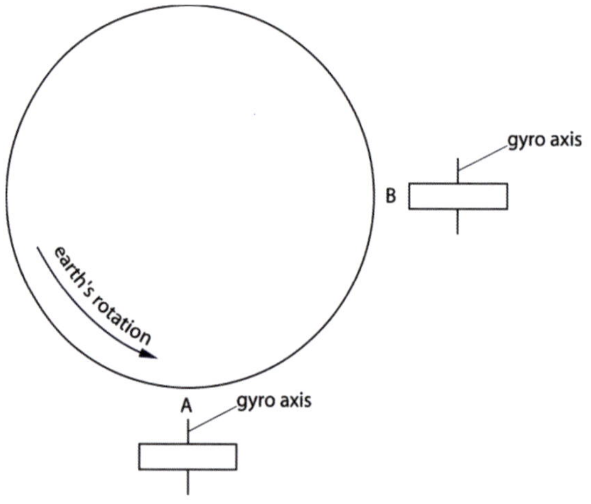

Figure 2.6

It can therefore be seen that drift at the Poles is 15°/h and 0 at the equator, whilst topple is 0 at the Poles and 15°/h at the equator. At intermediate latitudes drift and topple are calculated as follows:

Drift = 15 sin (latitude) °/h
Topple = 15 cos (latitude) °/h

Note that drift is clockwise in the Northern hemisphere and the eastern end of the gyro axis appears to rise in the case of a toppling gyro. The reverse occurs in the Southern hemisphere.

An additional drift/topple occurs if we put the gyro on a platform, such as an aeroplane, and fly east or west. We would now be carrying the gyro in space in the same way as the Earth is and this will cause transport drift and transport topple.

Transport drift = change of longitude x sin (latitude) °/h
Transport topple = change of longitude x cos (latitude) °/h

2.1.5.3.1 Calculation of Transport Drift

Transport drift is equal to Earth convergence (ch long sin lat). There are three cases to consider:

1) When the departure and destination points are known the d. long value is readily available for the whole flight, but the ***mean*** latitude for the flight must be used.

$$\text{Transport drift} = \text{ch long} \sin(\text{mean lat})\ ^\circ/\text{h}$$

2) When the flight is E/W at a particular ground speed (G/S), the latitude is as quoted but the ch long value must be derived from the groundspeed using the departure formula as follows:

$$\text{Transport drift} = \frac{G/S}{60} \tan \text{lat}\ ^\circ/\text{h}$$

3) When the groundspeed quoted is appropriate to a track other than E/W, mean latitude for the flight must be used. The E/W component must also be used. The E/W component must also be used. The formula is:

$$\text{Transport drift} = \frac{G/S}{60} \cos\theta \tan \text{lat}\ ^\circ/\text{h}$$

Where θ is the angle between track and E/W. For example, if an aircraft is tracking 300° then θ =300 – 270 = 30°, if the aircraft is tracking 045°, then θ =090 – 045 = 45°

2.1.6 Power Sources For Gyros

In order to assume the properties of a gyroscope the gyro wheel (or rotor) must be rotated. It follows that this will require the application of some power. In addition, when considering a tied gyro, we must also apply a controlling force and this requires a power source. Conventional gyroscopes in aircraft are either air driven or electrically driven.

2.1.6.1 Air Driven Gyros

These are widely used on small aircraft and are still found on some large aircraft in the role of stand-by or emergency instruments.

2.1.6.1.1 Principle of Operation

In the air driven gyro, the gyro is contained in an airtight case. The case is attached to a vacuum source by a pipeline, This source is normally an engine driven vacuum pump but, in very simple aeroplanes, may be a venturi tube attached to the outside of the fuselage. The gyro wheel has buckets cut in the outer rim (Figure 2.7). It is encased in a shroud, which acts as the inner gimbal and has a pipeline attached. This pipeline terminates at a small opening that is designed to direct the airflow onto the buckets. The shroud has an exhaust port to allow air to escape to the outer case. The pipeline from the inner gimbal is fed through the inner gimbal axis along the outer gimbal and through its axis then to a filter system that covers a hole in the outer case. Now when the vacuum is applied the pressure in the outer case will drop. Replacement air entering the system from outside the case will pass through the filter, through the piping system and will impact on the buckets on the rotor. The air then escapes from the rotor shroud and this escape path can be designed to provide a controlling force to 'tie' the gyro.

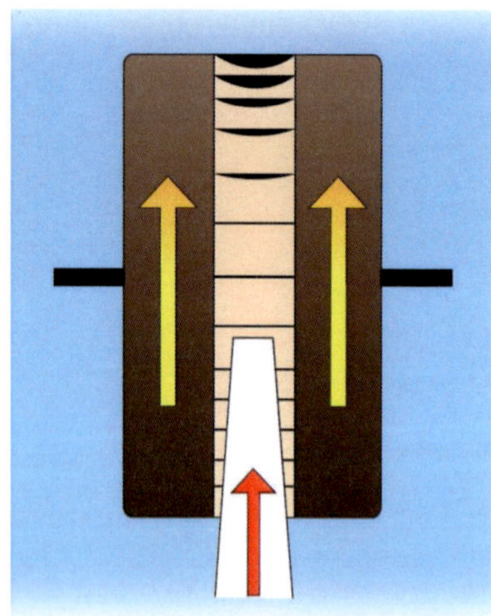

Figure 2.7 Air Driven Gyro

2.1.6.1.2 Problems

The air driven gyro suffers from a number of problems and these limit its usefulness. Full rigidity will not be reached until the rotor speed has built up. The engine driven vacuum pump does not apply power until the engine(s) are running so the gyros will not be operational for some time.

In a venturi type system, the gyros will not become available until the aeroplane is airborne. The speed of the rotor depends on the mass of air flowing through the system (mass flow). As the aeroplane climbs, the air density falls and the mass flow reduces. The rotor speed reduces as a consequence of this and gyro rigidity will deteriorate.

Also, a clear unimpeded flow of air is required. If the filters on the inlet line are blocked or partially blocked, this will affect gyro rigidity. Another major drawback of the air driven gyro is the need to provide airtight joints where the inlet pipes pass through the inner and outer gimbal axes. This severely limits the degree of freedom around these axes.

2.1.6.1.3 Advantages

An air driven gyro is cheap, easy to maintain and, in the event of an emergency, can operate without electrical power.

2.1.6.2 Electrical Gyros

The vast majority of gyroscopes used in aeroplanes today are electrically driven. There are two main types used:

- 24V DC motor
- 115V 3 phase AC 'squirrel cage' induction motor.

2.1.6.2.1 Operating Principle

In the 24V DC type, the spin axis carries the stator of a simple DC motor, while the gyro rotor is also the rotor for the DC motor. Power is fed through slip rings at each axis from a 24V DC bus. The AC gyroscope also uses the technique of placing the stator at the centre of the system with the rotor arranged to rotate around it. In the same way as above, the power supply to the stator is fed through slip rings at the axes. AC gyros are capable of higher rotational speeds than the DC ones and they are therefore the favoured option when high rigidity is required. In both types of gyro, emergency power supply may be available from appropriate sources.

2.1.6.2.2 Problems

Electrical gyros depend on their power supply and these gyros tend to be more expensive than the air driven counterparts.

2.1.6.2.3 Advantages

- Higher rigidity is possible
- More consistent RPM
- Unaffected by altitude
- Less restricted freedom to rotate around axes
- Instrument case is completely sealed – this excludes dirt and it can even be temperature compensated to prevent heating/cooling effects on the components (if necessary).

2.2 Directional Gyro

The Directional Gyro Indicator employs a horizontal axis tied gyro. It is manually aligned with the direct reading magnetic compass and, in light aircraft, is used as the primary heading reference. It is absolutely essential that its indications be checked, at regular intervals and after aerobatic flight, against the direct reading magnetic compass.

2.2.1 Description

The instrument can be either air driven or electrically driven. In the air driven version the instrument consists of an air-driven horizontal axis gyro, rotating at approximately 10000 rpm.

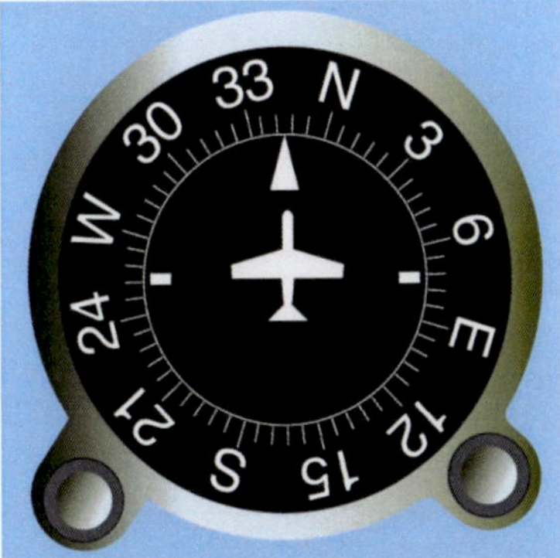

Figure 2.8 Directional Gyro Indicator

Externally the front of the instrument case has a circular scale that is graduated 0° to 360° in 10° divisions. (Figure 2.8) Below the window is a knob. This is used to cage the gyro and rotate the gyro assembly when setting a heading.

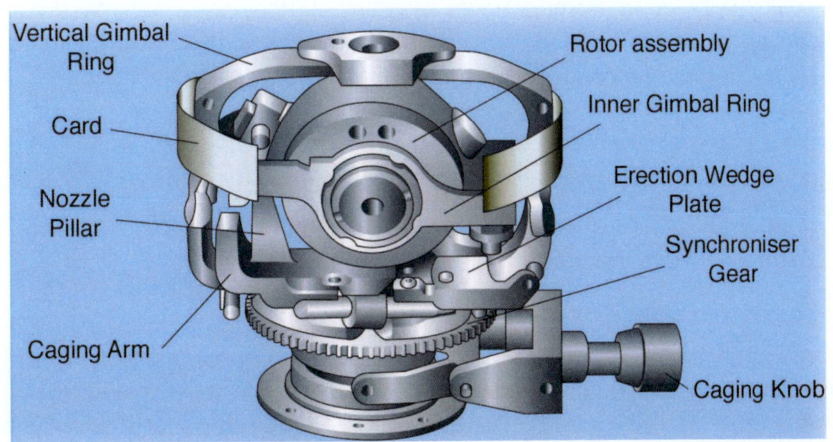

Figure 2.9 Assembly

Figure 2.9 shows the internal mechanism of the instrument. In the air driven version shown, the horizontal gimbal has a freedom of movement of ± 55° when it is un-caged. The nozzles of the air jet are attached to the vertical gimbal. In this older type the indicator scale is carried on the ring mounted on the outer gimbal. On newer models, the synchronising gear also drives a sequence of gears to connect the movements of the gyro around the vertical axis to the vertical scale illustrated in Figure 2.8.

The gyro is initially erected by the caging mechanism so that the gyro spin axis is brought into the horizontal plane. The gyro rotor is spun by the action of air entering through the jet and attaining operating rpm about five min after full suction is developed by the vacuum pump. The air jet also maintains the rotor spin axis in the horizontal plane as shown in Figure 2.10. If the gyro topples, a component of the jet force will act at right angles to the rotor and produce a precessing force to erect the gyro. In the electrical version, the motor is an AC 'squirrel cage' giving a high RPM. Initial erection is by use of the caging device but thereafter the gyro is tied so that it maintains the spin axis horizontal to Earth's surface.

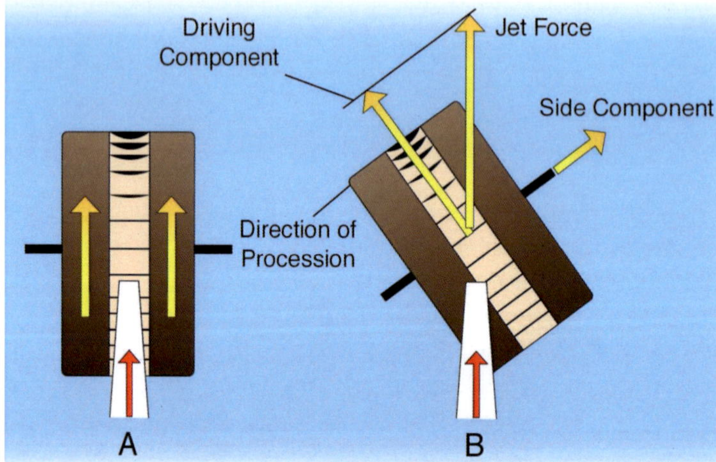

Figure 2.10 Forces on a air driven gyro

2.2.1.1 Errors

2.2.1.1.1 Real Drift and Tilt

The gyro is subject to both real drift and topple. These are caused by imperfections in manufacture.

2.2.1.1.2 Apparent Drift

The gyro is subject to apparent drift, caused by Earth rate and transport wander. A fixed rate of compensation for this apparent wander may be applied by means of balancing (latitude) nuts attached to the gimbals. The rate of compensation is calculated for the latitude of operation of the aircraft; no compensation for transport wander is made apart from periodic resetting of the instrument to the magnetic compass heading. Drift rate can be as much as 15°/h and for this reason the instrument should be aligned with the magnetic heading shown on the direct reading compass every 15 min whilst in flight.

Any topple experienced by the gyro will be corrected by the air jet erection system. The gyro is also subject to gimballing error (occurs when the gyro is displaced with its gimbal rings not mutually perpendicular to each other) during manoeuvres, but these will disappear once level flight is resumed.

2.2.1.2 Use of the Direction Indicator (DI)

2.2.1.2.1 Basic DI

On small basic aeroplanes and some older aeroplanes, the direction indicator is the primary heading reference used for maintaining the required heading. Because of the various drift errors that we have just considered, great care must be exercised in the use of the DI. Pre-departure, when the DI has achieved rigidity, we should use the heading set knob to align the gyro with the magnetic compass. Periodically, during the pre flight process and during taxi to take-off, we should compare the two headings and make sure that the gyro is not showing large drift rates. Once in flight the DI should be checked and reset against the magnetic compass at intervals of about 15 min. It is absolutely essential that this should only be done with the aeroplane in level and unaccelerated flight.

2.2.1.2.2 Advanced Use

In areas where the Earth's magnetic field does not provide a stable heading reference, it is necessary to base our headings on an unmonitored DI. The DI used is of a very sophisticated design in which the friction effects have been reduced to a minimum, however it still suffers from apparent drift errors. We must be able to calculate these in order to compensate for them.

For these calculations we must remember that there are two sources of drift:

- Real (mechanical) drift, which is a result of mechanical imperfections such as
  - Slight imbalance of the rotor/gimbal system
  - Bearing friction
  - Mechanical or electrical latitude correction
- Apparent drift which results from the fact that the Earth directional reference system rotates in space while the directional gyro maintains a constant direction in space – i.e. the meridians change alignment with respect to the gyro datum. There are two accountable factors that cause this:
  - Earth rotation, known as Earth Rate
  - East/West transport, known as Transport Wander

2.2.1.2.3 Calculation of Total Drift

The following mnemonic is useful for calculating total drift:

	Cause of drift	Northern Hemisphere	Southern Hemisphere
Ernie	Earth Rate	**-**	**+**
Loves the	Latitude Nut	**+**	**-**
TErrible	Transport East	**-**	**+**
TWins	Transport West	**+**	**-**

Consider the following example.

2.2.1.2.4 Example

The DI of an aeroplane has its latitude compensator set to correct for operations in latitude 45° N. The aeroplane flies eastwards along the parallel of 60°N at a ground speed of 240 KT. What drift rate (°/h) should be expected if the gyro is free from random drift errors?

Solution

The gyro will experience three sources of drift.

1. A real drift from the fixed latitude correction.
2. Apparent drift due to latitude of operation.
3. Apparent drift due to transport in an easterly direction.

	Cause of drift	Northern Hemisphere	
Ernie	Earth Rate	-	-15 sin 60 = -12.99
Loves the	Latitude Nut	+	+15 sin 45 = +10.61
TErrible	Transport East	-	-240/60 tan 60 = -6.93
TWins	Transport West	+	0
		Total drift =	-9.3 °/h

By comparing the actual DI heading with the expected one (derived from these calculations), the pilot could use this information to establish the real (random) drift error.

2.3 Artificial Horizon

2.3.1 Description

In instrument flight conditions, when the natural horizon cannot be seen, it is essential that the pilot be provided with an indication of the aeroplane's attitude with respect to the Earth's vertical reference. The Artificial Horizon or Attitude Indicator provides this reference.

The gyro horizon, or artificial horizon as it is frequently called, employs a vertical spin axis Earth gyro having freedom of movement in all 3 planes (i.e. 2 degrees of freedom) and indicates the aircraft attitude relative to the pitch and roll axis. The gyro spin axis is maintained vertical with reference to the centre of the Earth, so that a bar positioned at 90° to the spin axis represents the local horizon. A symbol representing the aircraft is fixed to the instrument case, as shown in Figure 2.11. On some instruments this is adjustable up or down by the pilot to suit his eye level and the pitch trim setting. In flight, aircraft movement about the pitch or roll axis is indicated instantaneously by case movement relative to the horizon bar, which is held in the local horizontal by gyro rigidity.

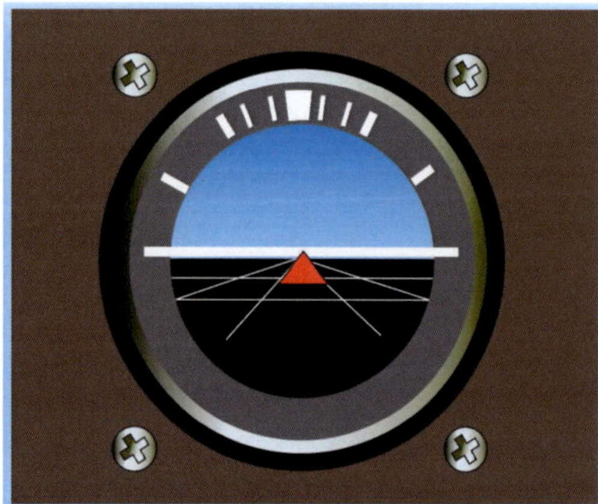

Figure 2.11 Artificial horizon

2.3.2 Display

A typical version of a vacuum-driven artificial horizon is shown below. The rotor of the gyro is mounted within a sealed case forming the inner gimbal, which in turn is pivoted in a rectangular shaped outer gimbal. A background plate representing the sky is fixed to the front end of the outer gimbal and carries a bank pointer, which registers against a bank-angle scale. The outer gimbal has freedom in the rolling plane through 110° either side of the central position, while the inner gimbal is limited to ±55° about the pitching plane. In both cases movement is limited by resilient stops to prevent internal damage to the instrument.

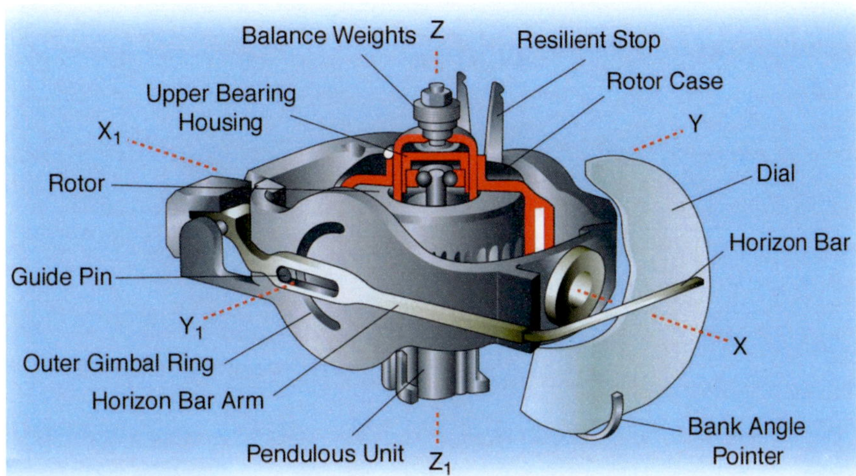

Figure 2.12 Gyro assembly

2.3.3 Operation – Pitch

Any movement relative to the inner gimbal is transmitted to the horizon bar arm through a guide pin on the inner gimbal. The guide pin engages the horizon bar arm through a curved slot in the outer gimbal, as shown in Figure 2.12. During level flight the aircraft's vertical axis is parallel to the rotor spin axis, and the guide pin is central in the slot with the horizon bar centralised. During climb or descent the rotor, and hence inner gimbal, remains rigid with reference to the local vertical, whilst the outer gimbal and instrument case move with the aircraft. Such movement, relative to the inner gimbal, causes the guide pin to become displaced in the slot, taking the horizon bar arm with it, providing an indication of dive or climb.

2.3.4 Operation – Roll

Bank indication is given by an index on the sky plate. The index reads against a scale printed on the glass face of the instrument. When an aircraft banks, the rotor, inner gimbal and outer gimbal remain rigid in level position while the instrument case, and hence printed scale, move with the aircraft; thus the position of the sky plate index indicates bank angle against the scale.

Air is evacuated from the instrument case and gyro housing (inner gimbal) by a vacuum pump. With the vacuum system in operation a depression is created within the instrument, so that the surrounding atmosphere enters the instrument through a filtered inlet passing through channels to jets mounted within the inner gimbal. Air issuing from the jets impinges on buckets cut into the periphery of the rotor, thus importing an even driving force to the rotor causing, it to rotate at approximately 13 000 rpm.

2.3.5 Construction and Operation - Electrically Driven Instrument

An example of an electrically driven gyro is shown below. It is made up of the same basic components as the vacuum-driven type; the exception is the vertical spin axis gyroscope, which is of the squirrel-cage induction motor type.

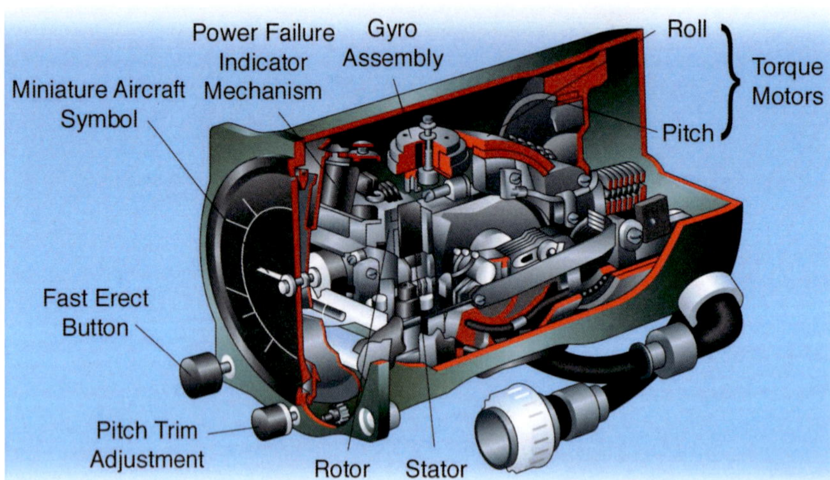

Figure 2.13 Inside an electrically driven instrument

One of the essential requirements of a gyroscope is to have the mass of the rotor concentrated as near to the periphery as possible, thus ensuring maximum inertia. However, an induction motor normally has its rotor revolving inside the stator, and to make one small enough to be accommodated within the space available in a modern miniaturised instrument would result in too small a rotor mass and hence inertia. But, by designing the rotor and its bearings so that it rotates outside the stator, then for a given size of motor (electrical gyro) the mass of the rotor is concentrated further from the centre and thus gyro inertia (rigidity) is increased.

This "squirrel-cage motor" is the method used not only in the gyro horizon but also in many instruments employing electrical gyroscopes. The motor assembly is carried in a housing that forms the inner gimbal. This is supported in bearings by the outer gimbal, which in turn is supported on a bearing in the front glass and rear casing of the instrument. The horizon bar assembly is in two parts pivoted at the rear of the outer gimbal and working in a manner similar to that already described. The instrument employs a torque motor erection system, operation of which will be described later. Use of electrics provides a rotor speed of approximately 22 500 rpm, whilst failure of power supply is indicated by a solenoid-actuated "OFF" flag appearing in the face of the indicator.

2.3.6 Remote Vertical Gyro

On many modern aeroplanes, the attitude indicator is fed from a remote vertical gyro unit normally sited in the avionics bay. This gyro works in the same way as the electrical gyro just described except that it is not linked directly to a presentation. The pitch and bank data is fed to the remote (panel mounted) indicator by means of an electrical synchro transmission system. The same attitude information can also be fed to the autopilot so that it uses the same data as the pilot is seeing. The biggest advantage of the remote vertical gyro is that it can provide greater degrees of freedom and the indicator can be constructed to present all attitudes with virtually unlimited freedom.

2.3.7 Gyro Horizons - Erection Systems

A system is required for erecting the gyroscope to its vertical position and to maintain the axis in that position during operation. The system adopted depends on the type of gyro; however, they are all of the gravity sensing type and in general fall into two categories, mechanical and electrical.

2.3.7.1 Mechanical – Pendulous Vane Type

A pendulous vane unit is used with the air-driven gyro. It is fastened to the underside of the rotor housing and consists of four knife-edged, pendulously suspended vanes, fixed in diametrically opposed pairs on two shafts supported in the unit body. One shaft is parallel to axis $Y - Y_1$, (pitch axis), with the other parallel to $Z - Z_1$, (roll axis) of the gyroscope. In the sides of the unit body are four small, elongated ports, one located under each vane. Suction air, having spun the gyro rotor, is exhausted through the ports and the reaction of these diametrically opposed streams of air applies a force to the unit body.

The vanes, under the influence of gravity, always hang in the vertical position and it is this feature that is used to govern the airflow from the ports and to control the forces applied to the gyroscope through the reaction to exhausting air. When the gyroscope is in the vertical position, the knife-edges of the vanes bisect each port, making all four port openings equal. In this position all the air reactions are equal and resultant forces about each axis are in balance.

If the spin axis is displaced from the vertical, as at Figure 2.14 (a and b), the pair of vanes on axis Y – Y_1, remain vertical, thus opening port D and closing port B. The increased reaction of air at the fully open port results in a torque being applied to the body in the direction of the arrow (obeying the law of precession) about the pitch axis Y – Y_1. The spin axis will thus be returned to the local vertical when the vanes again bisect the ports to equalise air reactions.

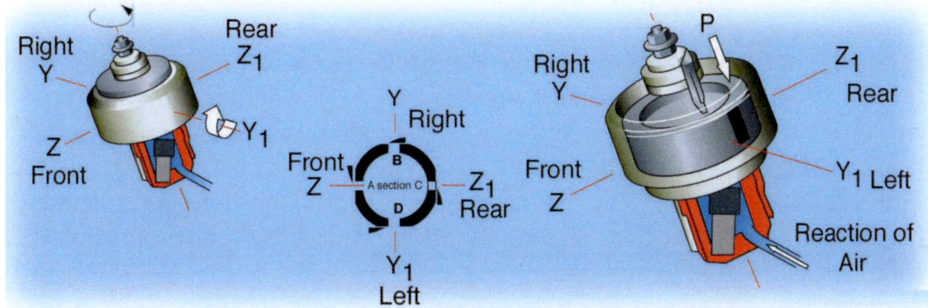

Figure 2.14 Vertical spin axis

2.3.7.2 Electrical – Torque Motor and Levelling Switch System

The torque motor electrical system, which is used in a number of electrically operated gyro horizons, consists of two torque control motors independently operated by mercury levelling switches mounted one parallel to the longitudinal axis and one parallel to the lateral axis. The lateral switch detects displacement of the gyroscope in roll and is connected to the torque motor mounted across the pitch axis, as shown below. Displacement in pitch is detected by the longitudinal switch, which is coupled to a torque motor mounted across the roll axis. Each levelling switch consists of a sealed glass tube containing three electrodes and a small quantity of mercury.

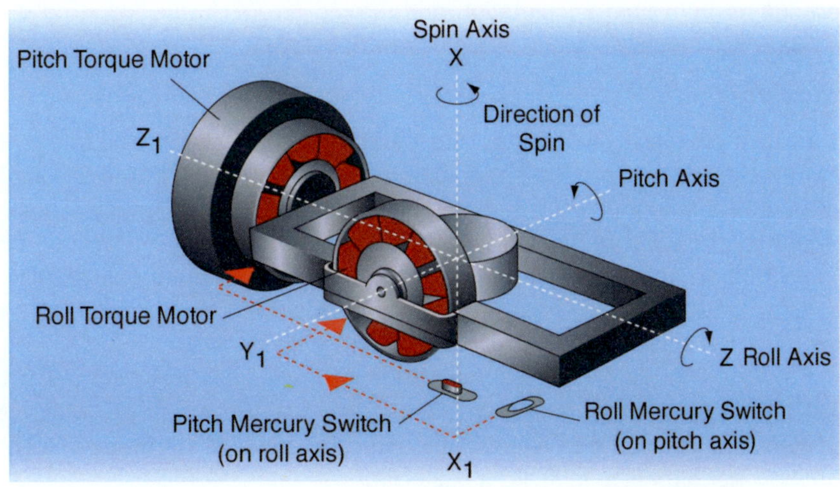

Figure 2.15 Position of torque motor and levelling switch

When the gyro is running and in its normal operating position, the mercury in the levelling switches ties at the centre of the tubes and is in contact only with the centre electrode; the two outer electrodes, which are connected to the respective torque motors, remain open. The auto-transformer reduces the voltage to a nominal value (20V) which is then fed to the centre electrode of the switches; there is thus no current flow to the torque motors.

If the gyro is displaced about, say the pitch axis in Figure 2.15, the pitch-levelling switch will be displaced and the mercury will roll in the direction of pitch to make contact with an outer electrode. This completes the electrical circuit to the laterally mounted pitch torque motor, energising the motor to apply a torque force which, when moved according to the law of precession, will become a force on the gyro about the pitch axis returning the spin axis to the vertical. At this time the pitch levelling mercury switch will return to its normal operating position with the mercury element now only in contact with the central electrode, thereby breaking the circuit to the pitch torque motor via one of the outer electrodes.

2.3.7.3 Electrical – Fast Erection

2.3.7.3.1 Operation

On many electrically operated gyro horizons employing the torque motor method of erection, there is a roll cut out switch. This is designed to prevent false erection signals being sent to the erection torque motors during a prolonged turn. In this arrangement, if the gyro rotor spin axis becomes more than 10° misaligned from the vertical, a commutator switch, fitted to the outer gimbal ring interrupts the current flow between mercury switches and torque motors on completion of turn, and to bring the gyro to its operational state as quickly as possible, a fast erection system is provided. This system by passes the roll cut out switch and applies a higher than normal voltage to the erection motors.

2.3.7.3.2 Fast Erection

If the gyroscope exceeds the appropriate limits of movement from the vertical, it must be brought back to normal as quickly as possible. This is achieved by pushing in the fast-erection switch. Output from the torque motors is thereby increased and the greater torque increases the erection rate from the normal 5° per minute to between l20° and 180° per minute, depending on design. However, to prevent overheating of the torque motor, the fast-erection switch must not be used continuously for longer than 15 s, nor used when the gyro is vertical.

2.3.8 Errors

The artificial horizon suffers from both acceleration and turning errors. In the following discussion the gyro rotor is assumed to rotate anti-clockwise when viewed from above.

2.3.8.1 Acceleration Errors

Sometimes known as take-off errors, since they are most noticeable during this stage of flight. The two components that introduce the errors are the pendulous unit and the vanes. In the air-driven instrument, the pendulous unit, Figure 2.14, makes the rotor housing (inner gimbal) bottom-heavy. Thus, when the aircraft accelerates, a force due to the unit's inertia is effective at the bottom, acting aft towards the pilot. This force is precessed through 90° in an anti-clockwise direction, lifts up the right-hand side of the outer gimbal, and hence the sky-plate attached to the outer gimbal rotates anti-clockwise, indicating a false starboard turn on the bank angle index.

During acceleration both longitudinally mounted side vanes are thrown back, with the result that the starboard side port opens and the port side closes; reaction occurs on the starboard side, precessed through 90°, the reaction lifts the inner gimbal to indicate a false climb.

In the case of the electrically driven gyro horizon, the inner gimbal does not have a pendulous erection unit hanging below it and is therefore not subject to apparent turn component of acceleration error. However, the mercury in the longitudinally mounted switch will hang back and complete the circuit to the pitch torque motor, causing the instrument to show a false climb.

In summary, therefore, acceleration errors on the air-driven instrument result in an apparent climbing turn to starboard being indicated, while the electrically driven instrument will show only a false climb in the same circumstances

2.3.8.2 Turning Errors

During a turn the laterally mounted vanes of the air-driven gyro horizon will be displaced due to centrifugal force acting outwards from the centre of the turn. Thus one port will be open while the opposite port will be closed. Reaction will be set up in the fore and aft axis of the aircraft, which, having precessed through 90°, will lift the outer gimbal to port or starboard. This results in a false bank indication.

Centrifugal force also causes the pendulous unit to swing outwards away from the centre of the turn. The force affects the inner gimbal, giving a false indication of climb or descent. The combined effect of the two forces is to displace the gyro rotor in two planes. In modern gyroscopes the gyro axis is off set from the true vertical to counteract these errors, but the correction is only valid for a given rate of turn. The sole effect on an electrically driven gyro is to displace the mercury in the lateral mercury switch, to complete the circuit via one or other of the outer electrodes to the roll torque motor, resulting in a false bank indication.

In summary, turning error will cause the air-driven gyro horizon to give a false indication of turn and climb or descent, while an electrically driven gyro will give only a false bank indication

2.3.8.3 Compensation

Some compensation is made for these errors by arranging the vertical axis of the gyro to be tilted away from the real vertical when the indicator shows zero pitch or bank. This has the effect of moving the circle, prescribed by the top of the spin axis during a turn, so that it is centred over the top of the centre of the gyro and thus minimises the error.

2.3.9 Standby Attitude indicator

Many modern aircraft employ integrated flight systems. These include indicators that can display not only pitch and roll attitude data, from a remotely located vertical axis gyroscope, but also associated guidance data from radio navigation systems. It could, therefore, be concluded that there is no longer a need for a gyro horizon. However, there is an airworthiness requirement to meet the case of possible failure of the circuits controlling the display of aircraft attitude. Thus, the gyro horizon still has a part to play, if only in the role of standby attitude indicator.

2.3.9.1 Principle

The gyroscope is of the electrically operated type and powered during normal operation by the aircraft's 115V 3-phase supply. Failure of normal power supplies is sensed and a static inverter, which is powered by 28V DC from the battery bus bar, automatically supplies the standby gyro horizon (attitude indicator). Power from such a source is always available, thereby ensuring that attitude indications are displayed.

In place of the conventional stabilised horizon bar method of displaying pitch and roll, a stabilised spherical element is adopted as the reference against an aircraft symbol. The upper half of the element is coloured blue (sky) to display climb attitudes, while the lower half is black, to display descending attitudes. Each half is graduated in l0° increments up to 80° climb and 60° descent. A pointer and scale indicate bank angle in the normal manner. The indicator has a pitch-trim adjustment and a fast-erection facility. When the knob is rotated to its "IN" position, the aircraft symbol may be positioned through ±5° variable pitch trim. Pulling the knob out and holding it energises a fast-erection circuit.

2.4 Turn and Balance Indicator

2.4.1 Introduction

The turn and balance indicator, previously known as the turn and bank indicator, was the first instrument on the blind flying panel to use a gyro. It is essentially two instruments in one case: a turn component to show the rate (speed) and direction of turn; and a balance component to show whether the aircraft is perfectly balanced in the turn, skidding out of the turn or sliding into the turn. We will, therefore, study separately the two components of the instrument. The dial presentation of a typical instrument is shown below.

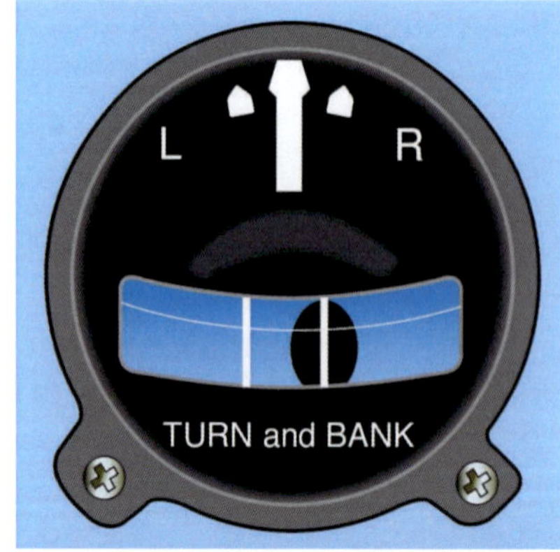

Figure 2.16 Turn and slip indicator

2.4.2 Turn Indicator

The instrument employs a horizontal spin axis gyro, the rotor being mounted to spin in the fore and aft axis of the aircraft. The gyro has freedom of movement in the rolling plane only and is, therefore, a "rate gyro". The rotor is either electrically driven and includes a power failure warning flag, or is driven by an air jet which impinges on buckets cut into the rim of the rotor. Both rotor-drives are structured to produce a rotor speed of approximately 9000 rpm; low rotor speeds being employed as in level flight, the gyro axis is maintained in the horizontal by use of one or more springs, as shown in Figure 2.17.

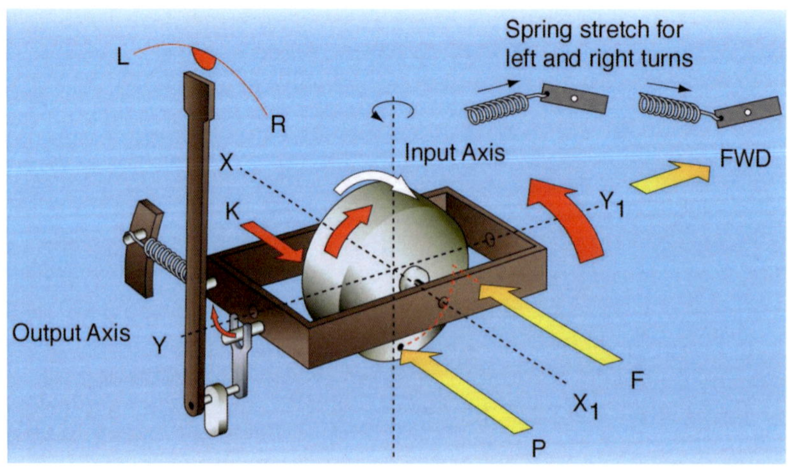

Figure 2.17 Turn indicator axis

2.4.2.1 Gyro and Gimbal Movement

From Figure 2.17 it is readily apparent that the turn indicator differs markedly from the type of gyro used in other instruments, in that it has only one spring-restrained gimbal ring, the spring restraining gimbal movement about the aircraft's fore and aft axis. When the instrument is in its normal operating position, the

spring restraint will ensure the rotor spin axis is always horizontal and the turn pointer will be at the zero datum mark.
As the aircraft enters a turn, say to the left, the gyro axis, being rigid, opposes the turn and a force is experienced about the vertical input axis. The gimbal ring will also turn, but as the rigidity of the gyroscope resists this turning movement, it will precess about axis "$Y - Y_1$". A turn to the left causes a force to be applied at the front pivot of the gimbal ring, which is the same as applying a force at point F on the rim of the rotor. Following the property of precession, the force will act at a position 90° removed from the point of application in the direction of gyro rotation, i.e. at point P, thus causing the gimbal ring to tilt about the fore and aft axis. A pointer connected to the gimbal ring would also move, and in doing so would indicate the direction of turn. However, in addition to direction, we wish to know the rate of turn, and this is a function of the retaining spring connecting the gimbal ring to the instrument case.

2.4.2.2 Spring Operation

Considering again an aircraft turning to the left, the gyroscope, in precessing, will stretch the spring until the force it exerts prevents further deflection of the gyro. Since the force exerted at P is a function of the angular momentum of the gyroscope and rate of turn, then the force exerted by the spring is proportional to gimbal ring deflection and is a measure of the rate of turn.

As the gimbal ring is deflected by force P, the stretched spring (Figure 2.17) will exert a downward force on the left-hand end of the gyro spin axis. This may be seen as a force pressing on the left hand lower part of the gyro rotor, i.e. opposite to force P. This force, when precessed through 90°, will become a rotational force about the input axis acting at point K on the rotor rim. By reference to Figure 2.17, it can be seen that force K is therefore acting in the same direction as the original turning force F. This is called Secondary Precession.

As the rate of turn is established, force F becomes a constant value. When force K reaches the same value, a situation is achieved where two forces of equal value are acting for opposing purposes, force F is due to rigidity of the gyro, and force K is a precessing force. At this stage the gyro cannot tilt any further, and whatever tilt angle has been attained is due entirely to force F.

2.4.2.3 Calibration

The rate of turn as shown by pointer displacement is thus a function of gyro tilt. Scale is calibrated in what are termed standard rates and, although seldom marked on the instrument, are classified by the numbers 1 to 4, corresponding to turn rates of 180°, 360°, 540° and 720° per minute respectively. On commercial aeroplanes the scale is normally only graduated to indicate rate 1 turns. Turns in excess of this rate are not normally performed in these aeroplanes as they are uncomfortable for the majority of passengers and they also impose unnecessarily high loads on the airframe.

2.4.2.4 Damping

A piston and cylinder system, for damping out oscillations of the gyroscope, is also incorporated and is adjusted so that the turn pointer will respond accurately to fast rate of turn changes while at the same time reacting to a definite turn rate without pointer oscillation.

2.4.2.5 Effect of Air leaks

If the instrument case of an air-driven gyro is not airtight, air will be drawn into the case via the leaks, resulting in a loss of efficiency.

The product of an air leak in a turn and balance indicator will be a reduction in rotor speed and the pointer will indicate a lesser rate of turn; similarly, if the speed is too high, the pointer will indicate a higher rate of turn than that being flown

2.4.3 Balance Indication

This part of the instrument uses one of two mechanical methods to indicate that the aircraft is correctly banked for the rate of turn. In the most common method, the force of gravity acts upon a pendulous weight in the form of a ball in a liquid filled tube. The ball maintains the true vertical in straight and level flight. In this position there is no slip or skid and the indication is as shown at Figure 2.18(A). At (B), the aircraft is shown turning to the left and having a certain bank angle. The indicator case and scale move with the aircraft and, because of the turn, centrifugal force in addition to gravity acts on the ball and displaces it outwards away from the centre of the turn. However, when the turn is executed with the correct bank angle, there is a balanced condition between the two forces of gravity and centrifugal, and the ball remains in the zero position. An increase of airspeed during the turn would increase both the bank angle and centrifugal force, but so long as the bank angle is correct, the ball will remain at the zero position, lying along the new resultant of the two forces.

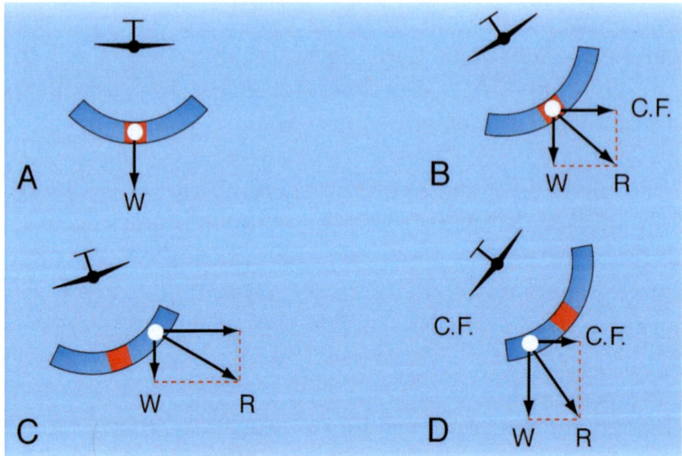

Figure 2.18 Balance Indicator

2.4.4 Slip and Skid

If the bank angle for a particular rate of turn is incorrect, say the turn is under banked, as in Figure 2.18 (C), the aircraft will tend to skid out of the turn. In such conditions, centrifugal force will predominate, displacing the ball away from the zero position in the opposite direction to that in which the turn is being made. When the turn is over-banked, as at Figure 2.18 (D), the aircraft will slip into the turn and the force of gravity will predominate, displacing the ball away from the zero position in the same direction as the turn.

Some older models of turn and balance indicator employ a pendulous weight attached by a mechanical linkage to a pointer. The principle of operation is the same in that the same forces are acting on a pendulous mass. The only difference is the appearance of the presentation.

From the foregoing, the rule of interpretation is that if the rate of turn pointer and the balance pointer, or ball, are displaced in the same direction, the aircraft is slipping into the turn. If they are displaced in opposite directions, the aircraft is skidding outward from the centre of turn. If turn is indicated and balance indicator is in zero position, it is a balanced turn

2.4.5 Typical Indicators

The mechanism of a typical air driven turn and balance indicator is shown in Figure 2.19.

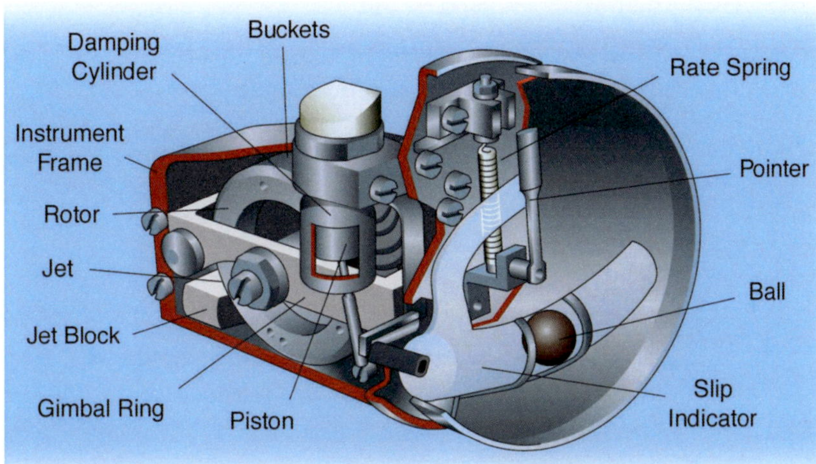

Figure 2.19 Air Driven Turn and Balance Indicator

2.4.6 Pre-flight Checks

For an electrical instrument, check that the "OFF" flag has disappeared. During taxi, check that the needle indicates a turn in the correct direction and that the ball indicates a slip.

2.4.7 Faults

The most likely fault is a rotor speed that differs from the design RPM. If the rotor speed is lower than design, both the gyro rigidity and the precessional forces are reduced. Of these, the reduction in the precessional forces is the most important as they will no longer be able to overcome the spring tension to the same degree. The Turn indicator will therefore under read.

Under speed of the rotor under indicates the rate of turn

2.5 Turn Co-ordinator

A turn co-ordinator is a development of the turn and balance indicator and is used in place of such instruments in a number of small, general aviation aircraft. The primary difference is in the location of the precession axis of the rate gyroscope. The gyroscope is spring-restrained and is mounted so that the axis is at about 30° with respect to the aircraft's fore-and-aft axis, as shown in Figure 2.20, thus making the gyroscope sensitive to banking as well as turning of the aircraft.

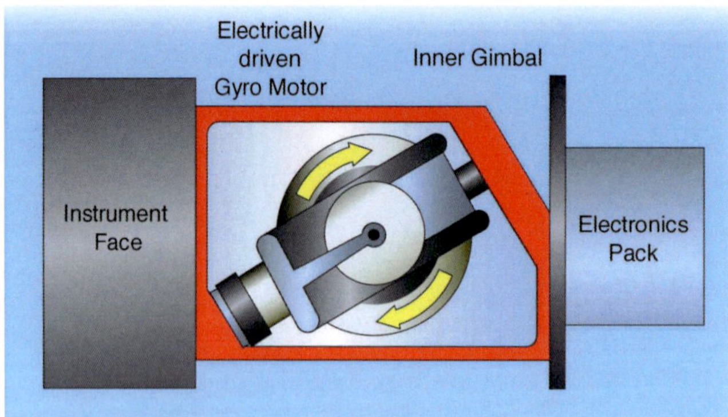

Figure 2.20 Inside a turn co-ordinator

2.5.1 Display

The turn co-ordinator integrates both the rate of roll and the rate of turn, so as to give a presentation of what the aircraft is actually doing, not what it has done. It indicates the two rates on a display similar to that shown in Figure 2.21. The aeroplane symbol of the turn co-ordinator moves in the direction of turn or roll, unlike the artificial horizon where the symbol is fixed to the instrument case and the horizon bar moves.

The annotation "No pitch information" is sometime given on the indicator scale so as to avoid confusion in pitch control that might result from the instrument's similarity to a gyro horizon. The instrument is NOT an attitude indicator.

Figure 2.21 Turn indicator

2.5.2 Operation

It is possible (although of little practical value) to roll an aeroplane into a bank and keep it straight with the rudder; in this situation the ball of the balance indicator would be displaced, but the bank needle of a turn indicator would show no turn. The turn co-ordinator in similar circumstances would also show no turn; however, it would show a roll while the bank was being applied, which the turn and balance indicator would not if no yaw were present.

As the wing of the aircraft is lowered, even very slightly, the turn co-ordinator will immediately show a deviation from straight and level flight, whereas the turn and balance indicator will show nothing until yaw is present. In essence, therefore, the turn co-ordinator anticipates a change from straight and level flight, while a turn and balance indicator measures a deviation, thereby enabling the pilot to anticipate the resulting turn. The pilot can then control the turn to the required rate as indicated by the alignment of the aircraft with the outer scale. The gyroscope is a DC motor operating at 6000 rpm. However, some types of turn co-ordinator may employ an AC motor supplied from a solid state inverter housed within the instrument. Damping of the gyroscope is achieved by using silicon fluid or by a graphite plunger in a glass tube.

2.6 Gyro Stabilised Platforms

2.6.1 Inertial Navigation Systems

Inertial Navigation Systems (INS) provide aircraft velocity and position by continuously measuring and integrating aircraft acceleration. INS use no external references, are unaffected by weather, operate day/night, and all corrections for Earth movement and for transporting over the Earth's surface are applied automatically. The products of an INS are: position (lat/long), speed (KT), distance (nautical miles), and other navigational information. The quality of information is dependent on the accuracy of initial (input) data and the precision with which the system is aligned (to True North). The basis of an Inertial Navigation System (INS) is the measurement of acceleration in known directions. Accelerometers detect and measure acceleration along their sensitive (input) axes.

The output is integrated, first to provide velocity along the sensitive axis, and a second time to obtain the distance along the same axis

The process of integration is used because acceleration is rarely a constant value.
For navigation in a horizontal plane, two accelerometers are necessary and are placed with their sensitive axes at 90° to each other. In order to simplify our understanding we will assume that they are aligned with True North and True East.

To avoid contamination by gravity, the accelerometers must be maintained in the local horizontal, (i.e. there must be no influence from gravity along the sensitive axes). To keep this reference valid, the accelerometers are mounted on a gyro-stabilised platform capable of maintaining the correct orientation as the aircraft manoeuvres

2.6.2 Accelerometers

2.6.2.1 Principles and Construction

The principle of an accelerometer is the measurement of the inertial force that displaces a mass when acted on by an external force (acceleration). The simplest form is shown in the diagram at Figure 2.22. The mass is suspended in a cylindrical casing in such a way that it can move relative to the case when the case (aircraft) is accelerated. The retaining springs dictate the position of the mass: at rest it is centrally placed and the mass will appear to remain stationary when a horizontal force is applied. The final position of the mass is controlled by the pull of the springs and the displacement of the mass is proportional to acceleration.

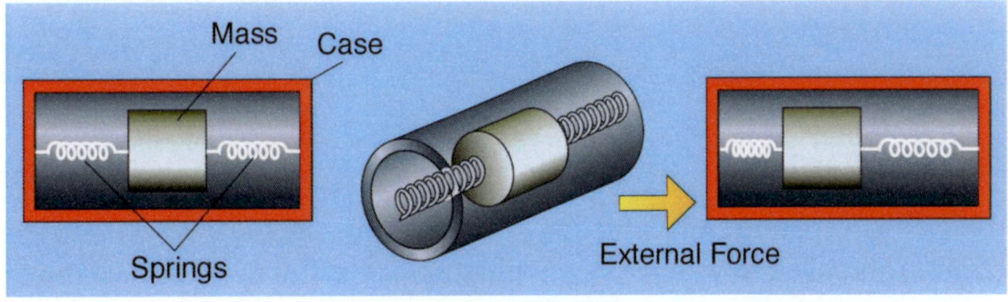

Figure 2.22 Accelerometer

Another form of accelerometer is based on the angular displacement of a pendulum under acceleration at the pivot point (called a force-rebalance accelerometer). Figure 2.23 is a diagrammatic representation of such an accelerometer. With the outer case at rest (and horizontal) or when moving at a constant velocity, the pendulum is central and no pick-off current flows. When accelerated left or right, the pendulum deflects and this is detected by the pick-off coils; by feeding the current to the restoring coils, the pendulum is drawn back to the central position and the magnitude of the current to hold the pendulum central is now proportional to acceleration. In practice, the movement of the pendulum is very small indeed - the reason for this is to prevent cross coupling, which occurs when the pendulum departs from the vertical and is subject to gravity.

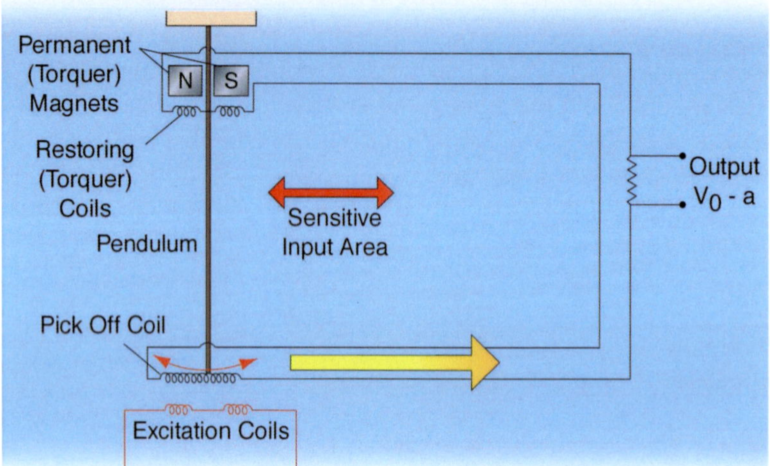

Figure 2.23 Accelerometer inputs and outputs

Figure 2.24 illustrates an example of the force-rebalance accelerometer. The inner tube is the pendulum arm, and the restorer coil and the pick-off coil form the inertial mass or pendulum. In all the types described, the current in the restoring circuit is proportional to the acceleration along the sensitive axis. This is known as the output.

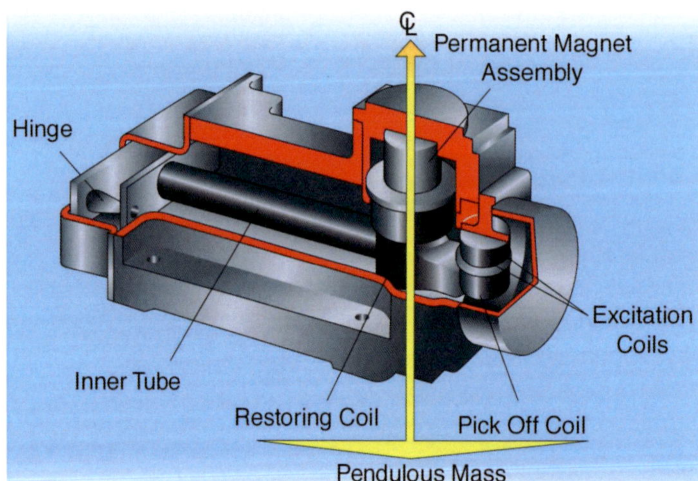

Figure 2.24 Force re-balance acceleromater

2.6.3 Gyro Stabilised Platform

For navigation in a horizontal plane (with respect to the Earth) we must keep the sensitive axis of the accelerometers horizontal and aligned with a known geographical axes system. Alternatively the equipment must be designed so that it can recognise the alignment of the accelerometers and can determine the horizontal vector components of any sensed accelerations. For our purposes we will initially assume a “North aligned” system.

In Inertial Navigation Systems, the accelerometers are normally mounted on a gimballed platform. A system of gyro control is used to keep this platform in the horizontal, aligned and independent of aeroplane pitch, roll or yaw

2.6.3.1 Gyros/Platform Stabilisation

The accelerometers in an INS are mounted on a platform that is kept level and aligned with true north. To maintain this stabilisation, rate gyros are mounted on the platform and are oriented so that they sense manoeuvres of the aircraft - pitch, roll, yaw. Rate integrating gyros are used in INS to achieve the requisite high accuracy. Immersing the gimbal and rotor assemblies in fluid reduces gimbal friction. An example is shown at Figure 2.25. Any torque (rotation) about the input (sensitive) axis causes the inner can to precess about the output axis, i.e., there is relative motion between the inner and outer cans. The pick-off coils sense this and the output is proportional to the input turning rate. To avoid any temperature errors, the whole unit is closely temperature controlled.

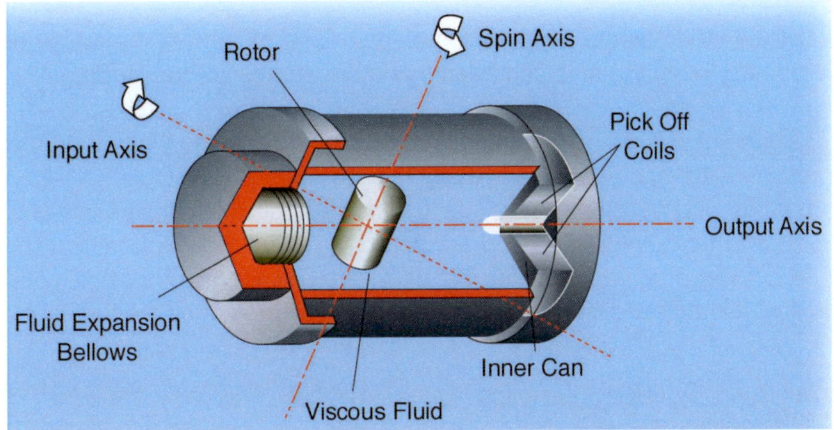

Figure 2.25 Gyro axis

> The operation of INS depends on the N/S and E/W accelerometers being held horizontal and correctly aligned. To achieve this, the accelerometers are placed on a platform, which is mounted within a gimbal system

The diagram at Figure 2.26 shows a stable platform for an aircraft heading north. The platform is isolated from aircraft manoeuvres of roll and pitch by the gimbals. Thus, by the sensing gyros and follow-up torque systems, the platform is maintained Earth horizontal and directionally aligned.

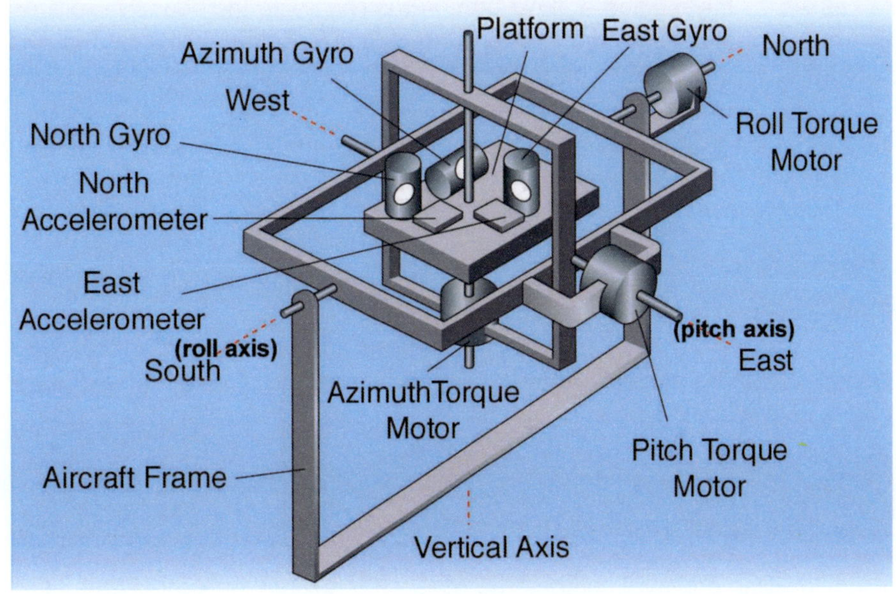

Figure 2.26 Gyro platform

In the diagram, the north gyro will be sensitive to roll and the east gyro to movements in the pitch axis. Any yaw will be detected by the azimuth gyro and all 3 rate gyros will turn the respective motors to maintain alignment. If the aircraft heads east, the east gyro will sense roll and the north senses pitch; for all intermediate headings, the simultaneous action of the rate gyros/torque motors is computed and the appropriate corrections applied.

In summary, the platform isolates the accelerometers from angular rotations of the aircraft and maintains the platform in a fixed orientation relative to the Earth. The assembly (accelerometers, rate gyros, torque motors, platform and gimbal system) is known as the stable element

2.6.3.2 Setting-Up Procedures

The accuracy of an INS depends on the alignment in azimuth and attitude of the stable element, i.e. it must be horizontal (level) and aligned to the selected heading datum, normally True North.

The levelling and alignment processes must be conducted on the ground when the aircraft is stationary

As already indicated, gyros and accelerometers used in INS are normally fluid filled and it is necessary to bring the containing fluid to its correct operating temperature before the platform is aligned. Thus the first stage in the sequence is a warm-up period where the gyros are run up to their operating speeds and the fluid is temperature controlled. When these have been achieved, the alignment sequence begins.

2.6.3.2.1 Levelling

Coarse levelling is achieved by driving the pitch and roll gimbals until they are at 90° to each other; the platform is then erect to the aircraft frame.

Fine levelling follows this initial process. In this process any acceleration detected by the accelerometers is assumed to be gravity. The output(s) are used to drive the appropriate torque motors until there is zero acceleration sensed.

2.6.3.2.2 Alignment

"Gyro compassing", or fine alignment, is automatically initiated once the platform has been levelled

Where the platform is not accurately aligned with True North, the E/W accelerometer will sense an acceleration force caused by the rotation of the Earth; if it is lying with the sensitive axis exactly E/W, then the Earth's rotation has no effect. But, and this is normally the case when the INS is switched on, if the alignment is not accurate, there is an E/W output and this is used to torque the platform until the E/W output is reduced to nil.

Note: Within the value of Earth rate affecting the E/W accelerometer is a component dependent on the cosine of latitude. Therefore, for an aircraft at very high latitudes, this component gets very close to zero and makes alignment to True North virtually impossible.

The effect of latitude on the fine alignment process limits the initial alignment to mid-latitudes and equatorial regions and this limits the usefulness of the North aligned system

The complete process of levelling and gyro compassing takes a period of time that varies from equipment to equipment but is, for a conventional gyro system, unlikely to be much less than 15 to 20 min.

During this time the aeroplane must not be moved as the accelerations will upset the process and prevent the platform from aligning. However, loading, wind gusts, etc will not affect the process

The processes of fine levelling and gyro compassing require corrections to be applied that are dependent on the system being "told" the accurate value of the present latitude. If the wrong latitude is put in the alignment process will be unsuccessful.

Gross latitude errors will cause failure to align. Small latitude errors will cause poor alignment and degraded accuracy

A wrong set up longitude will not affect the alignment process but will affect the accuracy of subsequent positions. This is because the INS is a dead reckoning (DR) system and, like any DR navigation, if you start with a wrong position all subsequent positions will be wrong.

The inter-relationship between levelling and alignment is complex - any slight discrepancy in the one affects the other. It is therefore important that from the moment fine levelling is completed the necessary correction to keep the platform horizontal with respect to the Earth is applied. The Earth waits for no man and rotates continuously. Remember that this is a gyro-stabilised device and the gyros want to maintain spatial rather than terrestrial rigidity. So the platform has to be "tilted" as the Earth moves round to maintain terrestrial horizontality.

2.6.4 Inertial Navigation System (Operation)

The final step towards an integrated INS is to provide the necessary corrections to keep the stable element in the local horizontal and to process the output of the accelerometers.

A simple INS is shown in schematic form at Figure 2.27. The N/S distance is added to initial latitude to give present latitude, while the departure E/W has to be multiplied by the secant of the latitude to obtain change in longitude. The accelerometer outputs are integrated with respect to time to obtain velocity, and then a second time to obtain distance. The accelerometer output may be either in voltage (analogue) form, or in pulse form, for analogue and digital systems respectively. Remember that the output of first stage integration is the value velocity and of the second is distance along the sensitive axis of the accelerometer. The translation of detection by the accelerometers at 90° to each other into present position expressed in lat/long is also illustrated at Figure 2.27.

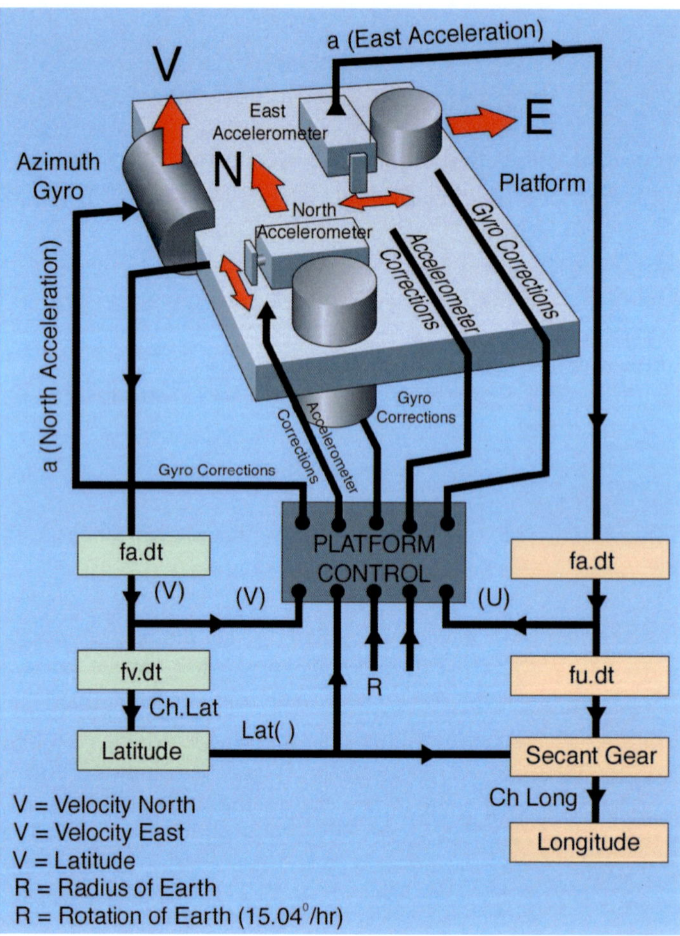

Figure 2.27 INS

2.6.4.1 Corrections

Accelerometers and gyros have sensitive axes, which extend infinitely in straight lines; i.e. they operate with respect to inertial space. But the Earth is not like that - local vertical axes are not constant because the Earth is a curved surface and it also rotates. Corrections for Earth rate and transport wander have to be made, as do those for accelerations caused by the Earth's rotation. Any control gyro is rigid in space and, in order to maintain an Earth reference, it must be corrected for both Earth rate and transport wander. Further correction for Coriolis (sideways movement caused by Earth rotation except if at the equator) and the centripetal acceleration, the latter caused by rotating the platform to maintain alignment with the local vertical reference frame, must also be applied.

2.6.4.1.1 Gyro Corrections

Due to Apparent Wander:

Earth Rate Drift:- The azimuth gyro must be torque compensated for Earth rate. This compensation allows for the familiar 15 sin (lat)°/h.

Earth Rate Topple:- The north gyro must be torque compensated at a rate of 15 cos (lat)°/h.

Due to Transport Wander:

Transport Wander Drift:- Transport wander causes misalignment of the gyro input (sensitive) axis at a rate varying directly with speed (along the sensitive axis) and latitude. For a correctly aligned platform, the speed in an E/W direction is the first integral of easterly acceleration, i.e. the output of the east accelerometer. Latitude is also calculated by the platform and, given these two values the INS computer can calculate and apply the correction for transport wander drift.

Transport Wander Topple:- A stabilised platform, which is transported across the surface of the Earth, will appear to topple in both the E/W and N/S planes. To keep the platform locally horizontal, transport wander corrections must be applied to the pitch/roll torque motors by the appropriate amounts.

2.6.4.1.2 Acceleration Corrections

Applying the apparent wander corrections implies turning the platform, even though it is only by small amounts, about its axes. Moving the spatial reference to make the platform "keep up" with the changing Earth reference causes acceleration errors. To remove these, acceleration error corrections must be applied. This rotation becomes extreme as we approach the vicinity for the poles.

Coriolis

This sideways force affects the output of both N/S and E/W accelerometers; it is caused by the rotation of the Earth about its axis. An aircraft following an Earth referenced track will follow a curved path in space. The very small error is computed and the necessary corrections applied to the outputs of the accelerometers.

Centripetal Acceleration

A body moving at a constant speed in a circle (such as an aircraft flying over the surface of the Earth where the centre of the Earth is the centre of the circle) has a constant acceleration towards the centre of the Earth. This acceleration will affect the accelerometers on an inertial platform and corrections to compensate for this movement are made and applied to the outputs of the accelerometers.

The above corrections to the gyros and the accelerometers in an INS are summarised in the following table. It is unlikely that the student would be required to calculate these corrections, but you are expected to be aware that they exist.

AXIS	GYROS		ACCELEROMETERS	
	EARTH RATE	TRANS. WANDER	CENTRPTL	CORIOLIS
North	$\Omega \cos \lambda$	$\frac{U}{R}$	$\frac{-U^2 \tan \lambda}{R}$	$-2\Omega U \sin \lambda$
East	Nil	$\frac{-V}{R}$	$\frac{UV \tan \lambda}{R}$	$2\Omega v \sin \lambda$
Azimuth/Vertical	$\Omega \sin \lambda$	$\frac{U \tan \lambda}{R}$	$\frac{U^2 + V^2}{R}$	$2\Omega U \cos \lambda$
V = Velocity North U = Velocity East λ = Latitude R = Radius of Earth Ω = Rotation of Earth (15.04°/ hr.)				

2.6.5 The Schuler Period

Schuler postulated an "Earth pendulum" with length equal to the radius of the Earth, its bob (plumb weight) at the Earth's centre and point of suspension at the Earth's surface. If the suspension point of such a pendulum were to be accelerated over the Earth's surface, inertia and gravity would combine to hold the bob stationary at the Earth's centre and the shaft of the pendulum would remain vertical throughout. If the bob of an Earth pendulum were disturbed, as it is when the aircraft is the suspension point, it would oscillate with a period of 84.4 min.

It can be shown that an INS platform which is "tied" to the Earth's vertical possesses the characteristics of an Earth pendulum; once disturbed, it will oscillate with a "Schuler Period" of 84.4 min

2.6.6 Errors

The errors of INS fall into three categories:

- Bounded Errors
- Unbounded Errors
- Inherent Errors

2.6.6.1 Bounded Errors

Errors that build up to a maximum and return to zero within each 84.4 min Schuler cycle are termed bounded errors. The main causes of these errors are:

(a) platform tilt, due to initial misalignment
(b) inaccurate measurement of acceleration by accelerometers
(c) integrator errors in the first integration stage

In practical terms, to the aviator this means that the output of the INS will be correct three times every Schuler Period; once when the period starts and then again at the end. In the middle, at 42.2 min, it is again correct. At 21.1 min the error will be a maximum high (say) and at 63.3, a maximum low. So, for an INS where the platform has been slightly disturbed, the real ground speed is 500 KT and the bounded error is carrying maximum variation of 7 KT in ground speed, then:

Period (min)	0	21.1	42.2	63.3	84.4
INS G/S (KT)	500	507	500	493	500

It can be seen that the error averages out over time.

2.6.6.2 Unbounded Errors

2.6.6.2.1 Cumulative Track Errors

These errors arise from misalignment of the accelerometers in the horizontal plane resulting in track errors. The main causes of these errors are:

(a) Initial azimuth misalignment of the platform
(b) Wander of the azimuth gyro

2.6.6.2.2 Cumulative Distance Error

These errors give rise to cumulative errors in the recording of distance run. The main causes are:

(a) Wander in the levelling gyros. NOTE: wander causes a Schuler oscillation of the platform, but the mean recorded value of distance run is increasingly divergent from the true distance run
(b) Integrator errors in the second stage of integration

In both cases above, position error is the most obvious result. The largest single contribution is real wander of the gyros. The sensitivities of an INS system expose any inaccuracies in the manufacture of rate integrating gyros and despite tight tolerances (less than 0.01°/h is normal) real wander is the culprit in unbounded error.

2.6.6.3 Inherent Errors

The irregular shape and composition of the Earth, the movement of the Earth through space and other factors provide further possible sources of error. Such errors vary from system to system, depending upon the balance achieved between accuracy on one hand and simplicity of design, reliability, ease of construction and cost of production on the other.

2.6.6.4 Radial Error

The radial error of an INS is an indication of the continuing serviceability of the INS. Its determination is frequently called for on the "voyage report" at the end of the flight. It is a calculation that is sometimes asked for in examinations. It is derived from the following:

$$\text{Radial error} = \frac{\text{Distance of final ramp position from INS position (NM/ hour)}}{\text{Elapsed time in hours}}$$

Watch out when calculating the distance between two positions; latitude must be considered.

2.6.7 Advantages of the Inertial System

- Indications of position and velocity are instantaneous and continuous
- Self contained; independent of ground stations.
- Navigation information is obtainable at all latitudes and in all weathers
- Operation is independent of aircraft manoeuvres.
- Given TAS, the W/V can be calculated and displayed on a continuous basis
- If correctly levelled and aligned, any inaccuracies may be considered minor
- as far as civil air transport is concerned.
- Apart from the over-riding necessity for accuracy in pre-flight requirements there is no possibility of human error.

2.6.8 Disadvantages

- Position and velocity information does degrade with time.
- Not cheap and is difficult to maintain and service.
- Initial alignment is simple enough in moderate latitudes when stationary, but difficult above 75° latitude.
- Alignment can not be carried out in flight.

2.6.9 Alternative Systems

The system described in the previous is fairly straightforward to understand but it suffers from severe latitude limitations such as alignment at high latitudes. Platform rotation rates at high latitudes become extreme and in the worst case an aeroplane crossing the pole would require the platform to rotate in azimuth by 180° in an instant. This gives extreme errors to the accelerometers.

For these reasons most modern systems that employ gyro stabilised platforms do not use a North aligned system.

The preferred option is to use a Wander Azimuth system. In this the platform is levelled as normal but, instead of physically gyro-compassing the platform, the alignment of the horizontal accelerometers is determined by calculation from the sensed tilt outputs of the two gyros having horizontal sensitive axes. Provided the computer has an accurate value for the present latitude of the system it can calculate the maximum tilt rate that the gyros could be experiencing. By comparing this to what is being measured the alignment of each gyro can be determined and so therefore can the alignment of the platform and the accelerometers.

Using this technique, the computer keeps a record of the platform azimuth alignment corrections and adds them to the initial sensed alignment mathematically. The platform does not have to be physically rotated and so the system becomes usable at high latitude.

2.6.10 INS Data and Applications

This paragraph describes the control, operation and displays of a conventional INS. The following diagrams and accompanying text demonstrate what can be expected from an INS when the various display switch selections are made.

2.6.10.1 *Mode Selector Unit (MSU)*

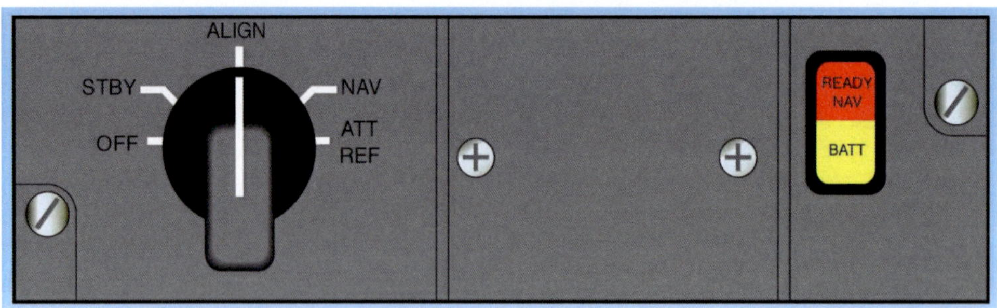

Figure 2.28 MSU

SELECTION	**MEANING**
OFF	Power OFF
STBY	Power ON
TEST or INSERT (data) may be carried out	Platform erects to aircraft axes System NOT affected by aircraft movement
ALIGN	Automatic alignment commences; aircraft must NOT BE MOVED when ALIGN mode is selected. System can withstand loading/gust movement
"READY NAV"	light (green) illuminates at end of alignment sequence
NAV	"READY NAV" extinguishes.
Platform in operational mode, all gyro and accelerometer corrections applied Selector switch heavily indented in NAV position to prevent accidental movement of switch to any other position. In NAV mode, the INS navigation computer requires a feed of TAS from the air data computer in order to calculate and present wind values. In addition, it cannot provide steering signals unless the data in respect of way points, course, etc have been correctly loaded into the Command Display Unit (CDU).	
ATT REF	Selected if NAV mode fails Continues to provide pitch, roll, and heading
CDU L/R displays go blank	Extinguishes red WRN lamp on CDU
When in ATT REF (Altitude Mode) the system will continue to provide the necessary attitude data for operation of dependant equipment such as attitude indicators, EFIS, AFCS.	
BATT	Red battery warning lamp. Informs that back-up power is in action

2.6.10.2 *Command /Display Unit (CDU)*

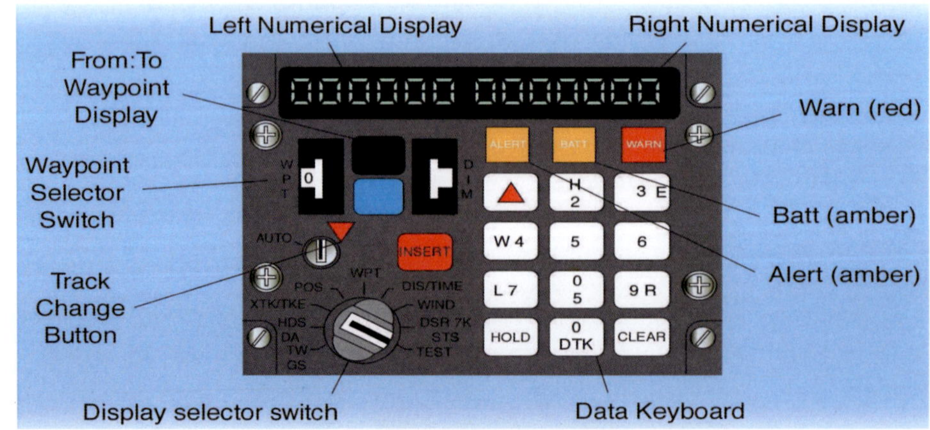

Figure 2.29 CDU

The character positions on the L/R displays is as follows:

POSITION	LEFT DISPLAY PANEL	RIGHT DISPLAY PANEL
TK/GS	PRESENT GC TRACK to the nearest tenth of a degree	PRESENT groundspeed to the nearest knot
HDG/DA	PRESENT HEADING to the nearest tenth of a degree	DRIFT ANGLE left or right of heading to the nearest degree
XTK/TKE	CROSS TRACK DISTANCE left or right of desired track to the nearest tenth of a nm	TRACK ANGLE ERROR left or right of desired track to the nearest degree
POS	PRESENT POSITION to nearest tenth of a minute of latitude	PRESENT POSITION to nearest tenth of a minute of longitude
WPT	WAYPOINT POSITION to nearest to nearest tenth of latitude	WAYPOINT POSITION to the nearest tenth of a minute of longitude
Note: The waypoint displayed is the one selected by the thumbwheel waypoint selector.		
DIS/TIME	GREAT CIRCLE DISTANCE to nearest tenth nm	TIME to the nearest minute at current groundspeed
Note: Depending on how other controls are set, this value can be one of the following : • from present position to next waypoint • from present position to any selected waypoint • from any waypoint to another waypoint.		
WIND	WIND DIRECTION to the nearest degree	WIND SPEED to the nearest knot
Note: This function is only available if TAS is supplied to the computer. Without TAS the display panels stay blank.		
DSR TK/STS	DESIRED (INITIAL) GC great circle track between the two waypoints	TRACK SYSTEM STATUS Various codes indicating status and serviceability according to status and elections.

WARNING LIGHTS

ALERT
An amber alerting light illuminates two minutes before reaching the next waypoint. In MAN the light will start to blink as the waypoint is passed and will continue to do so until the waypoint change is made manually when the light will go out. In AUTO the Automatic Flight Control System (AFCS) on command from the INS, will alter heading as necessary at the waypoint; the light will go out and the INS will update the waypoint FROM/TO display.

BAT
An amber light which illuminates whenever the system is operating on standby batteries, following loss of aircraft electric power to the INS. Normally 15 or 30 min standby battery power is available. If normal aircraft electric power is not restored to the INS before this power runs out the whole system automatically shuts down and the red BATT light on the Selector Panel illuminates.

WARN
A red light, which illuminates whenever a self-checking system in the computer detects an out-of-tolerance condition. When this light illuminates the Data Selector should be turned to DSRTK/STS, the Action and Malfunction Codes should be checked and the INS Operating Manual consulted before further action is taken.

2.7 Strap Down System

2.7.1 Inertial Reference Systems (IRS)

An IRS works on the same fundamental principles as the INS:

- measuring vector accelerations
- determining the horizontal components of these accelerations
- integrating these to obtain vector velocities and distances
- adding these to a start position to obtain a present position.

The fundamental difference between the INS and the IRS is that the IRS is a "Strap Down System". In this, three accelerometers are strapped or fixed to the airframe. They are mounted at 90° to each other, one aligned along each axis of the aeroplane

Solid state gyros are used to detect and determine the rate of rotation around each of the aeroplane's axes.

2.7.2 Solid State Gyros

A solid state gyro has no moving parts. It is not really accurate to describe it as a gyro but it can do what many gyros do, and can achieve a significantly higher level of accuracy and serviceability.

There are currently 3 types of solid state gyro suitable for aviation applications. Of these, only one is not yet available for commercial aviation, namely the Nuclear Magnetic Resonance Gyro (NMRG). The Ring Laser Gyro (RLG) and the Fibre Optic Gyro (FOG) are both available and operate on similar principles. Accordingly, the RLG is explained in some detail and a brief mention is made of the FOG towards the end of this Chapter.

2.7.3 Ring Laser Gyro

Unlike conventional, or spinning wheel, gyros that are maintained in a level attitude by a series of gimbals, the RLG is fixed in orientation to the aircraft axes. Changes in orientation caused by aircraft manoeuvre are sensed by measuring the frequencies of 2 contra-rotating beams of light within the gyro.

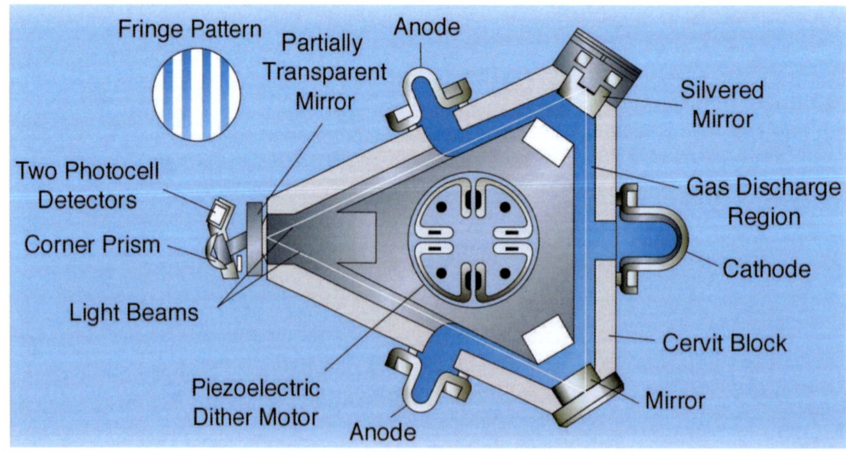

Figure 2.30 Ring laser gyro

A triad (3) of RLGs, with sensitive axes mutually perpendicular, is utilised. A block diagram of one of them is shown at Figure 2.30. The example shown has a triangular path of laser light the path length being normally 24, 32 or 45 cm. Other models have a square path, i.e. one more mirror. The RLG is produced from a block of a very stable glass ceramic compound with an extremely low coefficient of expansion. The triangular cavity contains a mixture of helium and neon gases at low pressure through which a current is passed. The gas (or plasma) is ionised by the voltage causing helium atoms to collide with, and transfer energy to, the neon atoms. This raises the neon to an inversion state and the spontaneous return of neon to a lower energy level produces photons which then react with other excited neon atoms. This action repeated at speed creates a cascade of photons throughout the cavity, i.e. a sustained oscillation, and the laser beam is pulsed around the cavity by the mirrors at each corner.

The laser beam is made to travel in both directions around the cavity. Thus, for a stationary block, the travelled paths are identical and the frequencies of the 2 beams will be the same at any sampling point. But, if the block is rotated, the effective path lengths will differ - one will increase and the other decrease. Now sampling at any point will give different frequencies and the frequency change can be processed to give an angular change AND a rate of angular change.

By processing the frequency difference between the 2 pulsed light paths, the RLG can be used as both a displacement and a rate gyro. There is a limit of rotation rate below which the RLG will not function: because of minute imperfections (instrument error) in the mirrors, one laser beam can "lock-in" to the other and therefore no frequency change is detected - the RLG has ceased to be a gyro. The situation is the RLG equivalent of gimbal-lock in a conventional gyro. One solution is to gently vibrate the RLG. 'The complete block is vibrated, or "dithered", by a piezo-electric motor at about 350Hz: the dither mechanism, literally the only moving part of the RLG, prevents "lock-in" of the 2 laser beams. The outputs of the RLG are digital, not mechanical, and the reliability and accuracy should exceed those of a conventional gyro by a factor of several times.

2.7.4 Fibre Optic Gyros

Like the RLG, the FOG comprises a triad of gyros mutually perpendicular to each other and similarly three accelerometers. The FOG senses the phase shift proportional to angular rate in counter-directional light beams travelling through an optical fibre. Although dimensionally similar, the FOG benefits from less weight and is cheaper, but, the fibre optic is not quite as rugged or efficient (more instrument error) than the RLG.

2.7.5 System Description

Strap-down systems dispense with the gimbal mounted stable element. The sensitive axes of both the accelerometers and the RLGs are in line with the vehicle body axes. There is no isolation from vehicle movement and so the outputs represent linear accelerations (accelerometers) and angular rates (RLGs) with respect to the 3 axes of the aircraft.

The RLGs are not required to stabilise the accelerometers but provide vehicle orientation - the already familiar horizontal and True North alignment are the reference axes. This is done in a mathematical method much the same as we saw for the azimuth calculations in a wander azimuth system. The orientation data is used to process (modify) the accelerometer outputs to represent those which, under the same conditions, would be output by accelerometers actually in the N, E and vertical planes. The transform matrix (a quaternion) can only be generated by digital computation, i.e., the quaternion is the analytical equivalent of a gimballed system.

2.7.5.1 Alignment

Although the assembly is "bolted" to the aircraft frame, an RLG INS still needs to be aligned to an Earth reference. Instead of levelling and aligning a stable platform, the speed and flexibility of a digital computer allows a transform to be calculated and compiled. 'The transform is a mathematical solution as to where the horizontal and True North lie with respect to the triad of RLGs and accelerometers. Full alignment takes less than 10 min at the end of which an offset to each output of the RLGs and accelerometers is established which determine local horizontal and True North references. These initial calculated values are applicable at that place on that heading at that time. The Earth will certainly move on and if the aircraft moves as well, the vital references must be safeguarded. This is done by making sure that the NAV mode is engaged. The complexities of 3-D motion, i.e. the interactions of pitch, roll and yaw, require a fairly extensive mathematical and trigonometrical juggle to be conducted at speed. The answer lies in a series of functions, which make up a mathematical matrix. Try to think of it as the reverse of the techniques in a conventional INS. Instead of creating a reference from a gimballed system, a reference is created from data taken from a completely different set of values. If the aircraft heading has not been altered since the RLG INS was last used, then a rapid alignment taking 10 -15 s is possible. If the aircraft is also fitted with Global Positioning Systems GPS -

satellite positional systems), it is possible to re-align an RLG INS in flight - a significant advantage over conventional systems.

2.7.5.2 Control/Display and Output

Control and Display of RLG INS is very similar to that of the conventional INS. Some more recent models have abandoned the familiar turret Display Selector Switch all outputs being displayed on pages of information selected by the crew and changes being made menu driven keypad actions.

In Figure 2.31, a block schematic of input/output functions for a typical IRS is shown and it can be seen that the emphasis is not solely on INS data but integrates navigation aids and equipment also. Note the multitude of data to the Horizontal Situation Indicator (HSI). The HSI may be an electro-mechanical instrument or it may be part of an Electronic Flight Information System (EFIS) display.

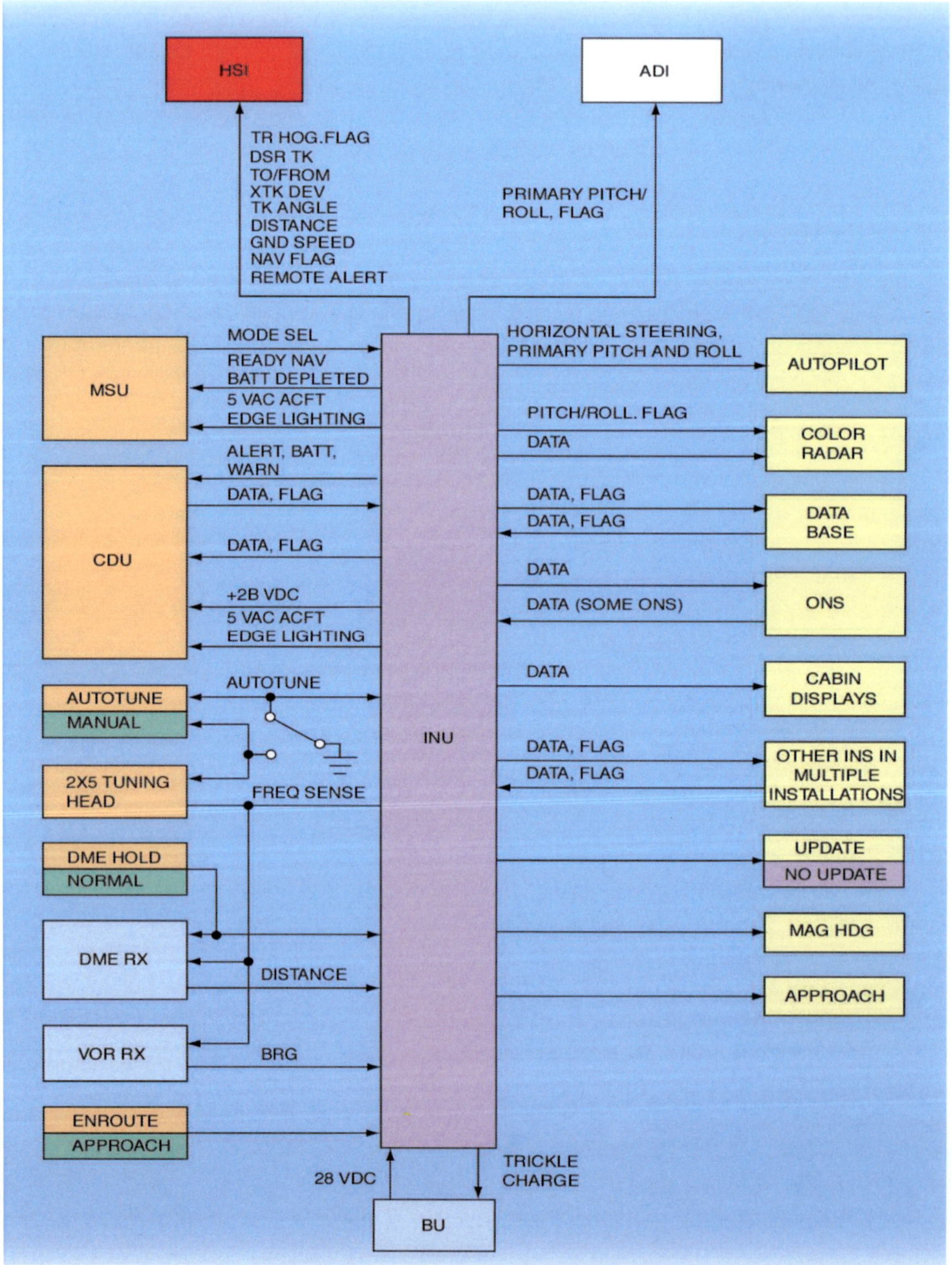

Figure 2.31 Components of the INS

Self-Assessment Test 2

1. The rigidity property of a gyro is best explained by a knowledge of:
A) Newtons 2nd Law of Motion
B) Newtons 3rd Law of Motion
C) Newtons 1st Law of Motion
D) Boyles and Charles Laws of Motion

2. When a force is applied to a spinning gyro the effect is evident:
A) 45° forward in the direction of rotation
B) 30° forward in the direction of rotation
C) Immediately in line with the plane of rotation
D) 90° forward in the direction of rotation

3. The basic types of gyro are as follows:
A) Space and Tied gyros
B) Tied and Rate gyros
C) Space (free), Earth, Tied and Rate gyros
D) Earth, Free and Rate gyros

4. A Space (free) gyro is defined as a gyro having:
A) Three degrees of freedom
B) Two degrees of freedom
C) One degree of freedom
D) Freedom in the longitudinal sense only

5. A rate gyro is defined as having:
A) One degree of freedom
B) Two degrees of freedom
C) Three degrees of freedom
D) Freedom in the longitudinal sense only

6. A Tied gyro is used in:
A) Compass and artificial horizon instruments
B) Turn Co-ordinator instruments
C) Turn and slip indicators
D) Direct Reading Compasses

7. In Appendix A, the turning force will cause the gyro to precess about the:
A) XX axis
B) YY axis
C) Plane of rotation
D) ZZ axis

8. The gyroscope arrangement in Appendix B has:
A) One degree of Freedom
B) Two degrees of Freedom
C) Three degrees of Freedom
D) Freedom about the spin axis only

9. The gyroscope in Appendix C is:
A) A Tied gyro
B) An Earth gyro
C) A Rate gyro
D) A Space gyro

10. A Displacement Gyro has:
A) Two degrees of Freedom and may be used as a heading reference, and in INS and aircraft instruments
B) One degree of Freedom and is used in INS systems only
C) Two degrees of Freedom and is used in INS only
D) Three degrees of Freedom and can be used in INS systems only

11. Wander is the generic term for gyro drift and may be summarized as follows:
A) Real Wander and Apparent Wander; Real Drift, Real Topple; Apparent Drift, Apparent Topple
B) Transport wander and Earths Rate
C) Real Wander, Real Topple, Transport Wander and Earths Rate
D) Apparent Topple, Apparent Drift

12. The amount of apparent drift shown by a horizontal axis gyro aligned with a local meridian and located in turn at the Equator, N45° and the Poles is:
A) No drift at the Latitude and 15 Sin Lat °/h at the Equator and the Poles
B) No drift at the Equator, 15° Sin Latitude at N45° and 15°Cos Latitude at the Poles
C) No drift at the Equator, 15° Cos Latitude at N45° and no drift at the Poles
D) No apparent drift at the Equator, 15 Sin Latitude °/h at N45° and 15°hour apparent drift at the poles

13. Apparent topple shown by a vertical axis gyro located at the Equator, N45 and the Pole is:
A) No topple at the equator, or the Poles and 15 Sin Latitude ° /h at N45°
B) 15 °/h topple at the Equator, 15 Cos °/h at N45° and no topple at the poles
C) 15 °/h topple at the poles, 15 Tan Latitude °/h at N45° and no topple at the Poles
D) Zero topple at any station

14. The following fundamental mechanical definitions provide the basis of some of the laws of gyrodynamics:
A) Momentum = mass X velocity
Angular velocity = momentum X velocity in radians
Angular momentum = velocity / radius
B) Angular momentum = mass X velocity
Momentum = velocity X radius
Angular velocity = mass X velocity X radius X π
C) Momentum = mass X velocity
Angular velocity = velocity / radius (measured in radius/second)
Angular momentum = Linear momentum X radius
D) Momentum = Linear momentum X radius
Angular velocity = mass X velocity
Angular momentum = $\frac{\text{Mass X Velocity}}{\text{Gyro diameter}}$

15. Assuming a horizontal axis gyro is at N30° and the spin axis aligned with a meridian. What will be the apparent drift:
A) 7.5°
B) 15°
C) 3.25°
D) Nil

16. The main advantages of electrically driven gyros over air driven gyros are:
A) Constant RPM at all heights
Sealed instrument case
Heat generated produces instability
Subject to turning and acceleration errors
B) Sealed instrument case – no dust or corrosion
Operating temperatures more stable
C) Largely immune to turning and acceleration
Higher RPM giving greater rigidity and less precession
D) Higher RPM giving more rigidity and less precession
Constant RPM at all heights
Sealed instrument case – no dust or corrosion
Heat generated in windings more stable
Largely immune to turning and acceleration errors

17. The source of air for suction operated gyros is:
A) An engine driven vacuum pump
B) An engine driven vacuum pump or a venturi tube attached to the outside of the fuselage
C) An air bottle
D) An electrically operated vacuum pump

18. The gyro rotor of an air driven gyro takes the form of a:
A) Ring of buckets (pelton wheel) which are cut into the surface of the gyro
B) Impulse/reaction turbine similar to that of a gas turbine
C) Propeller which is positioned in an air blast
D) Bicycle chain driven sprocket wheel

19. Earths rate compensation is provided by:
A) An offset gimbal ring
B) An offset air jet
C) A latitude nut correct for one latitude
D) Tables

20. Earths rate is:
A) 15 Sin latitude °/h at an increasing heading in the Northern hemisphere
B) 15 Cos latitude °/h at a decreasing heading in the Southern hemisphere
C) 15 Tan latitude °/h at an increasing heading in the Southern hemisphere
D) 15 Sin latitude °/h at a decreasing heading in the Northern hemisphere

21. If no corrective action was taken, an aircraft would, if maintaining a constant DG heading:
A) Turn left continuously in the Northern hemisphere
B) Turn right continuously in the Southern hemisphere
C) Turn right continuously in the Northern hemisphere
D) Maintain a straight and level constant path over the surface of the Earth

22. Transport drift is calculated from the basic formula:
A) 15 Sin latitude °/h
B) Change in longitude Sin MEAN lat
C) D.long Tan lat
D) D.long Cos lat

23. If a flight track is East/West at a particular groundspeed (G/S), the transport drift formula becomes:
A) $G/S \times \frac{\text{Tan lat}}{60}$ °/h
B) D.long Tan Lat X G/S
C) $D.long \times \frac{\text{Cos Lat}}{60} \times G/S$ °/h – Transport Drift
D) $G/S \times \text{Cos}\,\theta\, \frac{\text{Tan lat}}{60}$ °/h = Transport Drift

24. If a flight track is other than East or West, the Transport Drift is found by using the following formula where mean latitude is used and θ is the angle between track and East/West:
A) Transport Drift = $\text{Sin}\,\theta\, \text{Cos}\,\theta\, \frac{\text{Tan}\,\theta}{G/S \times 60}$ °/h
B) Transport Drift = $G/S \times \text{Cos}\,\theta\, \frac{\text{Tan}\,\theta}{60}$ °/h
C) Transport Drift = D.long X Cos θ X G/S X 60 Tan θ
D) Transport Drift = Lat X Sin Track Angle / Track X 60

25. A Latitude Nut is fitted to a DI to compensate for:
A) Transport drift
B) Coriolis
C) RPM changes on an air-driven gyro
D) Earths rate compensation

26. The Turn and Balance Indicator uses a:
A) Space gyro to indicate turn rate and a pendulum to indicate slip or skid
B) Pendulum to indicate turn rate and a tied gyro to indicate slip or skid
C) Rate gyro to indicate turn rate and a pendulum to indicate slip or skid
D) Pendulum to indicate turn rate and an Earth gyro to indicate slip or skid

27. Rates of turn are:
A) Rate 1 = 180°/min; Rate 2 = 270°/min; Rate 3 = 360°/min; Rate 4 = 720°/min
B) Rate 1 = 90°/min; Rate 2 = 180°/min; Rate 3 = 360°/min; Rate 4 =720°/min
C) Rate 1 = 90°/min; Rate 2 = 180°/min; Rate 3 = 360°/min; Rate 4 = 540°/min
D) Rate 1 = 180°/min; Rate 2 = 360°/min; Rate 3 = 540°/min; Rate 4 = 720°/min

28. If the rotor RPM of a gyro reduces below the normal operating speed range (circa 10 000 RPM), the instrument will:
A) Underread the rate of turn and the pendulum will show a slip indication
B) Overread the rate of turn and the pendulum will indicate normally
C) Overread the rate of turn and the pendulum will show a skid indication
D) Underread the rate of turn and the pendulum will indicate normally

29. If a turn indicator is correctly tuned to an average operating TAS at a Rate 1 turn, any change in TAS will cause the instrument to generally:
A) Underread the rate of turn in most cases
B) Overread the rate of turn
C) Not be affected by the rate of turn
D) Underread at rates of turn in excess of Rate 4

30. A rate gyro comprises of a:
A) Horizontal gyro carried in a single horizontal gimbal with the gyro axis lying athwartships
B) A horizontal gyro carried in a single vertical gimbal with the gyro axis lying parallel to the aircraft vertical axis
C) A vertically mounted gyro with two freedoms of movement and an athwartships spin axis
D) A vertically mounted gyro with a vertical axis superimposed on a single gimbal

31. Refer to Appendix D, the attitude situations are:
A) Straight and level
Balanced Rate 1 turn
Rate 2 turn to the right with slip
Rate 2 turn to the left with skid
B) Straight and level
Rate 2 right turn – balance
Rate2 right turn – with slip
Rate 2 right turn – with skid
C) Straight and level
Rate 2 left turn – balanced
Rate 2 left turn – with skid
Rate 2 left turn – with slip
D) Straight and level
Rate2 right turn – balanced
Rate 2 right turn – with skid
Rate 2 right turn – with slip

32. The turn co-ordinator when compared with a turn and balance indicator will show:
A) A turn only if yaw is present
B) Will show a change in flight path but only if the aircraft was not rolling at the time
C) Pitch changes at all times
D) Will show a change in flight path if a roll is initiated; the turn and balance indicator will only show turn rate if yaw is present

33. The gyro of an air driven artificial horizon is maintained in the vertical position by a:
A) System of suspended vanes fixed to a pendulous weight
B) Mercury switch
C) Liquid levelling switch
D) Torque motor driven in series with the gyro

34. The OFF flag of an electrically driven Turn and Balance Indicator will be out of view whenever:
A) Electrical power is applied
B) Electrical power fails
C) Electrical power is applied and the gyro has run up to speed
D) The gyro has run up to speed only

35. The principle of the turn element of a turn and balance indicator is that of:
A) Indicating spring force deflection only
B) Measuring the difference in magnitude between processional forces versus spring pressure
C) Measuring spring force against the deflection of the case
D) Displacing the gyro by the resultant centrifugal force during the turn and measuring the deflection

36. If the gyro speed of the turn element of a Turn and Balance Indicator is greater than the design speed, the indicated rate of turn will:
A) Be lower than the actual rate of turn
B) Be unaffected
C) Vary as usual depending on the rate of yaw
D) Be greater

37. During carrying out an instrument check during taxy, a turn is made the slip pointer of a turn and balance indicator will show a:
A) Skid out if the turn
B) Slip into the turn
C) Skid into the turn
D) Slip out of the turn

38. Assuming the aircraft is turned right onto the runway to line up. During the turn the ball in a balance indicator will indicate:
A) A move to the right
B) Remain central
C) A move to the left
D) None of these

39. If the gyro speed of the turn element of a Turn and Balance Indicator is lower than the design speed, the indicated rate of turn will:
A) Be lower than the actual rate of turn
B) Be unaffected
C) Vary as usual depending on the rate of yaw
D) Be greater

40. The gyro of a Turn and Slip Indicator is a:
A) Vertically mounted rate gyro fitted along the fore and aft axis of the aircraft
B) Horizontal axis rate gyro mounted in a horizontal ring in the athwartships axis
C) Horizontal axis rate gyro mounted in vertical ring on the fore and aft aircraft axis
D) Vertically mounted gyro fitted along mounted in a horizontal ring in the athwartships

41. INS relies on:
A) Satellite radio positioning waves to fix position
B) Accelerometers and a rate gyro stabilized platform to measure acceleration and velocity and keep a continuous log of progress from initial erection to shut-down
C) Accelerometers only to fly the aircraft along a given set of waypoints
D) Accurate inputs from a remote indicating compass and artificial horizon to maintain the aircraft on the desired course

42. Accelerometers detect and measure acceleration the data is integrated twice:
A) Once to measure vertical acceleration; twice to measure track
B) Once to measure cross track error; twice to measure altitude
C) Once to measure desired track; twice to measure velocity
D) Once to measure velocity; twice to measure distance along same axis

43. A force re-balance accelerometer is constructed as follows:
A) A mass is magnetically held centrally in a tube. When the aircraft accelerates in that axis, the mass moves in the appropriate direction and generates an error signal which is amplified and supplied to the relevant system
B) A free hanging pendulum displaced by aircraft acceleration, generates a corrective signal
C) A mass is held centrally in a tube by springs. Movement of the mass produces an output which is proportional to acceleration
D) An independent gyro stabilized mass is affected by acceleration. When this occurs, an output is produced which is supplied to the relevant system

44. Rate gyros are used in the INS equipment to:
A) Stabilizes the platform horizontally upon which are mounted the gyros
B) Provide rate/rate input signals for use by the control surface actuators
C) Generate basic altitude stabilization signals for direct use by the autopilot
D) Accept inputs from the vertical reference units which in turn, stabilize the integrated output

45. The following gyro corrections are provided by the INS alignment system:
A) Apparent wander, transport wander and acceleration corrections
B) Apparent wander, transport wander, acceleration corrections, Coriolis and centripetal acceleration
C) Transport wander, acceleration and Coriolis corrections
D) Coriolis corrections, Earth's rate and centripetal acceleration

46. The Schuler period is based on the:
A) Movement of the gyro stabilized platform when under g loading
B) Rate at which a rate gyro unit is self erecting over a period of 84.4 min
C) Movement of vertical reference units during the alignment process
D) Displacement of the pendulous mass used 'tie' the platform to Earth vertical. The period of movement is 84.4 min and these are sometimes called bounded errors

47. A cumulative track error arises from:
A) Consistently inaccurate DME fixing information
B) Schuler period distortions
C) Pendulous malfunctions in the levelling platform
D) Initial azimuth misalignment of the platform and/or wander of the azimuth gyro

48. Radial error is the:
A) Distance of the final ramp position from INS position divided by the elapsed time in NAV mode, in NM per hour
B) Distance from the last known waypoint position to the start of the flight in NM per hour
C) Angle of the levelling platform compared to the calculated angle
D) Distance of the final ramp position from INS position in radians per NM

49. When ALIGN is selected on an INS MSU, the aircraft:
A) Can be moved regardless
B) Cannot be moved otherwise the setting up procedure will have to be restarted
C) Must be in stable, level flight path conditions
D) Flight checks must be stopped under alignment is complete

50. When the READY NAV illuminates:
A) All azimuth functions may be selected
B) The gyro platform is about to be levelled
C) The MSU switch may be set to NAV
D) STBY is selected under the lamp goes out

51. IF ATT REF is selected on the MSU:
A) Pitch, roll and heading information together with all signals to the autopilots, is available
B) The red light is extinguished
C) Stand by battery power is made available for abnormal operation
D) Pitch roll and heading information is available to the flight instruments (EFIS) only

52. A red light on the MSU illuminates to:
A) Signify that standby power to the INS (probably an integral battery) is powering the system
B) Indicate that an overheat has occurred
C) Show that ALIGN has been selected but not accepted by the system
D) STBY should not be selected until the READY NAV light is illuminated

53. Pos 0 on the waypoint selector switch of an INS CDU is:
A) Waypoint 10
B) Present position
C) To do with the initialising sequence for aligning the INS when STBY is selected
D) Used only on the ground to select present position

54. The DIS/Time selector on the CDU when selected:
A) Selects the distance and time between the first and the last waypoints programmed into the system
B) Displays the DIS/TIME on MSU between selected waypoints
C) Displays DIS/TIME on the CDU between selected waypoints
D) Displays DIS/TIME on the CDU provided the aircraft is airborne

55. An IRS is basically a:
A) More accurate version of an INS where a basic platform, upon which are mounted accelerometers and which is maintained in the level position by rate gyros, provides controlling signals to the relevant systems
B) Platform, levelled by accelerometers and upon which rate gyros are mounted to provide controlling signals to relevant systems
C) Very much more accurate version of an INS and which is a strap down system with no levelling platform. Three accelerometers are strapped or fixed to the airframe and the output of solid state gyros (Ring Laser Gyros (RLG)) is mathematically resolved to produce acceleration and rate of change of movement about the aircraft axes
D) Modified electro-magnetic compass system that uses a solid state gyro (RLG) to measure aircraft heading and to integrate radio information when in the RNAV mode

56. Fibre optic gyros (FOG) operate on the principle of:
A) Utilizing the phase shift of light beams inside a fibre optic when subjected to acceleration and rate of change of acceleration. The output is used in the relevant systems in the same way as RLG and conventional gyros
B) The use of light beam phase shift to measure acceleration; RLG measure rate of change
C) Using light beam phase shift to measure conventional gyro wander and, through the action of a light sensitive torque motor, maintain gyro erection
D) Light beam phase shift caused by acceleration; conventional gyros measure rate of change

57. The main disadvantage of laser ring gyros is:
A) A 40 minute warm up time
B) High capital cost
C) High power requirement
D) Analogue output

58. RLG systems can only be aligned in flight:
A) By reselecting ALIGN and NAV
B) By selecting OFF then STANDBY
C) If the aircraft is equipped with GPS
D) When position information is provided by twin DME or VOR and a collocated DME

59. To prevent lock-in of the two laser beams of a RLG a:
A) Cam operated shaft is arranged to sequentially alter the length of the laser beam and therefore the frequency, at regular intervals
B) Mathematical matrix which alters the angles of laser beam transmission
C) Mirror adjusting system which alters the angle of reflection of the laser beam at set intervals
D) Dither motor that gently vibrates the whole of the RLG assembly at approximately 350HZ

Appendix A

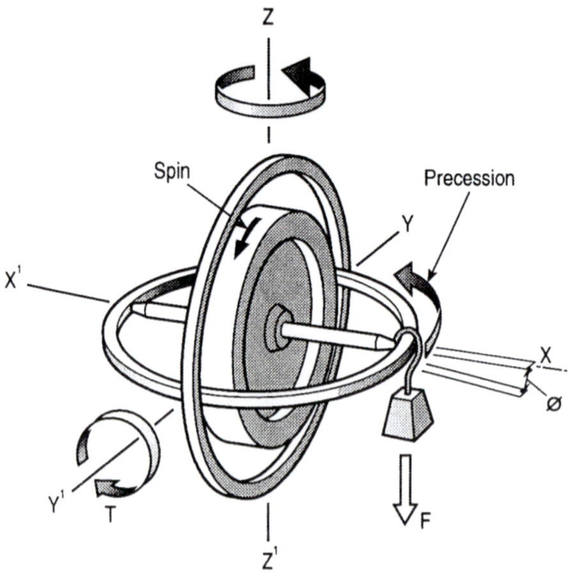

F = turning force

Appendix B

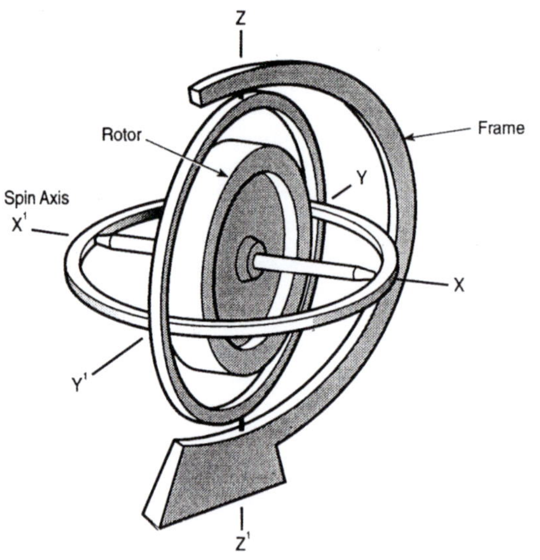

Appendix C

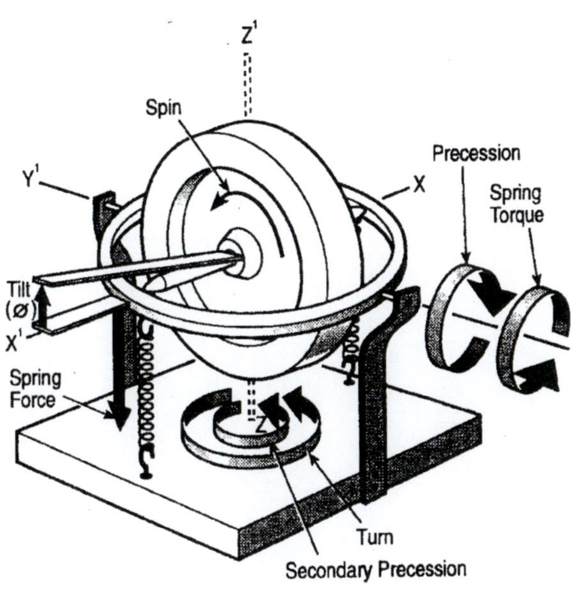

Appendix D

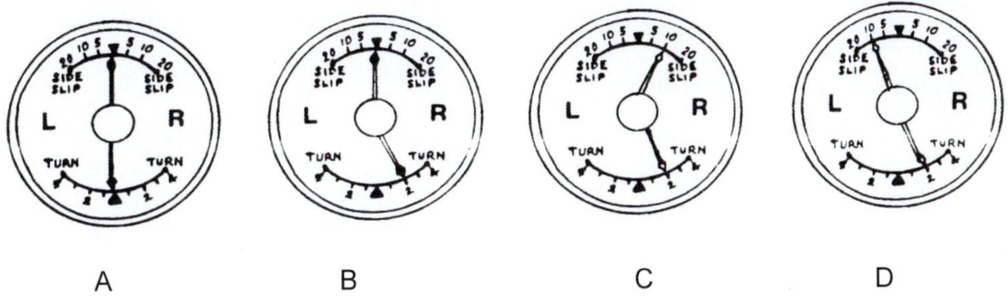

A B C D

Self-Assessment Test 2 Answers

1	C	21	C	41	B
2	D	22	B	42	D
3	C	23	A	43	C
4	B	24	B	44	A
5	A	25	D	45	B
6	A	26	C	46	D
7	D	27	D	47	D
8	B	28	D	48	A
9	C	29	A	49	B
10	A	30	A	50	C
11	A	31	B	51	D
12	D	32	D	52	A
13	B	33	A	53	B
14	C	34	C	54	C
15	A	35	B	55	C
16	D	36	D	56	A
17	B	37	A	57	B
18	A	38	C	58	C
19	C	39	A	59	D
20	D	40	B		

CHAPTER 3
Magnetism and Compasses

3.1 Principles of Magnetism

Direct reading magnetic compasses were among the first of the airborne flight instruments to be introduced into aircraft. The primary function of the direct reading compass was to show the direction in which the fore and aft axis of an aircraft was pointing (heading) with reference to the Earth's local magnetic meridian. However, the direct reading magnetic compass has now been overtaken as a heading reference instrument by the gyro magnetic compass and Inertial Reference Systems. The direct reading compass is now relegated to the standby role, although its carriage in all types of aircraft is still a mandatory requirement. The operating principles of direct reading compasses are based on the fundamentals of magnetism, and on the reaction between the magnetic field of a suitably suspended magnetic element and the magnetic field surrounding the Earth. It is therefore useful to have a basic understanding of the fundamentals before proceeding further.

3.1.1 Magnetic Properties

The three principle properties of a simple permanent bar magnet that must be understood are:

- It will attract other pieces of iron and steel.
- Its power of attraction is concentrated at each end of the bar.
- When suspended so as to move horizontally, it always comes to rest in an approximately north - south direction.

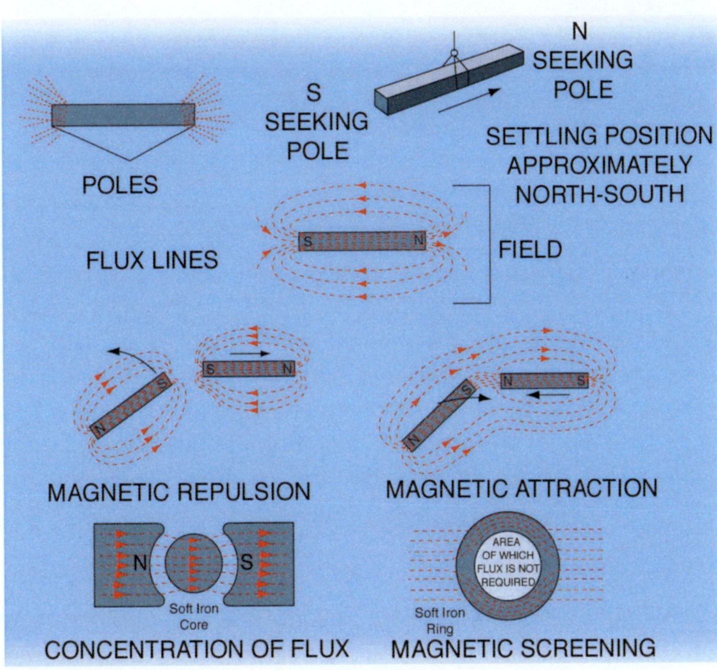

Figure 3.1 Lines of Magnetic Flux

The second and third properties are related to what are termed the poles of a magnet. The end which seeks north being called the north or red pole, and the end which seeks south the south or blue pole.

3.1.2 Magnetic Attraction

When two such magnets are brought together so that both North or both South poles face each other, a force is felt between the magnets which will keep them apart. However, if one magnet is turned round so that a north pole faces a south pole, a force will again be created between the magnets, but this time it will pull them together. Like poles repel and unlike poles attract is a fundamental law of magnetism. The force of attraction or repulsion between the two magnets varies inversely as the square of the distance between them.

3.1.3 Magnetic Field

The region in which the force exerted by a magnet can be detected is known as a magnetic field. This field has a magnetic flux that may be represented in direction and intensity by lines of flux. The directions of the lines of flux outside a magnet are from the North to the South Pole. The lines are continuous and do not cross one another so that, within the magnet, flow is from the South to the North Pole. If two magnetic fields are brought close together, the lines of flux again do not cross one another, but together form a distorted field consisting of closed loops. Magnetic flux is established more easily in some materials than in others. All materials, whether magnetic or not, have a property called “reluctance” which resists the establishment of magnetic flux and equates to the resistance found in an electric circuit.

3.1.4 Magnetic Moment

The magnetic moment of a magnet is the tendency for it to turn or be turned by another magnet. It is a requirement of aircraft compass design that the strength of the moment is such that the magnetic detection system will rapidly respond to the directive force of a magnetic field.

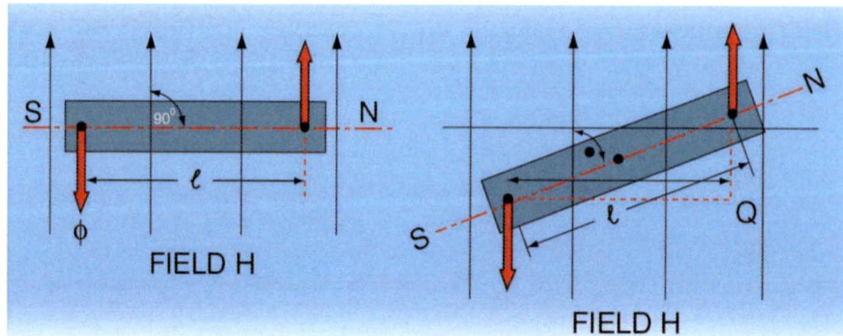

Figure 3.2 Magnetic moment

In Figure 3.2 a pivoted magnet of pole strength “S” and magnetic axis “l” is positioned at right angles to a uniform magnetic field “H”. In this situation the field will be distorted in order to “pass through” the magnet. In resisting the distortion the field will try to pull the magnet round until it is correctly aligned with the field. As the forces applied to the magnet act in opposite directions, the magnet's moment (M = S (pole strength) x l (length of magnetic axis)) will work as a couple swinging the magnet into line with the magnetic field. The greater the pole strength and the longer the magnetic moment, the greater will be the magnet's tendency to align itself quickly with the applied field. Additionally, the greater will be the force it exerts upon the surrounding field or upon any magnetic material in its vicinity.

3.1.5 Magnet in a Deflecting Field

The figure below shows a magnet situated in a uniform magnetic field of strength H_1 and subject to a uniform deflecting field of strength H_2, acting at right angles to H_1. Assuming the magnet is at an angle θ to field H_1 the torque due to H_1 is (magnetic moment) m $H_1 \sin \theta$. The torque due to H_2 is m $H_2 \cos \theta$. Thus, for the magnet to be in equilibrium, $m H_1 \sin \theta = m H_2 \cos \theta$, and therefore the strength of the deflecting field H_2 is $H_1 \tan \theta$.

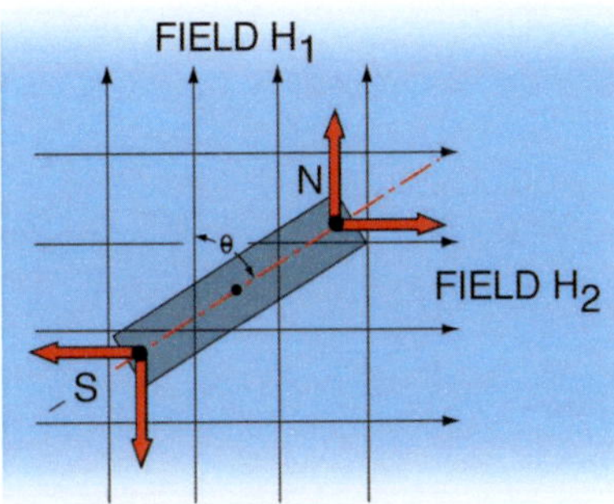

Figure 3.3 Magnet in a field

3.1.6 Period of a Suspended Magnet

If a suspended magnet is deflected from its position of rest in a magnetic field, the magnet is immediately subject to a couple urging the magnet to resume its original position. When the deflecting influence is removed, the magnet will swing back, and if undamped the system will oscillate about its equilibrium position before coming to rest. The time taken for the magnet to swing from one extremity of oscillation to the other and back again is known as the "period" of the magnet.

As the magnet approaches alignment, the amplitude of the oscillations gradually decreases but the period remains the same and cannot be altered by adjusting amplitude. The period of a magnet depends upon its shape and size or mass (factors which effect the moment of inertia), its magnetic moment and the strength of the field in which it is oscillating. The period growing longer as the magnet's mass is increased and becomes shorter as the field strength increases.

3.1.7 Hard Iron and Soft Iron

"Hard" and "soft" are terms used to describe various magnetic materials according to the ease with which they can be magnetised. Metals such as cobalt and tungsten steels are of the "hard" type since they are difficult to magnetise, but once in a magnetised state, they retain the magnetism for a considerable length of time. This long-term magnetic state is known as "permanent magnetism". The power which hard iron has of resisting magnetisation or, if already magnetised, of resisting demagnetisation, is known as its "coercive force". Metals which are easily magnetised, e.g.: silicon iron, and which generally lose their magnetised state once the magnetising force is removed, are known as "soft iron". These terms are also used to describe the magnetic effects occurring in aircraft.

3.2 Terrestrial Magnetism

The planet Earth is surrounded by a weak magnetic field that culminates in two internal magnetic poles situated near the North and South geographic poles. That this is true is obvious from the fact that a magnet, freely suspended at various locations within the Earth's magnetic field, will settle in a definite direction. This alignment, in respect to true North, depending on the location of the observer. A plane passing through the magnet and the centre of the Earth would trace on the Earth's surface an imaginary line called a "magnetic meridian", as shown below.

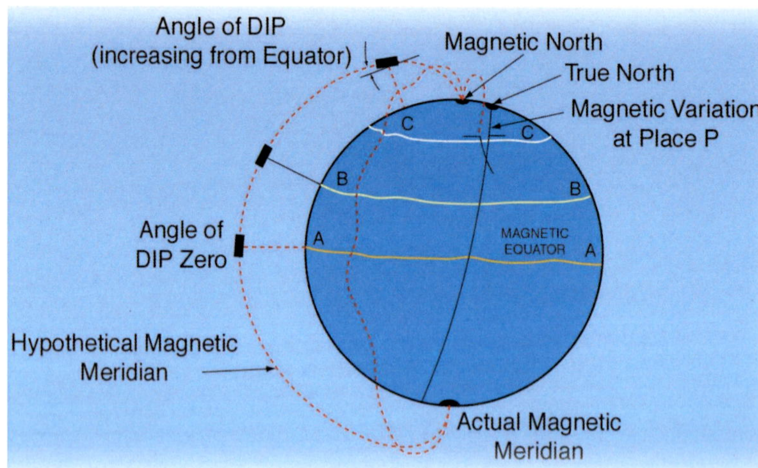

Figure 3.4 Terrestrial magnetism

It would thus appear that the Earth's magnetic field is similar to that which would be expected at the surface if a short but very powerful bar magnet were located at the centre of the planet. This partly explains why the magnetic poles cover relatively large geographic areas, due to the spreading out of the lines of force, and it also provides for the lines of force being horizontal in the vicinity of the equator. However, the precise origin of the field is not known, but for purpose of explanation the bar magnet at the Earth's centre analogy is most useful in visualising the general form of the Earth's magnetic field, as it is currently known to be.

The Earth's magnetic field differs from that of an ordinary magnet in many respects. Its points of maximum intensity are not at the magnetic poles, as they are in a bar magnet, but occur at four other positions, known as magnetic foci, two of which are near the magnetic poles. Also, the magnetic poles themselves are continually changing position by a small amount and at any point on the Earth's surface the field is not constant, being subject to changes both periodic and irregular.

3.2.1 Magnetic Variation

In a similar manner, as meridians and parallels are constructed with reference to the geographic poles, so magnetic meridians and parallels may be plotted with reference to the magnetic poles. If a map were prepared showing both true and magnetic meridians, it would be seen that the meridians intersect each other at angles varying at different points on the Earth's surface. The horizontal angle contained between the true and magnetic meridians at any place when looking north is known as magnetic variation (or declination).

3.2.2 Effect of Variation

When the direction of the magnetic meridian inclines to the left of the true meridian, the variation is said to be "west"; inclination to the right of the true meridian is said to be variation "east".

+ sign indicates Easterly variation and a - sign Westerly variation

Variation can change from 0° in areas where the magnetic meridians run parallel to the true meridian, to 180° in places located between the true and magnetic north poles. At some locations on Earth, where the ferrous nature of the rock deposits disturbs the Earth's magnetic field, abnormal magnetic anomalies occur. These may cause large changes in the value of variation over very short distances. While variation differs all over the world, it does not maintain a constant value in any one place, and the following changes, which are not constant in themselves, may occur:

- Secular changes which occur over long periods, due to the changing position of the magnetic poles relative to the true poles.
- Annual change which is a small seasonal fluctuation super-imposed on a secular change.

- Diurnal (daily) changes which appear to be caused by electrical currents flowing in the atmosphere as a result of solar heating.
- Magnetic storms associated with sunspot activity. These may last from a few hours to several days, with intensity varying from very small to very great. The effect on aircraft compasses obviously varies with intensity, but both variation and local values of magnetic field will be modified whilst the "storm" lasts.

Information regarding magnetic variation and its changes is printed on special charts of the World, which are issued every few years. An example of such a chart is shown below. The lines, drawn on the chart, joining places that have the same value of variation are called "isogonals"; those drawn through places which have zero variation are known as "agonic" lines.

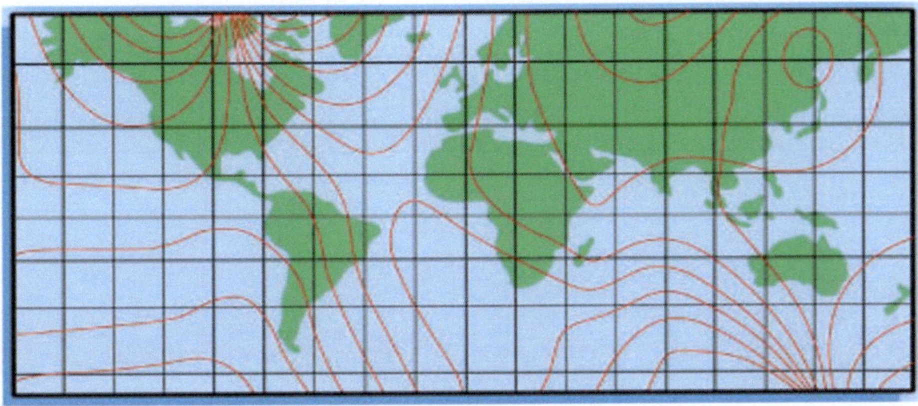

Figure 3.5 Isogonal lines

3.2.3 Magnetic Dip

As stated earlier, a freely suspended magnetic needle will settle in a definite direction at any point on the Earth's surface, aligning itself with the magnetic meridian at that point. However, it will not lie parallel to the Earth's surface at all points, because the Earth's lines of magnetic flux (force) are themselves not horizontal, as can be seen in Figure 3.4. The lines of force emerge vertically from the north magnetic pole, bend over to parallel the Earth's surface, and then descend vertically at the south magnetic pole. If, therefore, a magnetic needle is transported along a meridian from north to south, it will at the start have its red end pointing down; near the magnetic equator the needle will be horizontal; whilst at the southern end of its travel the blue end will point Earthwards.

3.2.4 Dip Angle

The angle that lines of force make with the Earth's surface at any given place is called the "angle of dip". Dip varies from 0° at the magnetic equator to virtually 90° at the magnetic poles. Dip is conventionally positive when the red end of a freely suspended magnetic needle is below the horizontal and negative when the blue end dips below the horizontal. The angle of dip at all locations undergoes changes similar to those described for variation and is also shown on charts of the world. Places on these charts having the same value of magnetic dip are joined by lines known as "isoclinals", while one which joins places having zero dip is known as an "aclinic line". This is the magnetic equator.

3.2.5 Earth's Total Magnetic Force

When a magnetic needle freely suspended in the Earth's field comes to rest, it does so under the influence of the total force of the Earth's magnetic field at that point. The value of this total force at a given place is not easy to measure, but in any case seldom needs to be known. It is usual, therefore, to resolve the total force into a horizontal component termed "H" and a vertical component termed "Z". If the value of dip angle (θ) for the particular location is then known, the total force can readily be calculated.

3.2.6 Practical Effect of H and Z

Knowledge of horizontal component "H" and vertical component "Z" is of considerable practical value, as both are responsible for inducing magnetism into the various ferrous metal parts of the aircraft (both hard and soft iron) which lie in their respective planes.

H is the directive (horizontal) force, Z is the vertical force

Both components may, therefore, be responsible for providing a deflecting or deviating force around the aircraft's compass position, a force whose value must be determined and calibrated against if the compass is to provide a worthwhile heading reference. The relationship between dip, horizontal, vertical and total force is shown in Figure 3.6. From the figure it can be seen that "H" is of maximum value at the magnetic equator and decreases in value towards the poles. Conversely, "Z" is zero at the magnetic equator and, together with the value of dip, increases towards the poles.

Dip is zero at the Equator and maximum at the Poles

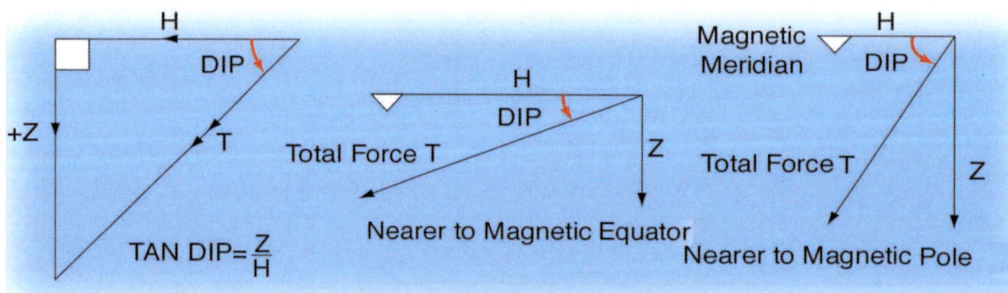

Figure 3.6 Dip angle

3.3 Aircraft Magnetism

A challenge to the designers of aircraft compasses is that aircraft are themselves magnetised in various degrees and that a direct reading compass must be located where the pilot can readily see it, namely the cockpit area. In this location the compass is surrounded by magnetic material and electrical circuits. Such magnetic influence provides a deviation force to the Earth's magnetic field which will cause a compass needle to be deflected away from the local magnetic meridian. Fortunately the deviation caused by aircraft magnetism can be analysed and resolved into components acting along the aircraft major axes; thus action can be taken to minimise the errors, or "deviations" as they are more properly called, resulting from aircraft magnetism.

Deviation is a correction from compass heading to get magnetic heading

3.3.1 Types of Aircraft Magnetism

Essentially there are two types of aircraft magnetism, which can be divided in the same way that magnetic materials are classified according to their ability to be magnetised.

3.3.1.1 Hard Iron Magnetism

This is of a permanent nature and is due to the presence of steel or steel alloy parts used in the main strength components of the aircraft structure in power plants and other equipment

The Earth's magnetic field will influence the molecular structure of ferrous parts of the aircraft during construction while it is lying on one heading for a long period. Hammering and working of the materials will play their part in molecular alignment and hence magnetisation of component parts.

3.3.1.2 Soft Iron Magnetism

Soft iron magnetism is of a temporary nature and is caused by metallic parts of the aircraft, which are magnetically soft or highly permeable, becoming magnetised due to induction by the Earth's magnetic field

Typically, this is associated with frames, stringers and light ferrous alloys. The effect of this type of magnetism is dependent on heading and attitude of the aircraft and its geographical location.

3.3.1.3 Components of Hard Iron Magnetism

It is useful to know the following conventions in the study of magnetism:

- Letters indicate the various components that cause deviation. Those for permanent hard iron magnetism are given in capitals, and those for induced soft iron magnetism are in small letters.
- Positive deviations (those deflecting the compass needle to the right) are termed easterly, while negative deviations (deflection of the needle to the left) are termed westerly.
- Positive (E) deviations are added (+) to the compass indications to obtain magnetic direction. Negative (W) deviations are subtracted (-) from the compass indication to obtain magnetic direction.

The total effect of hard iron magnetism at the compass position is likened, as in Figure 3.7, to a number of bar magnets lying longitudinally, laterally and vertically about the compass position. To analyse the effect of hard iron, the imaginary bar magnets are annotated as "Component P", "Component Q" and "Component R". The components will not vary in strength with change of heading or latitude, but may vary with time due to a weakening of the magnetism in the aircraft. Algebraic signs are allocated to these components depending upon the position of the blue polarity (in respect of the compass). Blue poles to the nose, to the right (starboard) and to the bottom are termed positive (+) as shown.

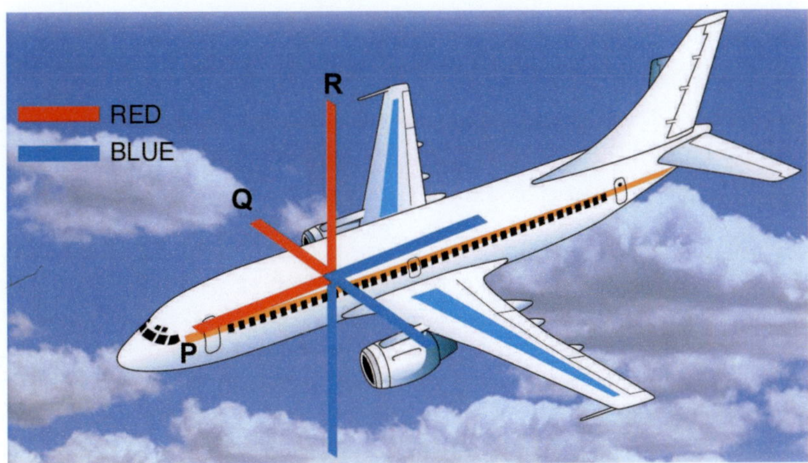

Figure 3.7 Effect of hard iron magnetism

When an aircraft is heading north, the imaginary magnet due to component P will, together with the compass needle, be in alignment with the aircraft's fore and aft axis and Earth's component H, thus P will add or subtract to the directive force H but will not cause any deviation. If the aircraft is now turned through 360^{0}, then as it commences the turn (ignoring compass pivot friction, liquid swirl, etc) the magnet system will remain attracted to the Earth's component H. However, component P, which will still be acting in the aircraft's fore and aft axis, will cause the compass needle to align itself in the resultant position between the directive force H and the deflecting force P. This will make the needle point so many degrees east or west (of north), depending on the polarity of P. The deviation will increase during the turn, being a maximum on east and west and zero on north and south. Deviation resulting from a positive P is shown in Figure 3.8.

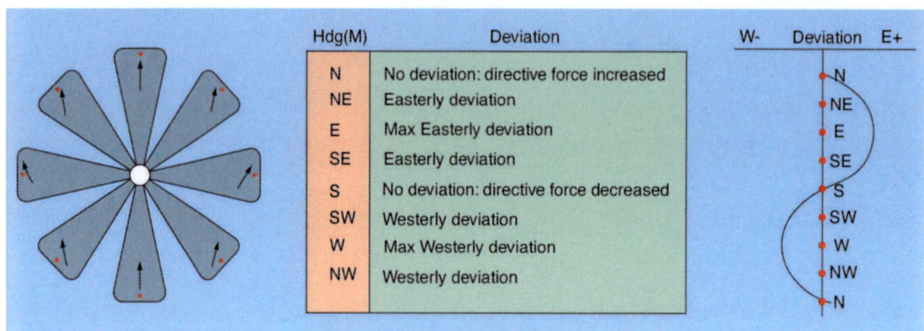

Figure 3.8 Deviation

This is a sine curve with P proportional to sin Hdg(M); thus:

Deviation = P sin Hdg(M)

Component Q produces a similar effect, but displaced by 90°. Since the component acts along the aircraft's lateral axis (wingtip to wingtip), the resultant deviation is at a maximum on North and South. Zero deflection is given on east and west when the component is aligned with the directive force H and is adding to or subtracting from the directive force acting on the compass. Deviations resulting from a negative Q (blue pole to the left of compass position) are shown in Figure 3.9. This is a cosine curve with Q proportional to cosine Hdg (M); thus:

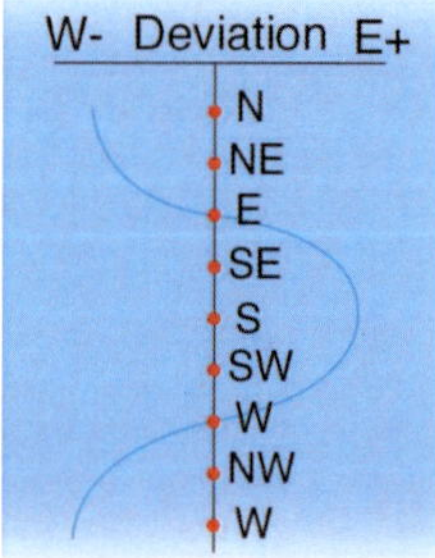

Figure 3.9 Deviation

Deviation = Q cos Hdg(M)

Component R acts in the vertical and when the aircraft is in level flight has no effect on the compass system. If, however, the aircraft flies with its longitudinal or lateral axis other than horizontal, then component R will be out of the vertical and a horizontal vector of the component will affect the compass system. Figure 3.10 demonstrates the effect of this and shows that an element of R would affect components P and Q. A similar situation occurs when a tail wheel aircraft is on the ground. Although the value of R may vary, because the angles of climb or dive for most aircraft are normally small, any deviation resulting from component R is correspondingly small. Other errors affecting direct reading compasses due to turns and accelerations are such as to make errors due to R of no practical significance, while the circuitry of remote indicating compasses is such that turn errors are virtually eliminated and the effect of component R is negligible.

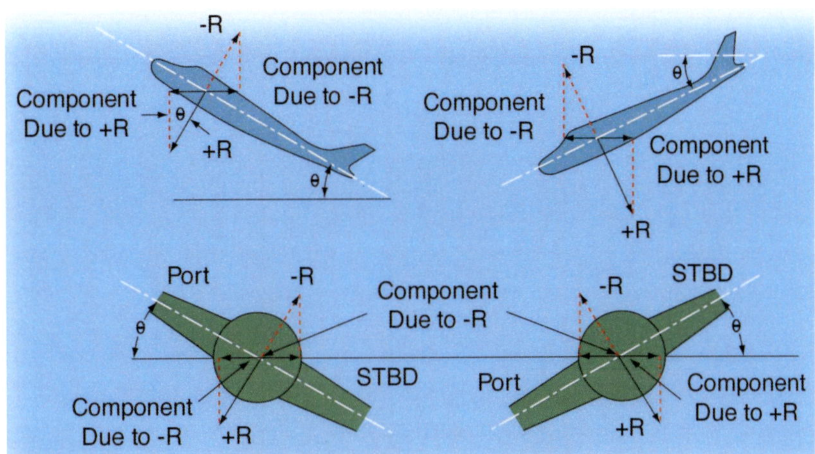

Figure 3.10 Magnetic influence

3.3.1.4 Components of Soft Iron Magnetism

Soft iron magnetism, effective at the compass position, may be considered as originating from soft iron rods adjacent to the compass position in which magnetism is induced by the Earth's magnetic field. Although as already discussed the field has two components, H and Z, in order to analyse the effect of soft iron H must be split into two horizontal components, X and Y, which together with Z can then be related to the three principal axes of the aircraft. Figure 3.11 shows how the polarities and strengths of X and Y change with change of aircraft heading as the aircraft turns relative to the direction of component H. Component Z acts vertically through the compass and therefore does not effect the directional properties of the magnet system.

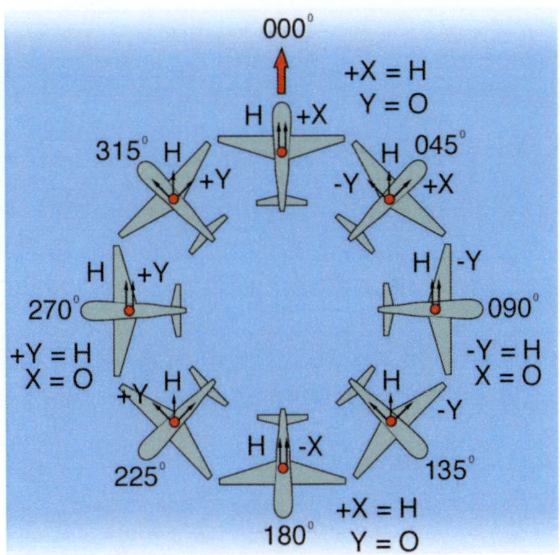

Figure 3.11 Different polarities

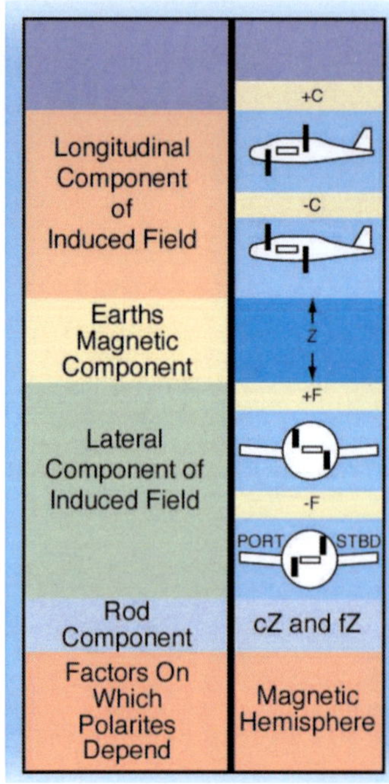

Figure 3.12 Different polarities

When an aircraft is moved to a new geographic location, then, because of the change in the Earth's field strength and direction, all three components of soft iron magnetism will change. However, the sign of Z will only change if the aircraft changes magnetic hemisphere.

Magnetic induction due to soft iron is visualised as soft-iron rods disposed about the compass position. These soft iron components are indicated conventionally by small letters "a" to "k" which are then related to the Earth field components X, Y and Z. Of all the soft iron components, we are only really interested in cZ and fZ. They do not change polarity with change of heading and they act in the same manner as hard iron components P and Q respectively. In Figure 3.12, cZ and fZ can be represented as pairs of vertical soft iron rods positioned respectively fore and aft and athwart the compass position. In the Northern Hemisphere (magnetic) the lower pole of each rod would be induced with "red" magnetism.

You should remember that the strength and polarity of these rods is a function of the vertical component of the Earth's magnetic field. Polarity will change when the aeroplane crosses the magnetic equator.

3.3.2 Determination of Deviation Coefficients

Before action can be taken to minimise the effect of hard iron and soft iron magnetism on an aircraft's compass, it is necessary to determine the deviations caused by the components of aircraft magnetism on various headings and the value of such deviations are analysed into "Coefficients of deviation".

There are five Coefficients of deviation, named A, B, C, D and E. Of these, D and E are soft iron and cannot be compensated on an aeroplane's compass. They will not be given any further consideration in this manual. This leaves the following coefficients:

- ***Coefficient A*** which is usually constant on all headings and results from misalignment of the compass (Apparent A). A peculiar arrangement of horizontal soft iron can give a similar effect (Real A).
- ***Coefficient B*** which results from deviations caused by hard iron P + soft iron cZ, with deviation maximum on east and west.
- ***Coefficient C*** which results from deviations caused by hard iron Q + soft iron fZ, with maximum deviation on north and south.

We will consider how each Coefficient can be calculated.

3.3.2.1 Coefficient A

Coefficient A is calculated by taking the algebraic sum of the deviations on a number of equally spaced compass headings and dividing the sum by the number of observations made. Usually readings are taken on the four cardinal and four quadrantal headings, thus:

$$\text{Coefficient A} = \frac{\text{Deviation on N} + \text{NE} + \text{E} + \text{SE} + \text{S} + \text{SW} + \text{W} + \text{NW}}{8}$$

3.3.2.2 Coefficient B

Coefficient B represents the resultant deviation due to the presence either together or separately of hard iron component P and soft iron component cz. Coefficient B is calculated by taking half the algebraic difference between deviations on compass heading east and west, hence:

$$\text{Coefficient B} = \frac{\text{Deviation on East} - \text{Deviation on West}}{2}$$

You will recall it may also be expressed for any heading as:

Deviation = B sin (heading)

3.3.2.3 Coefficient C

Coefficient C represents the resultant deviation due to the presence either together or separately of hard iron component Q and soft iron component fz. Coefficient C is calculated by taking half the algebraic difference between deviations on compass heading north and south, hence:

$$\text{Coefficient C} = \frac{\text{Deviation on North} - \text{Deviation on South}}{2}$$

Coefficient C may also be expressed (for any heading) as:

Deviation = C cos (heading)

3.3.3 Total Deviation

Accepting the foregoing, the total deviation on an uncorrected compass for any given direction of aircraft heading (compass) may be expressed:

Total deviation = A + B sin Hdg + C cos Hdg

This is true provided there are no other deviating effects (such as Coefficients D and E) around the compass.

3.3.4 The Compass Swing

In order to determine by what amount compass readings are affected by aircraft magnetism, a special calibration procedure, known as "compass swinging", is carried out so that deviations may be determined, coefficients calculated and the deviations compensated.

3.3.4.1 When Is A Compass Swing Required?

Before reviewing the mechanics of the compass swing, there are certain occasions or events requiring that the instrument should be swung; these are:

- On acceptance of a new aircraft from manufacture.
- When a new compass is fitted.
- At Periodic intervals as specified in maintenance schedules.
- After a major inspection.
- Following a change of magnetic material in the aircraft.
- If the aircraft is moved permanently or semi-permanently to another airfield involving a large change of magnetic latitude.
- Following a lightning strike or prolonged flying in heavy static.

- After standing on one heading for more than four weeks.
- When carrying ferrous (magnetic) freight.
- Whenever specified in the maintenance schedule.
- For issue of a C of A.
- At any time when the compass or residual deviation recorded on the compass card are in doubt.

3.3.4.2 EASA Certification Specification (CS) Limits

CS 25 for large aeroplanes requires that a placard showing the calibration of the magnetic direction indicator (compass) in level flight with engines running must be installed on or near the instrument. The placard (compass residual deviation card) must show each calibration reading in terms of magnetic heading of the aircraft in not greater than 45° steps.

The compass after compensation may not have deviation in normal level flight > 10° on any heading

In general, the distance between a compass and any item of equipment containing magnetic material shall be such that the equipment does not cause a change of deviation exceeding 1°, nor shall the combined effect of all such equipment exceed 2°. The same ruling shall apply to installed electrical equipment and associated wiring when such equipment is powered up. Change in deviation caused by movement of the flight or undercarriage controls shall not exceed 1°.

The effect of the aeroplane's permanent and induced magnetism, as given by coefficients B and C with associated soft iron components shall not exceed:

Coefficient	Direct Reading Compass (degrees)	Remote Reading Compass (degrees)
B	15	5
C	15	5

After correction the greatest deviation on any heading shall be 3° for direct reading compasses and 1° for remote indicating compasses

3.3.4.3 Compass Swing Procedure

The term compass swing has already been mentioned, as has the occasions when a swing is necessary; let us now look at what is involved. Although there are a number of methods by which a swing may be achieved, the usual method involves an engineer with a landing or datum compass. The compass is mounted on a tripod and is located well in front or, in some circumstances, behind the aircraft, so that the engineer can sight accurately along the fore and aft line. In these modern times calibration is normally in the hands of an experienced compass adjuster, with a pilot only being called on occasionally to drive the aeroplane. The procedure is split into two phases, correcting and check swing.

3.3.4.3.1 Correcting Swing

- Ensure compass is serviceable.
- Ensure all equipment not carried in flight is removed from the aircraft.
- Ensure all equipment carried in flight is correctly stowed.
- Take the aircraft to swing sight (at least 50 m from other aircraft and 100 m from a hangar).
- Ensure flying controls are in normal flying position, engines running, radios and electrical circuits on (as far as is practicable).
- Position aircraft on a heading of south (M) and note deviation (difference between datum compass and aircraft compass reading).
- Position aircraft on a heading of west (M) and note deviation.

- Position aircraft on a heading of north (M) and note deviation. Calculate Coefficient C and apply it direct to compass reading. If applicable, set required corrected heading on compass grid ring or set heading pointer.
- Place compass corrector key in micro-adjuster box using winder which is across (at 90°) to compass needle and turn key until compass needle shows corrected heading. Remove key.

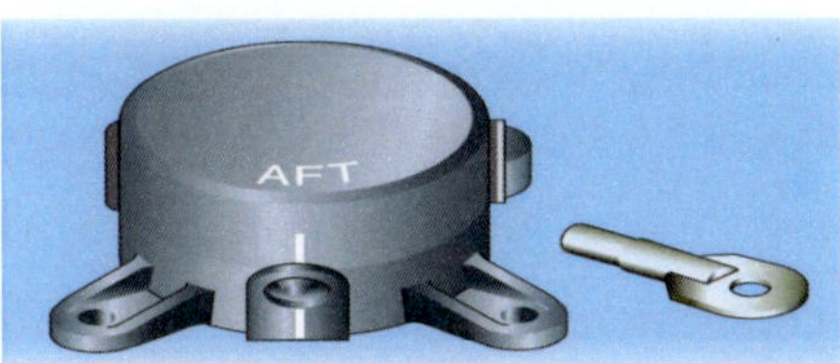

Figure 3.13 Compass corrector key

- Position aircraft on a heading of east (M) and note deviation. Calculate Coefficient B and correct for B in the same manner as for Coefficient C.

3.3.4.3.2 Check Swing

- Carry out a check swing on eight headings, starting on southeast (M), noting deviation on each heading.
- Calculate Coefficient A on completion of check swing and apply to compass reading. Set required corrected heading on compass grid ring or set heading pointer. Loosen compass, or, for remote indicating instrument the detector head retaining screws, and rotate until compass needle indicates correct heading. Re-tighten retaining screws.
- Having applied A algebraically to all deviations found during the check swing, plot the residual (remaining) deviations and make out a compass deviation card for placing in the aircraft.

3.3.4.4 Compass Swing - Example

Correcting Swing

	Datum Compass HDG (M)	Aircraft Compass HDG (C)	Deviation
S	182	180	+ 2
W	274	270	+4
N	000	354	+6
Coefficient C = $\frac{+6-(+2)}{2}$ = +2		Therefore make compass read 356	
E	090	090	0
Coefficient B = $\frac{+0-(+4)}{2}$ = -2		Therefore make compass read 088	

Check Swing

DATUM COMPASS	AIRCRAFT COMPASS	DEVIATION	RESIDUAL DEVIATION (After comp A)
136	131	+5	+2
183	181	+2	-1
225	221	+4	+1
270	268	+2	-1
313	308	+5	+2
000	358	+2	-1
047	044	+3	0
092	090	+2	-1

$$\text{Coefficient A} = \frac{25}{8} = +3$$

Finally a deviation card is produced showing residual deviations against headings (M) and placed in the aircraft adjacent to the compass position.

3.3.5 Deviation Compensation Devices

The compass swing being complete, we now have coefficients B, C and A, but how do we make use of the coefficients to correct or offset the compass needle by an amount in degrees equivalent to deviation?

3.3.5.1 Mechanical Compensation

The majority of mechanical deviation compensation devices consist of two pairs of magnets, each pair being fitted into a bevel gear assembly made of non-magnetic material. The gears are mounted one above the other, so that in the neutral position one pair of magnets is parallel to the aircraft's fore and aft plane for correction of Coefficient C, while the other pair lays athwartships to correct for Coefficient B. By use of the compass correction key, a small bevel pinion may be turned, thus rotating one pair of bevel gears. As can be seen from Figure 3.14, the pairs of magnets are thus made to open, creating a magnetic field between the poles to deflect the compass needle and correct for Coefficient B or C, depending which pair of magnets are used.

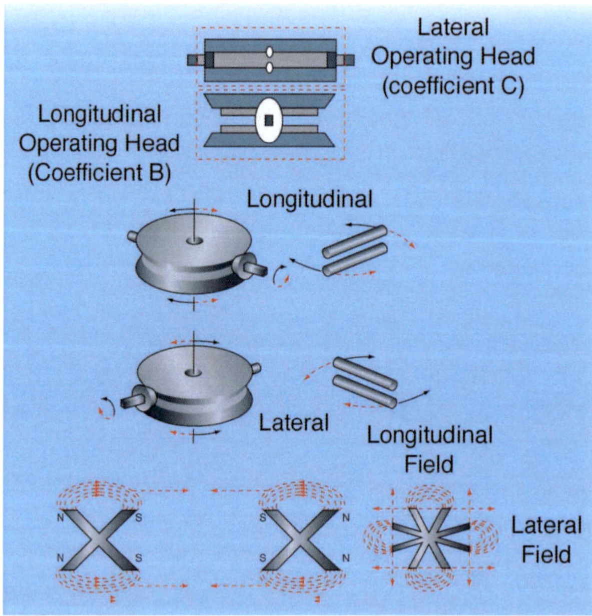

Figure 3.14 Mechanical compensation

The micro-adjuster unit is normally mounted below the compass needle assembly in the “P” type direct reading compass and above the needle assembly in compass of the “E” series. These will be covered in greater detail in the next section.

3.3.5.2 Electrical Compensation

The exact design and construction of the electro-magnetic compensator depends on the compass manufacturer. However, they all follow a similar concept whereby two variable potentiometers are connected to the coils of a flux detector unit. The potentiometers correspond to the Coefficient B and C magnets of a mechanical compensator and, when moved with respect to calibrated dials, they insert very small DC signals into the flux detector coils. The magnetic fields produced by the signals are sufficient to oppose those causing deviations and accordingly modify the output from the detector head via the synchronous transmission link to drive the gyro and hence the compass heading indicator to show corrected readings.

3.4 The Direct Reading Magnetic Compass

The basis of the direct reading magnetic compass is simply a magnetic needle which points to the northern end of the Earth's magnetic field installed in an instrument of dimensions and weight that makes it suitable for use in aircraft. It is mandatory, under the CS 25, for modern civil transport aircraft to carry a direct reading non-stabilised magnetic compass as a standby direction indicator. The most commonly found direct reading compass is the "E" type illustrated below.

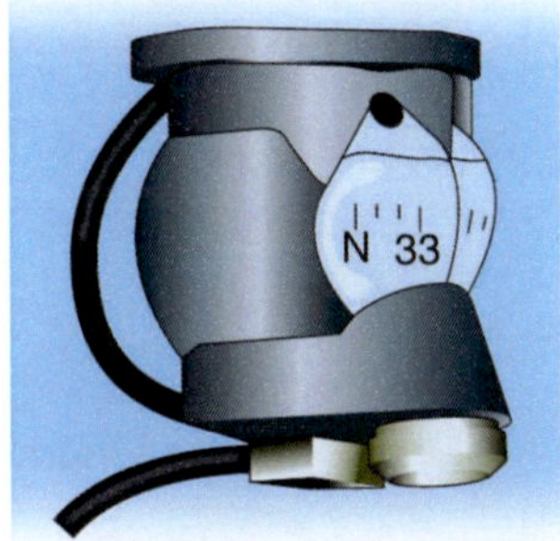

Figure 3.15 Typical compass

3.4.1 Principle of Operation

For a direct reading compass to function efficiently, its magnetic element must:

- Lie horizontal, thereby sensing only the horizontal or directive component of the Earth's field.
- Be sensitive, in order to operate effectively down to low values of "H".
- Be aperiodic or dead-beat, to minimise oscillation of the sensitive element about a new heading following a turn.

3.4.1.1 Lying Horizontally

The first requirement, that of lying horizontally, is obtained by making the magnet system pendulous. This is achieved by mounting the magnets, below the needle pivot, as in Figure 3.16. Thus, when the system is tilted by the Earth's vertical force "Z", the C of G moves out from below the pivot away from the nearer Earth pole, thereby introducing a righting force upon the magnet system and reducing the effect of "Z". The compass needle will take up a position along the resultant of the two forces, "H" and reduced effect of "Z". In temperate latitudes the final inclination of the needle is approximately 2° to 3° to the horizontal.

At about 70° north or south, the compass is virtually useless (called the 6 micro-Tesla zone)

It must be stressed that the displacement of the C of G is a function of the system's pendulosity, it is not a mechanical adjustment. It will, therefore, work in either hemisphere without further adjustment.

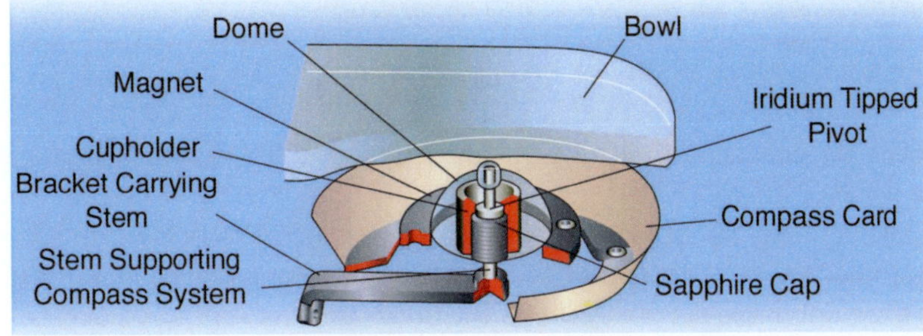

Figure 3.16 Assembly

3.4.1.2 Sensitivity

The second requirement, of sensitivity, is achieved by increasing the pole strengths of the magnets used, so that it remains firmly aligned with the local magnetic meridian. Sensitivity is aided by keeping pivot friction to a minimum by using an iridium-tipped pivot moving in a sapphire cup. Filling the compass bowl with a liquid reduces the effective weight of the magnet system. This also serves to lubricate the pivot.

3.4.1.3 Aperiodicity

The third requirement is aperiodicity. If a suspended magnet is deflected from its position of rest and then released, it will tend to oscillate around the correct direction for some time before stabilising. This is obviously undesirable, as it could, at worst, lead to the pilot chasing the needle. Ideally then, the compass needle should come to rest without oscillation.

3.4.1.4 Achieving the Requirements

- The compass bowl is filled with methyl alcohol or a silicon fluid, and damping filaments are fitted to the magnet system.
- The lever of the magnet system is kept short but the strength remains high. This maximises directional force whilst reducing the moment of inertia.
- The buoyancy of the fluid reduces the apparent weight of the system and the weight is concentrated as close to the pivot as possible, to further reduce the turning moment.

The liquids used in the compass bowl must be transparent, have a wide temperature range, a low viscosity, high resistance to corrosion and should be free from any tendency towards discoloration in use.

One disadvantage of using a liquid in the compass bowl is that, in a prolonged turn, it will turn with the aircraft, taking the magnet system with it and thus affect compass readings. To offset in part the effect of "liquid swirl", a good clearance is provided between damping wires and the side of the compass bowl. However, liquid swirl does delay the immediate settling of the system on a new compass heading. Although the liquid in the compass bowl has a wide temperature range, it will expand and contract with variation of temperature. It is, therefore, necessary for all direct reading compasses to be fitted with some form of expansion chamber, thus ensuring that the liquid neither bursts a seal, or contracts, leaving vacuum bubbles.

3.4.2 "E" Type Compass Description

The majority of the standby compasses in use today are of the card type shown in Figure 3.16. These compasses have a single circular cobalt steel magnet, to which is attached the compass card, mounted so as to be close to the inner face of the bowl, thereby minimising errors in observation due to parallax. The card is graduated every 10° with intermediate indications being estimated. Heading observations are made against a lubber line on the inner face of the bowl. Suspension of the system is by means of an iridium-tipped pivot revolving in a sapphire cup. The bowl is moulded in plastic, painted on the outside with black enamel, except for a small area at the front through which the vertical card can be seen. This part of the bowl is so moulded that it has a magnifying effect on the compass card. The damping liquid is silicon fluid, and a bellows type expansion chamber located at the rear of the bowl compensates for changes in liquid volume, due to temperature variation. The effects of deviation Coefficient B and C are compensated for by permanent magnet corrector assemblies secured to the compass mounting plate.

3.4.3 Serviceability Tests - Direct Reading Compass

- Check liquid is free from bubbles, discoloration and sediment.
- Examine all parts for luminosity.
- Test for pivot friction by deflecting the magnet system through 10-15° each way; note the readings on return - should be within 2° of each other.
- Periodically test for damping by deflecting the system through 90°, holding for 30 s to allow liquid to settle, and timing the return through 85°. Maximum and minimum times are laid down in the manufacturer's instrument manual, usually about 6.5 to 8.5 s.

On older "P" type compasses, of which there are still a few around, the following additional checks must be carried out:

- Ensure grid ring rotates freely through 360° and that the locking device functions positively.
- Test suspension of bowl by moving gently in all directions and check that there is no metal to metal contact.

3.4.4 Acceleration and Turning Errors

In the search for accuracy of an indicating system, it is often found that the methods used to counter an undesirable error under one set of circumstances create other errors under different circumstances. This is precisely what happens when the compass system is made pendulous to counteract the effect of dip by displacing the C of G and thus making the instrument effective over a greater latitude band. Unfortunately, having done this, any manoeuvre which introduces a component of aircraft acceleration either east or west from the aircraft's magnetic meridian will produce a torque about the magnet system's vertical axis, causing it to rotate in azimuth to a false meridian.

There are two main elements resulting from these accelerations, namely "Acceleration Error" and "Turning Error". Before we examine these more closely, let us see what would happen to a plain pendulum, freely suspended in the aircraft fuselage. If a constant direction and speed were maintained, the pendulum would remain at rest. However, if the aircraft turns, accelerates or decelerates the pendulum will be displaced from the true vertical, because inertia will cause the centre of gravity to lag behind the pendulum pivot, thus moving it from its normal position directly below the point of suspension.

Since the magnet system (in the compass) is pendulous, any acceleration or deceleration in flight will result in a displacement of the C of G of the system from its normal position. A torque will therefore be established about the vertical axis of the compass, unless the compass is on the magnetic equator where the Earth field vertical component "Z" is zero.

3.4.4.1 Acceleration Error

The force applied by an aircraft when accelerating or decelerating on a fixed heading is applied to the magnet system at the pivot, which is the magnet's only connection with the remainder of the instrument. The reaction to the force must be equal and opposite and must act through the C of G, which is below and offset from the pivot (except at the magnetic equator). The two forces thus constitute a couple which, dependent on heading, will cause the magnet system to change the angle of dip or to rotate in azimuth.

Figure 3.17(a) shows the forces affecting a compass needle when an aircraft accelerates on a northerly heading (the observer is looking eastwards at the compass system). Since both the pivot "P" and C of G are in the plane of the local magnetic meridian, the reactive force "R" will cause the northern or pole ward end of the system to dip further, thus increasing the angle of dip without any needle rotation. Conversely, when the aircraft decelerates on north, Figure 3.17(b), the reaction tilts the needle down at the south end. The opposite of these reactions will be observed when accelerating/decelerating on north along the meridian in the Southern Hemisphere.

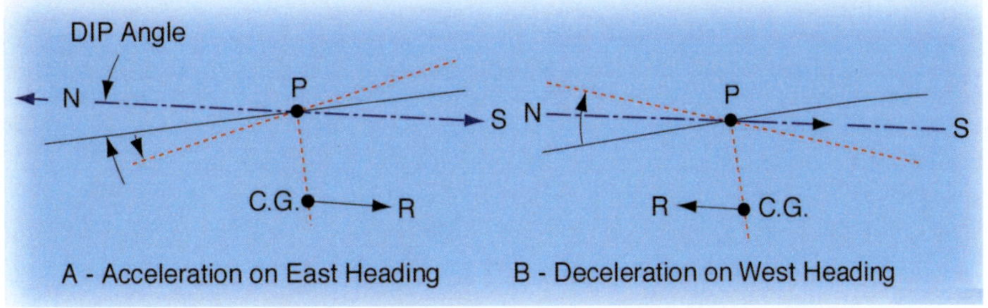

Figure 3.17 Errors on various headings

> When an aircraft flying in either hemisphere changes speed on headings other than north or south, the change will result in azimuth rotation of the magnet system, and hence there will be errors in heading indication

When an aircraft flying in the Northern Hemisphere, accelerates on an easterly heading (decelerates on a Westerly heading), as in Figure 3.18 the accelerating force will act through the pivot "P", and the reaction "R" will act through the C of G. Unless the value of "Z" is zero the two forces will now form a couple, turning the needle in a clockwise direction. Action of "R" will also cause the magnet system to tilt in the direction of acceleration, and thus the pivot and C of G will no longer be in line with the magnet meridian. The magnets

will come under the influence of "Z", as shown in the second diagram of Figure 3.18 providing a further turning moment in the same direction as the force "P/R" couple.

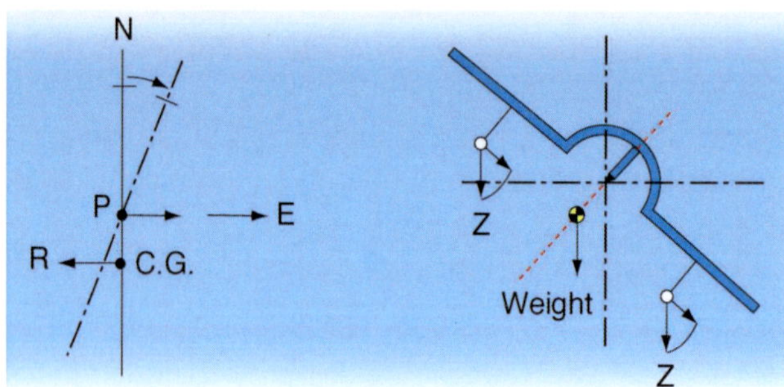

Figure 3.18 Principle of acceleration errors

When the aircraft decelerates on east, the action and reaction of "P" and "R" respectively will have the opposite effect , as shown below causing the assembly to turn anti-clockwise with all forces again turning in the same direction.

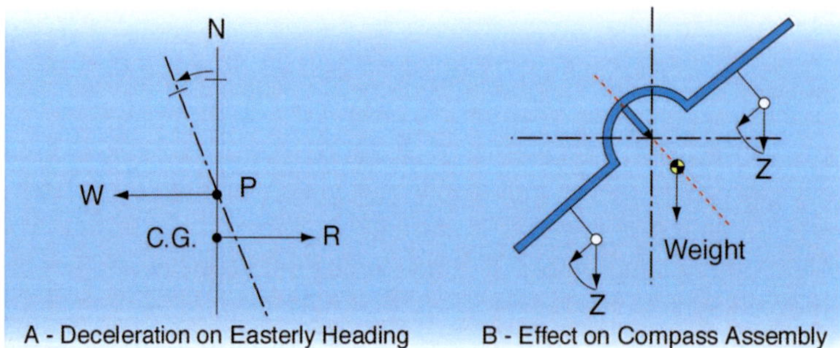

Figure 3.19 Principle of deceleration errors

To summarise, errors due to acceleration and deceleration:

Hdg	Speed	Needle turns	Visual Effect
East	Increase	Clockwise	Apparent turn to north
West	Increase	Anti-clockwise	Apparent turn to north
East	Decrease	Anti-clockwise	Apparent turn to south
West	Decrease	Clockwise	Apparent turn to south

Note:

1. In the Southern Hemisphere, errors are in opposite sense.
2. No error on north or south as reaction force acts along the needle.
3. Similar errors can occur in turbulent flight conditions.
4. No error on magnetic equator, as value of "Z" is zero and hence pivot and C of G are co-incident.

3.4.4.2 Turning Error

When an aircraft executes a turn, the compass pivot is carried with it along the curved path of the turn. The centre of gravity (of the magnet system) being offset from the pivot is subject to the force of centrifugal acceleration acting outwards from the centre of the turn. Further, in a correctly banked turn the magnet system will tend to maintain a position parallel to the athwartship (wing tip to wing tip) plane of the aircraft and will therefore now be tilted in relation to the Earth's magnetic field. As before, the pivot and C of G will no longer be in the plane of the local magnetic meridian. The needle will be subject to a component of "Z", as shown in Figure 3.20, causing the system, when in the northern hemisphere, to rotate in the same direction as the turn and further increase the turning error.

The extent and direction of Turning Error is dependent upon the aircraft heading, the angle of bank (degree of tilt of the magnet system) and the local value of "Z". However, turning errors are maximum on north/south and are of significance within 35° of these headings.

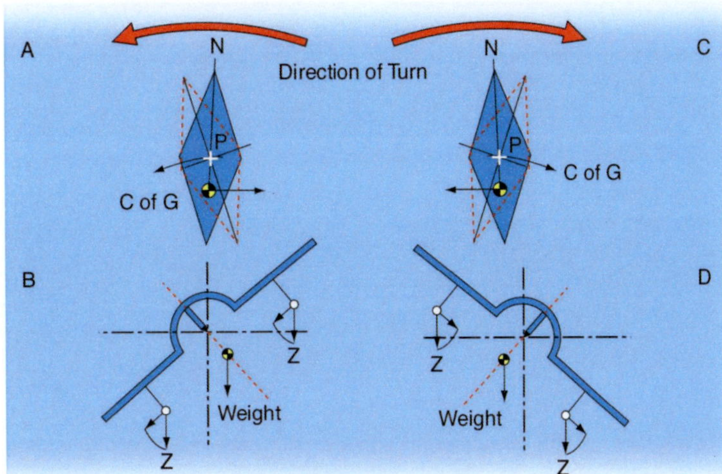

Figure 3.20 Principle of turning errors

Figure 3.21(a) shows the needle of a compass in an aircraft flying on a northerly heading in the Northern Hemisphere. The north-seeking end of the compass needle is coincident with the lubber line. The aircraft now turns east. As soon as the turn is commenced, centrifugal acceleration acts on the system C of G. This causes it to rotate in the same direction as the turn. Since the magnet system is now tilted, the Earth's vertical component "Z" exerts a pull on the northern end, causing further rotation of the system. The same effect will occur if the heading change is from north to west in the Northern Hemisphere. Figure 3.21(b) to (h) summarises pictorially the effect on the compass needle of differing turns in the northern and southern hemispheres.

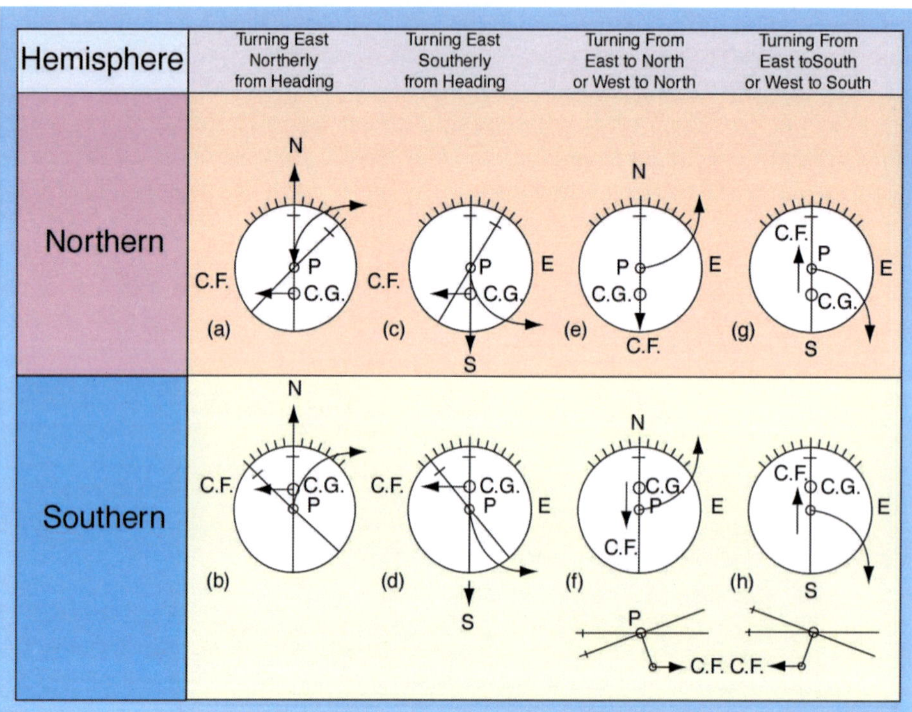

Figure 3.21 Turning errors

As mentioned earlier, the speed of system rotation is a function of the aircraft's bank angle and rate of turn, and, depending on those factors, three possible indications may be registered by the compass:

- A turn in the correct sense, but smaller than that carried out when the magnet system turns at a slower rate than the aircraft.
- No turn when the magnet system turns at the same rate as the aircraft.
- A turn in the opposite sense when the magnet system turns at a faster rate than the aircraft.

When turning from a southerly heading in the Northern Hemisphere onto east or west, the rotation of the system and indications registered by the compass will be the same as when turning from north, except that the compass will over-indicate the turn.

In the Southern Hemisphere the south magnetic pole is dominant and, in counter-acting its downward pull on the compass magnet system, the C of G moves to the northern side of the pivot. If an aircraft turns from a northerly heading eastward, the centrifugal acceleration acting on the C of G causes the needle to rotate more rapidly in the opposite direction to the turn, thus indicating a turn in the correct sense but of greater magnitude than that actually carried out. The turn will thus be over-indicated. Turning from a southerly heading onto east or west in the Southern Hemisphere will, because the C of G is still north of the compass pivot, result in the same effect as turning through north in the Northern Hemisphere.

3.4.5 Liquid Swirl Errors

So far no mention has been made regarding motion of the liquid in the compass bowl. Ideally it should remain motionless to act as an effect damping medium preventing compass oscillation (aperiodicity). Regrettably, this is not so and the liquid turns with and in the same direction as the turn; its motion thus adds to or subtracts from needle error, depending on relative movement.

3.4.6 Turning Errors Summary

To summarise turning error for the Northern Hemisphere:

Turn Direction	Needle Movement	Visual Effect	Liquid Swirl	Corrective Action
Through north	Same as aircraft	Under indication	Adds to error	Turn less than needle shows
Through south	Opposite to aircraft	Over indication	Reduces error	Turn more than needle shows

Note:

- In Southern Hemisphere, errors are of opposite value.
- In turns about east and west, no significant errors, since forces act along needle.
- Northerly turning error is greater than southerly, as liquid swirl is additive to needle movement.

3.5 Gyro Magnetic Compasses

In its most basic form, a gyro magnetic compass is a system in which a magnetic detecting element monitors a gyroscope indicating element to provide a remotely displayed indication of heading. This combination of the better properties of a magnetic compass (determination of direction relative to a geographical location) and the gyroscope (rigidity) was a logical step in the development of heading display systems for use in aircraft.

3.5.1 Basic Principle of Operation

The manner in which the modern techniques are applied to gyro compass systems depends on the particular manufacturer; for the same reason the number of components comprising an individual system may vary. However, the fundamental operating principles of the main components, as seen in Figure 3.22, are the same and are dealt with in this section in general terms rather than the specifics of a particular manufacturer's instrument.

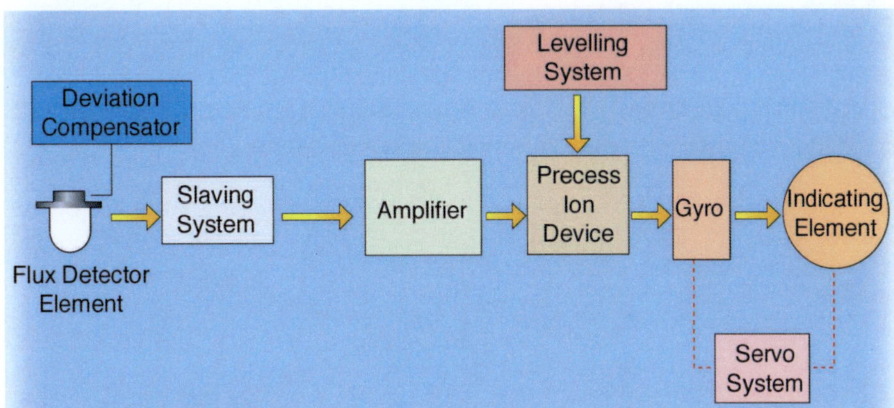

Figure 3.22 Gyro Magnetic Compass

3.5.2 Flux Detector Element

Unlike the detector element of the simple magnetic compass, the element used in all remote indicating compasses is of the fixed-in-azimuth type which senses the effect of the Earth's magnetic field as an electro-magnetically induced voltage.

If a highly permeable magnetic bar is exposed to the Earth's field, the bar will acquire a magnetic flux. The amount of flux so produced will depend on the magnetic latitude, which governs the strength of the Earth's horizontal component "H" and the direction of the bar relative to the direction of component "H".

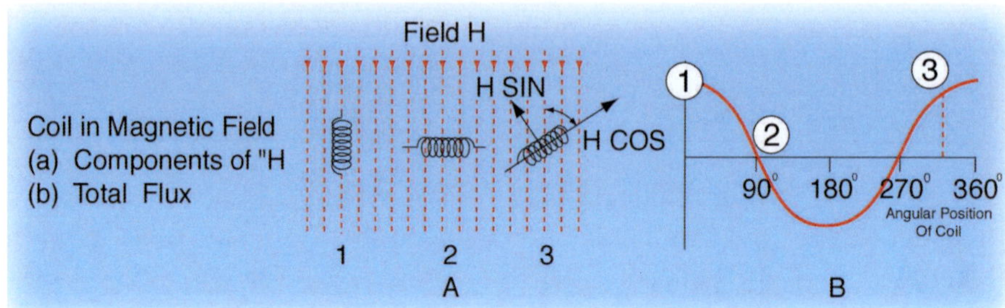

Figure 3.23 Rotating coil in a magnetic field

In Figure 3.23(a) the bar is replaced with a single-turn coil which is placed in the Earth's field with its longitudinal axis parallel to the magnetic meridian. In this case the magnetic flux passing through the coil is maximum. Rotating the coil through 90°, so that it is at right angles to the field, will produce zero magnetic flux, while rotating through a further 90°, to re-align the coil with field H, but this time in the reverse direction, will again produce maximum flux, but in the opposite algebraic sense.

Figure 3.23(b) summarises this and shows a cosine relationship (zero flux at 90° and maximum flux at 0°) between field direction and coil alignment. If the aircraft was on a heading of 030°(M), the flux intensity would be H cos30°. Similarly, the flux intensity due to the Earth's magnetic field on a heading of 150°(M) would again be H cos30°, but the direction of flow will have reversed (Cos 150° is negative). However, on a heading of 330°(M) the induced flux ('3' in Figure 3.23(b)) would be of the same sign and value as for a heading of 030°(M).

It can be seen, therefore, that such a simple system is impracticable. Firstly, in order to determine the magnetic heading it is necessary to measure the magnetic flux in the coil and there is no simple way of doing this; secondly, the ambiguity in heading must be solved. However, a basic principle has been established which may be adapted to give direction measurement.

3.5.2.1 Flux Detection

Firstly, the problem of converting flux into a measurable electrical current. This is simple if the flux produced was a "changing flux", for, according to Faraday, "Whenever there is a change of flux linked with a circuit, an EMF is induced in the circuit". It can already be seen that for an aircraft at any given position and direction, the flux produced will be constant in value. If this steady flux could be converted to a changing one, then a current representing heading would flow. This is achieved in the gyro-magnetic compass through a device called a Flux Valve. Figure 3.24 shows a flux valve in diagrammatic form.

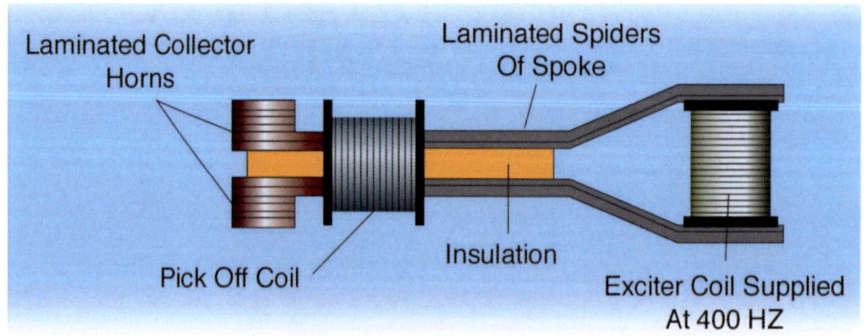

Figure 3.24 Flux detector

The flux valve consists of two bars of highly permeable (easily magnetised and de-magnetised) material, bars A and B in Figure 3.24. They are mounted on a common hub. This is wound with a coil, known as the Primary Coil, which is connected in series to an AC power source at 400 Hz. Around both bars is wound a pick-off coil, called the Secondary Coil. The effect of passing an alternating current through the primary coil is shown in Figure 3.25. The current used is of such strength that at the peak it saturates both the primary and secondary coils. However, the flux produced will have no effect on the secondary coil, since at an instant of time the two bars produce flux of equal and opposite (sign) intensity, such that the total flux is zero. In practice this situation does not occur, since a bar placed horizontally in the Earth's magnetic field has always present in it the field component "H" (unless the aircraft is near the north or south magnetic pole). The component of H produces a static flux in both bars of the flux valve. This adds a bias to the system which, when added to the variable flux produced by the alternating current, saturates the bars (cores) of the flux valve before the AC reaches its peak, as seen in Figure 3.26. Thus the coils become saturated before the AC has peaked. The effect of this is that, from the moment total saturation is reached, the flux resulting from intake of Earth magnetism will start to fall. On a graph of total flux in cores A and B, this will show as a curved variation to the straight line, or more simply, as a "Change in Flux", Figure 3.27. This changing flux (Faraday's Law) will result in an EMF or voltage being induced in the secondary coil that is proportional to the component of H along the axis of the flux valve.

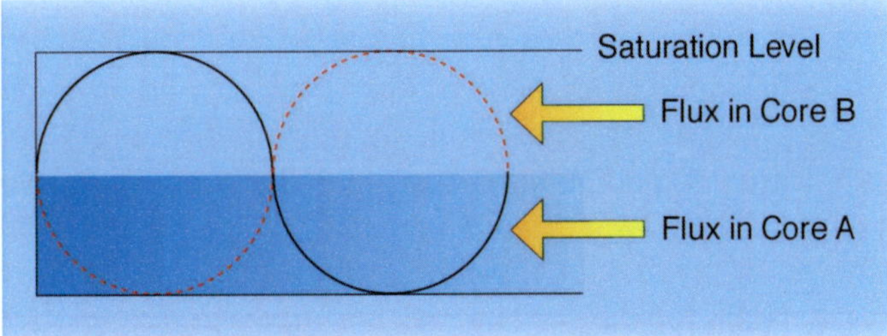

Figure 3.25 Total Saturation of Primary Coil

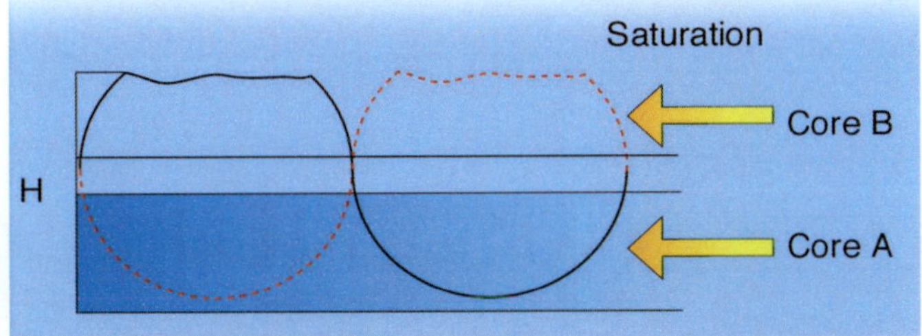

Figure 3.26 Pictorial Summation of Total Flux

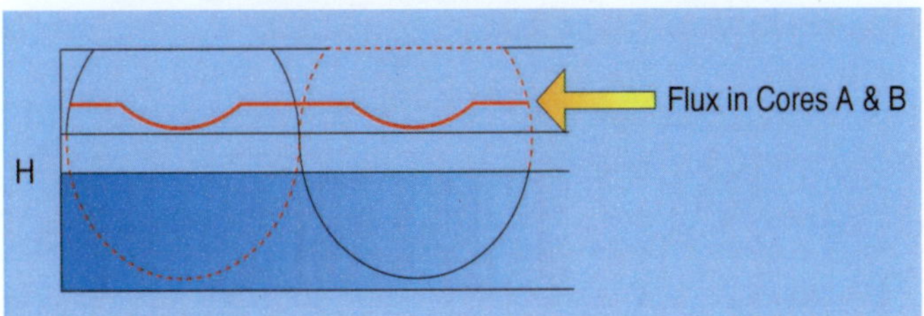

Figure 3.27 Change of Flux producing EMF in Secondary Coil

Having solved the problem of flux detection, that for resolution of direction is relatively simple. The single flux valve, as we have seen, has ambiguity over four headings, although two of these have different algebraic signs to the remaining two. The solution that is used in the gyro-magnetic compass is to employ two or more separate flux valves. It is still possible, however, to align the compass 180° in error, but the instrument will itself detect this and immediately start to precess to the correct heading.

3.5.2.2 Detector Unit

Construction of a typical flux detector element is shown in diagrammatic form below, from which it can be seen that the primary windings of the single spoke flux valve are replaced by a centrally located exciter coil serving all three spokes. A laminated collector horn is located at the outer end of each flux valve to concentrate the lines of Earth magnetic force along the parent spoke, thereby increasing sensitivity.

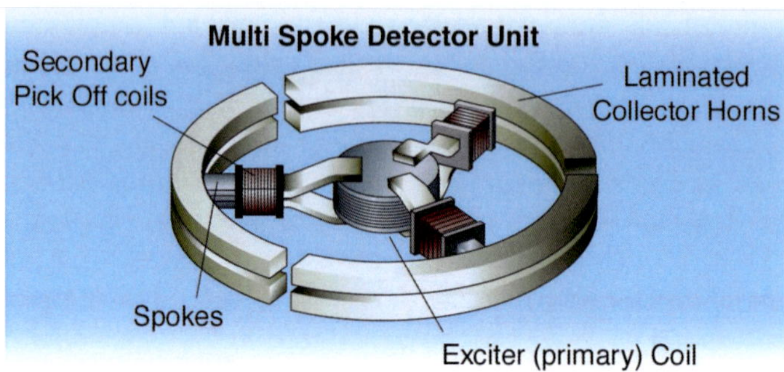

Figure 3.28

Figure 3.29 is a sectional view of a typical practical detector unit. The spokes and coil assemblies are pendulously suspended from a universal joint which permits limited freedom in pitch and roll to enable the element to sense the maximum value of "H". There is no freedom in azimuth. The unit's case is hermetically sealed and partially filled with fluid to damp out oscillation of the element. The complete unit is secured in the aircraft structure, in a wing or fin tip, well away from the deviating influence of electronic circuits and the main body of the airframe. Fixing is by means of a flange containing three slots for screws. One slot has calibration marks to permit correction for Coefficient A error. Provision is made at the top of the instrument case for installation of a deviation-compensating device.

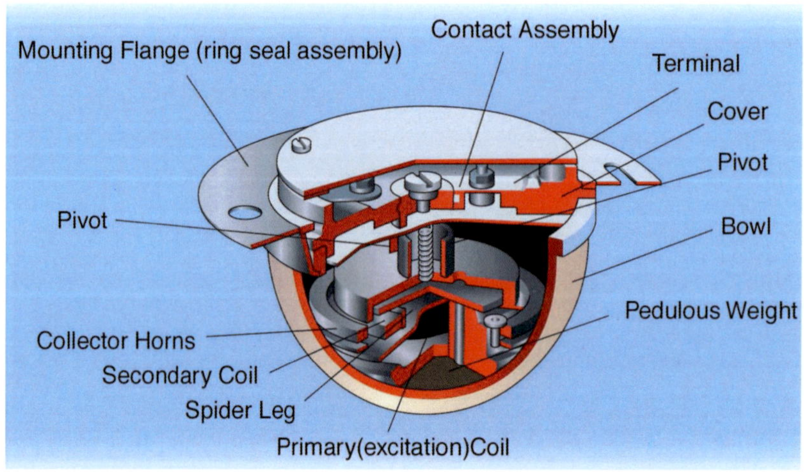

Figure 3.29 Detector Unit

3.5.3 Slaved Gyro Compass/Remote Indicating Compass(RIC)

Use of a remotely located detector unit requires that the directional reference established by the unit is electronically transmitted to another location in the aircraft, where it is used to monitor the action of a gyro or be displayed on an indicator as a value of aircraft heading. The principle of monitoring through transmission systems is essentially the same for all types of gyro magnetic compass.

3.5.3.1 Operation

Consider Figure 3.30. When the flux detector is positioned steady on one heading, say 000°, then a maximum voltage signal will be induced in the pick-off coil (secondary winding) A, while coils B and C will have voltages of half strength and opposing phases induced in them. These signals are fed to the corresponding legs of the stator of a synchro receiver, where voltages reproduced combine to establish a resultant field across the centre of the stator. The resultant is in exact alignment with the Earth's field passing through the detector unit. If the rotor of the synchro receiver is at right angles to the resultant, no voltage will be induced in the windings. In this position, the synchro is in a "null" position, and the directional gyro being monitored will also be aligned with the Earth field resultant vector; thus the heading indicator will show 000°. Now look at figure Figure 3.30 (Synchro Transmission/Receiver System

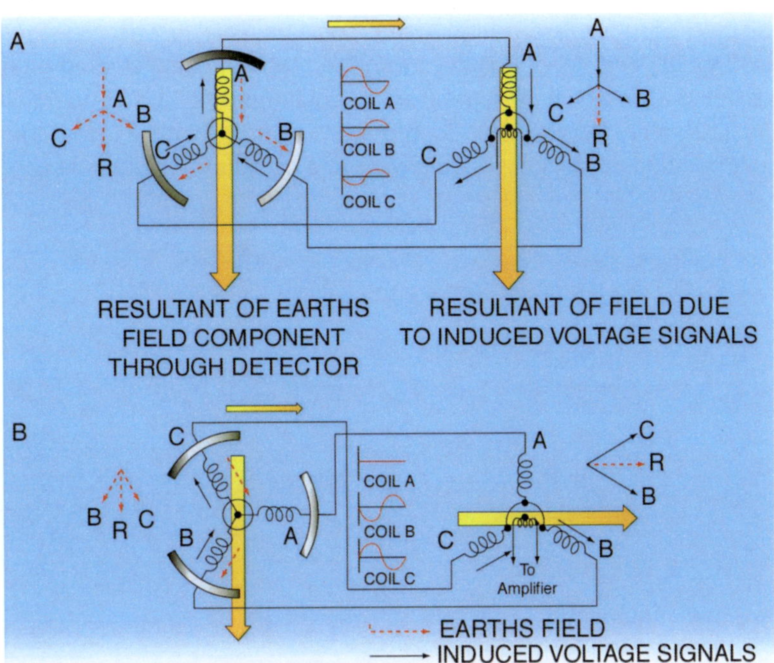

Figure 3.30 Operation

The aircraft has turned through 90° to the right, the disposition of the flux valve pick-off coils will therefore be as shown. No signal voltage will be induced in coil A. Coils B and C will have increased voltages, with that in C being opposite in phase to B . The resultant voltage (across the receiver synchro stator) will have rotated through 90° and, assuming that the synchro and gyro were still in their original positions, the resultant will now be in line with the synchro rotor. It will, therefore, induce a maximum voltage in the rotor. This error voltage signal is fed to a slaving amplifier. There it is phase-detected and amplified before being passed to a slaving torque motor. The action of this motor precesses the gyro and synchro rotor until the synchro rotor reaches a null position at right angles to the resultant of the field induced in the synchro receiver. The system will now again be in a position of stability, the aircraft having turned through 90°. With the receiver rotor mounted on the shaft of a directional gyro (DG) (Figure 3.31) if the gyro drifts or is misaligned, an error signal will be created in the receiver rotor.

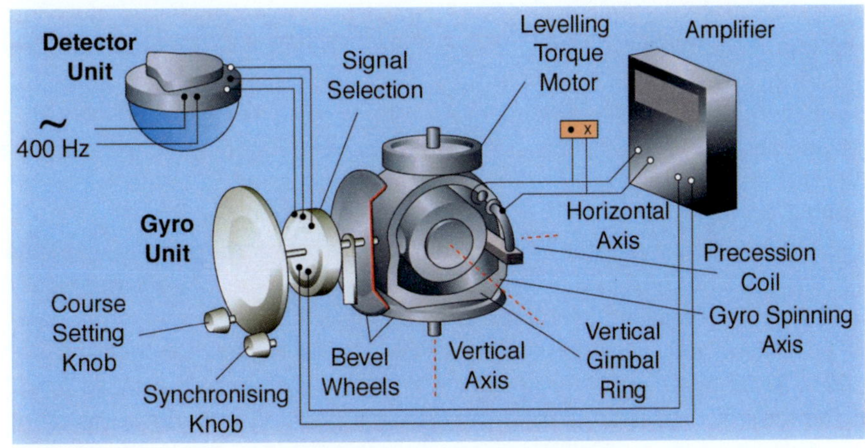

Figure 3.31 Inputs to the gyro

3.5.4 Receiver Rotor Output

The output from the receiver rotor should be fed to an amplifier to boost its power and then to a rectifier. From here it can be fed to a torque motor fitted around the DG horizontal axis. The signal from the receiver rotor will now apply a torque to the gyro and will precess it around the vertical axis until the rotor, on the shaft of the gyro, is again aligned with the zero output signal position. This system has used the signal from the detector unit to stabilise the DG and keep it aligned with the magnetic field sensed by the detector unit. The system would be ideal for use in an aircraft where the equipment fit only requires one or, at most, two heading outputs. It is therefore, very similar to the type of unit found in many light, general aviation aeroplanes. Where more heading outputs are required a more complex system is necessary.

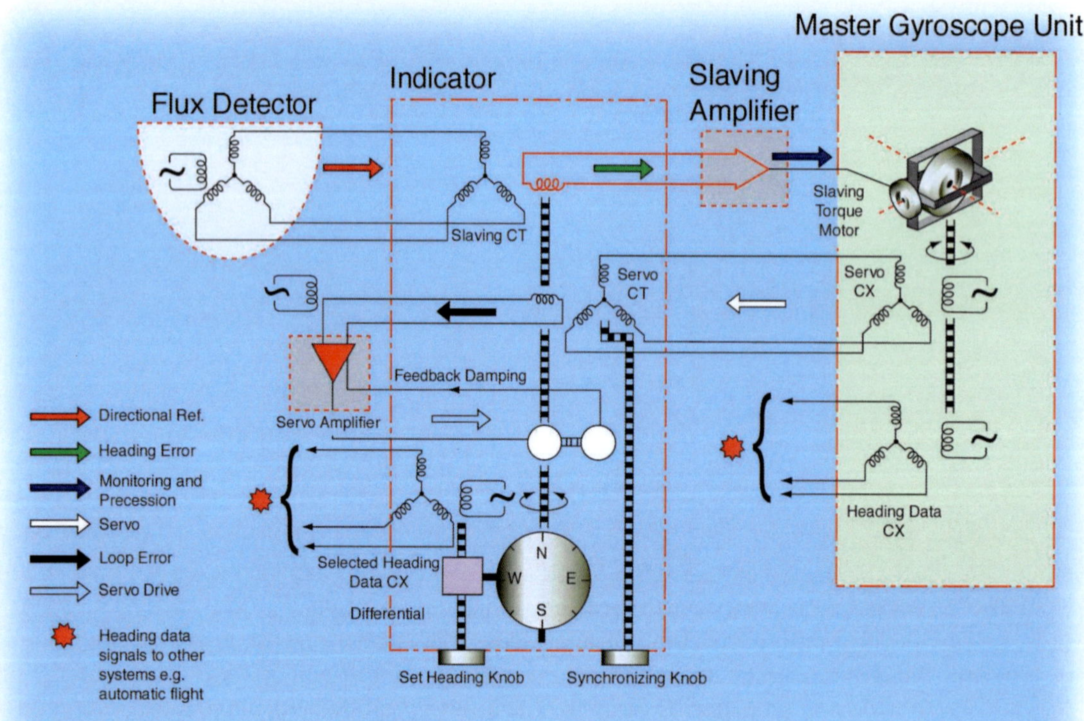

Figure 3.32 Receiver Rotor Output

3.5.5 Remote Indicating Compass

The synchronous transmission link between the three principle components of a more complex modern gyro magnetic compass system is shown in Figure 3.32. The basic principles of monitoring (already described) apply to this system. Because the indicator is a separate unit, it is necessary to incorporate additional synchros into the system, to form what is called a servo-loop. The rotor of the loop transmitter synchro (CX), mounted in the master gyro unit is rotated whenever the gyro is precessed, or slaved, to the directional reference (detector unit). The rotor of the transmitter synchro in the gyro unit is fed with AC current, and thus a voltage is induced in each of the legs of the stator which is reproduced in the legs of the receiver synchro (CT) located in the indicator unit. If the rotor of the CT synchro does not lie in the null of the induced field, a voltage will be created in the rotor. This is fed to the servo-amplifier and then to a motor which is mechanically coupled to the CT servo-rotor and the rotor of the slaving synchro (CT). Thus both rotors and the dial of the heading indicator are rotated, the latter to indicate the correct heading. The rotor of the receiver synchro and that of the slaving synchro are so coupled that when rotation is complete, both rotors will lie in the null position of the fields produced in their stators, and hence no current will flow. The servomotor also drives a tacho-generator that supplies feedback signals to the servo-amplifier, to damp out any oscillations in the system. Provision is made to transmit heading information to other locations in the aircraft through the installation of additional servo-transmitters in the master gyro unit and the heading indicator.

3.5.6 Gyroscope Element

In addition to the use of efficient synchro transmitter/receiver systems, it is also essential to employ a gyroscope that will maintain its spin axis in a horizontal position at all times. A gyro erection mechanism is therefore essential. This consists of a torque motor mounted horizontally on top of the outer gimbal with its stators fixed to the gimbal and its rotor attached to the gyro casing. The torque motor switch is generally of the liquid level type, as in Figure 3.33, and is mounted on the gyro rotor housing, or inner gimbal, so as to move with it.

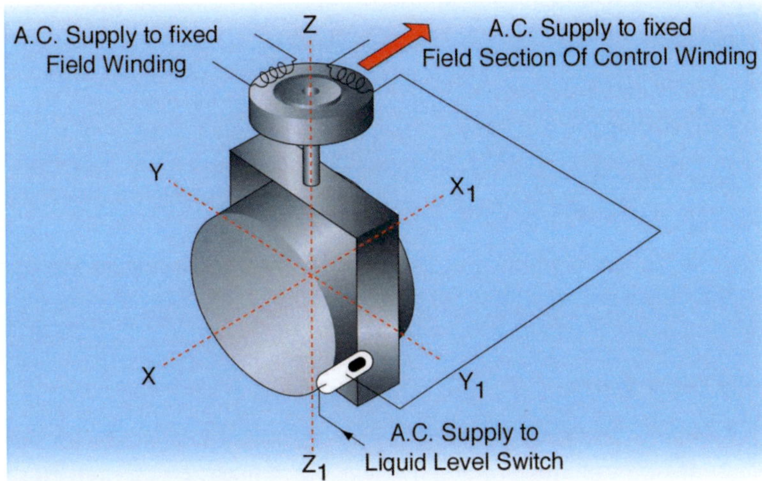

Figure 3.33 Gyroscope elements

When the gyro axis is horizontal, the liquid switch is open and no current will flow to the levelling torque motor. When the axis is tilted, however, the liquid completes the contact between the switch centre electrode and an outer electrode, providing power in one direction or another to the torque motor. The direction of current decides the direction of torque. The torque applied will precess the gyro axis back into the horizontal, at which time the liquid switch will be broken. Depending on the type of compass system, the directional gyroscope element may be contained in a panel-mounted indicator, or it may be an independent master gyro located at a remote part of the aircraft. Systems adopting the master gyro are now the most commonly used, because, in serving as a centralised heading source, they provide for more efficient transmission of the data to flight director systems and automatic flight control systems with which they are now closely linked.

3.5.7 Heading Indicator

An example of a fairly basic type of dial indicator, used with modern gyro magnetic compasses, is shown at Figure 3.34. In addition to displaying magnetic heading, it is also capable of showing the magnetic bearing to the aircraft with respect to ground stations of the radio navigation system - ADF (Automatic Direction Finding) and VOR (Very High Frequency Omni-directional Range). For this reason the indicator is generally referred to as a Radio Magnetic Indicator (RMI). The radio aspects of the RMI and its use as an aid to navigation are covered in the Radio Navigation Study Guide.

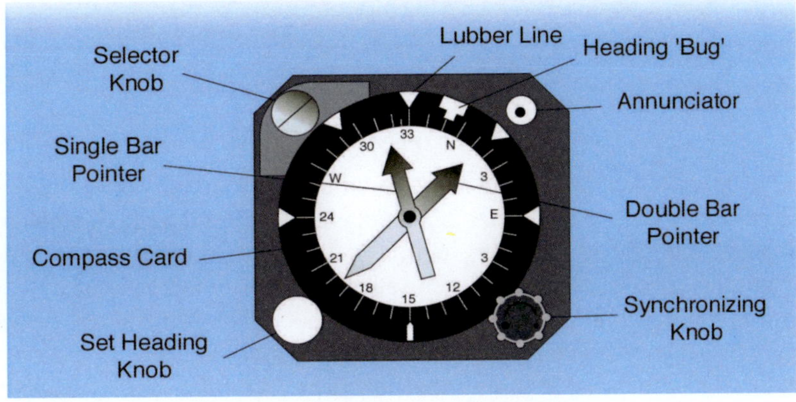

Figure 3.34 Heading display

In order that the pilot may set a desired heading, a 'set heading' knob is provided. It is mechanically coupled to a heading bug, so that rotation of the knob causes the bug to move with respect to the compass card. For turning under automatically controlled flight, rotation of the set heading knob also positions the rotor of a CX synchro, which then supplies twin commands to the autopilot system. On more modern equipment, the main heading references will be found on the EFIS and/or HSI.

3.5.8 Modes of Operation

All gyro compass systems provide for the selection of two modes of operation:

SLAVED – in which the gyro is monitored by the detector element, and

FREE GYRO – in which the gyro is isolated from the detector unit and functions as a straightforward directional gyroscope

The latter operating mode is selected when a malfunction in the monitoring mode occurs or the aircraft is flying in latitudes where the value of H is too small to be used as a reliable reference (e.g. the 6 micro-Tesla zone).

3.5.9 Synchronising Indicators

The function of the synchronising indicator, or annunciator as it is more usually known, is to indicate to the user that the gyro is synchronised with the directional reference sensed by the detector unit

The synchronisation indicator may be integrated with the heading indicator or it may be a separate unit mounted on the aircraft instrument panel. The annunciator is activated by monitoring signals from the detector head to the gyro slaving torque motor and is therefore connected into the gyro slaving circuit.

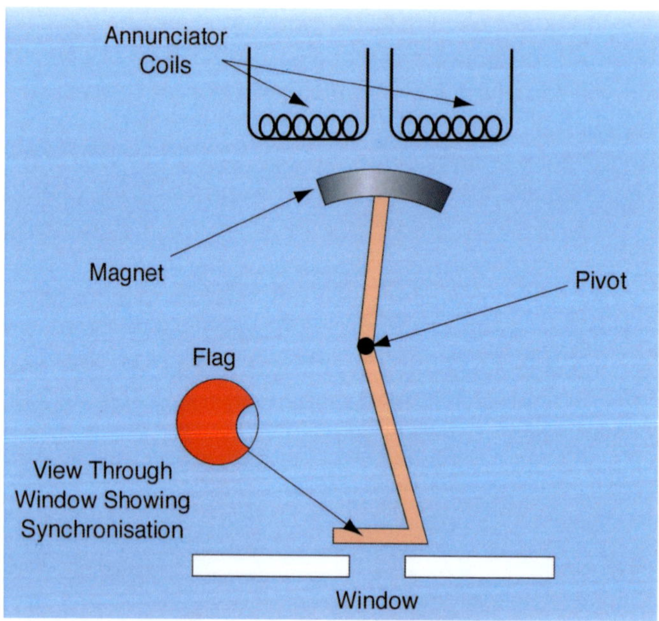

Figure 3.35 Typical annunciator

Figure 3.35 shows a typical annunciator. It consists of a small flag marked with a dot and a cross, which is visible through a window in one corner of the heading indicator (if so mounted). A small magnet is located at the other end of the shaft, positioned adjacent to two soft-iron cored coils connected in series with the precession circuit. When the gyro is out of synchronisation with the detector head, a current flows through the coils, attracting the magnet in one direction or the other such that either a dot or a cross shows in the annunciator window. With a synchronised system, the annunciator window should be clear of an image; however, in practice the flag moves slowly from dot to cross and back again, serving as a most useful indication that the system is working correctly.

3.5.10 Manual Synchronisation

When electrical power is initially applied to a compass system operating in the “slaved” mode, the gyroscope may be out of alignment from the detector head by a large amount. The system will start to synchronise, but, as the rate of precession is normally low (1° to 2° per minute), some time may elapse before synchronisation is achieved. To speed up the process, a manual synchronisation system is always incorporated.
The principle of manual synchronisation may be better understood by reference to Figure 3.34. The heading indicator incorporates a manual synchronisation knob, the face of which is marked with a dot and a cross and is coupled mechanically to the stator of the servo (CT) synchro. When the knob is pushed in and rotated in the direction indicated by the annunciator, the synchro stator is turned, inducing an error voltage into its rotor. This is fed to the servo-amplifier and motor which drives the slave heading synchro rotor and gyro, via the slaving amplifier and precession torque motor, into synchronisation with the detector head. At the same time the synchro (CT) rotor is driven to the null position and all error signals are removed; the system is synchronised.

3.5.11 Operation in a Turn

To better understand the operation of the gyro magnetic compass, let us study its performance in a turn. (Refer to Figure 3.32). As the aircraft enters a turn, the gyroscope maintains its direction with reference to a fixed point (rigidity) and the aircraft thus turns around the gyro. The rotor of the servo synchro CX is rotated, and error signals are generated in the stator which are passed to and reflected in the stator of the servo synchro CT located in the heading indicator. The rotor of the servo synchro CT will now no longer lie in the null of the induced field. A voltage will thus be generated which will be passed via the servo amplifier to the servo-motor M. The servo-motor will drive the face of the indicator round, so that the compass card keeps pace with the turn and at the same time will drive the rotor of the servo-synchro CT and the slaving synchro round again, keeping pace with the turn. During all this time the detector unit, which is fixed in azimuth, is being turned in the Earth's magnetic field; therefore, the flux induced each spoke of the detector unit is continuously changing. This results in a rotating field being produced in the stator of the slaving synchro CT, which would normally result in a change in flux being detected by the rotor of the slaving synchro and passed as an error signal to the precession circuit. However, as we have already seen, the rotor of the slaving synchro is already rotating under the influence of the synchro motor. Since the speed and direction of rotation of the rotor matches that of the stator field, hence no error signal is present for transmission to the precession circuit and hence no gyro precession occurs. When the aircraft resumes straight and level flight, rotation of the servo-synchro CX rotor ceases. There is no further field change between stators and therefore no current flow in the servo-loop. Rotation of the heading indicator display ceases and the system is now electrical “at rest”, but still in a fully synchronised condition. In a steep and prolonged turn, a slight de-synchronisation may occur due to the introduction of a small component of Z, while the detector head is out of the horizontal for a protracted period of time. However, on coming out of the turn, the compass card will rapidly resume the correct heading through the normal precession process.

Apart from this small error in a prolonged turn, the system is virtually clear of turning and acceleration errors

3.5.12 Advantages of the Gyro Magnetic Compass

The advantages of the gyro magnetic compass over a DI or direct reading instrument are:

- The DI suffers from real and apparent drift and has to be reset in flight. Also, when resetting to the magnetic compass, the aircraft must be flown straight and level, whereas the detector unit constantly monitors the gyro magnetic compass.
- The detector unit can be installed in a remote part of the aircraft, well away from electrical circuits and other influences due to airframe magnetism.

The flux valve technique used in the detector unit senses the Earth's magnetic meridian rather than seeking it. This makes the system more sensitive to small components of H. The unit will provide a heading reference to a much higher magnetic latitude than the direct reading magnetic compass

- Turning and acceleration errors are minimised because:

1. The detector unit is fixed in azimuth
2. The precession signals aligning the compass are kept to a low value (typically 5° / min)
3. There is a roll cut out switch that isolates the precession system during turns at bank angles of greater than 10°

- The compass may be detached from the detector unit by a simple switch election to work as a DI. A normal DI is therefore not required
- The system can readily be used to monitor other equipment: autopilot, Doppler, RMI
- Repeaters can be made available to as many crew stations or equipment as are desired

3.5.13 Disadvantages of the Gyro Magnetic Compass

- It is much heavier than a direct reading compass
- It is much more expensive
- It is electrical in operation and therefore susceptible to electrical failure
- It is much more complicated than a DI or a direct reading compass

Self-Assessment Test 3

1. There are three principle properties of a magnet:
A) The power of attraction is concentrated in the middle of the magnet
It will attract other pieces of iron or steel
When left suspended it will adopt a N – S direction
B) The power of attraction is concentrated at the ends of the magnet
It will attract other pieces of iron and steel
When left suspended it will adopt a N – S direction
C) The power of attraction is concentrated at the ends of the magnet
It will attract non-ferrous material
When left suspended it will adopt a N – S direction
D) The power of attraction is concentrated at the ends of the magnet
It will attract ferrous material
When left suspended it will adopt an E – W direction

2. The force of attraction between two magnets varies:
A) Directly as the square of the direction between them
B) Indirectly as the cube of the direction between them
C) Inversely as the square of the distance between them
D) Inversely as the cube of the distance between them

3. Reluctance is said to be:
A) The amount of resistance a material may have to being magnetized
B) The amount of resistance a material may have to being demagnetized
C) Has no relevance to magnetism
D) The ease with which hard iron can be magnetized

4. Isogonic lines:
A) Join all points having the same magnetic deviation
B) Join all points having zero variation
C) Are concerned with the difference in magnetic dip in different parts of the Earth
D) Join all points having the same magnetic variation

5. Agonic lines:
A) Join all points having zero variation
B) Join all points having zero deviation
C) Join all points having the same magnetic dip
D) Join all points having the same value of Z

6. The letters H and Z are assigned to particular functions as follows:
A) Z is the horizontal component; H is the vertical component
B) H and Z represent the Easterly and Westerly components, respectively, of the Earth's magnetic field
C) H is the horizontal component; Z is the vertical component
D) H and Z represent the two elements of the vertical magnetic field

7. The following qualities are given to the H and Z factors:
A) At the Magnetic Equator, H is minimum and Z is maximum
B) At the poles, Z is maximum and H is minimum
C) At the poles, H is maximum and Z is minimum
D) At the Magnetic Equator or the Poles, H and Z have similar values

8. The Angle of Dip is calculated from the following formula:
A) $\text{Tan dip} = \frac{Z}{H}$
B) $\text{Tan dip} = \frac{H}{Z}$
C) Tan dip = HZ
D) Tan dip = H – Z

9. Assume the angle of dip is 64° and the value of H = 1.5 units. What is the value of Z:
A) 1.3481
B) 0.0174
C) 1.3668
D) 3.0754

10. The magnetic total force (T) is calculated from the formula:
A) $T = \frac{Z}{\text{tan dip}}$
B) $T = \frac{Z}{\text{cos dip}}$
C) T = HZ
D) $T = \frac{Z}{\text{sin dip}}$

11. Variation, deviation and grivation are defined as follows:
A) Variation is the angle between True North and Grid North
Deviation is the angle between True North and Compass North
Grivation is the angle between Compass North and grid North
B) Grivation is the angle between True North and Magnetic North
Variation is the angle between Magnetic North and Grid North
Deviation is the angle between Compass North and Grid North
C) Variation is the angle between True North and Magnetic North
Deviation is the angle between Magnetic North and Compass North
Grivation is the angle between Magnetic North and Grid North
D) Deviation is the angle between True North and Magnetic North
Variation is the angle between Compass North and grid North
Grivation is the angle between Compass North and True North

12. Hard iron and soft iron magnetism is due primarily to:
A) Hard iron – manufacturing processes and is permanent
Soft iron – induced by the Earth's magnetic field and is temporary
B) Hard iron – induced by the Earth's magnetic field and is temporary
Soft iron – manufacturing processes and is permanent
C) Hard iron – induced by aircraft electrical systems and is temporary
Soft iron – induced by natural phenomena and is permanent
D) Hard iron – induced by natural phenomena and is temporary
Soft iron – induced by aircraft electrical systems and is permanent

13. The three components of permanent magnetism are:
A) P – fore and aft; Q – vertical; R – athwartships
B) P – fore and aft; Q – athwartships; R – vertical
C) P – vertical; Q – athwartships; R – fore and aft
D) P – athwartships; P – vertical; R – fore and aft

14. Coefficients A, B and C are a follows:
A) A varies on all headings and is a factor of electrical induction
B hard iron P deviations maximum on N and S
C hard iron Q deviations maximum on E and W
B) A Hard iron P deviations and its maximum on E and W
B varies on all headings and is maximum on N and S
C Hard iron Z and is usually constant on all headings
C) A Soft iron P deviations and is constant on all headings
B Hard iron Q deviations and is maximum on N and S
C Hard iron P deviations and is constant on all headings
D) A Usually constant on all headings and result from a misaligned compass
B Hard iron P with maximum deviation on E and W
C Hard iron Q with maximum deviation on N and S

15. The method used for the calculation of Coefficient A is as follows:
A) Divide the sum of the deviations measured at the cardinal points by 4
B) Find the average of the sum of the deviations measured at the 8 main compass points
C) Coefficient on A = Deviation on East minus deviation on West divided by 2
D) Coefficient A = Deviation x Cos heading

16. The method used for the calculation of Coefficient B is as follows:
A) Find the average of the sum of the deviations measured at the 8 main compass points
B) Deviation divided by the Cosine of the heading
C) Deviation divided by the Sin of the heading
D) Deviation on North minus deviation on South divided by 2

17. The method used for the calculation of Coefficient C is as follows:
A) Deviation on North minus deviation on South divided by 2
B) A + B Sin hdg + C Cos hdg
C) Find the average of the algebraic sum of the deviations noted on the eight compass headings
D) Deviation divided by Sin heading

18. Total compass deviation equals:
A) A + B Sin Hdg + C Tan Hdg
B) A + B Sin Hdg + C Cos Hdg
C) A + B Tan Hdg + C Cos Hdg
D) A + B Sin Hdg minus C Cos Hdg

19. The effect of magnetic dip (Z) on an E type compass is compensated in part by:
A) Liquid levelling switches
B) Gyro compensation
C) Automatic leveling to compensate for azimuth error
D) The pendulous effect of the magnets mounted below the compass needle

20. Permanent magnet assemblies fitted to the compass mounting plate compensate for:
A) Coefficient A
B) Coefficients B and C
C) Coefficients A, B, C, D and E
D) Large values of Z when approaching N70° and S70°

21. E Type compass acceleration/deceleration errors in the Northern Hemisphere are summarized as follows:

	Hdg	Speed	Needle Turns	Visual Effect
A)	East	Increase	Clockwise	Apparent turn to North
	West	Increase	Anti-clockwise	Apparent turn to North
B)	North	Increase	Clockwise	Apparent turn to East
	South	Decrease	Anti-clockwise	Apparent to East
C)	East	Decrease	Clockwise	Apparent turn to North
	West	Decrease	Anti-clockwise	Apparent turn to South
D)	East	Increase	Anti-clockwise	Apparent turn to West
	West	Decrease	Clockwise	Apparent turn to South

22. In turns about East or West, E Type compass reading errors are:
A) Particularly significant
B) Shows turning errors opposite in direction to the turn
C) Insignificant
D) Maximum about a North/South axis

23. In turns through North and South in the Northern Hemisphere, E Type compass errors are as follows:

	Turn Direction	Needle Movement	Visual Effect	Liquid Swirl	Corrective Action
A)	Through North	Same as aircraft	Under indicates	Adds to error	Turn less
		Same as aircraft	Over indicates		
	Through South			Adds to error	Turn more
B)	Through North	Same as aircraft	Under indicates	Adds to error	Turn less
		Opposite to aircraft	Over indicates		
	Through South			Reduces error	Turn more
C)	Through North	Opposite to aircraft	Over indicates	Reduces error	Turn more
		Same as aircraft	Under indicates	Adds to error	
	Through South				Turn less
D)	Through North	Opposite to aircraft	Under indicates	Adds to error	Turn more
		Same as aircraft	Over indicates		
	Through South			Reduces error	Turn less

24. The principle of operation of a gyro magnetic compass is as follows:
A) The outputs of a flux detector and a tied gyro are integrated and amplified, and used to drive the relevant compass and automatic flight control systems. The flux detector output aligns the gyro
B) The output of a flux detector is used to drive the selected compass system only
C) The output of an space gyro is used to supply compass heading information to the selected compass system
D) None of the above

25. The flux detector operates on the principle of:
A) Magnetic field detection and the use of an induced emf from the flux detector element as it passes through the Earth's magnetic field
B) Magnetic field detection and sampling
C) Gyro stability and precession control
D) Direct coupling to the heading drive mechanisms of the compass system

26. An annunciator indicates:
A) Gyro erect
B) Flux detector serviceable
C) Compass system synchronized
D) Compass system coupled to AFCS

27. A gyro magnetic system has two modes of operations:
A) Altitude and compass
B) Compass and DG or GYRO
C) SLAVED or DG
D) MAP and VOR

28. The Directional Gyro in a remote indicating compass is levelled by a:
A) Gimbal operated micro switch
B) Liquid levelling switch
C) FAST ERECTION button
D) Mechanical precession

Self-Assessment Test 3 Answers

1	B
2	C
3	A
4	D
5	A
6	C
7	B
8	A
9	D
10	D
11	C
12	A
13	B
14	D
15	B
16	C
17	A
18	B
19	D
20	B
21	A
22	C
23	B
24	A
25	A
26	C
27	C
28	B

CHAPTER 4
Radio Altimeter

4.1 Introduction

Using Frequency Modulated Continuous Wave techniques (FMCW), radio altimeters provide a continuous indication of height above the surface immediately below the aircraft, up to a maximum of 5000'. They are particularly suited to low altitude terrain clearance measurement and for provision of height data to GPWS and Autoland (ILS) equipment. The radio altimeter is instantaneous and accurate, but gives no indication of high ground ahead. As the height measurement is absolute, flight over undulating terrain will result in variations in the indications of aircraft height on the radio altimeter display.

4.2 Principle of Operation

A radio altimeter consists of a transmitter / receiver and integral timing device, a transmitter aerial, a receiver aerial and a display of some type. The elapsed time from transmission of an electromagnetic wave to reception back at the aircraft after ground reflection is measured. As long as the path followed by the wave is vertical, down and up, then the elapsed time is a function of aircraft height. The measurement of time is made by changing the frequency of the transmission at a known rate, then measuring the change in frequency by the time the reflected energy is received back at the aircraft. The greater the height, the greater the frequency change.

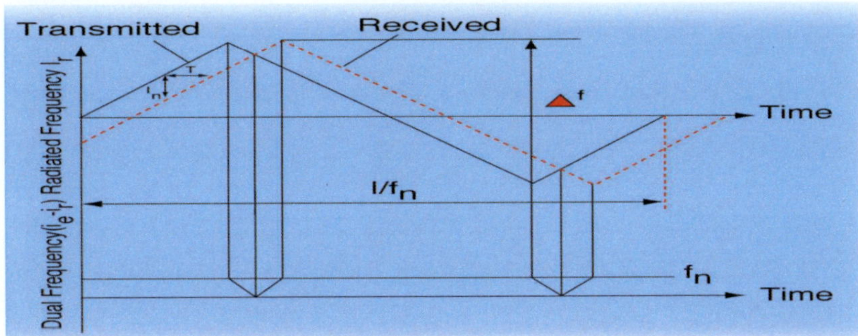

Figure 4.1 Illustration of operation

It is not possible, within the frequency allocation, to change the frequency (FM) indefinitely, and so the modulation sweeps between upper and lower frequency limits, normally by 60 MHz. At Figure 4.1, the base frequency is 4270 MHz and the upper limit is 4330 MHz - the variation, or modulation, is made as shown. Throughout the cycle there will be two very short periods when the modulation changes from +ve to -ve and vice-versa; apart from during these short periods, which can be excluded from height calculation, the instantaneous frequency difference is proportional to aircraft height. Sweep-rates are normally in the order of 500 times per second. It is possible for an aircraft to be at a height such that the returning wave arrives after a complete frequency sweep, and this would give an erroneous height solution. To overcome this ambiguity, the sweep rate is made low, i.e. the time for a sweep is made longer, so that all normal heights within the range of the radio altimeter are covered.

4.3 Display

Normal display maximum altitudes (2500' or 5000') are obvious from the conventional dial display, but not so apparent from the moving vertical scale presentation. The circular displays are linear up to 500' and logarithmic from 500' - 2500' (or 5000'), making the lower range of heights easier to read more accurately.

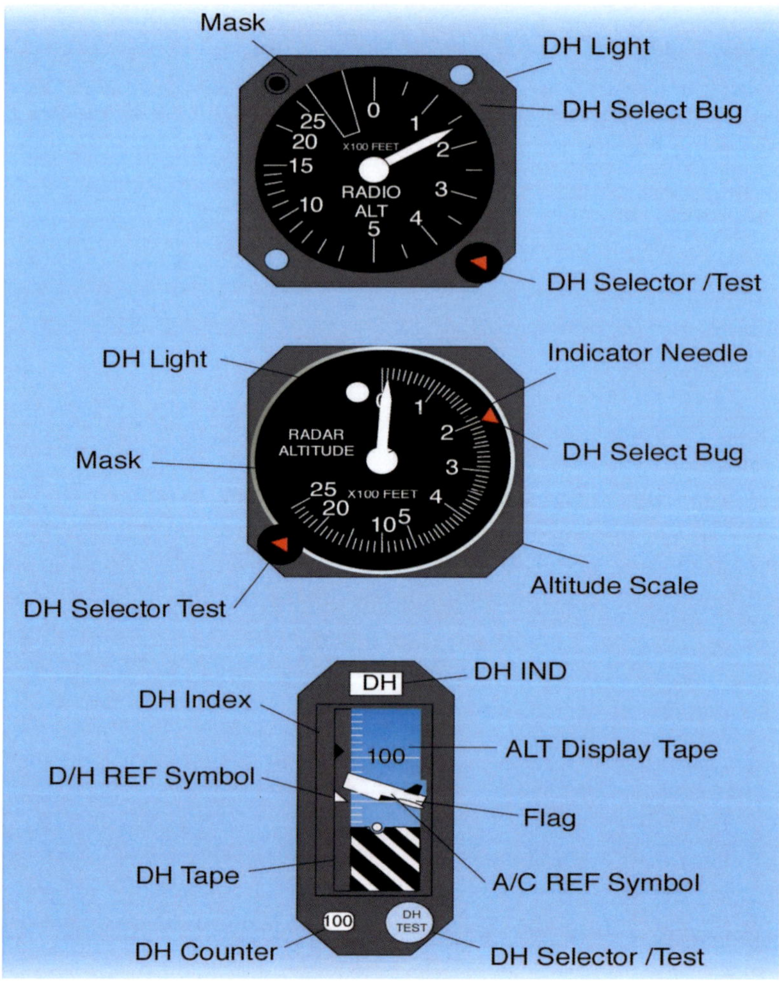

Figure 4.2 Aircraft Dislays

All radio altimeter displays have a setting control for a decision height, at which point a warning will be given. The height can be set by positioning an outside cursor against the required height on the scale. The setting control will normally double as a PTT (press-to-test) facility which, when engaged, drives the display to a predetermined value - normally 100'.

With reference to the top display, an OFF or FAIL flag will be visible when:

The equipment is switched off;

There is a power failure;

A TX, Rx, or display fault occurs.

The returning signal is too weak;

Signals are reflected from the airframe.

The height pointer is hidden from view behind the mask when:

The equipment is switched off;

A Tx, Rx, or display fault occurs;

The aircraft climbs beyond the equipment height limit

4.4 Warnings

Both light and / or audio warnings are given for departure from the height limit indicator. Visual warnings are:

AMBER above selected height
GREEN ± 15' of selected height
RED 15' below selected height

Where only a single light is fitted, the DH light will flash continuously when the aircraft goes below the set height until the aircraft climbs or until the DH value is set lower

4.5 Accuracy

The accuracy of the radio altimeter is expected to be:

0 - 500': ±2' or 2% of height, whichever is the greater.
Above 500': 5 % of height.

4.6 Errors

Given that the sweep-rate is compatible with the height performance of the installation, the only two errors that might occur are:

Leakage - It is necessary to separate the Tx and Rx antenna on the underside of the aircraft to avoid leakage, i.e. spilling through of side-lobes directly into the Rx antenna. Placing the antenna a distance apart is generally adequate screening.

Mushing - Because the antenna are apart, the closer the aircraft is to the ground, then the Tx antenna, reflection point and Rx antenna form a triangle. It follows that the path distance travelled by the wave is greater than twice the vertical height between surface and aircraft, as illustrated in Figure 4.3. This causes inaccuracies very close to the ground and is known as "mushing error".

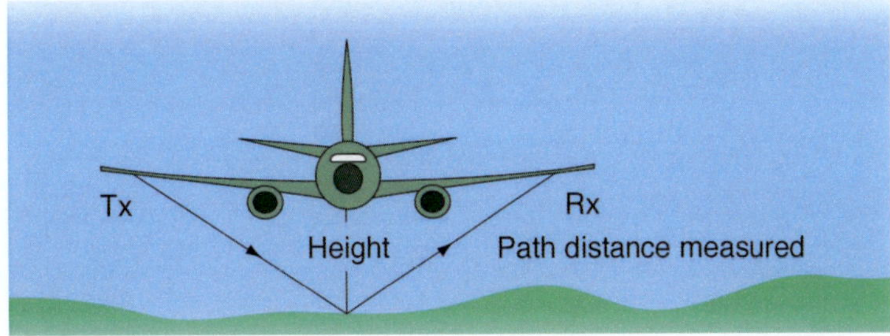

Figure 4.3 Separating antenna reduces Leakage but causes Mushing Errors

4.7 Advantages of Radio Altimeters

- Indication of actual (absolute) height is given
- Provides an easy crosscheck with barometric altimeter for terrain clearance
- Provides a warning signal at DH

4.8 Outputs

Outputs from the Radio Altimeter can be fed directly or via a data bus to:

- Automatic Flight Control System (for ILS coupling)
- Global Positioning Navigation System
- Flight Director

- Electronic Flight Instrumentation System
- Flight Management Computer

Self-Assessment Test 4

1. The normally accepted operating height range of a radio altimeter is:
A) Surface to 4000'
B) 1 000' to 5000'
C) Surface to 8000'
D) Surface to 5000'

2. The main uses of a radio altimeter are:
A) Terrain and collision avoidance
B) GPWS and terrain avoidance
C) Height above terrain measurement, height data to GPWS and autoland equipment
D) GPWS and height data to GPWS

3. The main components of a radio altimeter system are a:
A) Transmitter/receiver, integral timing device, transmitter and receiver aerials and a display indicator
B) Transmitter/receiver, integral timing device, transmitter aerials and a display indicator
C) Transmitter and transmitter aerial, integral timing device and a display indicator
D) Transmitter/receiver, transmitter and receiver aerials and a display indicator

4. Radio Altimeters operate in the:
A) SHF range
B) VHF range
C) UHF range
D) HF range

5. The modulation sweep between upper and lower frequency ranges is:
A) 70 MHz
B) 60 kHz
C) 30 MHz
D) 60 MHz

6. The usual indications and controls located on a radio altimeter are as follows:
A) DH selector, DH warning light
B) Altitude indicator needle, DH selector/TEST control, DH warning light and an ON/OFF flag
C) Altitude indicator needle, a DH selector and warning light
D) DH selector and warning light, and an adjustable mb scale

7. A radio altimeter OFF flag will be visible on the following occasions:
A) A power failure only
B) The received signal is weak only
C) Equipment is switched OFF, a power failure or a system component failure
D) A weak received signal only

8. When a single DH warning light is fitted:
A) The light will be illuminated continuously if the aircraft is above the selected height
B) The lamp will remain on steady if the aircraft goes below the selected height
C) The lamp will flash if the aircraft goes below the selected height or until the height is changed or the aircraft climbs above the selected height
D) The lamp will be lit continuously if the aircraft goes below the selected height

9. Radio altimeter accuracy is:
A) ± 50' throughout the range
B) ± 25' throughout the range
C) 5% of the height below 500' and ± 2' above 500'
D) 0 to 500': ± 2' or 2% of the height whichever is the greater; above 500': 5% of the height

10. It is necessary to separate the transmitter and receiver aerials of a radio altimeter to prevent:
A) Leakage
B) Mushing
C) Gravitas
D) Synchronous lock in due to phase shift in the respective aerials

11. Radio altimeter outputs can be fed directly or via a data bus to the following systems:
A) AFCS, auto-thrust control and EFIS
B) AFCS, flight director, EFIS, FMC
C) AFCS, VOR attenuation, EFIS, FMC
D) AFCS, ADF and VOR attenuation, EFIS, FMC

Self-Assessment Test 4 Answers

1	D
2	C
3	A
4	A
5	D
6	B
7	C
8	C
9	D
10	A
11	B

CHAPTER 5
Electronic Flight Instrument Systems (EFIS)

5.1 Introduction

Electronic display systems are replacing the electro-mechanical type of instruments for several important reasons. Firstly, the technology of screen displays, whether CRT, LED or flat panel, has demonstrated the high reliability necessary for safe operations. Secondly, by using a sizeable screen, more information can be integrated into a single presentation well positioned in the pilot's preferred line of sight. Thirdly, colours and clarity of presentation make the information easily absorbed and understood. Finally, by being able to select the information he/she considers is relevant at the time, the pilot can concentrate (without having to scan a large instrument panel) on the task at hand. This can be done in the confidence that, should any irregularity occur in an undisplayed system, a warning interruption will be made on the display in use.

In a computerised, highly integrated system such as EFIS, both hardware and software architectures must be well matched. An EFIS must be capable of interfacing with multiple avionics, flight control and radio navigation equipment (long and short-range). This infers rapid, accurate analogue/digital conversion and vice-versa. An important feature of any EFIS system is that it must provide a full-time automatic crosscheck between pilot/co-pilot displays and provide an alert where discrepancies are found. As an example, one commercially available system reacts to 13ft. difference in radio altitude and 0.5 dot ILS localiser / glideslope difference between displays. There are, of course, many other integrity checks continuously in progress.

5.2 Components of the EFIS

An Electronic Flight Instruments System (EFIS) installation will normally consist of:

- 3 (Left, Centre, Right) Symbol Generators (SG)
- 2 Control Panels (CP)
- 2 Attitude Director Indicators (ADI), and
- 2 Horizontal Situation Indicators (HSI)

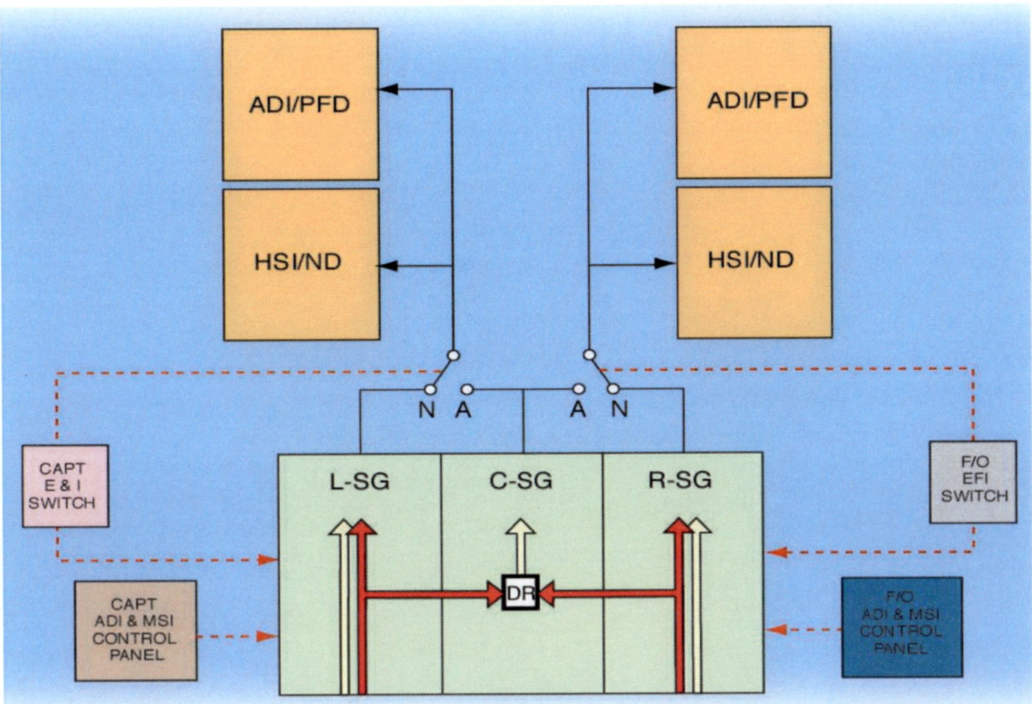

Figure 5.1 General Components of an EFIS

These instruments depend on the Flight Management Computer for flight progress and map background data, the Inertial Reference System for attitude and heading data and the symbol generator. You should be aware that, just to add to the confusion and make you believe that something that has a simple logic is extremely complicated, there are many different terms used to describe the same item. As examples of this the ADI and the HSI are frequently referred to as the Primary Flight Display (PFD) and the Navigation Display (ND) respectively.

5.2.1 EFIS Symbol Generator

The central part of the EFIS is the symbol generator (SG). It receives inputs from many avionics systems. It processes data and generates the proper outputs for presentations on the ADI and HSI. When the SG's are powered, displays are provided on the appropriate ADI and HSI. When not powered the displays are blank. When the LIGHTS TEST switch on the overhead panel (or a test switch on the supplying symbol generator) is pushed the ADI and HSI will display a maintenance test pattern. A message stating 'TEST OK' or 'TEST FAIL' and the name of the failed component appears at the end of the test. This test is inhibited in flight.

Various failure conditions may be displayed on each ADI or HSI. A blank screen results when a power failure or "over temperature" condition exists. Partial loss of colour capability may cause an odd colour presentation. When information is not reliable or radio signals are not received, the display is removed. Numeric indications are replaced with dashes. If aeroplane equipment fails a failure flag is displayed.

5.2.2 Instrument Comparator Unit (ICU)

ADI and HSI data faults detection and comparison monitoring is accomplished by the Instrument Comparator Unit (ICU). The system monitors the following ADI and HSI data for cross-cockpit agreement of:

- Attitude (pitch and roll)
- Heading
- Track

When conditions are detected outside parameters, the appropriate Master Warning light illuminates, an aural signal sounds and an appropriate EICAS message appears. ICU comparison monitoring is inhibited when both pilots are using the centre symbol generator.

5.3 EFIS Control

The ADI and HSI Control Panels provide control of symbology options, modes, ranges and brightness for the respective ADI and HSI displays, and selection of radio altimeter decision heights. Figure 5.2 illustrates a typical control unit.

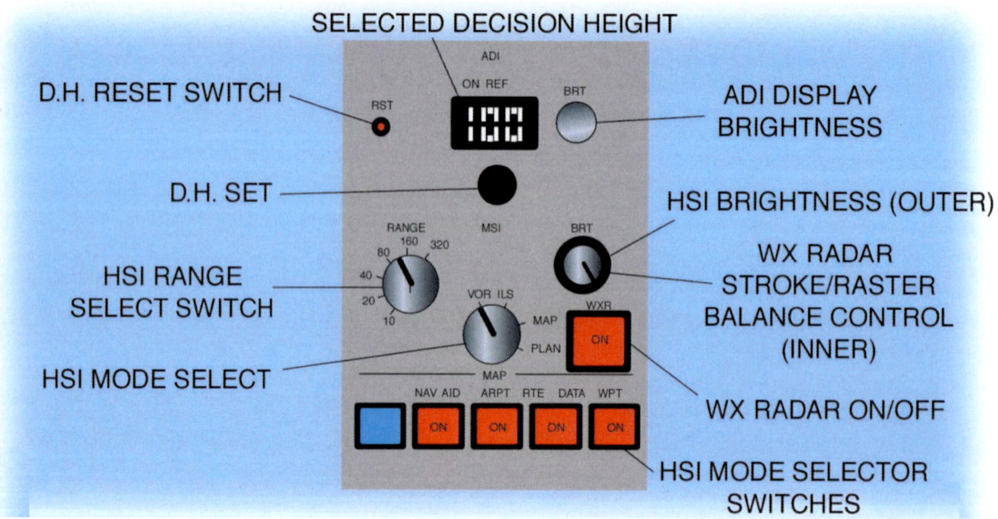

Figure 5.2 Control Unit

5.4 Attitude Director Indicator (ADI)

The ADI (Figure 5.3) presents conventional aeroplane attitude indications, flight director commands and deviation from localiser, glideslope and selected airspeed. Flight Mode displays (AFS operating modes), ground speed, radio altitude, and decision height are also displayed. Attitude information is provided by the respective IRS (Captain's ADI-L IRS, F/O ADI - R IRS). The centre IRS is an alternate source. The colour presentation may be found in Section 5.7.

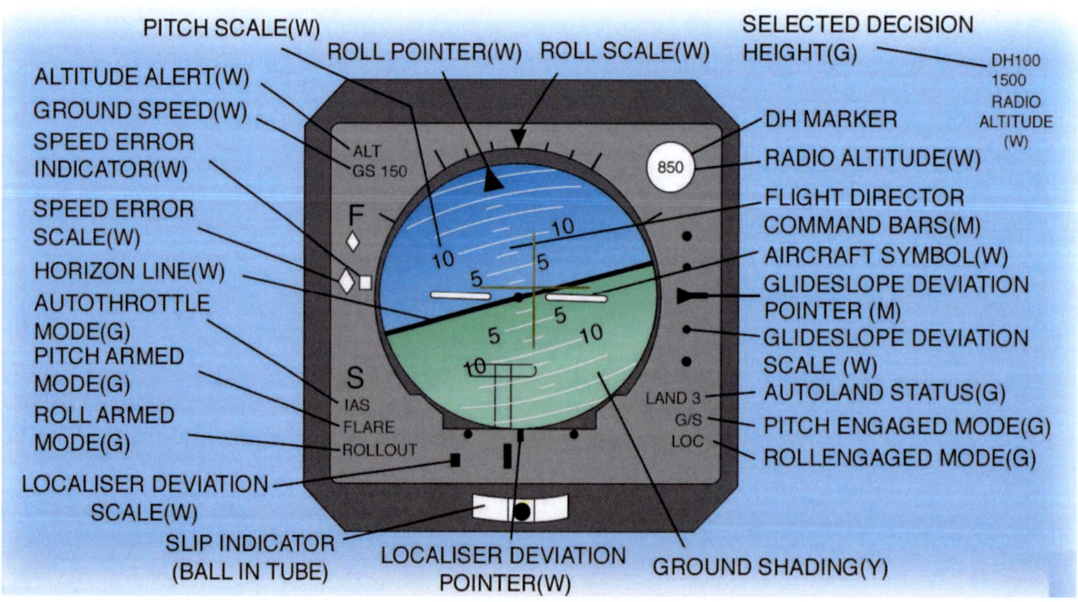

Figure 5.3 ADI/PFD

During pre-flight attitude data is unavailable until the associated IRS has completed alignment and entered the navigation mode. The ATT (attitude) flag does not appear in this case.

A flight director failure in either axis causes the respective command bar to disappear. If both axes become unreliable, both command bars disappear and the FD flag appears. IRS alignment must be completed before flight director commands can be displayed.

When the normal data sources for the ADI are not available an associated Instrument Source Selector Panel provides access to alternate data.

The selected decision height is normally displayed digitally, except from 1 000' to touchdown when the selected decision height is displayed as a decision height marker on the circular radio altitude display.

When below 1 000' RA the digital radio altitude is replaced with a ring and scale representing radio altitude along with a digital altitude readout (as illustrated).

On descent at selected decision height plus 50', an aural alert chime sounds at an increasing rate until reaching the DH. At DH the ring and scale change from white to amber, the DH marker changes from magenta to amber, and ring, scale and DH marker, flash for several seconds

RA display is blank above 2 500' AGL.

The ADI localiser deviation pointer sense is reversed whenever the aircraft's track is more than 90° from the ILS front course. This is to ensure that the ADI deviation pointer is usable on a back-course approach, and to retain compatibility between HSI and ADI localiser deviation directions in all circumstances.

ILS Deviation Monitoring alerts the crew of ILS deviations during an autopilot or flight director approach. With APP selected on the MCP, below 500' AGL, if more than one dot for one second in glideslope deviation or more than one fifth dot for one sec in localiser deviation occurs, the respective localiser or glideslope scales change colour from white to amber and the pointer flashes. This alert condition ceases when localiser and/or glideslope parameters return to within their normal limits.

5.5 Horizontal Situation Indicator

The HSI presents a selectable, dynamic colour display of flight progress and plan view orientation. Various display modes presented include MAP, PLAN, ILS and VOR. Heading is provided by the respected IRS (CAPT HSI - L IRS, F/O HSI - R IRS). The centre IRS is available as an alternate source for that data.

The HSI compass rose is automatically referenced to magnetic north when between 73°N and 60°S latitude with the NORM/TRUE switch in NORM and to true north when above those latitudes. Additionally, the compass rose may be referenced to true north by manually selecting TRUE with the NORM/TRUE switch regardless of the latitude.

TRU is displayed at the top of the HSI enclosed by a white box when the HSI is referenced to True North. When the HSI is referenced to true north and the aircraft descends 2 000' at more than 800 fpm the box changes from white to amber, flashes for 10 s and then remains amber. The box returns to white when the aircraft climbs 2 000' at more than 500 fpm. A green box is displayed around the M for 10 s when the HSI is returned to magnetic referencing.

Track is supplied by the FMC. The opposite FMC is available as an alternate source. If track information from the FMC is unreliable, it is automatically supplied by the IRS.

The MAP mode (see Figure 5.4) presents information against a moving map background. Displayed information includes symbology representing: -

- Heading,
- Routes,
- Curved trend vector,
- Range to altitude,
- Wind,
- Distance,
- Estimated time of arrival.

and selected navigation data points programmed into the Flight Management Computer. You should be familiar with the colours and symbology used and, to this end, an appendix to this chapter provides a comprehensive listing. Note that some symbols will vary from manufacturer to manufacturer.

MAP mode is the recommended mode of display for most phases of flight.

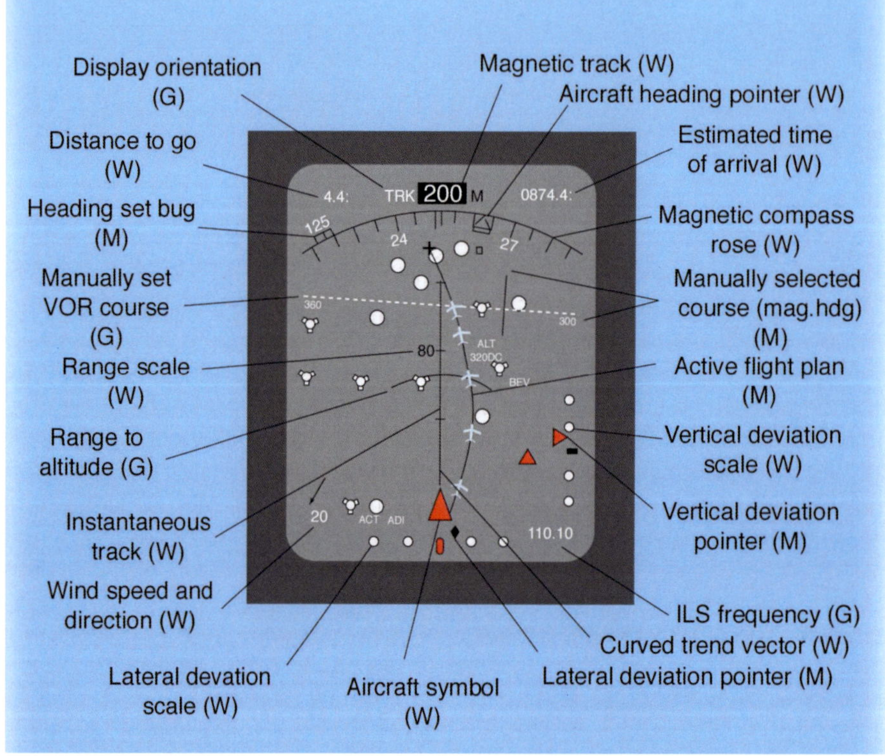

Figure 5.4 MAP Mode

The PLAN mode (see Figure 5.5) presents, on the bottom 2/3 of the HSI a static map background with active route data oriented to True North. Pilot action on the FMC CDU is required to sequence through the active route for viewing. The top part of the HSI maintains a display of track and heading information as in the MAP mode.

Figure 5.5 PLAN Mode

The VOR and ILS modes (see Figure 5.6) present expanded track scale with heading orientation. Wind information, and system source annunciation is provided with conventional VOR/ILS navigation information. A conventional full compass rose VOR and ILS mode is also available.

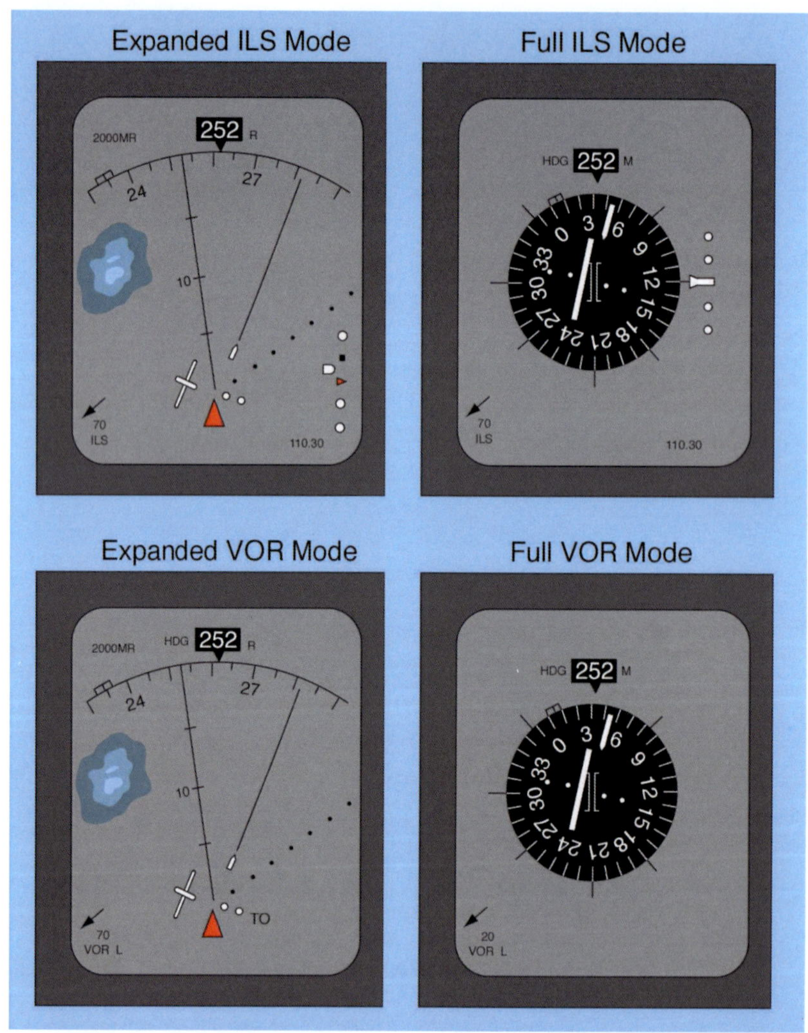

Figure 5.6 VOR/ILS mode display

The HSI displays weather radar data in cyan, green, amber, red and magenta. Red is used for areas of greatest return intensity and therefore the highest risk area for intense turbulence. Reductions in return intensity are indicated by a change of colour from magenta to red to amber then to green.

Cyan and amber are also used for message displays.

Weather radar data can only be displayed when the system is on and the respective HSI is in VOR, ILS or MAP mode.

When Weather radar (Wx) is displayed in VOR or ILS mode, the scale shown applies only to the Wx radar display, and not to the deviation display.

During pre-flight, heading/track data is unavailable until the associated IRS has completed alignment and entered the navigation mode. HDG (heading) flags do not appear in this case.

In addition to previously mentioned EFIS failure indications, other discrepancy messages can be displayed on the HSI. For example WXR/MAP RANGE DISAGREE, indicates both Flight Management Computers and weather radar range disagree with the control panel range data

5.6 Heading Reference Switch

A Heading Reference Switch is installed on the centre instrument panel and permits selection of a magnetic or true heading reference for each HSI, each RMI, each FMC, the Autopilot Flight Director System (AFDS) and each Flight Control Computer (FCC).

The AFDS uses true heading only when the switch is in TRUE. If TRUE is selected when the AFDS is in HDG SEL mode, it changes to HDG HOLD. HDG SEL may be re-selected.

5.7 Appendix

The following symbols can be displayed on each PFD/ND depending on the EFIS control panel switch selection. Symbols can be displayed with different colours but the general colour presentation is as follows:

GREEN (G)	engaged flight mode displays, dynamic conditions
WHITE (W)	present status situation, scales, armed flight mode displays.
MAGENTA (M) pink	command information, pointers, symbols, 'fly-to' condition.
CYAN (C) blue	non-active and background information.
RED (R)	WARNING
AMBER (A)	cautionary information, faults, flags
BLACK (B)	blank areas, 'off' condition.

SYMBOL	NAME & (colour)	MODE APPLICABLE	REMARKS
200NM/4.4 NM or DME124/DME24.6	DISTANCE DISPLAY (W)	PLAN; MAP; Or VOR/ILS	Distance is displayed to next FMC waypoint(nm) or tuned navaid (DME)
HDG 268 M	HEADING Orientation (G) Indicator (W) Reference (G)	PLAN; MAP; Or VOR/ILS	Box displays actual heading. Lat. 73N to 60 S (M) Above those (T)
0835.4	ETA display (M, W)	MAP; PLAN	Indicates ETA at active waypoint based on present GS
	Selected heading marker (M)	PLAN; MAP; Or VOR/ILS	Indicates heading set in MCP. Dotted line extends from marker to aeroplane symbol to assist in tracking marker when it is out

			of view.(except in PLAN)
24 27	Expanded Compass Rose (W)	PLAN; MAP; Or VOR/ILS	Compass data provided from IRS. 360° available but approx. 70°in view.
0 3 6 9 12 15 18 21 24 27 30 33	FULL COMPASS ROSE	FULL VOR FULL ILS	Compass data from selected IRS
80	PRESENT TRACK LINE & RANGE SCALE (W)	MAP;ILS; VOR	Predicts ground track from present heading and winds. Range mark is one half selected range.
	AEROPLANE SYMBOL (W)	MAP; VOR; ILS	Represents the aeroplane and indicates its position at the apex of the triangle.
	AEROPLANE SYMBOL (W)	FULL VOR; FULL ILS	Represents the aeroplane and indicates its position at the centre of the symbol.
AMBOY	WAYPOINT: ACTIVE (M) INACTIVE (W)	MAP; PLAN	Active – Represents the waypoint the aeroplane is currently navigating to. Inactive – Represents a navigation point making up the selected active route.
	ALTITUDE RANGE ARC (G)	MAP	When intersected with the track line, it predicts the point where the reference altitude will be reached.
	TREND VECTOR (W)	MAP	Predicts aeroplane directional trend at the end of 30, 60 and 90-second intervals. Based on back angle and ground speed. 3

			segments are displayed when selected range is greater than 20NM. 2 segments are displayed on the 20NM scale and one segment on the 10NM scale.
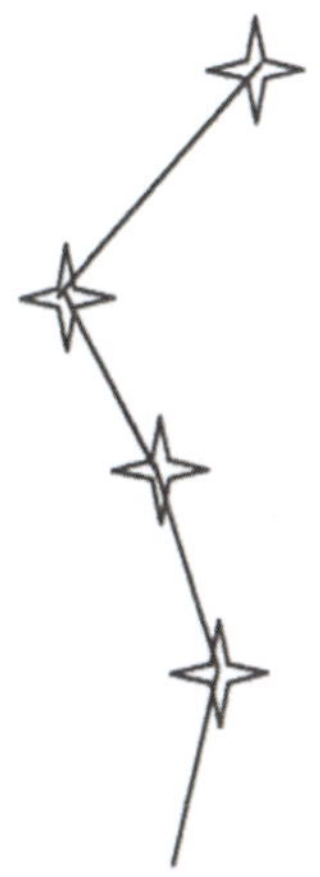	ACTIVE ROUTE (M) ACTIVE ROUTE MODS (W) INACTIVE ROUTES (C)	MAP; PLAN	The active route is displayed with continuous lines (M) between waypoints. Active route modifications are displayed with short dashes (W) between waypoints. When a change is activated in the FMC, the short dashes are replaced with a continuous line. Inactive routes are displayed with long dashes (C) between waypoints.
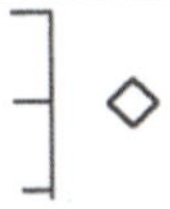	VERTICAL POINTER (M) AND DEVIATION SCALE (W)	MAP	Displays vertical deviation from selected vertical profile (pointer) in MAP mode during descent only. Scale indicates ± 400 feet deviation.
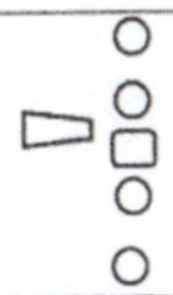	GLIDESLOPE POINTER (M) AND DEVIATION SCALE (W)	ILS	Displays glideslope position and deviation in ILS mode.
	DRIFT ANGLE POINTER (W)	FULL VOR; ILS	Displays difference between FMC track angle and IRS heading.
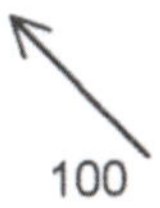 100	WIND SPEED AND DIRECTION (W)	MAP; VOR; ILS	Indicates wind speed in knots and wind direction with respect to the map display orientation and compass reference.

	OFFSET PATH AND IDENTIFIER (M)	MAP; PLAN	Presents a dot-dash line parallel to and offset from the active route after selection on the FMC CDU.
N	NORTH POINTER (G)	PLAN	Indicates map background is oriented and referenced to true north.
O T/D	ALTITUDE PROFILE POINT AND IDENTIFIER (G)	MAP	Represents an FMC calculated point and is labelled on the flight plan as, T/C (top of climb), **T/D** (top of descent) and S/C (step climb).
	WEATHER (G,A,R) MAPPING RADAR RETURNS (G,A,R)	MAP; VOR; ILS	Multicoloured returns are presented when either WXR On switch is pushed. Most intense areas are displayed in red. Lesser intensity amber and lowest intensity green.
	HOLDING PATTERN (M)	MAP; PLAN	A fixed size holding pattern symbol appears when a hold entered in RTE. The pattern increases to the correct size when the HSI range is 80 or less and the aircraft passes the waypoint prior to the holding pattern.
	PROCEDURE TURN (M)	MAP; PLAN	A fixed size procedure turn symbol appears when entered in the RTE. The symbol increases to the correct size when HSI range is 80 or less ad the aeroplane passes the waypoint prior to the procedure turn.

Symbol	Name	Mode	Remarks
 KJFK 22R	AIRPORT IDENTIFIER AND RUNWAY (W)	MAP; PLAN	Appears when selected on FMC CDU. Available when HSI range is 80, 160 or 320NM.
	AIRPORT AND RUNWAY(W)	MAP; PLAN	Appears when selected on FMC CDU. Available when HSI range is 10, 20 or 40NM. Dashed line represents a 14.2 NM extended runway centre line ending at threshold.
 **ABC**	SELECTED FIX CIRCLE (G) SYMBOL AND IDENTIFIER	MAP; PLAN	Presents a selected reference point (fix) via the FMC CDU FIX key. Can appear with any number of special map symbols (i.e. VOR, VORTAC, airport or waypoint, etc.) if contained in the existing data base.
 **ABC 150/35**	DOWN TRACK FIX (DNTKFX) conditional (W) active conditional (M)	MAP; PLAN	Defines the intersection of selected fix radials and present track. Appears with fix identifier and route data.
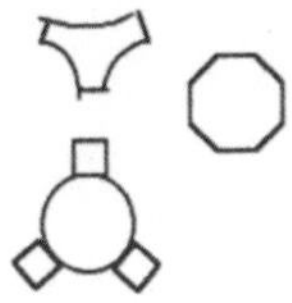	VOR (C) DME/TACAN (C) VORTAC (C)	MAP	When NAVAID switch is ON, all appropriate navaids in range appear in addition to those navaids which are standard or active waypoints and those which are tuned (G)
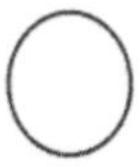 **KBOS**	AIRPORT (C)	MAP	When the ARPT switch is ON, airports within the map area are displayed. Origin and destination airports are always displayed independent of ARPT switch.
 **KILMR 12000 0835Z**	ROUTE DATA (M, W)	MAP; PLAN	When the RTE DATA switch is ON, altitude and ETA for route

			waypoints can be displayed
△ **ARK**	OFF ROUTE WAYPOINT (C)	MAP	When WPT switch is ON, database waypoints not on the selected route are displayed.
	COURSE INDICATOR (M) AND DEVIATION SCALE	VOR; ILS; FULL VOR, ILS	Displays ILS course when ILS mode is selected and valid signals are present. VOR course is displayed when VOR mode is selected and valid signals are present.
VOR L/R ILS	SOURCE NAV DATA (G)	VOR; ILS	Displays source of nav radio data based on EFI control selection.
	SELECTED COURSE POINTER (W) AND LINE (M)	VOR; ILS	Displayed selected course as appropriately set by the VOR course selector or ILS Front Course Selector.

Self-Assessment Test 5

1. A typical EFIS installation consists of the following components:
A) A FMS, two signal generators, one ADI and one PND
B) Three signal generators, two control panels, two ADI and two HSI
C) Two signal generators, one control panel and two HSI
D) Three vital service busbars, two ADI and two HSI

2. When the LIGHTS TEST switch is pressed, the:
A) TESK OK, or TEST FAIL message together with the name of the failed component appears at the end of the test only
B) Multi functional display located on the ADI only is switched to TEST mode and the failed component is highlighted
C) Multi functional display located on the HSI only is switched to TEST mode and the failed component is highlighted
D) ADI and HSI display a maintenance test pattern, a TEST OK or TEST FAIL message together with the name of the failed component appears at the end of the test

3. If the normal data sources for an ADI are not available:
A) Alternate data is switched to the relevant ADI by selections made on an associated Source Selector Panel
B) No alternate data is available and the facility is lost
C) Alternate data is only available in flight and is switched from the associated Source Selector Panel
D) TEST modes, operative on the ground only, are used to pinpoint the failed component. No alternate data is available

4. The Radio Altitude Indicator is ordinarily blank above:
A) 3 000’
B) 1 000’
C) 2 500’
D) 850’

5. Localiser and Glideslope scales change from white to amber and the pointers flash when:
A) Localiser and glideslope deviations occur which exceed a specific safe tolerance
B) Localiser and glideslope deviations occur which remain within capture limits
C) Localiser and glideslope signals deviations have been corrected and are now within tolerance
D) Localiser and glideslope signals have failed and pointer deviations should be ignored

6. The radio altitude digital read out is replaced with a ring and scale below:
A) 500’
B) 1 000’
C) 2 000’
D) 2 000’

7. When within 50' of the selected DH:
A) An aural alert whistle sounds until DH, at DH the ring and scale change from blue to amber with series numbers and the ring, scale and symbols remain lit continuously until touch down
B) An aural alert horn sounds until DH, at DH the ring and scale change from amber to white, the DH marker changes from blue to green and all symbols flash red for thirty seconds
C) An anural alert chimes until DH, at DH the ring and scale change from white to amber, the DH marker changes from magenta to amber and the ring, scale and DH marker flash for several seconds
D) A visual marker flashes red and green, at DH the ring and scale change from amber to green, the DH marker changes from purple to amber and the DH ring and scale and DH marker flash for several seconds

8. Fail operational with regard to autopilots means that:
A) Duplex control will only disconnect an autopilot if there is a disturbance to the aircraft flight path
B) That if one failure in a system occurs there will be no degradation of performance nor any disturbance to the aircraft flight path
C) The failed system is isolated but only after a change in aircraft flight path has been detected
D) A triplex system will only detect a failure is there is a disturbance to the aircraft flight path

9. Fail soft is the ability of a system to:
A) Fail but without producing excessive deviations from the aircraft flight path
B) Withstand failures in duplicate operation so as to leave the aircraft in a safe attitude
C) Constantly monitor inputs and outputs to the autopilot to ensure monitoring of the system
D) Re-arrange AFCS software to enable adjustment to be made to system commands for stability purposes

10. When the HSI is selected to the expanded ILS mode:
A) Holding patterns can be displayed
B) Radar returns cannot be displayed
C) A full size compass rose is displayed
D) Only the appropriate compass rose arc is displayed on the instrument

11. The triangle symbol represents:
A) A selected course pointer and is available on the ADI when VOR or ILS is selected; it is coloured magenta
B) An active waypoint and is available on the HSI when MAP, PLAN or VOR is selected; it is coloured green
C) An inactive VOR beacon and is available on the ADI when MAP, VOR or ILS is selected and is coloured red
D) The aeroplane and indicates its position at the apex of the triangle; it is available on the HSI when MAP, VOR or ILS is selected and is coloured white

12. The triangle symbol represents:
A) The waypoint to which the aircraft is currently navigating or an inactive waypoint; it is coloured magenta or white respectively; it is available on the HSI when in the MAP or PLAN mode
B) An inactive waypoint and is coloured blue; it is available on the ADI when ILS, VOR or weather radar is selected
C) An aeroplane symbol, it is coloured green and is available when MAP, ILS or VOR is selected; it is located on the ADI
D) A drift angle pointer; it is coloured green, it is in view at all times and is located on the HSI

Self-Assessment Test 5 Answers

1	B
2	D
3	A
4	C
5	A
6	B
7	C
8	B
9	A
10	D
11	D
12	A

CHAPTER 6
Flight Management Systems

6.1 Role of FMS

Essentially, the FMS accepts information, processes that information to provide either or both of the following:

- Performance advisory functions
- Full flight management

In the advisory role, the system advises the flight crew as to the optimum settings to use in order to obtain the optimum performance. The flight crew must manipulate the controls in order to maximise the available benefits. Most early FMS units were restricted to this role.

In the 'flight management' role, the FMS is interfaced with the engine 'Power Management Control' (PMC) and the Automatic Flight Control System (AFCS).

This isolates the flight crew from the control loop and allows the FMS to act in a totally integrated fashion providing optimum control of engine power and total flight path control.

Modern FMS units can operate in the advisory role but are capable of providing a full flight management. Indeed, their primary functions are to manage:

- Aeroplane performance
- Flight planning
- Navigation
- Three-dimensional guidance

The advisory role is a secondary function. In this role, it feeds suitable flight deck displays, such as a map (for orientation) and bugs on the ASI and EPR gauges (to assist in manually flying precise flight profiles). This relieves the flight crew so that they can attend more closely to the tasks of monitoring and decision making.

The tasks that can be conducted by a modern FMS within a totally integrated system are illustrated below.

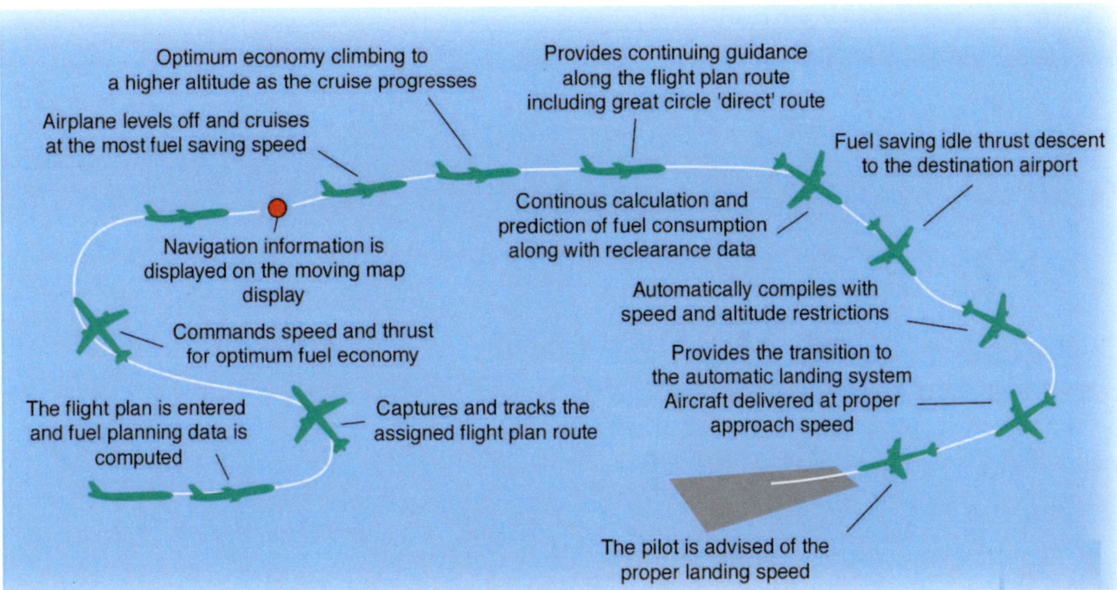

Figure 6.1 Practical use of the FMS

It is obvious that the FMS is now a major piece of equipment and yet, repeatedly, it is the unit that appears to be the most misused and, in many cases, most misunderstood. Let us see if we can remove some of the mystery and make you confident in its function, abilities and use.

6.2 FMS Components

An FMS will consist of two major units:

- Flight Management Computer (FMC)
- Command Display Unit (CDU)

The CDU is the means by which the flight crew can communicate with the computer. Figure 6.2 illustrates a typical CDU.

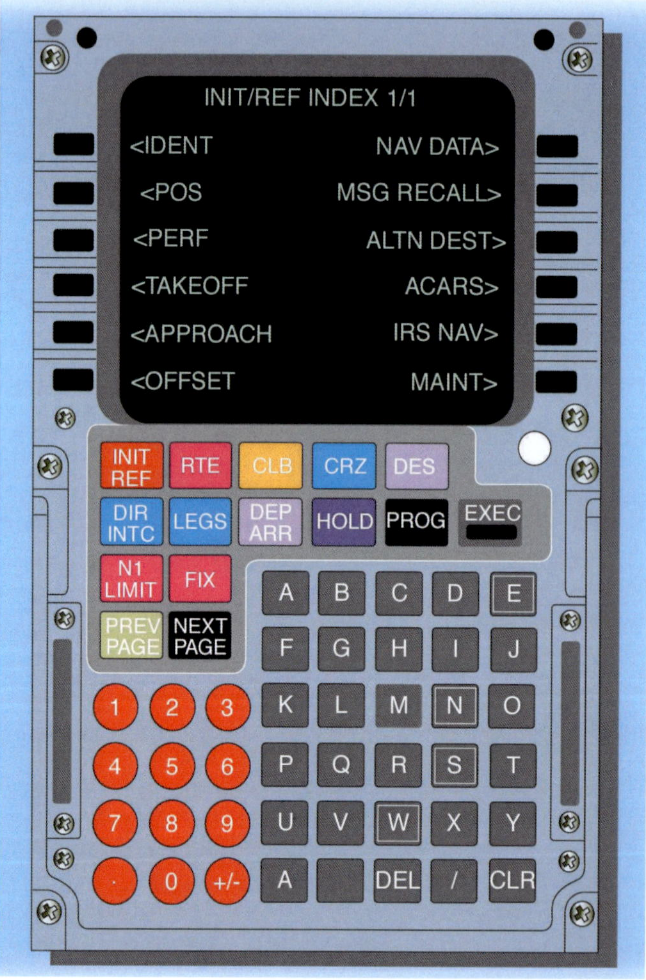

Figure 6.2 CDU

The upper part of the control display unit is dominated by an alpha/numeric CRT screen while the lower part has a keyboard. Using this keyboard, the plot can enter the desired vertical and lateral flight plan data into the FMC.

The FMC combines the pilot-entered information stored in its memory and information fed from external sources (e.g. navigation data, air data and engine data). From this information the computer calculates the present position and derives pitch, roll and thrust commands that will optimise the flight profile.
The computer will send these commands to the AFCS and PMC and will transmit the advisory information to the flight deck displays.

On a totally integrated system there are two other control panels which we need to consider. These are:

- the AFCS Mode Control Panel (MCP)
- the EFIS Control Panel (ECP)

Figure 6.3 illustrates the information flow to, within and from the FMS components.

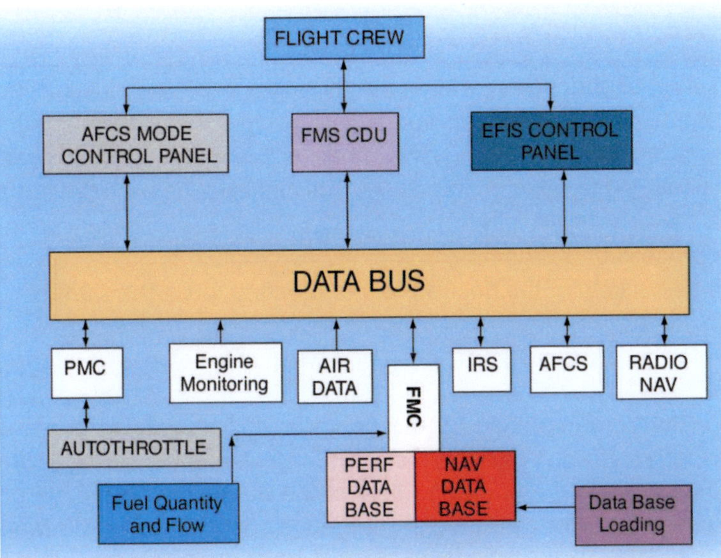

Figure 6.3 FMS inputs

On most modern aeroplanes there are two FMS units. These are usually arranged as illustrated below.

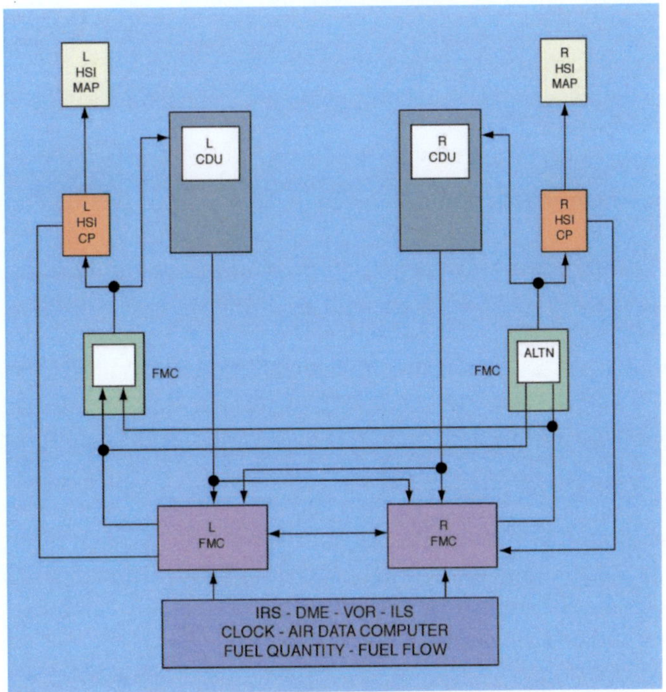

Figure 6.4 Inputs to the entire system

By virtue of the cross-coupling, loading data into one CDU will feed both FMC's. It is therefore advisable to nominate one CDU for data loading while using the other to monitor or cross check the data being loaded. In this arrangement each CDU and EFIS map display will relate to its own computer, i.e. left FMC feeds left CDU and left EFIS. If the FMC switch is placed to "ALTN" position, the related CDU and EFIS displays will be connected to the other computer. This level of interconnection enables all functions to be achieved provided at least one CDU and one FMC is operating.

6.3 CDU and FMC Terminology

"Active" refers to flight plan information that is currently being used to calculate lateral (LNAV) or vertical (VNAV) guidance commands. For example; the active waypoint is the point the system is currently navigating toward; the active performance (VNAV) mode is the climb, cruise or descent speed schedule currently being used for pitch and thrust commands. ACT is displayed in associated page titles.

"Activate" refers to the process of designating one of the two routes as active. It's a two step process. First, push the ACTIVATE line select key for the desired routes. Second, push the illuminated EXEC key.

"Altitude Constraint" refers to a crossing restriction at a waypoint.

"Cost Index" is a figure that is determined by the operator and is used to bias the computations for the speed schedule. It is based on a trade off to get the optimum balance between minimum fuel and least time. The index is determined by dividing the operating cost of the aeroplane by the cost of fuel. If fuel costs are high the number is low. A cost index of zero results in an econ speed equal to the maximum range speed.

"Econ" refers to a speed schedule that is calculated to minimise the operating cost of the aeroplane. The economy speed is based on a cost index that is entered into the CDU during pre-flight.

"Enter" refers to the process of typing or line selecting characters into the CDU scratch pad line and then line selecting the desired location for the data.

"Erase" refers to removing modified data from the system by pushing the line select key adjacent to the word ERASE.

"Execute" refers to making entered data part of the active flight plan by pushing the illuminated EXEC key.

"Inactive" refers to route, climb cruise or descent information that is not currently being used to calculate LNAV or VNAV commands.

"Initialise" refers to the process of entering data into the CDU that is required to make the system operative.

"Message" refers to information the system automatically writes in the scratch pad to inform the pilot of some condition.

"Modified" refers to active data that has been changed. When modification is made to the active route or performance mode, MOD is displayed in associated page title, ERASE appears next to one of the line select keys and the EXEC key illuminates. Pushing the ERASE line select key removes the modification. Pushing the EXEC key changes the modified data to the active status.

"Prompt" refers to something displayed on the CDU to aid the pilot in accomplishing a task. It may be some boxes or dashes to remind the pilot to enter information on the associated line, or perhaps a word to indicate what action is required next.

"Resynchronisation" is the automatic process of one FMC loading data in the other when a significant difference between the two FMC's is detected.

"Select" refers to pushing a key to obtain the desired data or action.

"Speed Restriction" refers to a pilot entered airspeed limit below a specified altitude.

"Speed Transition" refers to an automatically entered airspeed limit below a specified altitude.

"Waypoint" refers to a point in the route. It may be a fixed point such as a latitude and longitude, VOR or NDB station, intersection on an airway, or a conditional point. An example of a conditional point is "when reaching 1000'".

6.4 Flight Management Computer (FMC)

The FMC will normally include three different types of memory as follows:

Bubble Memory	holding the bulk of the navigation and performance data base
RAM	holding specific navigation and performance data down loaded from the Bubble Memory
PROM	holding the operating programme. This can be altered by CDU input

The two data bases held in the Bubble Memory are of fundamental importance.

The Performance database provides the FMC with the data required to calculate pitch and thrust commands

Additionally, the relevant data can be displayed and this reduces the need for the pilot to refer to a performance manual during flight. The data stored includes:

- aeroplane drag characteristics
- engine performance characteristics
- maximum, optimum, minimum altitudes
- speeds and speed limits

Your maintenance group can refine this data, for individual aeroplanes, by entering correction factors for drag and fuel flow.

The Navigation database contains numerous elements of data related to the normal operational area of the operator and type of aeroplane

Each data package is originated in the Flight Operations department and is loaded onto a magnetic tape. Then, using a portable data transfer unit connected to the FMC, the data is loaded into the Bubble memory.

There are normally two Navigation Databases – one active and one inactive. To cover changes in navigational data and procedures, each navigation database is renewed at intervals not exceeding 28 days

The navigation database contains items such as:

ITEM	DATA HELD
Radio Aids	identifier; position; frequency; type of aid; DME elevation; VOR magnetic variation; ILS category and centre line bearing; Maximum distance aid can be tuned (at normal cruise altitude)
Waypoints	ICAO identifier; type (en-route/terminal) Position (latitude/longitude)
En-route Airways	designator; outboard magnetic course
Airports	ICAO four letter identifier; position; elevation; alternates
Runways	ICAO identifier; number; length; heading; threshold position; final approach fix (FAF) Ident; Any threshold displacement.
Airport Procedures	ICAO code; type (SID, STAR, ILS, RNAV etc) runway number/ transmission; path and termination code.
Company Route	origin airport; destination airport; route number; details of SID, route, STAR, approach.

6.5 The CDU

As explained, the CDU is the interface between the crew and the computer systems. The appearance and arrangement of CDUs will vary slightly from type to type but if you are familiar with one you will find it considerably easier to develop a good level of understanding of another quite rapidly.

We will use a fairly representative model in our studies here. Figure 6.5 illustrates our model and labels the relevant portions.

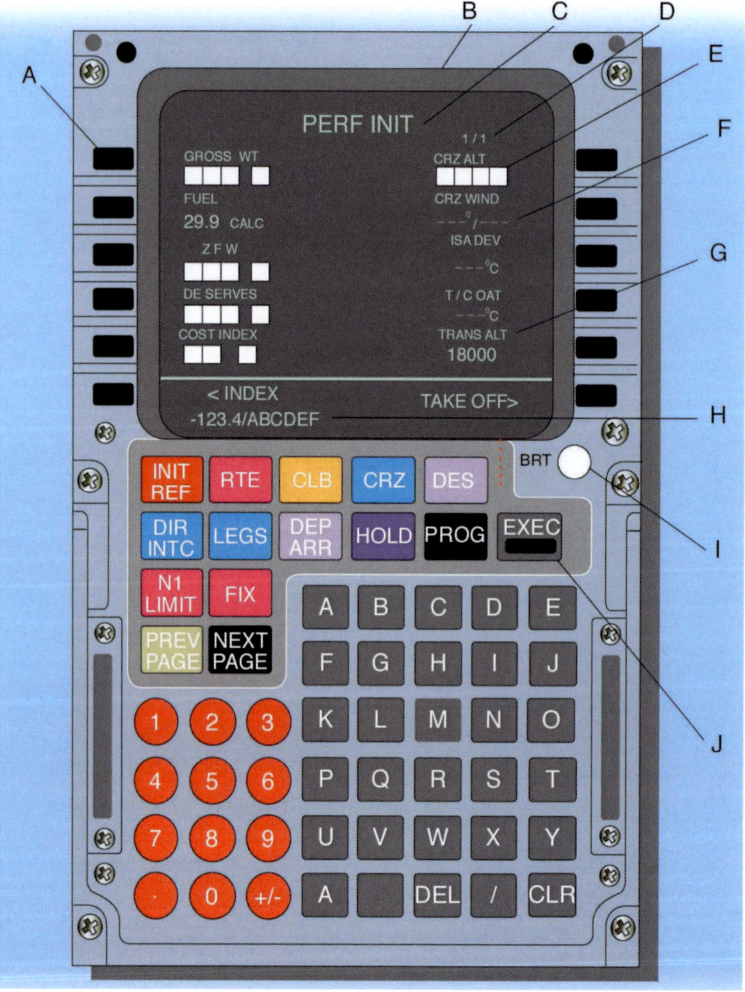

Figure 6.5CDU

A – Line Select Keys. (Six Each side of screen) Push to select or enter data on adjacent line.

B – CDU Display. Displays page of data selected by function, mode or Line Select key.

C – Page Title. Indicates type of data displayed. When in lateral or vertical navigation modes displays ACT or MOD to indicate status of page.

D – Page Number. First digit represents page number. Second digit indicates total number of related pages.

E – Boxes. Indicates data required by the FMC for full navigation capability. Data will be entered from scratch pad using Line Select key.

F – Dashes. Indicates data entry is required by the system. If known, the data should be keyed in and transferred from the scratch pad using the appropriate Line Select key.

G – Line Title. Indicates type of data on lie. Will be blank if data is not recognised by the FMC.

H – Scratch Pad Line. This is the bottom line of the display. Displays: -

- System generated messages to the Crew
- All keyboard entries (before they are transferred to the required line).
- Data being moved from one line to another

I – Display brightness control.

J – Function and Mode Keys. This block of keys allows selection of data for display or executes changes. It provides a rapid access to the data most often used.

Now that we are familiar with the role of the FMS and its appearance, the next logical step is to look at how we use it. In this we will assume that a twin unit, configured as we saw in Figure 6.4, is what we are working on.

6.6 CDU Operation

The following descriptions are generic in their application. FMS units vary from type to type and you must be sure that you are totally familiar with the type to which you are converting. During your conversion course you must spend time on this familiarisation process using both the operations manual and the fixed base simulator or other training device available. Remember that, like so many of the good things in life, "hands on" practice is best.

6.6.1 General Rules

These rules are drawn up to assist you in making full and effective use of the FMS.

- To avoid errors, work in a slow deliberate manner while operating the CDU. Avoid pushing more than one key at a time. Avoid entering data in both CDUs at the same time. Do not push CDU keys when the system is going through a resynchronisation. Resynchronisations take about 30 s to complete. During this time one map and CDU shows a failed condition while the other CDU displays the RESYNCING OTHER FMC message.
- When selecting a CDU page read the page title to ensure the correct page appears.
- Check that the scratch pad line is blank before trying to enter data on the line. Use the CLR key as required to blank the scratch pad.
- When entering data on the scratch pad line ensure that it is correct before continuing with the procedure.
- Use care when pushing line select keys to ensure the correct key is being pushed.
- Confirm that data displayed on the CDU is correct before pushing the EXEC key. If an error has been made, correct the erroneous data or push the ERASE line select key and then restart the procedure. Data cannot be entered on a blank line.
- Messages that commonly indicate an error has been made are:- NOT IN DATABASE, INVALID ENTRY and INVALID DELETE.

6.6.2 Pre-Flight

During pre-flight, information from the flight plan and load sheet is entered into the CDU. This information defines the starting point of the flight for initialisation of the inertial reference systems, the desired route to the destination to initialise LNAV, and performance information to initialise VNAV. If necessary, the CDU may be used to modify the flight plan while in flight.

Although the CDU may display many pages of information, proper page selection is not difficult.

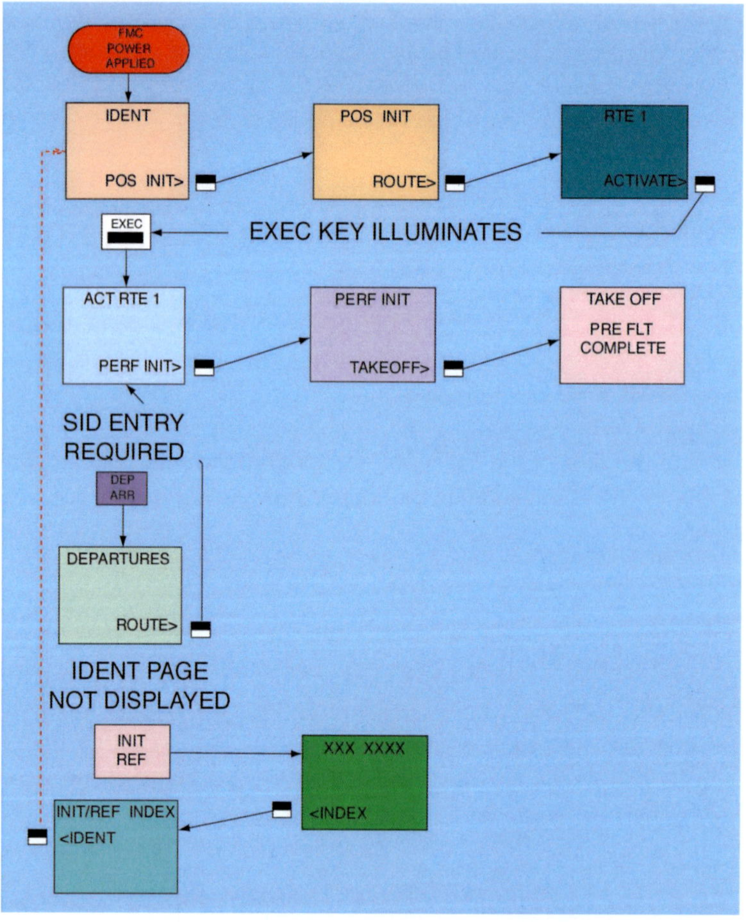

Figure 6.6 "Start-up" Page Sequences

Automatic display of some pages, as well as visual prompts on the CDU, provides assistance in selecting the appropriate page for most tasks. For example, the diagram at Figure 6.6 illustrates how, at initial electrical power application, the CDU displays the appropriate page for starting the pre-flight.

After checking and entering the necessary data on each pre-flight page, the lower right line select key is pushed to select the next page. When ACTIVATE is selected on the route page the EXEC key illuminates. The EXEC key should then be pushed to complete the task of making the route active before continuing the sequence.

If a Standard Instrument Departure (SID) must be entered into the route the DEP/ARR key is pushed. After selecting the desired SID the lower right line select key is again used to proceed with the pre-flight sequence.

When the TAKEOFF REF page is reached it displays PRE-FLT COMPLETE in confirmation that all required pre-flight entries have been made.

If the IDENT page is not displayed at the beginning of the pre-flight, (this will occur on occasions such as during a through flight) the lower part of the diagram shows how the IDENT page can be selected by starting with the INIT. REF (initialisation) key.

6.6.3 En-route

In-flight the CDU is used to modify the flight plan and display navigation and performance information.

The first step is to select the appropriate page of data by pushing the Function/Mode key that says what you want to do. For example, DIR - go direct; CLB - change climb conditions; HOLD - enter or exit holding pattern, etc. Then, if required, enter the desired modification.

For example, to fly from present position direct to a waypoint, push the DIR/INTC key and enter the waypoint in the box prompts that appear. Or to answer a "what if" type question, select the page that displays the desired information and enter the modified conditions. The CDU then displays predictions of what will happen if the modification is executed. The pilot then has the option of erasing or executing the modification.

6.6.3.1 Lateral Navigation

LNAV guidance outputs from the FMC are normally great circle courses between the waypoints that make up the active route. However, when a procedure stored in the FMC database is entered into the active route the FMC can supply commands to maintain a constant heading, track or follow a DME arc, as required to comply with the procedure.

The FMC determines present position using inputs from the IRS, DME, VOR and localizer receivers. The FMC uses its calculated present position to generate lateral steering commands along the active leg to the active waypoint.

While the aeroplane is on the ground the FMC calculates present position based only on data received from the IRS systems. To function the FMC requires a present position input from at least one IRS. Since inertial systems accumulate position errors as a function of time, the position information being used by the FMC is slowly accumulating errors. These position errors can be detected by observing the position of the aeroplane on the HSI map. If an extended ground delay occurs and a significant map error is noticed the IRS should be realigned and present position re-entered.

While the aeroplane is in flight the FMC refines its position calculations based on inputs from the three IRS, DME, VOR, and ILS. The refinement of position calculations is made by use of two DME stations, if available, or one DME and one co-located VOR. During an ILS approach the position can also be refined by use of localizer signals.

Normally the FMC automatically tunes the VOR and DME to provide the best available signals for updating the FMC calculated present position. However, the pilot can select frequencies manually and the FMC can continue to use the signals for position updating.

6.6.3.2 Vertical Navigation

6.6.3.2.1 Climb and Cruise

After takeoff, VNAV mode will engage after a thrust reference other than take off is selected and the MCP altitude window is set to an altitude above the aeroplane. Once VNAV is engaged, the MCP may be set to any altitude, even below the aeroplane, without causing a level off; VNAV mode disengages however, if the MCP altitude is intercepted before reaching the FMC cruise altitude.

The VNAV profile that the FMC commands, if not modified by the pilot, is a climb with climb thrust at the airspeed limit associated with the origin airport until above the limit altitude, then climb at economy speed to the entered cruise altitude. During climb, remain within all altitude constraints that are part of a SID entered into the active route. Cruise at economy speed until reaching the top of descent point. Thrust is limited to maximum cruise thrust.

If flying the climb speed profile would cause a violation of an altitude constraint the UNABLE NEXT ALT message appears. The pilot must manually select a different speed that provides a steeper climb angle.

The diagram at Figure 6.7 shows a climb profile containing waypoint altitude constraints and a lapped transition with a limit of 250 KT below 10 000'. The diagram also shows normal mode annunciations that appear on the ADI.

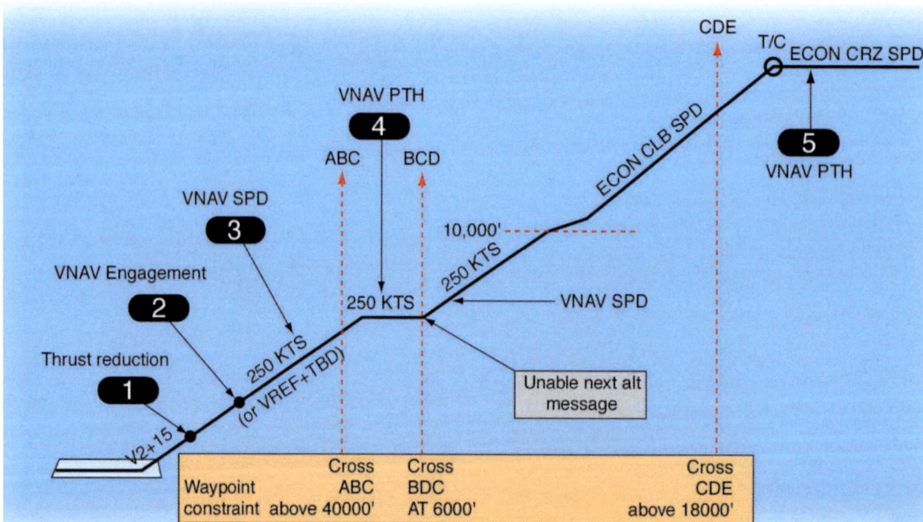

Figure 6.7 Climb profile

6.6.3.2.2 Descent

When a (E/D) point is entered the FMC calculates a descent path. (An E/D is a waypoint altitude constraint that requires a descent from cruise altitude. The E/D normally is entered on the "legs" page as a result of selecting a STAR or APPROACH).

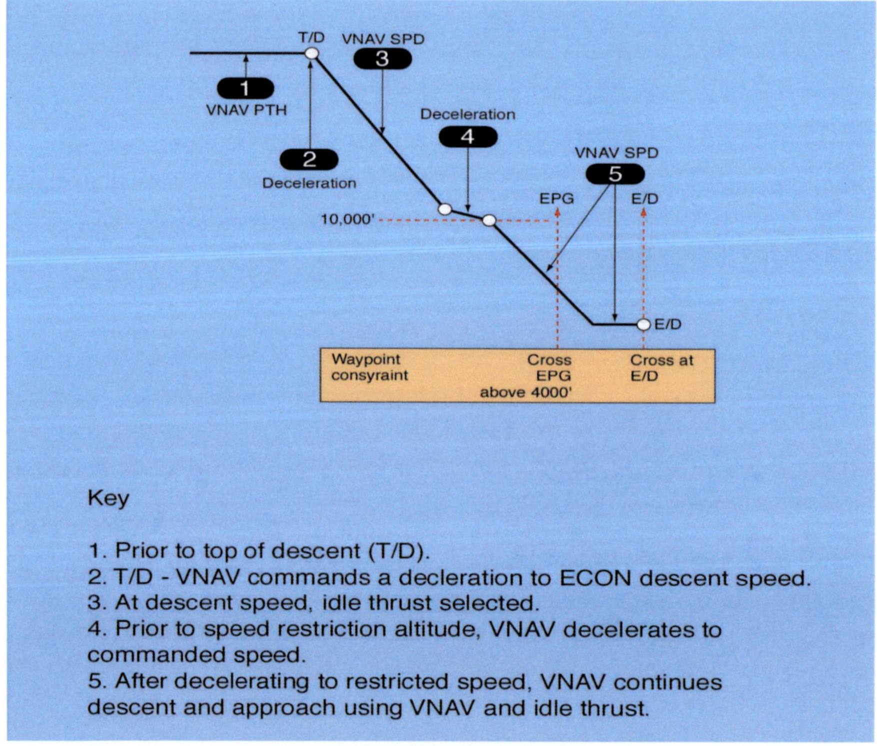

Figure 6.8 Descent path

The descent path (Figure 6.8) begins at the calculated TOD and passes over waypoints so as to comply with altitude constraints. The path to the first constraint assumes the use of idle thrust, speed brakes retracted, a wind speed that decreases with altitude and the appropriate target speed. Normally, the target speed is economy above 10 000' and 240 KT below 10 000' until necessary to begin a deceleration to reach the final approach fix (FAF) inbound at 170 KT. Target speeds may be changed by entries on the legs or descent page. Wind and thrust assumptions may be changed on the descent forecast page.

If the MCP is set to an altitude below the aeroplane, when the TOD point is reached the FMC commands idle thrust and pitch to track the descent path. VNAV disengages if MCP altitude is reached before the lowest altitude constraint. During descent the MCP may be set to an altitude above the aeroplane without VNAV disengaging or stopping the descent.

If an unexpected (not entered on descent forecast page) headwind is encountered, that causes a significant decrease in airspeed, thrust increases to regain the target speed. If the auto-throttle is not engaged, a THRUST REQUIRED message is displayed. If an unexpected tailwind is encountered, that causes a significant increase in airspeed, the DRAG REQUIRED message is displayed. If airspeed reaches a limit the aeroplane flies the limit speed even if it must leave the path.

For VFR and non-precision approaches, the FMC computed path is built to a point that is 50' over the approach end of the runway. It is the pilot's responsibility not to descend below MDA until adequate visual contact has been achieved. At the missed approach point the vertical profile initiates a climb to the missed approach altitude, using climb thrust.

6.7 Operational Notes

When operating in LNAV and VNAV modes, monitor system operation for undesired pitch, roll or thrust commands. If undesired operation is noticed switch over to the heading select and flight level change modes.

The system should be carefully monitored for errors following activation of a new data base, resynchronisation, power interruption or IRS failure.

During twin IRS operation each FMC uses a different IRS for position calculations. The IRS positions are not averaged as during normal operation. This can result in a difference between the two HSI maps and descent paths when radio updating is not available.

When operating significantly off the active route, the active waypoint may not change as it is passed. When the LNAV mode is armed it can only capture the active leg. It will not capture an inactive leg in the active route. The DIRECT TO or INTERCEPT LEG/COURSE TO procedures may by used to make the desired leg active.

When the same waypoint is used more than once in the route, certain route modifications (such as DIRECT TO and HOLD) use the first waypoint.

Some standard instrument departures contain a heading vector leg. These show on the CDU LEGS page as a VECTORS waypoint and on the map as a magenta line leading away form the aeroplane symbol or waypoint. If VNAV mode is engaged, the DIRECT TO or INTERCEPT LEG/COURSE TO procedure may be used to restore waypoint sequencing.

When entering airways into a route page the beginning and ending waypoint must be in the database. Otherwise the route segment must be entered as a DIRECT leg.

Occasionally a procedure in the database contains a hidden discontinuity that appears on the LEGS page as ---- for the inbound course.

If an ILS procedure is entered into the active route, and it contains a leg to intercept the inbound course, LNAV mode will not sequence past the (INTERCEPT) waypoint until the LOC. mode engages.

If engines are not shutdown on landing, a cruise altitude entry must be made prior to the next flight to ensure that the vertical profile is rebuilt. If in descent and a diversion to another airport is entered, a cruise altitude entry must be made to rebuild the vertical profile.

When operating outside the FMC navigation database area the following operating characteristics will be noticed:

Origin, destination and runways can not be entered into the route. However, any origin that is in the database may be entered. An origin entry is required for VNAV operation.

All waypoints must be entered as latitudes and longitudes.

The FMC will not use radio signals to update its calculated position and will not tune the VOR or DME.

The HSI may cannot display airports navaids or waypoints that are not in route.

6.8 Fuel Monitoring

The FMC receives fuel data from the fuel quantity system and EICAS.

The fuel quantity system provides a totaliser value that is displayed on Progress Page 2. When this value is displayed on the Performance Initialisation Page it is labelled SENSED.

The FMC also calculates a fuel quantity. Prior to engine start the calculated value is set to agree and track the totaliser value unless the pilot makes a manual fuel quantity entry. When the FMC receives a positive fuel flow signal (engine start) the calculated value is disconnected from the fuel quantity system until the engines are shutdown after the next flight. After start the calculated value decreases at the rate the fuel flow signals indicate. The calculated value is displayed on Progress Page 2. The calculated value is also displayed on the Performance Initialisation page where it is labelled CALC unless a manual entry of fuel quantity is made. In that case it's labelled MANUAL.

If fuel is loaded after the FMC receives a positive fuel flow signal the calculated value will not include the new fuel loaded. This could occur if the engines are shutdown at one location, then restarted to taxi to the fuelling location. Normal operation can be restored by making a manual Fuel quantity entry on the Performance Initialisation Page followed by deletion of the manual entry.

The fuel flow signals are also used for calculating the fuel used by the engines. FUEL USED is displayed on Progress page 2 and is reset to zero following a flight and then shutdown of both engines.

Beginning with engine start, the FMC monitors the fuel load on board as detected by the fuel quantity system totaliser and as calculated by the FMC using fuel flow inputs. If the FMC determines a significant difference between the totaliser and calculated values the FUEL QTY ERROR-PROG 2/2 message is displayed on the CDU scratch pad. The pilot may then select which value the FMC should use for fuel calculations for the remainder of the flight. The FMC also continually estimates the amount of fuel that will remain when the destination airport is reached if the active route is flown. If the estimate is less than the fuel reserve value entered on the Performance Initialisation Page the INSUFFICIENT FUEL message is displayed.

6.9 Flight Control and Management Summary

This paragraph is inserted to assist you to bring all these concepts together.

The FMS is capable of commanding the aircraft along a pre-selected lateral (navigation) and vertical path (performance), shortly after takeoff until the system captures the localiser and glideslope. A typical FMC receives twenty-four digital inputs and three discrete inputs, and outputs to nine different digital customers.

The FMC performs seven major functions (typical):

1. The input/output function of the FMC receives and transmits digital data to and from the various systems on board the aircraft, and checks that all received data is valid.
2. The CDU function of the FMC, formats updates and sends data to the CDU fix display, and provides alerting and advisory messages to the CDU for display on the scratch pad.
3. The bit and vc monitoring function of the FMC performs a self-test of the FMC during power up and upon request. It continuously monitors the FMS during normal operation. Failures would be recorded (on the memory disk) for retrieval at a later date.
4. The navigation function of the FMC houses the navigation data base, and is responsible for computing the aircraft's current position, velocity and altitude. It also selects and automatically tunes the VOR receivers and DME interrogators. The navigation function computes the aircraft's present position by determining the distance to two auto-tuned DME stations and GNSS, if installed. Positional information from the three IRUs is used to solve any ambiguity that may occur, or as a prime source when the aircraft is on the ground. Velocity is computed using IRU inputs, and altitude is computed using both IRU and ADC inputs.
5. The performance function of the FMC computes performance parameters (limits) and predictions for the vertical path of the flight profile, utilising the performance database and the CDU input data.
6. The guidance function stores the active vertical and lateral flight plan input from the CDU. Using the present aircraft velocity and position information calculated by the navigation function, the guidance function compares actual and desired position, and generates steering commands which are input to the appropriate flight control computer (FCC). Using the current computed vertical profile data from the performance function, the guidance function compares actual and desired altitude and altitude rate, and generates pitch and thrust commands which are input to the appropriate FCC and the thrust management computer (TMC).
7. The EFIS function of the FMC provides dynamic and background data to the EFIS symbol generator, and provides the navigation function with a list of the closest NAV aid array for auto tuning.

Self-Assessment Test 6

1. In the management role a FMS interfaces with the:
A) AFCS, PMC, FDC, HSI and ADI
B) ADI and HSI
C) PMC and the AFCS
D) AFCS and the FDC

2. The FMS consists of two major components, the:
A) ADI and HSI
B) PMS and HSI
C) AFCS and the PMC
D) Flight Management Computer (FMC) and the Command and Display Unit (CDU)

3. After take-off, VNAV will engage when:
A) A thrust setting other than take-off power is set and the altitude selected is, initially, above the aircraft current height
B) A steering command is initiated and the altitude is at least level with the current aircraft height
C) An IRS is operating and thrust management is available
D) There is no AFCS comparator operation and all system flags are clear

4. In flight, the FMS refines its position calculations by sampling inputs from:
A) VOR, ILS and ADF only
B) Three IRS, DME, VOR and ILS
C) DME, VOR and ILS only
D) Three IRS, VOR and ILS

5. In flight, the FMS refines its position calculations by using:
A) One DME, or two DME and a co-located VOR station
B) TACAN or, ADF, two DME, one DME and a co-located VOR
C) Two DME or, one DME and a co-located VOR station or ILS signals
D) TACAN or, two DME, or two MLS and co-located VOR station or ILS signals

6. A typical automatic VNAV programme is as follows:
A) After take-off reduce power to MCP and climb at best economy speed to the selected altitude; reduce power to that for best economy and cruise at V_{MR}
B) Maintain take-off thrust until after the noise abate profile and then set MCP until FL100, then climb at economy speed to the selected height. Reduce power to maximum cruise thrust and cruise at V_{MP}
C) After take-off, climb initially at maximum cruise thrust until at FL100 then climb at the recommended climb speed until at cruise altitude. Thereafter cruise at V_{MD}
D) After take-off, climb with climb thrust at the airspeed limit associated with the origin airport until above the limit altitude then climb at economy speed to the selected cruise altitude; cruise at economy speed at cruise thrust

7. Typical phases of flight for automatic flight operation are as follows:
A) Take-off and climb, enroute, approach and landing and go-around
B) Start up, taxi, take-off and landing
C) Take-off, climb, cruise and landing
D) None of the above

8. During take-off mode pressing a TO/GA button:
A) Engages the autothrottle in N1 mode and the throttles move to take-off thrust
B) Ensures disengagement of all automatic AFCS functions and ensures that the throttles cannot move to an unwanted position
C) Will select the autothrottle system to the ARM position in anticipation of the climb thrust setting
D) Is forbidden

9. Automatic thrust reduction to climb power occurs when:
A) VNAV, ALT ACQ or ALT HOLD is engaged
B) VNAV is selected only
C) RNAV is selected only
D) RNAV and VNAV are selected only

10. During the approach phase:
A) The glideslope can be engaged at any time
B) The glideslope can only be engaged after localiser capture
C) The localiser can only be engaged after glideslope capture
D) The localiser and glideslope are always engaged simultaneously

Self-Assessment Test 6 Answers

1	C
2	D
3	A
4	B
5	C
6	D
7	A
8	A
9	A
10	B

CHAPTER 7
Automatic Flight Control Systems (AFCS)

7.1 Flight Director Systems

In the 1960s, the increasing amount of information presented to pilots on the instruments, instead of easing their task, made it more difficult by increasing the scan and increasing the processing time necessary in order to make use of all the information. Even in the lowest technology aeroplane, problems associated with the scan, interpretation and analysis of the information became more and more apparent.

Various efforts were made to rationalise the process with the aims of:

- Reducing scan
- Simplifying interpretation
- Simplifying/removing the need to analyse

Reducing the Scan
In reducing the scan, it was recognised that the primary requirement was to provide the pilot with attitude and related aeroplane handling information. A secondary requirement was to provide a navigation display. Effectively, therefore, a need for two indicators was identified:

- a primary or attitude display
- a secondary or navigation display

The primary display is variously known as the Primary Flight Display (PFD) or Attitude Display Indicator (ADI). The secondary display is variously known as the Navigation Display (ND), Horizontal Situation Indicator (HSI) or (on an electronic unit) the MAP display.

Simplifying Interpretation
To simplify interpretation, clear presentations were utilised. These use colour (as and where beneficial), clear markings and symbology.

Information Analysis
To simplify or remove the need to analyse information, a computer is employed to process all the necessary inputs.

7.1.1 Flight Director (FD)

The product of these developments is the flight director. It consists of four components and two displays:

- Flight Director Computer (FDC)
- Signals (instrument) amplifier
- Mode Selector Panel (MSP)
- Annunciator Panel
- Attitude Director Indicator (ADI)
- Horizontal Situation Indicator (HSI)

The block schematic diagram below illustrates the information inputs and flow within the FD.

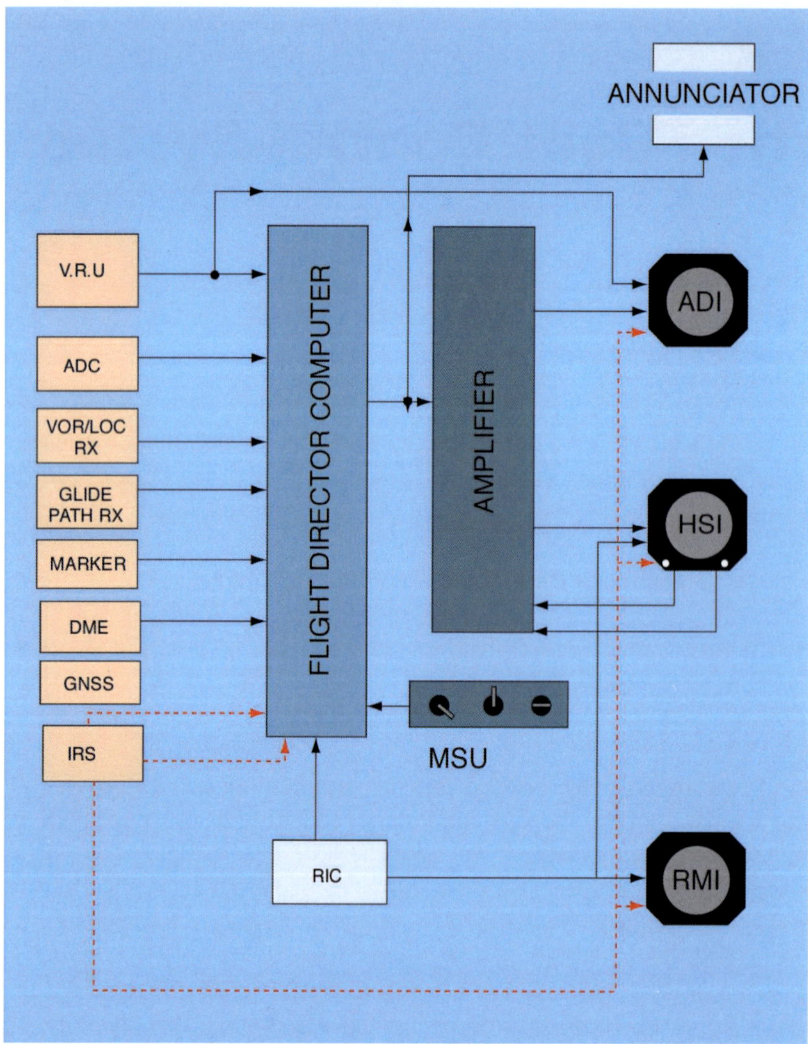

Figure 7.1 Flight Director

7.1.1.1 Flight Director Computer (FDC)

The information flowing to the FDC includes:

- Attitude information from the remote vertical gyro unit or IRS
- Heading information from the remote gyro magnetic compass, INS or IRS
- Air data information from an air data computer
- Navigation radio receivers
- VOR
- ILS localiser
- ILS glide path
- Marker beacons
- DME radio altimeter
- GNSS (where fitted)
- IRS may be used for position information on some units

On some FD installations the only data used from the ADC is altitude and vertical speed. In other units a target speed symbol is displayed and an angle of attack (probe) is used to determine the relationship between target and actual speeds.

7.1.1.2 Mode Selector Panel (MSP)

This information is processed, in a solid state digital computer, in accordance with the settings on the MSP. The computer output is in the form of attitude and steering commands that are fed to the displays and may also be fed to an AFCS. The MSP is the pilot's means of telling the FDC what is required in terms of flight phase commands. A MSP is illustrated below.

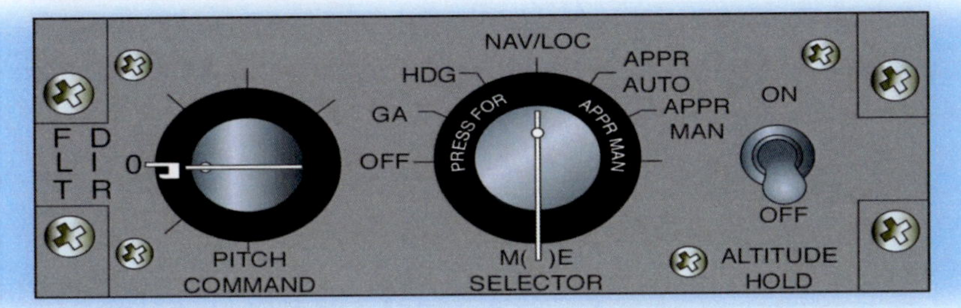

Figure 7.2 Mode selector Panel

The various selections which can be made are explained below:

OFF removes command processing and the command indications do not appear on the ADI

HDG in this position, the computer roll channel responds to the heading input and the heading selected on the HSI. In this mode, the pitch channel can be set to altitude hold by selecting ALT HOLD "ON". Alternatively, with ALT. HOLD "OFF", the pitch channel can be controlled manually by using a pitch command selector

NAV/LOC provides lateral guidance signals for the computer to process and pass to the roll channel. Pitch channel is controlled as in "HDG" mode

AUTO/APPR this mode uses the ILS localiser and glide path signals to provide both lateral and vertical guidance inputs to the computer. The computer processes these inputs and provides guidance signals on the roll channel throughout the approach. The pitch channel can be operated as in "HDG" or "NAV/LOC" but will automatically be cancelled at glide slope (GS) capture. After GS capture pitch commands are generated from a combination of pitch attitude and GS deviation signals

APPR MAN When selected, the system will automatically acquire the localise and glide slope regardless of aircraft position (this mode may be used to force GS capture from above)

GA this mode is selected for a "go around" after a missed approach. The computer signals the "command bars" to require a wings level pitch up attitude. This mode is automatically selected if the GA button on the throttle is activated

Other mode selectors (not shown in the panel configuration in Figure 7.2) may indicate the following manometric commands:-

"**IAS/MACH**" - mode selections may include speed hold modes. In these the computer will process data from the ADC, compare it to a present value and provide pitch commands as appropriate.

"**V/S**" - this mode provides pitch command guidance to maintain a pre-set rate of climb or descent.

Yet other modes may be encountered as different manufacturers have different presentations.

7.1.1.3 Mode Annunciator

This unit provides a visual reminder of the mode selected. This is usually in the form of a panel showing a number of coloured lights, one for each mode. As a mode is selected, the appropriate light illuminates. Mode annunciators come in many forms. Some are dedicated FD annunciators while others combine the FD and AFCS modes, normally with the FD annunciators to the left and the AFCS to the right.

7.1.1.4 Instrument Amplifier

This is the unit responsible for converting the outputs from the computer into command symbology positioning.

7.1.1.5 Attitude Direction Indicator (ADI)

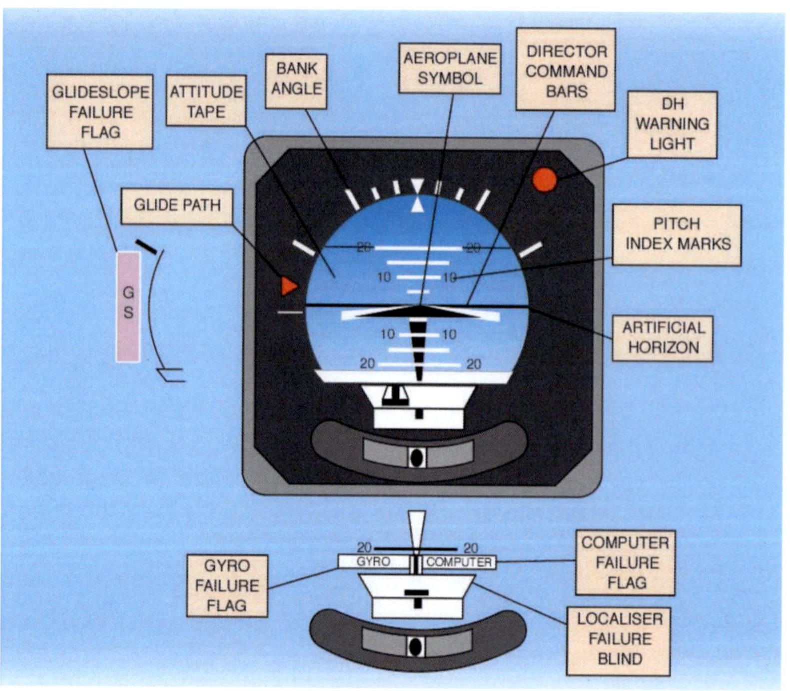

Figure 7.3 ADI

Essentially, the ADI appears like a sophisticated artificial horizon but it does not have an integral gyro. Servomotors connected to the receiver ends of a synchro system drive its attitude indications. These synchro systems (pitch and roll) are attached to a remote gyroscopic vertical reference unit (VRU). This makes it easier to provide almost unlimited degrees of freedom in attitude indication (90° pitch, 360° roll).
In addition to attitude, basic indications include:

- A slip (balance) indicator
- An ILS localiser deviation indicator on which full scale deflection represents 2.5° in azimuth
- A glideslope displacement on which full deflection of the needle occurs when the aircraft is 0.7° or more above or below the glidepath.

The ADI also shows a "fixed" symbolic aeroplane. In the example illustrated, this is in the form of a delta wing shape. When a mode is selected, command bars will appear. They are driven by servomotors controlled from signals originating at the FD computer and amplified at the instrument amplifier. On the example instrument, the command bars are in the form of a pair of wings. These "wings" are driven to assume an attitude position that, if complied with, will guide the aircraft to the required attitude.

It is important to note that the commands from the FD computer are modelled so that no command is given that will cause airframe stress levels to be exceeded

The following figures indicate commands as follows:

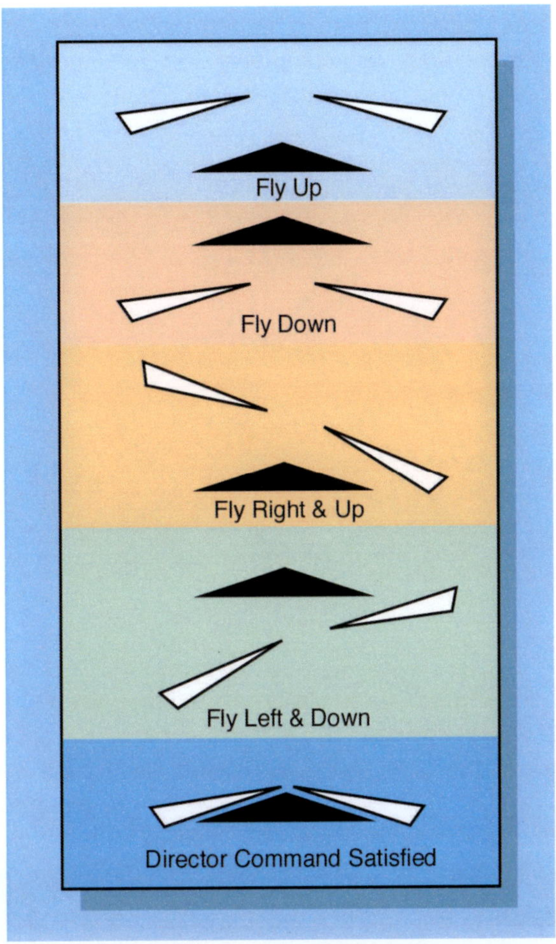

Figure 7.4 ADI Displays

An interesting point to note here is that, before take-off, using the "manual pitch" (on the mode selector), the pitch attitude for initial climb can be set on the command bars. As the aircraft takes off, it can be rotated until the aeroplane delta "fits" into the command wings at which point the climb attitude has been achieved.

When the aeroplane is approaching the target, the FD command bars will indicate the corrective action necessary in order to achieve the required transition to the new flight path. If, for example, the aeroplane is to climb to a specified cruise altitude, when the altitude acquisition signal is sent to the director's computer it will generate a "fly up" command. The pilot will fly the attitude that will place the aeroplane symbol into the command "wings". As the aeroplane approaches the target altitude the computer will generate a "fly down" command. In following this command the pilot will reduce the deck angle of the aeroplane progressively until the attitude for level cruise is reached as the aeroplane achieves the designated altitude.

Consider now the case of an aeroplane flying heading 090° which is to be turned right onto a new heading of 180°. As the heading select knob of the HSI is rotated to place the heading bug on 180° the command bars will generate a "fly right" command. As the aircraft banks into the turn at the correct bank attitude the aeroplane symbol will be centred within the command "wings"; as the desired heading is approached the aircraft must be rolled to a wings level position, therefore the command bars generate a "fly left" command. Following this command will result in the aircraft rolling out on a heading of 180°

Note:- with regard to VOR and LOC modes of operation, the localiser capture point varies with rate of change of beam deviation whilst the capture of a VOR radial occurs at a fixed value (usually 5° deviation)

A common alternative display uses command bars in the form of two bars, one horizontal representing pitch commands and one vertical representing roll commands. In this the aeroplane is flown towards the intersection of the bars. An example of this type is illustrated at Figure 7.5.

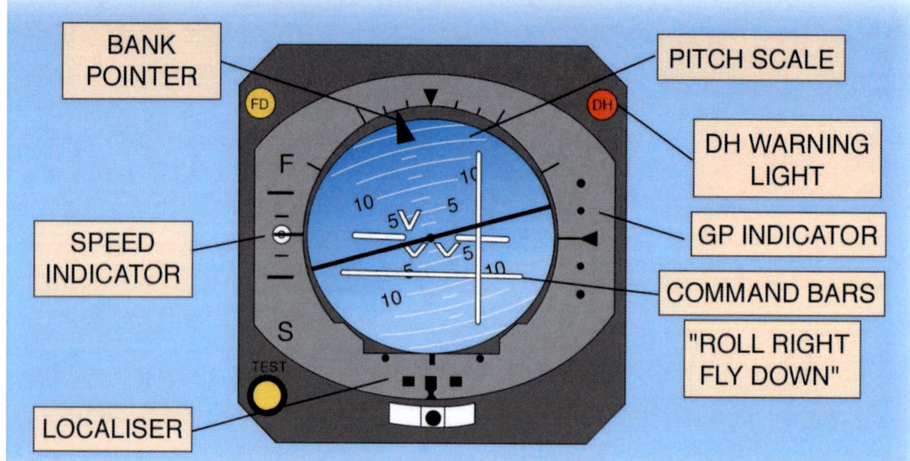

Figure 7.5 ADI Display

7.1.1.5.1 Warning Flags

These are provided in order to warn the pilot of a failure of an essential input. At least 3 such flags, each coloured red and identified by text, are provided:

- **GS** - In the event of failure of the glide slope signal this flag drops over the glide slope scale and prevents its use.
- **GYRO** - This flag appears in a prominent position if the attitude information input fails.
- **COMPUTER** - Flag appears when there is a detected failure in the computer, its outputs or the command signals.

7.1.1.6 Horizontal Situation Indicator (HSI)

A compass dominates the instrument display (see figure below). This is driven from the heading reference system (gyro magnetic or IRS) and rotates against a lubber line.

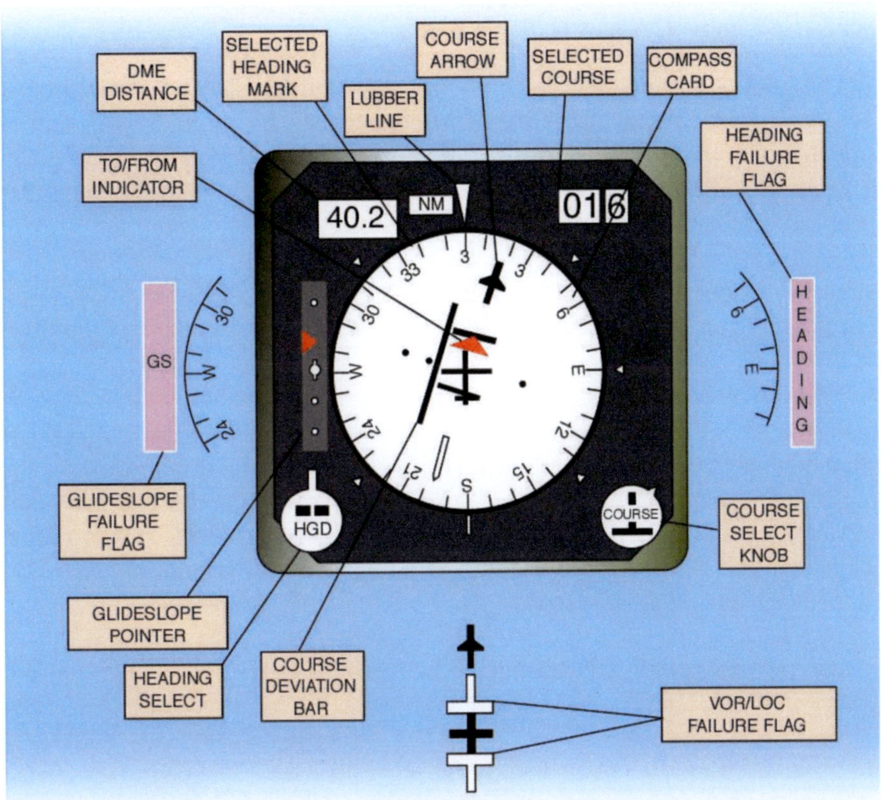

Figure 7.6 HSI

At the centre of the display is a fixed aeroplane symbol.

Inside the compass ring is the symbology that represents lateral guidance signals. This consists of:

- a course arrow adjusted/set by the course set knob
- a course deviation bar driven by signals from the VOR/LOC receiver (as appropriate)
- a course deviation scale on which each dot represents a displacement of 1° from the selected course or localiser
- a course deviation scale on which full deflection represents a displacement of 10° from the selected course or localiser so that each dot represents a displacement of 2°, or 2.5°, on a 5 dot, or 4 dot, instrument respectively.

In addition:

- Where the HSI is used in an RNAV mode, each dot represents a 1NM displacement except in RNAV APR mode where the scale is altered so that each dot represents 0.25 NM.
- To the left of the indicator is a glide path scale. This replicates the glide path indications on the ADI.
- Digital read outs are provided. The range figure is determined from a DME while the pilot selects the course.
- For intercept purposes the pilot may select a heading. This adjusts the position of the heading bug on the compass card.

7.1.1.6.1 Warning Flags

Warning flags, coloured red and identified by print, are provided as follows:

- **GS** - failure of glide slope signal. A flag covers GS indications
- **COMPASS** - indicates a failure of the heading reference
- **VOR/LOC** - appears if VOR or localiser (as appropriate) signals fail.

7.2 Automatic Flight Control Systems

An Automatic Flight Control System (AFCS) is a device designed to relieve the pilot from exercising direct control on a continuous basis. This allows him/her to concentrate on management and monitoring of the flight. The control provided by the AFCS exists at a number of levels as follows: -

- **Stability and Control Augmentation** – for an aeroplane to be controllable it must first be stable. This statement is applicable to both manual and automatic control.

Some aeroplanes suffer a degree of instability and the first function of the AFCS is to provide a stability augmentation. This must be capable of operating whether in AFCS or MANUAL mode of flight control.

- **Attitude Hold** – maintaining the attitude of the aeroplane around selected axes.
- **Flight Control** – the AFCS responds to externally sourced inputs such as altitude, airspeed, heading, navigational information. This is sometimes referred to as an "operational autopilot". In this the AFCS not only maintains a set condition but will follow changes of flight profile (e.g. track guidance, automatic approach, flare and landing) as dictated by inputs from such external sources. This provides a very accurate and responsive flight control. Although the external sources are not a part of the AFCS they must be integrated with it effectively if the system is to work.

A block schematic diagram at Figure 7.7 illustrates the possible flow of information to the AFCS.

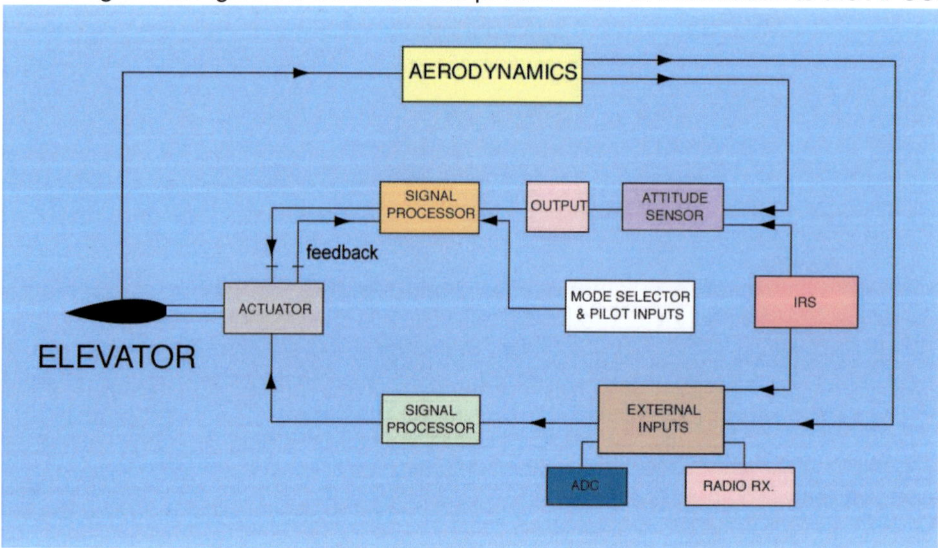

Figure 7.7 AFCS schematic

It is of passing interest to note that an average pilot will detect a 1° change of aeroplane attitude and apply the correct control response in about 0.8s. An autopilot can detect a much smaller disturbance (0.01° change of attitude) and apply the necessary control in about 0.16s.

7.2.1 Classification of an AFCS

The degree of complexity of the AFCS fitted to an aeroplane will be dictated by a number of factors such as:

- Size of aeroplane
- Age of the aeroplane
- General duration of flights
- Intended route structures
- Complexity of the aeroplane
- Number of flight crew
- Cost benefits achievable
- Safety benefits

An AFCS is classified according to the number of axes around which it exercises control. These classifications are as follows: -

- Single Axis – provides control (normally) around the roll axis.
- Two axes – provides control around two axes (normally the roll and pitch axes)
- Three Axes – providing control around pitch, roll and yaw.

7.2.2 Control Channels

A control channel serves each axis so we have the following: -

- Pitch channel
- Roll channel
- Yaw channel

7.2.2.1 Functioning of a Control Channel

Since each axis control channel works on the same basic principle we can look in depth at one channel and read it across to the others. Where differences do exist these will be dealt with channel by channel. In essence the autopilot control channel consists of an attitude detector, a signal processor (computer), a servomotor and a feedback loop. This forms a closed loop system (the inner loop) that is necessary for stable flight. Figure 7.8 illustrates these basic components.

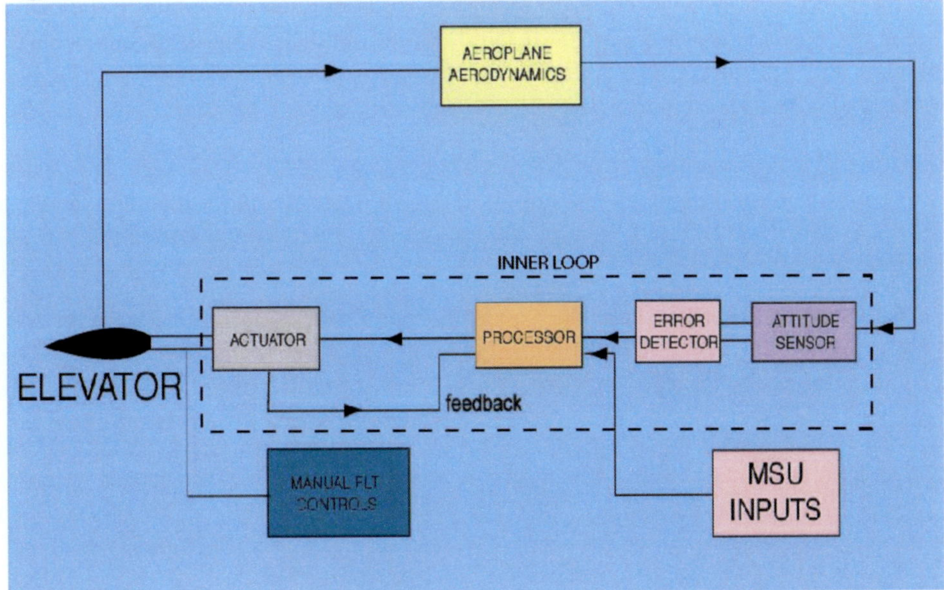

Figure 7.8 Inputs

The attitude sensor uses gyroscopes and/or accelerometers to sense attitude changes of the aircraft about its principle axes. The error detector unit is the source of the error signal. When the aeroplane pitch changes, as a result of some aerodynamic disturbance, an electrical pick off carries the displacement error signal to the signal processor. This processes the demand and determines the corrective control input required. It then sends the appropriate command as a signal to the actuator (or servomotor) and this moves the control surface in the appropriate direction and by the appropriate amount. In order to provide a stable system a feedback loop is included so that the computer is advised of control movement.

> Modes which use gyro outputs are usually inner loop modes and stabilise the aircraft (e.g. yaw damper, pitch attitude hold, wing levelling)

7.2.2.1.1 Command Facility

A facility must be provided for the pilot to enter a command. This is normally done through the Mode Control Panel (MCP) where commands to roll or pitch the aeroplane can be inserted. On the MCP, small controls are generally provided for both pitch and roll. Operation of these controls activates a synchro transmitter rotor or potentiometer that applies the appropriate command to the channel actuator. An example of a simple mode controller, such as fitted to a light twin engine aeroplane, is shown below.

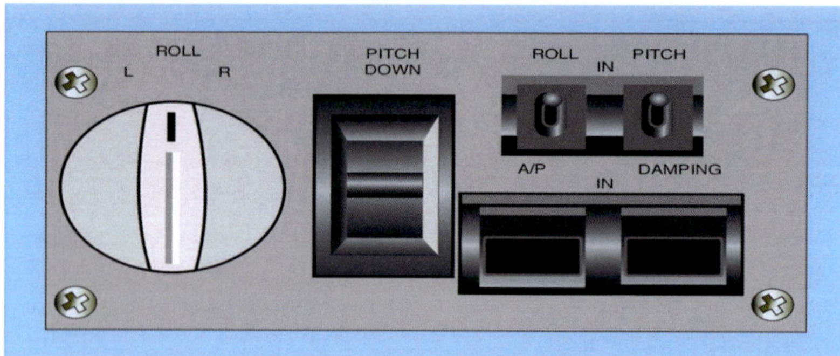

Figure 7.9 Aircraft selector

On some systems a Control Wheel Steering (CWS) mode of operation is provided. This enables the pilot to roll or pitch the aeroplane through the AFCS by using normal control forces on the control column. In this system the pitch and roll force transducers built into the control column or control stick detect forces applied by the pilot. The transducers may be in the form of piezo crystal elements in which the electrical resistance varies as they are put under pressure. The generated signal outputs, which are proportional to the input forces, are amplified and fed as output signals to the appropriate control channel where the controls are activated in proportion to the applied signal.

7.2.2.2 Attitude Sensor

Aircraft attitude is measured by a displacement gyro, whereas, rate of change of attitude is measured by a rate gyro.

7.2.2.2.1 Rate Gyro

The rate gyro, aligned with its sensitive axis parallel to the pitch axis, will detect a rotation of the aeroplane around an axis and will also be able to determine the rate of rotation being experienced. This makes this type of detection very attractive as the required control input is more correctly related to rate of rotation. Figure 7.10 illustrates the arrangement of rate gyros that would provide control around three axes.

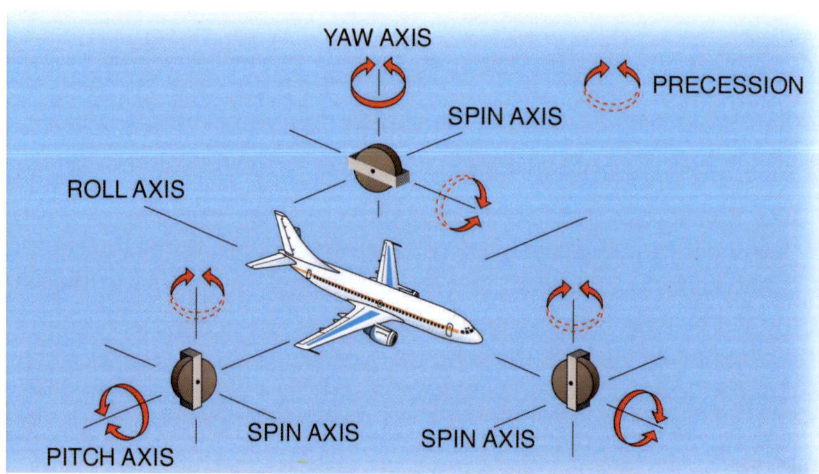

Figure 7.10 Rate gyro

7.2.2.2.2 Displacement Gyro

In this the attitude of the aeroplane is monitored against a vertical reference unit. When a displacement is sensed the computer determines the magnitude of the displacement and the corrective control input required as compensation for the displacement. The vertical reference can be from an integral gyro source or may be taken from an independent source such as a remote Vertical Reference Unit (VRU), INS or IRS.

You should note that, in many systems, the detector signal is derived from a combination of rate and displacement signals. This reduces the time delay incurred by deriving a rate from a displacement signal and has the advantage of "damping" the tendency to overshoot the correction, which is a common problem with the displacement type of system. You should also note that the pitch and roll channels are operated from the VRU but the yaw channel will require input from a horizontal axis tied gyro.

7.2.2.3 Processor

As has been indicated, the function of the signal processor (computer) is to process the displacement signal and determine the amount of control movement required to counteract the displacement. It must also monitor the feed back to ensure that the required control has been activated and that the desired effect is being achieved. The computations vary from the very simple in an attitude hold system to the very complex in a full multi-mode AFCS.

Examples of the computations and processes are as follows: -

- Amplification – Boosts the power of the detected signal to a sufficiently high level to act as an output.
- Integration/Differentiation – These are mathematical processes used to derive information such as attitude change from rate of rotation or vice versa.
- Limiting – Restricts range of parameter change e.g. pitch rate to a specific limit.
- Shaping – Modify the computer output so that the required flight path or handling characteristics are achieved.
- Programming – Individual processes designed to instruct the aeroplane to follow defined manoeuvres.

The signal processing power of the computer will vary according to the role and complexity of the AFCS.

7.2.2.3.1 Control Laws and Integration

In all of these computations, "control laws", which determine how the control demands are translated into control movements, are taken into account. A common form of the control laws as used in large transport aeroplanes in the pitch axis, is known as the C* control law. This provides stability of the aeroplane at a selected flight path angle and compensates for problems associated with flight at low airspeeds.

7.2.2.3.2 Manoeuvering

Within the computations, consideration is also given to the airframe loadings imposed by the manoeuvre. These are a function of the airspeed (dynamic pressure) and, as you would expect, require input from the ADC or other dynamic pressure source. On older or simple autopilots there is no allowance made for "gust loading" imposed in flight in turbulent conditions. In such conditions those autopilots should be disconnected and the aeroplane must be flown manually. In a more modern and complex system there is a function switch which, when operated, "softens" the control demands so that the aeroplane is allowed to ride with the gusts. This is achieved by increasing the "limits" argument in the computations. The switch should only be activated in turbulent conditions as it desensitises the autopilot.

7.2.2.4 Actuators

Actuators may be of the electro-mechanical, electro-hydraulic or electro-pneumatic type. In their design, consideration must be given to:

- a balance between range of control surface movement against rate of movement (in event of failure)
- rate of normal movement
- magnitude and accuracy of movement for control and/or stability.

7.2.2.4.1 Electro-Mechanical Actuator

These may be either DC or AC powered. In the DC system a motor is coupled to the flight control via an electro-magnetic clutch and a mechanical linkage. A feedback is provided from a potentiometer driven by the motor. In the AC system, the motors used may be either of the hysterisis type or of the two-phase induction type. A synchro transmission system provides information on the position of the control surface while a tachogenerator provides the necessary feedback to the computer.

7.2.2.4.2 Electro-Pneumatic Actuator

Figure 7.11 illustrates a typical actuator of this type. The valve assembly is operated electro-mechanically by signals from the AFCS computer. The power is supplied from a pneumatic feed taken from a source such as an engine driven pump or a compressor bleed from a turbine engine.

When a command input is received the opening of one valve is increased and the other is reduced. This produces a differential pressure in the two cylinders and results in a differential motion of the two rods causing a rotation of the output linkage and a resultant control movement.

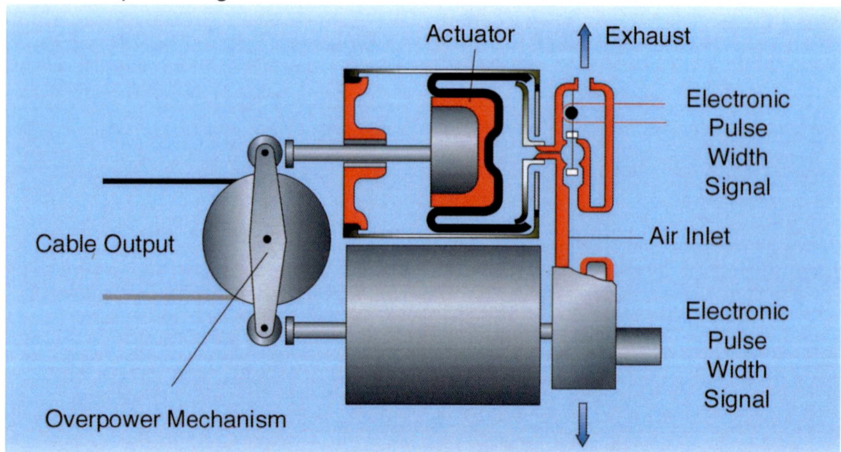

Figure 7.11 Electro-pneumatic actuator

7.2.2.4.3 Electro-Hydraulic Actuator

In most modern transport aeroplanes the primary flight controls are operated through Power Control Units (PCU) utilising the muscle of hydraulic power to activate the controls. It is possible to design these units to respond to signals from the AFCS computer and so to remove the need for independent servo actuators. A schematic of such a system is shown at Figure 7.12. The signal from the AFCS computer is fed to a solenoid, which operates a valve within the hydraulic system. This activates the control surface and a position transducer provides a feed back to the computer.

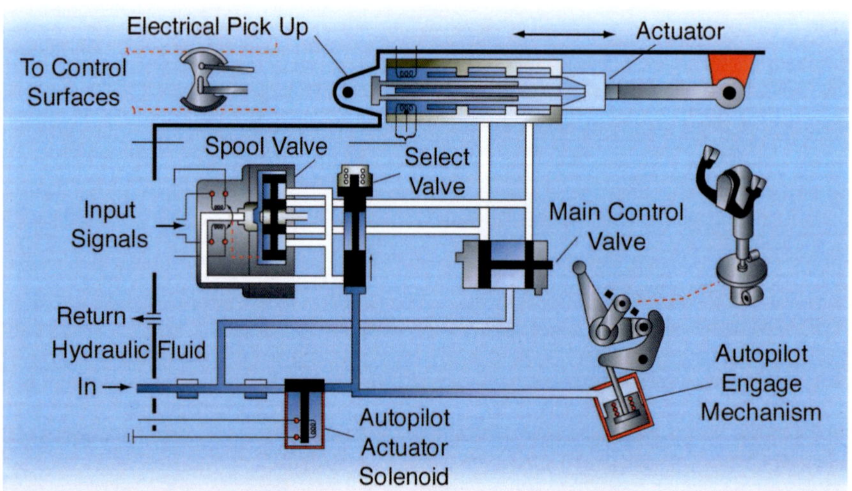

Figure 7.12 Schematic

7.2.2.5 *Enhancements*

Having looked at the basic components and principles of an attitude control system we will now consider some enhancements:

7.2.2.5.1 Rate Damping Systems

These are systems having more to do with stability than control. They will not return an aeroplane to a specific attitude but will stop a divergence developing. They are important in that they will: -

- Prevent unwanted divergence rates from developing.
- Will smooth rate demands commanded by the pilot.

7.2.2.5.2 System Protection

This is the critical function associated with any automatic system, the prevention of a runaway or other undesirable malfunction. We will look at some methods of achieving this but you should keep in mind that they are all going to achieve the same result, they are going to limit the authority of the actuator.

Comparators

In these systems, which are the most basic system protection devices, the outputs from both sensors and actuators are compared. If the attitude change being sensed is in the same direction as the actuator is applying control the comparator will disconnect the circuit.

Rate Trigger Systems

The characteristics exhibited by an aeroplane during a system runaway are very marked and are significantly different from normal flight characteristics. By knowing these rates a threshold can be introduced at which the system can be disconnected.

Duplex Systems

In such a system there are two complete control systems for each channel. These use independent sensors, computers, actuators and actuator power supplies. The two control systems are connected to the control surface. In the event of a runaway in one lane, the other lane will sense a disturbance and apply a corrective actuator input. The speed of response of this system (to a runaway) can be improved by using a comparator system. Where this is employed the positions of the individual actuators are monitored. The comparator examines the positions of the actuators and, if one is detected to be diverging at a significant (pre-set) rate, that channel is disengaged.

Triplex Systems

These are developments or extensions of the duplex system utilising three lanes on a control channel rather two. Monitoring of all three lanes is conducted continuously and a comparator circuit to detect a divergence of a lane. Voting takes place within the system to decide which lane is divergent and it is then closed down. This leaves the channel operational as a duplex system and it said to be “single failure survivable”.

Quadruplex Systems

As the name suggests this type uses four lanes and therefore provides additional redundancy.

Model Following

This system is not used except in association with another system such as a duplex system. It is basically a software fix in which the flight characteristics of the aeroplane are programmed into the AFCS computer. The computer can therefore determine the anticipated response for a given control demand and compare this with response detected by the sensors. In effect this gives a duplex system the properties of a triplex system.

Automatic Change of Gain

When a lane is shut down the remaining lanes must carry the additional load. This is achieved by automatically adjusting the gain of the system so that a given disturbance will demand a greater movement or rate of movement from the remaining actuator.

7.2.2.5.3 Cross-Coupling

When the ailerons are used to turn the aeroplane a yawing motion is set up. This has to be countered by the application of some rudder. In addition, the banked aeroplane now has its lift vector angled towards the low wing so that the vertical component is reduced – this requires an increase in pitch. These factors are taken into account so that, in order to obtain a balanced turn, although the primary action comes from the roll channel there will be secondary inputs from both the pitch and yaw channels. In two axes systems the roll and pitch channels work in conjunction to achieve this balance.

7.2.3 Stability Control

We have now looked at the components of the AFCS control channels and have some grasp of the vocabulary that is employed. In doing this we have considered only attitude control i.e. maintaining the aeroplane in the attitude set by the pilot and allowing the pilot to change that attitude through the control system. Now we will progress to looking at some other aspects of the AFCS such as stability augmentation and automatic trimming.

7.2.3.1 Stability Augmentation

The two most common stability problems that we are likely to encounter are: -

1. Dutch roll – this is an oscillation in yaw and roll. On some aeroplanes, especially ones with swept wings, this effect may not be dampened out by the natural stability of the aeroplane and the Dutch roll will become a divergent phugoid motion. This will require the introduction of some control and this is provided by the yaw damper system.
2. Tuck Under – this phenomena is encountered in aeroplanes flying at high subsonic, transonic or supersonic speeds. In these regimes there may be a significant rearward movement of the centre of pressure. In order to prevent this becoming an uncontrollable “nose down” motion, it is necessary to provide some form of compensation. This is done by the use of a Mach trim system.

7.2.3.1.1 Yaw Damper

This unit is designed to counteract the yawing tendency at an early stage of onset before it can develop the sympathetic roll motion associated with the onset of Dutch Roll.

It is operational whenever it is switched on and does not depend on the AFCS being active

Figure 7.13 illustrates the components of a typical Yaw Damper.

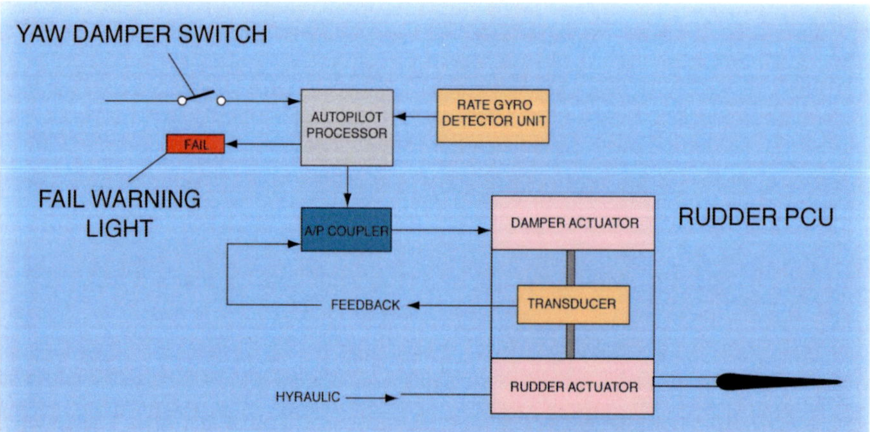

Figure 7.13 Yaw Damper

The sensor unit is a rate gyro that has its sensitive axis in the horizontal plane.

The rudder is therefore moved in proportion to the rate of yaw detected

This is contained within a unit known as the yaw damper coupler, which also contains the yaw damper circuit computer. The computer provides the functions of: -

- Filtering the detected error signals. In this the detected signal is compared to a reference signal before passing a command to the next stage of processing. This removes any error that can be caused by fuselage flexing.
- Integration of the filtered signals to form the servo signal input.
- Amplification of the servo signal.

The amplified servo signal is fed to the transfer valve in the yaw damper rudder actuator. This actuator is independent of the normal AFCS actuator. As the transfer valve moves it passes hydraulic fluid under pressure to the yaw damper actuator. In the mechanical linkage that connects the actuator to the main rudder actuator, the inputs from the yaw damper and from the rudder controls are added or subtracted so that the signal operating the rudder is the sum of both. A feedback is provide so that, when the yawing motion has been stopped the rudder will be returned to the normal position.

The operation of the yaw damper does not cause the rudder pedals to move

The yaw damper signal, for a given rate of oscillation, is varied inversely according to the airspeed. A signal from the Air Data Computer is used to achieve this. The yaw damper signal may also have to be modified for different configurations. Where this is necessary, a signal from the flap position indicator circuit is applied to a gain circuit on the yaw damper output. This increases the rate of response when the flaps are extended.

Confidence checking of the system is provided in two ways:

- An output from the feedback is relayed to an indicator on the flight deck. This shows the position of the rudder and provides a means of monitoring the damper operation. (On the B-737 this indicator shows rudder movement due to yaw damper operation only).
- A test circuit is provided. This simulates a yaw oscillation by applying torques to the sensor rate gyro. The displaced gyro causes an error signal to be generated that displaces the rudder. This movement is relayed to the flight deck indicators.

7.2.3.1.2 Mach Trim System

This system is attached to the pitch channel. It is designed as a sub-system and is therefore, like the yaw damper, can be operational irrespective of whether or not the AFCS is active

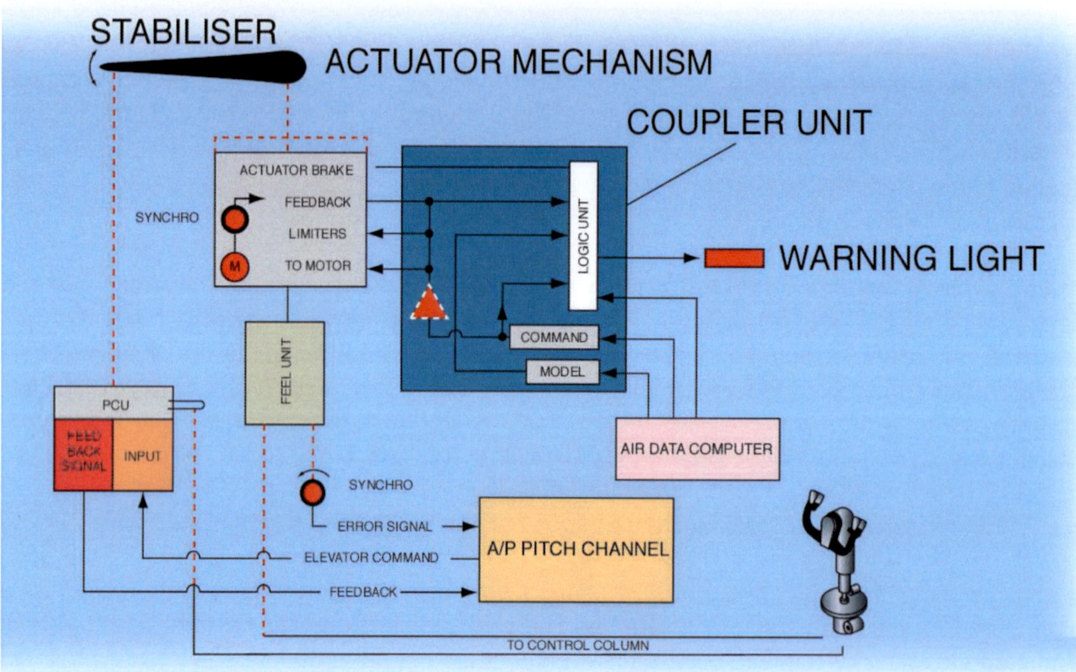

Figure 7.14 Mach trim system

Figure 7.14 illustrates the components of a typical system. The heart of the system is the coupler unit. This receives signals, corresponding to Mach number, from the ADC. Whenever these signals exceed the pre-set value (for the aeroplane type) the trim coupler unit releases the brake and the speed signal from the ADC is fed to the motor. This causes the stabiliser to move in such a way that the elevators are driven upward, counteracting any tendency to "tuck under".

Internal monitoring of the system provides a failure warning in the form of the illumination of a fail indicator light.

Although connected to the pitch channel the system is totally independent of the pitch control channel of the AFCS

7.2.4 Automatic Trim Control

The process of trimming an aeroplane is necessary in order to relieve the loads on the primary control and to leave the primary control with a full range of movement. Additionally, an aeroplane that is well trimmed is a more efficient. When the AFCS is active, trimming is maintained as a function of the AFCS.

Indeed, trimming is seen as so fundamental that the use of an AFCS without an active automatic pitch trim is prohibited

The design of the trim control varies significantly from type to type. In the following discussions we will look at two types: one for a general aviation twin engine aeroplane the other for a modern jet transport.
In the AFCS, trim control is usually provided only on the pitch axis.

Whenever an automatic control system takes control of an aircraft it must be done in a smooth manner without "snatching". The aircraft must be trimmed for the desired attitude before engaging the autopilot and the system must be synchronised to maintain that attitude whilst it is engaged.

The purpose of synchronisation therefore is to prevent snatching of the controls upon engagement of the automatic control system

7.2.4.1 *Small Aeroplane*

In a small aeroplane the elevators are operated by a system of cables that are powered either manually or electrically. In the sample automatic trim system (Figure 7.15) the sensor compares the tension of the "Up" elevator control cable with that of the "Down" control cable. If the elevator is subjected to an "up" command, the sensor will detect the imbalance of cable tension. This is used as an error signal and is amplified and sent to a motor. This drives the trim tab downward to a position such that the control cable tensions are reduced to a minimum. Since the extension of flaps is usually accompanied by a change in pitch, a "flap compensation" circuit may well be added to the command signal detection circuit. This will be operated by a relay attached to the flap position indicator.

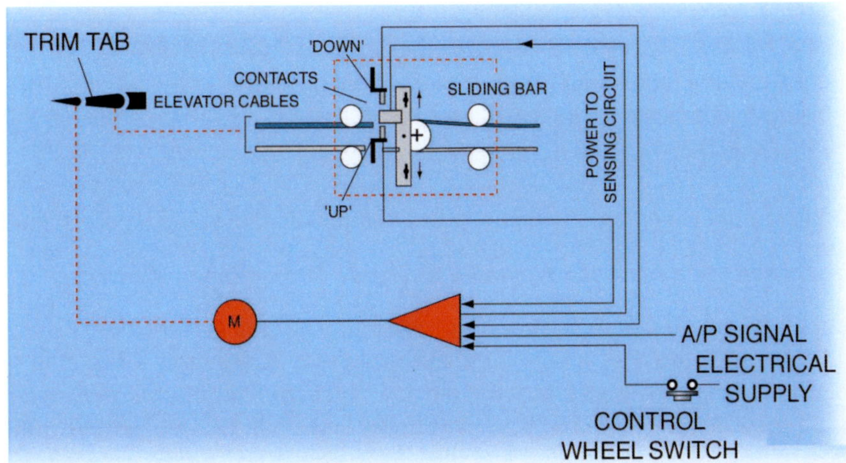

Figure 7.15 Auto Trim

When the aeroplane is being flown manually the pilot, using a control switch that controls the application of power to the servo system achieves the trimming.

7.2.4.2 *Large Aeroplane*

In large aeroplanes, where the elevators and stabiliser are likely to be hydraulically powered, the system is somewhat more complicated although it fulfils the same function. A block schematic of such a system is shown below.

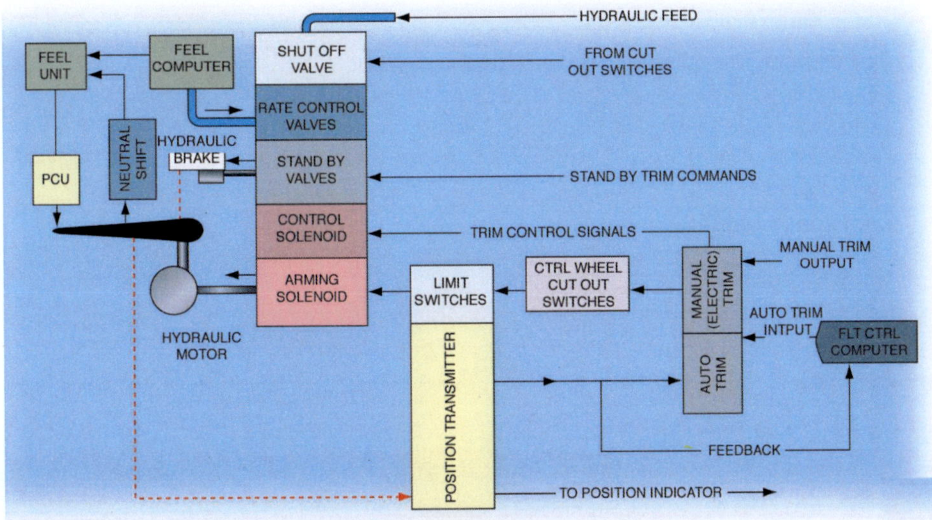

Figure 7.16 Complete system

In this example trimming is achieved by moving the stabiliser and leaving the elevators with full movement to control changes in pitch commanded by the AFCS.

Let us just follow the sequence of events associated with a nose down demand from the AFCS. The pitch control channel will activate the PCU and cause the elevator to displace downward. At the same time it will send a signal to the trim circuit. This circuit has a "threshold" which is dependent upon the relative positions of the stabiliser and the elevator. If the threshold is reached, the trim circuit will be activated and a signal will be passed to the solenoid. This will activate the hydraulic motor and reposition the stabiliser.

Feedbacks will allow the system to evaluate the new "neutral" position for the elevator and a signal will be sent to the elevator positioning circuit to drive it to that position. Limit switches are provided to prevent the stabiliser being driven beyond the pre-set limits. A stabiliser trim indicator shows the position of the trimming surfaces.

A fault detection circuit provides monitoring of the system. This gives the following outputs: -

- In the event of failure this activates a failure of the automatic trim a warning light in the flight deck.
- In the event of excessive trim input an aural alert will be activated.

The facility for manual trimming is provided just as it was in the simple system we considered above.

7.2.5 AFCS Control Inputs from External Sources (Outer Loop Control)

So far we have looked at the AFCS as a means of providing a stable flight profile for our aeroplane. In developing the system we have created a very sophisticated piece of equipment that can respond to both its own integral sensors and also to the pilot's manual inputs, either through the Mode Selector Panel (MSP) or through the use of Control Wheel Steering (CWS). It follows that, if it can respond to the pilot's inputs it should also be able to respond to commands from other sources. This is achieved by computing the necessary manoeuvres from inputs such as airspeed, altitude, magnetic heading, interception of radio beams, etc. It is to these sources that we now turn our attention.

The following table lists examples of outer loop control modes.

Pitch axis	Roll axis
Manometric (air data): Altitude select and hold Vertical speed Airspeed select and hold Mach hold Pitch hold Pitch trim Turbulence penetration Vertical navigation	Heading select and hold Bank hold Radio navigation: VOR Back beam Area navigation: Doppler Inertial heading
Instrument Landing System	
Glideslope	Localiser
Autoland	
Approach Flare	Runway align Roll out
Control Wheel Steering Touch Control Steering	

7.2.5.1 Manometric Locks

Manometric is a term used to refer to pressure derived inputs. In an AFCS, if we could supply information of sensed pressures we could create circuits that could use these measurements to maintain a given pressure altitude, airspeed, Mach number or vertical speed. All of these are effective about the pitch axis and so the control circuits will be built into the pitch control channel. Pressure (manometric) data may be derived from independent pressure sensors but, on modern aeroplanes, they will most likely be provided by outputs from the Air Data Computer (ADC).

7.2.5.2 Heading

This will be derived from a Remote Indicating Compass or, more commonly in modern aeroplanes, an IRS. Heading is maintained by use of the roll channel but input from the pitch channel and the yaw channel (if fitted) may be required in order to provide balanced turns.

When the heading select knob is rotated to select a heading an error signal is induced which is proportional to the difference between the aircraft's heading and the selected heading

7.2.5.3 Radio Navigation

Signals from the VOR, DME, GNSS, (or Loran) ILS and Radio Altimeter can be used to originate command signals.

VOR signals can be used for course definition and can provide command signals to the roll channel. Processed signals from the VOR and DME can provide an area navigation function and the outputs from this can issue command signals to the roll channel. In a similar way, processed signals from GNSS (or Loran) can also provide command signals affecting the roll channel. In the not too distant future the use of processed GNSS information may be available to effect control for vertical navigation and will input commands to the pitch channel as well.

ILS provides guidance along the localiser and down the glide path to a point from which a safe landing can be made. The localiser provides commands to the roll channel while the glide path commands are routed to the pitch channel.

7.2.5.4 Inertial Reference and Inertial Navigation Systems

These provide attitude references that can be used in place of the VRU that we discussed earlier. They also carry out a navigation function in which the associated computer determines the position of the aeroplane compares this with where the aeroplane is going and provides guidance signals. These guidance signals can be fed to the AFCS as command signals active through the roll channel.

All of the above can be fed directly to the AFCS but, on most modern aeroplanes, the inputs are fed to a Flight Management Computer (FMC) where they are processed, compared to a stored flight profile and the commands to the AFCS are originated as follows:

- The FMC creates profiles for both lateral navigation (LNAV) mode and vertical navigation (VNAV) mode.
- The LNAV outputs are predominately fed to the roll channel.
- In VNAV mode outputs will be fed to both pitch and roll channels (and sometimes to the yaw channel).

The simultaneous use of all this equipment together provides a powerful integrated management and control system.

7.2.6 Autoland Systems

This is the ultimate demand put on the autopilot. It is the unfortunate fact that, in aircraft operations, a large percentage of all accidents can be attributed to the approach and landing phase of a flight. This, coupled to the need for enhanced flight schedule reliability and the economic benefits that result, prompted considerable research into autoland. This research produced the first autoland aeroplanes in the late 1960s in the form of the British European Airways Trident fleet. Shortly after that the Lockheed L-1011 (Tristar) was introduced and systems then developed and improved as time went past.

At an early stage in development it was recognised that any system designed to carry out automatic landings under all visibility conditions would have to provide guidance and control better than that provided by the pilot looking at the outside world. Additionally, the systems would have to have a very high reliability factor.

7.2.6.1 Definitions

Automatic landing – an approach where the automatic flight control system maintains control down to the roll-out stage of the landing

Semi-automatic landing – an approach where the automatic flight control system flies to decision height (and lower in some cases) after which it is disengaged and the landing flown manually

7.2.6.2 Weather Minima

In low visibility operations, the weather limits for landing are given in the following terms runway visual range (RVR) and decision height (DH).

Runway visual range (RVR) – an an instrumentally derived value that represents the range at which high-intensity lights can be seen in the direction of landing along the runway. Its readings are transmitted to the air traffic controller who can inform the pilot of the very latest visibility conditions.

Decision height (DH) – the height above the runway threshold by which a go-round must be initiated by the pilot unless adequate visual reference has been established, and the position and approach path of the aircraft have been visually assessed as satisfactory to safely continue the approach or landing.

Minimum values of these two quantities, known as "weather minima", are specified by national licensing authorities for various types of aircraft and for various airports.

7.2.6.3 ICAO Categorisation

This is a system of categorisation adopted by ICAO describing low-visibility landing capabilities that are based on the principle that the probability of having adequate short visual reference, for the range of permitted decision heights, should be as high as possible. The categories described in the following table:

ICAO Category	Description
CAT 1	Operation down to minima of 200' decision height and RVR of 800 m with a high probability of approach success
CAT 2	Operation down to minima below 200' decision height and RVR of 800 m, and to as low as 100' decision height and RVR of 400 m with a high probability of approach success
CAT 3A	Operation down to and along the surface of the runway, with external visual reference during the final phase of the landing down to RVR minima of 200 m
CAT 3B	Operation to and along the surface of the runway and taxiways with visibility sufficient only for visual taxiing comparable to RVR value in the order of 50 m
CAT 3C	Operation to and along the surface of the runway and taxiways without external visual reference

These three categories also serve as an indication of the stages through which automatic approach and automatic landing development progresses, and therefore designate the capabilities of individual AFCS. In addition, they designate the capabilities of the ground guidance equipment available at the airport, in particular, ILS localiser/glide path and approach, runway and taxiway lighting.

In connection with automatic landing systems, the term "all weather operations" is frequently used. This term is frequently taken to mean that there are no weather conditions that can prevent an aircraft from taking-off and landing successfully. Be aware that this is not the case. At this time there is no automatic system that can perform the landing task in wind conditions in excess of those for which the aircraft has been certificated. Similarly, no present day automatic system can land an aircraft on a runway which, because of contamination by water, slush or ice, is not fit for such an operation.

7.2.6.4 Fundamental Landing Requirement

We require that the aeroplane should be controlled in such a way that:

- Its wheels make contact with the ground comfortably within the paved surface of the runway and that the landing point is not too far down the runway.
- It lands at a very low vertical velocity in order to avoid collapse of the landing gear.
- The speed at touchdown should be sufficiently low to allow the aeroplane to be brought to a halt within the remaining length of the runway.

Representative target figures are:

- Touchdown: 800' to 2300' from threshold within 27' of runway centreline
- Airspeed: at threshold 1.3 V_S
at landing 1.15 V_S
- Lateral velocity: 8 fps
- Sink rate: 0 to 5 fps
- Pitch Attitude: 0 to 5°
- Roll Attitude : 5°
- Airspeeds to be reduced from the approach margin of about 30% above the stall to about half this value by progressive reduction of engine power during the landing flare.
- Wings levelled prior to the actual landing.
- Drift "kick-off" before touchdown.

In descriptive terms a sink speed not greatly in excess of an optimum value of about 1 to 2 fps is required.

To achieve all the above requires that the aeroplane be controlled about all three axes simultaneously. In addition the airspeed must be controlled through engine power changes. The control function during the approach and landing manoeuvre is required on a highly repetitive basis, and although a number of parameters are to be controlled simultaneously, such control is only necessary for a comparatively short period of time. It is therefore well suited to automatic system operation.

7.2.6.4.1 System Integrity and Monitoring

Any such system, as well as being capable of achieving at least the targets spelled out above, must also be designed with the following aims:

- Achieving the highest integrity and reliability of systems bearing in mind that they need to be entrusted with very considerable authority over the controls of an aircraft, including the throttles, and in the presence of the ground.
- The provision of adequate monitoring information on the progress of the approach and landing manoeuvre, and which will enable the pilot to take over under the most critical conditions of a system malfunction in the presence of the ground.
- The substitution of the pilot's direct vision with an automatic externally referenced guidance system, having an integrity and reliability of the same high order as that demanded of the "on board" system.

7.2.6.4.2 System Reliability and Redundancy

Earlier we looked at devices designed to limit the authority of automatic control systems in the event of "runaway" conditions resulting from malfunctions. While such devices may be incorporated in the more conventional control systems, and thereby be generally effective for the intended purpose down to "break-off" heights, i.e. approach heights at which a control system is disengaged, this would not satisfy the requirements for systems designed for autoland. The setting of safety devices is dictated by two conflicting requirements.

- They must limit the effect of a "runaway" such that the pilot can effect a safe recovery;

- They must allow sufficient authority to the control system so that the required flight path can be followed accurately in the presence of disturbances.

A further factor limiting the application of safety devices (in the manner of conventional control systems) is their inability to protect against passive failures. While not producing flight path changes directly, these failures would nevertheless mean that the predetermined and accurate flight manoeuvre of automatic landing could not be maintained and so could set up an equally dangerous situation.

It follows therefore, that to achieve the objective of automatic landing, the operation of an AFCS must be of such a nature that it will:

- Not disturb the flight path as a result of an active malfunction.
- Have adequate authority for sufficiently accurate control along the required flight path.
- Warn of a passive failure.
- Not fail to complete the intended flight manoeuvre following an active or a passive failure.

In order to resolve these problems the concept of "system redundancy" is applied. This involves the use of multiple systems operating in such a manner that a single failure within a system will have an insignificant effect on the aeroplane's performance during the approach and landing operation.

7.2.6.4.3 Terminology

At this point we are going to introduce some more new terms and review some already covered. You must become familiar with them and, at least be able to select the correct name for a given definition as follows:

Fail-soft

The ability of a system to withstand a failure without endangering passenger safety and without producing excessive deviations from the flight path. An equivalent term that you may encounter is *"fail passive"*.

Fail-operational

This describes a system in which one failure (sometimes more) can occur, but leaves the overall system still functioning, and without causing degradation of performance beyond the limits required for automatic landing and roll-out. Alternative terms are *fail-active* and *fail-survival*.

Simplex

This term is usually used to define a single automatic control system and its appropriate number of sub-channels. Although various elements of the system may be duplicated, a single failure elsewhere will result in complete unserviceability. An equivalent term is *single (non-redundant)*.

Multiplex

This term is applied to a system comprising two or more sensibly independent simplex systems and sub-channels used collectively so that, in the event of a failure of a system or sub-channel, the remaining systems are alone capable of performing the controlling function. The number of systems and sub-channels adopted is qualified by the terms duplex, triplex and quadruplex as appropriate.

Duplex system is a system of two complete systems or channels which are interconnected, and which together provide continuous control. If comparison monitoring is provided, a duplex system can provide fail-operational capability. The term should not be confused with the terms duplicate-monitored or duplicate-redundancy. An equivalent term is *dual active with passive monitoring*.

Triplex system is a fail-operational system of three complete systems or channels which are interconnected and which together provide continuous control. In the event of failure of one of the systems or channels, that system or channel is out-voted by the other two and is automatically disengaged; control is therefore continued in duplex. In the event of a further fault in either of the two remaining systems or channels, they will both disconnect, and the aircraft is returned to the pilot in a trimmed and safe attitude. An equivalent term is *triple-redundant*.

Duplicate-monitored
This refers to a system comprising two systems in parallel and with separate power supplies. The components of both are designed to be either self-monitoring or to have their outputs checked by parallel comparator circuits. Only one system is engaged at any particular time, the other system being in a follow-up mode, and thereby serving as an active standby. In the event of a fault being shown up by the self-monitors or comparators of either of the systems, control is automatically changed over to the standby system.

Dual-dual
This term is used by some manufactures to define a twin "fail operational" control system having twin passive monitoring systems. It should not be considered synonymous to a duplex system, since the control systems may or may not be active simultaneously. In the event of a monitor detecting a failure in its associated system, the second system with its monitor is switched in.

Monitoring
In its strictest sense and, in particular, when applied to multiplex systems, this term defines the process of making comparisons either between two or more outputs (or inputs) or between an output (or input) and a selected datum. The monitoring process can also assume a limiting function; e.g. when it is set up to cause a system to disconnect whenever an output (or input) exceeds a prescribed limit.

Comparison monitor (or Comparator)
Monitor that operates on data supplied from comparable stages in two or more similar systems.

Equaliser
This is a device that adjusts the performance of the sub-systems, in multiplex systems, in order to remove differences between sub-system outputs that may arise other than as a result of fault conditions.

7.2.6.4.4 Automatic Landing Sequence
Now that we have come to grips with the terminology it is time to look at the sequence of events that takes place before, during and after an automatic landing. During this procedure you would make use of the MCP and an example of a more advanced unit is illustrated below.

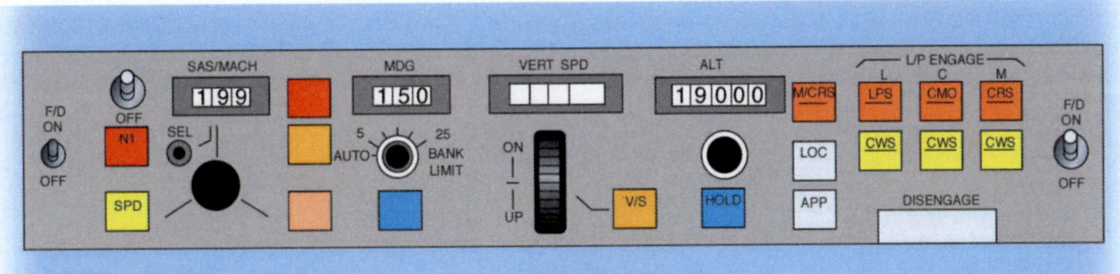

Figure 7.17 MCP

Following the pre approach briefing the FMS will be set for the appropriate approach and, at or about the final approach fix (FAF), the AFCS would be set to "approach" mode by pressing the APP button. This will arm the flight control system to capture the localiser and establish the aeroplane on the localiser inbound. It is at this time that the other flight control channels will also enter the APP mode so that the autoland system has the required level of system redundancy and becomes "Fail Operational".

Under normal conditions you would be below the glide path at this time so the effective controls would be under the influence of: -

- Lateral guidance from localiser - Roll channel
- Altitude from ADC - Pitch channel
- Attitude from IRS/ VRU - Roll & pitch channels

As the glide path intercept takes place (at about 1500') the aeroplane is established on the final approach and the flight control systems are "voted" into the approach control loop. Now things get a bit more active in the flight control system as the aeroplane is guided down the glide path, along the localiser meeting target speeds and with configuration changes as the landing configuration is established. The following channels become active.

- Lateral guidance from localiser - Roll channel
- Vertical guidance from glide path and radio altimeter - Pitch channel
- Speed control from the ADC - Autothrottle & pitch

At about 350' the stabiliser is repositioned so as to initiate a nose-up attitude. When the wheels are about 45' above the runway the "flare" mode is automatically initiated. In this the pitch control is taken away from the glide path (i.e. the glideslope signal is disconnected) and a pitch command is generated that will bring the descent rate to about 2 fps and, at about 12', drift is kicked off at the same time the autothrottles will be instructed to reduce engine thrust.

At about 5' wheel height the flare mode is disengaged as the aeroplane transitions to touchdown and roll out. At this time the elevators are given a signal to apply a nose down control so that the nose wheel will be lowered onto the runway. The autothrottle will remain in control of the engines until reverse thrust is demanded and the autopilot is disengaged.

At any time from 2000' down to the decision height, the crew can abort the approach. Pressing the TOGA switch on the throttle will cause the throttles to advance to a pre-set reduced thrust "go-around" value. A second press of the throttles will advance the engines to full power. This "go-around" phase will interact with the AFCS and will cause a "GA" annunciation on the ADI and the pitch channel generates a pitch up command so that the aeroplane will be placed in the correct climb attitude.

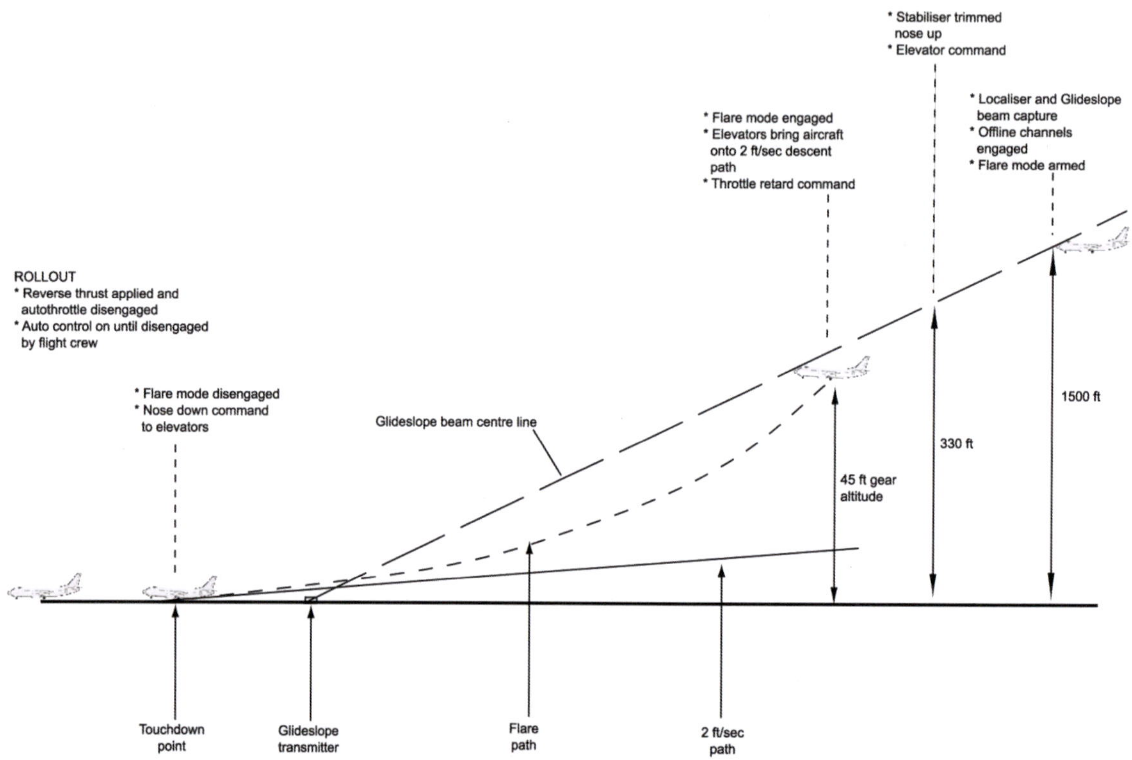

Figure 7.18 Automatic Landing Sequence

7.3 *Integrated Automatic Flight*

One of the biggest problems that people encounter with the advanced technology aeroplanes is to try to come to grips with how everything fits together and how it is used. Figure 7.19 is a block schematic showing the interconnections and interdependencies of the various equipments that we have now looked at. It is emphasised that this is an example only and will probably differ from the detail on your own aeroplane.

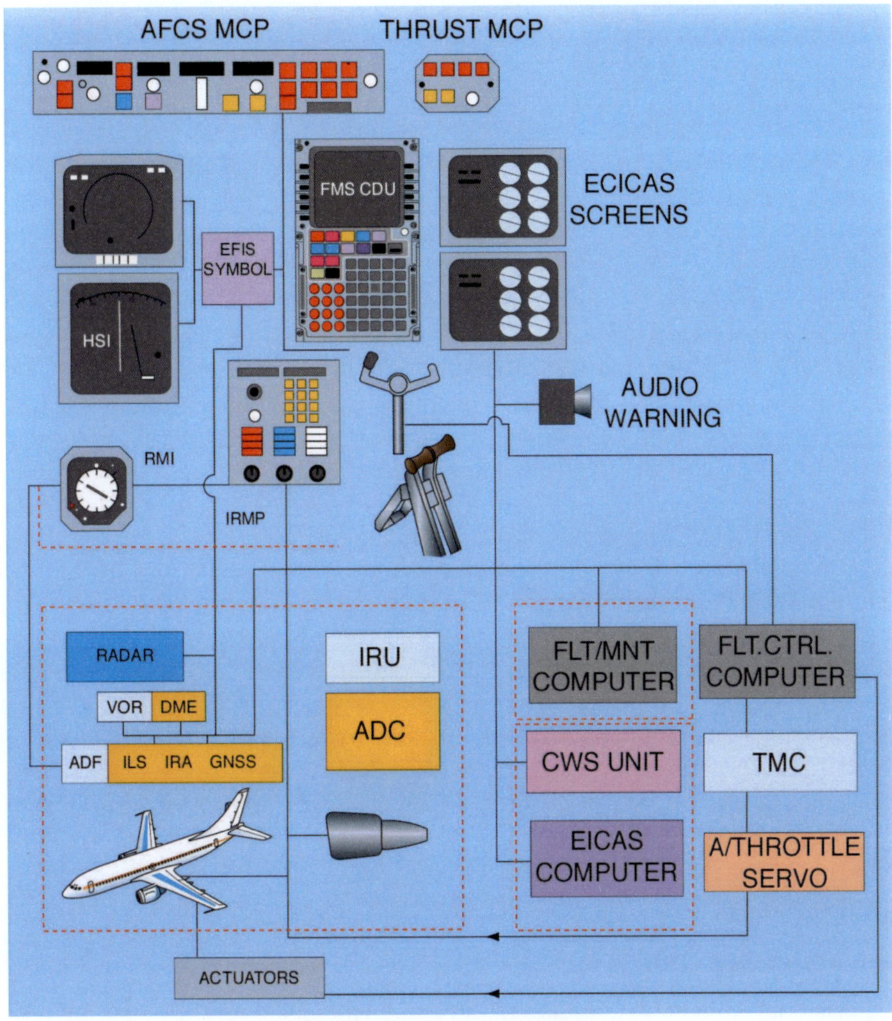

Figure 7.19 Auto flight

7.3.1 *Automatic Flight Operations*

The following is a brief discussion of a typical flight with an automatic flight system consisting of AFDS, A/T and FMC. Typical phases of flight for automatic flight operations are:

- Takeoff and climb
- Enroute
- Approach and landing
- Go-around

7.3.1.1 *Automatic Flight Takeoff and Climb*

Takeoff is a flight director only function of the TO/GA mode. Flight director pitch and roll commands are displayed, and the autothrottle maintains takeoff N_1 thrust limit as selected from the FMC. The autopilot may be engaged after takeoff. Both F/Ds must be ON to engage the takeoff mode prior to starting the takeoff. The F/D takeoff mode is engaged by pressing the TO/GA switch on either thrust lever. The Flight Mode

Annunciators display FD as the A/P status, TO/GA as the pitch mode, and blank for the roll mode. During takeoff, pushing a TO/GA switch engages the autothrottle in the N_1 mode. The A/T annunciation changes from ARM to N_1 and thrust levers advance toward takeoff thrust.

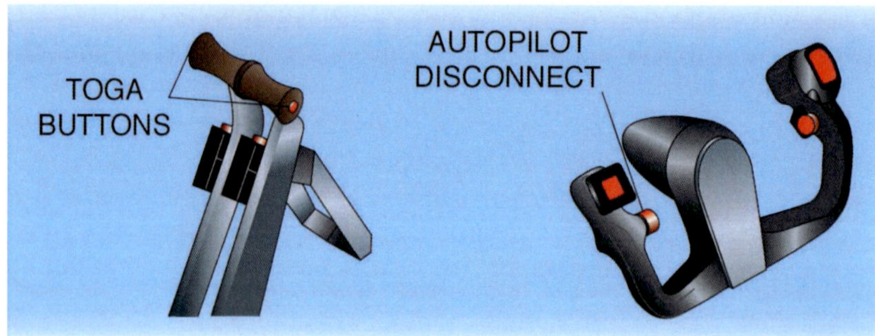

Figure 7.20 Auto flight controls

At 60 KT, the F/D pitch commands 15° nose up. At 64 KT the A/T mode annunciates THR HLD (throttle hold). At lift-off the pitch command remains at 15° until sufficient climb rate is acquired. Pitch then commands MCP speed (normally V_2) plus 20 KT. After lift-off the A/T remains in THR HLD until 400' RA is reached and approximately 18 s have elapsed since lift-off. A/T annunciation then changes from THR HLD to ARM and reduction to climb thrust can be made by pressing the N_1 switch. Automatic thrust reduction to climb power occurs when VNAV, ALT ACQ or ALT HOLD is engaged.

7.3.1.2 Automatic Flight En Route

The autopilot and/or the flight director can be used after takeoff to fly a lateral navigation track (LNAV) and a vertical navigation track (VNAV) provided by the FMC.

Other roll modes available are:

- VOR course (VOR/LOC)
- Heading select (HDG SEL)

Other pitch modes available are:

- Altitude hold (ALT HOLD)
- Level change (MCP SPD)
- Vertical speed (V/S)

7.3.1.3 Approach (APP) Mode - Dual A/Ps

Approach mode allows both A/Ps to be engaged at the same time. Dual A/P operation provides “fail-passive” operation through landing flare and touchdown or an automatic go-around. During fail passive operation, the flight controls respond to the A/P commanding the lesser control movement. If a failure occurs in one A/P, the second channel counteracts the failed channel such that both A/Ps disconnect with minimal aircraft manoeuvring and with aural and visual warnings to the pilot.

One VHF NAV receiver must be tuned to an ILS frequency before the approach mode can be selected. For a dual A/P approach, the second VHF NAV receiver must be tuned to the ILS frequency and the corresponding A/P engaged prior to 800' RA.

7.3.1.3.1 Localiser and Glide Slope Armed

After setting the localiser frequency and course, pressing the APP switch selects the APP mode. The APP switch illuminates, and VOR/LOC and G/S enunciate armed. The APP mode permits selecting the second A/P to engage. This arms the second A/P for automatic engagement after LOC and G/S capture and when descent below 1500' RA occurs.

7.3.1.3.2 Localiser Capture

Upon LOC capture, VOR/LOC annunciates captured, the previous roll mode disengages and the aircraft turns to track the LOC.

7.3.1.3.3 Glide Slope Capture

The G/S cannot be captured prior to localiser capture. The G/S can be captured from above or below. Capture results in the following:

- G/S annunciates captured
- Previous pitch mode disengages
- APP light extinguishes if localiser has also been captured
- Aircraft pitch tracks the G/S
- GA displayed on thrust mode display (N_1 thrust limit)

7.3.1.3.4 After Loc and Glide Slope Capture

Shortly after capturing both LOC and G/S and below 1 500' RA:

- The second A/P couples with the flight controls
- FLARE armed is annunciated
- A/P go-around mode arms but is not annunciated

800' Radio Altitude

The second A/P must be engaged by 800' RA to execute a dual channel A/P approach. Otherwise engagement of the second A/P is inhibited. Two autopilots (dual channel) are needed to do an auto land.

400' Radio Altitude

The stabiliser is automatically trimmed an additional amount nose up. If the A/Ps subsequently disengage, forward control column force may be required to hold the desired pitch attitude.

7.3.1.3.5 Flare

The A/P flare manoeuvre starts at approximately 50' RA and is completed at touchdown:

- FLARE engaged is annunciated and F/D command bars retract
- The A/T begins retarding thrust at approximately 27' RA so as to reach idle at touchdown.
- A/T FMA annunciates RETARD
- The A/T automatically disengages approximately 2 s after touchdown.
- Drift is kicked off by the yaw channel

7.3.1.4 Go Around

The A/P GA mode requires dual A/P operation.

With the first push of either TO/GA switch:

- The thrust advances toward the reduced go-around N_1 to produce 1 000 to 2 000 fpm rate of climb
- Pitch mode engages in TO/GA
- F/D pitch commands 15° nose up until reaching programmed rate of climb
- F/D pitch then commands manoeuvring speed for each flap setting
- F/D roll commands hold current ground track. FMA is blank

With the second push of either TO/GA switch, after A/T reaches reduced go-around thrust the A/T advances to the full go-around N_1 limit.

Self-Assessment Test 07

1. Information from the flight director computer is routed to:
A) An Autopilot
B) The ADI and HSI
C) All air data computers
D) The IRS, GNS and IRS

2. Inputs to the flight director are from the:
A) VRU or IRS only
B) Radio receivers, ADCs and IRS only
C) Autopilot
D) VRU or IRS (attitude information), heading source (INS, IRS or magnetic compass), air data information from an ADC and radio nav information from the VOR/LOC and glideslope receivers

The following 4 questions relate to selections made on a flight director mode control unit:

3. When AUTO/APPR is selected the:
A) Glideslope is captured, the HDG selector goes into the operating position and the localiser is disconnected
B) Heading mode is retained throughout until the glideslope is captured; thereafter, the heading mode is always in operation and the aircraft is controlled in azimuth by a combination of heading and localiser beam error signals
C) Localiser is captured and controls the flight director roll channel; when the glideslope is captured, other pitch selections are cancelled and the beam controls the flight director pitch channels
D) Localiser and glideslope are immediately captured and the flight director command bars respond to received beam deviation signals

4. When HDG is selected the:
A) Flight director roll channel responds to HSI heading commands only
B) Flight director roll channel responds to HSI heading commands and the pitch channel can be selected to altitude hold or controlled by the pitch command selector
C) Flight director roll channel is controlled by the heading selector
D) Localiser is used to back up the heading selection made on the HSI

5. The GA mode is operated by the:
A) Control column when it is pulled back into a pitch up position provided that GA is selected on the flight director control unit
B) Selection of the GA mode on the control unit or operation of the GA button on a thrust lever
C) Operation of the GA button on a thrust lever only
D) Selection of GA on the selector unit only

6. When the GA mode is engaged the:
A) Wings are levelled and the aircraft is pitched up an appropriate amount
B) Bank angle, if any, is maintained and the aircraft is pitched up from the landing attitude to level
C) Wings are levelled only
D) Aircraft is pitched up only

7. Generally there are at least three warning flags that can be displayed on an ADI as follows:
A) GYRO, AUTOPILOT DISCONNECT and COMPUTER
B) GS, GYRO and COMPUTER
C) GA, GYRO and GS
D) GA, AUTOPILOT CHANNEL FAULT and COMPUTER

8. DME distance is usually provided on the:
A) ADI
B) Flight director control panel
C) HSI
D) EFIS mode control panel

9. The two basic elements of an AFCS autopilot are as follows:
A) HSI and ADI displays
B) Attitude indication and control
C) Flight director commands and attitude hold
D) Stability and control

10. Autopilot stability control is provided by:
A) Gyroscopes (either VRU, INU or IRS) that detect pitch and roll attitude and rate gyros that detect the rate of change of pitch, roll and yaw attitude
B) Air data computers and heading detector systems
C) Gyros, ADCs and ratio nav information
D) Rad alt, GPWS and attitude hold

11. Each basic autopilot channel consists of the following components:
A) An attitude sensor, a VOR/LOC receiver, an actuator and a feedback loop
B) An attitude sensor, an error detector, an amplifier (processor), an actuator and a feed back loop; this is a closed loop
C) GPS, LORAN and IRS
D) An attitude sensor, an error detector, an amplifier, an actuator, a feed back loop, a VOR/LOC receiver, a compass system, IRS, INS and the radio altimeter

12. A rate gyro of the type used in an autopilot system will detect:
A) Aircraft attitude about the relevant axis
B) Rate of change of attitude about the relevant axis
C) Aircraft attitude about all axes
D) None of the above

13. An autopilot comparator system:
A) Is only found in the pitch channel
B) Compares the system requirement with the operation of the actuator
C) Operates when specified G loadings exceed a threshold value
D) Will only operate with hydraulic control systems

14. The channels of a duplex autopilot system:
A) Will disconnect completely if a failure is detected in one channel
B) Will provide warnings of an impending failure and the channel(s) are disconnected manually
C) Will provide warnings of an impending failure and will disconnect the failing channel automatically
D) Can only be disconnected by the control switches

15. A channel of a triplex system will:
A) Disconnect automatically when a failure occurs as soon as the aircraft responds to the failure
B) Only disconnect, even in the event of failure, when the relevant channel switch is selected to disconnect
C) Remain engaged until the autopilot is manually switched off
D) In the event of failure, disconnect automatically without disturbance to the flight path

16. A Mach trimmer is fitted to aircraft to provide:
A) Yaw damper correction as Mach No increases
B) Attenuation of roll error detection as Mach No increases
C) Correction to basic elevator control laws with varying Mach No
D) Compensation for an increasingly nose down trim condition as aircraft speed increases. This is caused by a rearward movement of the center of pressure and will cause 'tuck under' if not corrected

17. A yaw damper prevents:
A) Dutch roll and when in operation will cause the rubber pedals to move
B) Dutch roll but is only active when the autopilot is switched on
C) Dutch roll and is operative as soon as it is switched on; it will operate regardless of the engagement state of the autopilot and AFCS. On some aircraft, flap position will modify the rate of yaw damper operation
D) Tuck under

18. Manometric locks are to do with the:
A) Selection of MACH, IAS and HEIGHT acquire and hold functions for operation of the autopilot. Air data computers are connected to the aircraft pitot/static system and provide the appropriate feeds
B) Provision of air data information for operation of the mach trimmer
C) Attenuation of autopilot azimuth manoeuvre functions with regard to speed
D) Operation and selection of all pitch manoeuvres

19. When CWS is selected:
A) Manual inputs can be put into the system and once the aircraft is in the selected altitude, the autopilot can be fully engaged
B) All manometric locks disengage
C) All azimuth locks disengage
D) All locks disengage

20. A typical autoland sequence is as follows:
A) The aircraft is under the control of the ILS LOC and glideslope all the way down to touchdown
B) After acquisition of the glideslope the aircraft continues under ILS control until about 350'. At this point the aircraft adopts the pitch attitude of the last 300', say, and the glideslope is disconnected. At about 12' radio altimeter height (some aircraft 45') drift is kicked off and the aircraft flares onto the runway as idle power is selected
C) After initial acquisition of the glideslope, radio altimeters assist in controlling the aircraft down the glideslope to the runway. Drift is kicked ff and the aircraft flares.
D) After acquisition of the localiser, the radio altimeters control the points at which different aspects of the approach path are realized. The ILS glideslope controls the aircraft in pitch from acquisition to kick off drift

21. Auto-elevator trim is effective when the:
A) Centre of pressure is aft of the CG. This produces a nose-down moment which is negated by the operation of the system
B) CG is in the neutral position and the trim index is in the correct position on the control and trim indicator
C) Manual trim wheel is operated in the correct sense, the drive mechanism, is armed and then operated when the aircraft attitude changes. Further movement of the control wheel produces a further pitch change that is translated by the auto-trim system as a command. Aircraft attitude again changes and the resultant movement zeros the initial command
D) Initial pitch manoeuvre is sensed by the autopilot and operation of the primary control occurs; control cable movement usually operates micro-switches which, in turn, selects the appropriate trim operating mechanism and the trim tab (could be the whole stabilizer) moves in the correct direction. When the aircraft attitude changes, the resulting trim command is zeroed. At this point the trim tab (or stabiliser) will be set in the correct position and the main control will be neutral

22. AFCS inputs may be grouped under the following headings:
A) GNSS and manometric input only
B) Manometric and heading inputs only
C) Manometric locks, Heading, Radio Nav from VOR, DME, GNSS, ILS and Radio Altimeter
D) ILS, VOR, DME and Radio Altimeter only

23. Heading information is supplied to the:
A) Pitch channel only. Roll is provided by cross coupling to the yaw channel after engagement of the ILS glideslope
B) Yaw channel only. Roll is provided manually after reference to the turn and slip indicator
C) Roll and yaw channels only to ensure a balanced turn
D) Roll channel but to ensure a balanced turn and to ensure no loss of height, this may include the pitch and yaw channels

24. ICAO Autoland categories are decided by minimum RVR and decision height (DH) values. Categories 1, 2 and 3A categories are as follows:
A) CAT 1 – RVR = 1200 m, DH = 100’; CAT 2 – RVR = 300 m, DH = 150; CAT 3A – RVR = 1500 m, DH= 400’
B) CAT 1 – RVR = 600 m, DH 150 m, DH = 800’: CAT 2 – RVR = 150 m: CAT 3A – RVR = 50’, DH = 25’
C) CAT 1 – RVR = 800 m, DH = 200’: CAT 2 – RVR = 400 m, DH = 100’: CAT 3A – RVR = 200 m, DH = down to runway with external visual reference
D) CAT 1 – RVR = 100 m, DH = 150’: CAT 2 – RVR = 500 m, DH = 800’; CAT 3A – RVR = 700 m, DH = 1 000’

Self-Assessment Test 07 Answers

1	B
2	D
3	C
4	B
5	B
6	A
7	B
8	C
9	D
10	A
11	B
12	B
13	B
14	A
15	D
16	D
17	C
18	A
19	A
20	B
21	D
22	C
23	D
24	C

CHAPTER 8
Warning and Recording Equipment

8.1 Stall Warnings

In order to warn the pilot that the aeroplane is approaching a stall condition, a warning device is fitted. The design of this device varies and we will look at two representative situations. The first of these is typical of the type fitted in a light aeroplane, while the second will be more representative of the types fitted to transport aeroplanes.

8.1.1 Light Aeroplane Stall Warning

A stall warning sensor is in the form of flaps mounted on the leading edge of the wing. They are held in their non-active position by dynamic pressure resultant from the forward motion of the aeroplane. As the dynamic pressure falls (as a result of reducing air speed) the spring-loaded flap moves towards it's activating position.

At a pre-set angle of attack, an electrical circuit will be completed and a warning horn will be activated

This is usually a continuous sound that stops only when the angle of attack has been reduced, i.e. when air speed is increased.

To prevent the stall warning being activated during the landing or take-off, a squat switch is fitted to the landing gear. As long as there is weight on the gear the squat switch will cut out the warning horn circuit.

8.1.2 Transport Aeroplane Stall Warning

8.1.2.1 Stick Shaker

On most modern transport aeroplanes the sensor is an angle of attack or alpha sensor. As you will recall, an aeroplane will stall at a given angle of attack for a given configuration irrespective of weight. As the aeroplane's air speed is reduced, the angle of attack increases and the sensor detects this change. The sensor is connected to a stall warning system illustrated below.

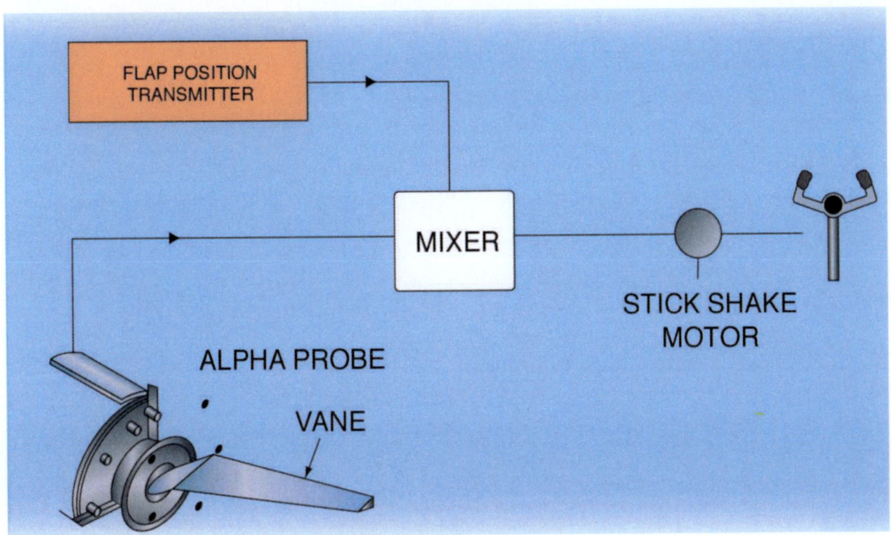

Figure 8.1 Stick Shaker

8.1.2.1.1 Operation

At the pre-set angle of attack the circuit is completed and a sector attached to the control column is activated

This motor vibrates the control column, imitating the effect of aerodynamic buffet.

A flap position signal is mixed with the alpha probe signal in order to compensate for configuration. A micro switch on the nose wheel gear de-activates the system whenever there is weight on the nose wheel gear

You should note that system design varies. On some aeroplanes, the sensor output may be processed through the ADC where it will be mixed with the flap position signal. It is normal to provide a "test" function. This activates the stick shaker by completing the circuit from the sensor to the motor.

8.1.2.2 Stick Pusher

On most aeroplanes the stall warning system is duplicated, and a stick pusher system incorporated into the system. At the design AoA, the contents of a nitrogen bottle is connected to a piston which pushes the control column forward.

8.1.2.2.1 Operating Sequence

The sequence assumes that full stall protection is fitted. As AoA increases, the system operate as follows:

1. At 5° AoA, auto-ignition operates and ensures igniters operate as AoA increases further.
2. At 12° AoA, the stick shakers operate.
3. At 15° AoA, the stick pushers operate.

The first phase ((1) and (2) above) is usually known as the stall ident phase; the latter stage in the stall warning phase. The system will operate at an earlier AoA rate of change is high.

8.1.2.3 Safety Devices

The system is cut-out if stall warning is not followed by stall ident within 60 s and also if a fault causes the stall ident system to be armed first. The system operating AoA is modified by slat (LE Flap), TE Flap and mach numbers.

8.2 Overspeed Warnings

This is another "air data" warning system provided as a means of preventing inadvertent speed increases beyond V_{MO} or M_{MO}.

The system is normally driven by outputs from the ADC but can be driven by an independent sensor unit in the form of interconnected altitude and airspeed capsules.

If the limiting speed, as shown by the bugs on the Mach/airspeed indicator, is exceeded an audio warning is activated. This makes a loud "CLACK CLACK" sound and the circuit is sometimes referred to as the "clacker" circuit.

A "Test" function is provided. When the button is pushed the "clacker" is activated.

The system provides the only audible warning of overspeed.

8.3 *Altitude Alert*

8.3.1 *CS Requirements*

An operator shall not operate a turbine propeller powered aeroplane with a maximum certificated take-off mass in excess of 5700 kg or having a maximum approved passenger seating configuration of more than 9 seats or a turbojet powered aeroplane unless it is equipped with an altitude alerting system capable of:

- Alerting the flight crew upon approaching a pre-selected altitude; and
- Alerting the flight crew by at least an aural signal, when deviating from a pre-selected altitude, except for aeroplanes with a maximum certificated take-off mass of 5700 kg or less having a maximum approved passenger seating configuration of more than 9 and first issued with an individual certificate of airworthiness in a EASA Member State or elsewhere before 1 April 1972 and already registered in a EASA Member State on 1 April 1995.

8.3.2 *Operation*

This system provides both aural and visual warnings of an aeroplane's reaching or deviating from a pre-selected altitude

The system utilises an output from a pressure altimeter (or ADC) and the pilot sets a target altitude on a control unit. The signal from the altitude sensor is mixed with the signal created by the control unit pre-set altitude. As long as the actual altitude and pre-set altitude are different there will be a signal difference.

Let us look at the sequence during a descent from 31000' to 12000'. Before leaving 31000' the pilot will set the control unit to 12000'. No warning will be given at this stage, as the signals are too different.

At about 1000' above the target altitude an aural warning will sound for two seconds and an alert light will be illuminated. The light will remain illuminated until about 300' above the target. If the aeroplane continues through the target altitude to 300' below the aural warning will sound and the light will again be illuminated.

8.4 *Ground Proximity Warning Systems*

Over the last 20 years or so it is estimated that over 50% of transport aircraft losses have been caused by "controlled" flights into the ground, for such reasons as inattention, confusion, vertigo, distraction, instrument reading error, poor visibility and navigation error. The GPWS is designed to prevent this sort of accident by giving flight deck crew advanced warning, both aurally and visually, of an unsafe flight condition close to the ground.

The radio altimeter and the Air Data Computer (ADC) are continuously monitored for aircraft height above the ground and barometric, rate of change of height; in this way, the rate of closure with the terrain immediately beneath the aircraft is continuously assessed. In a typical GPWS, a red PULL-UP light together with a WHOOP-WHOOP PULL-UP audible command will give warning of unsafe proximity to the ground. When the dangerous condition has been corrected, the warnings will cease and the system will reset itself automatically.

Note however, that the minimum OPS 1 requirements (see below) is an aural signal.

8.4.1 *OPS 1 Requirements*

(a) An operator shall not operate a turbine powered aeroplane having a maximum certificated take-off mass in excess of 5700 kg or a maximum approved passenger seating configuration of more than 9 unless it is equipped with a ground proximity warning system, except if otherwise permitted.

(b) The ground proximity warning system must automatically provide, by means of aural signals, which may be supplemented by visual signals, timely and distinctive warning to the flight crew of sink rate, ground proximity, altitude loss after take-off or go-around, incorrect landing configuration and downward glideslope deviation

8.4.2 General Operation

The GPWS is normally activated between 50' and 2450' above the surface - this height obviously being determined by the radio altimeter

The GPWS must never be de-activated (i.e. by pulling the circuit breakers) except when using approved procedures at those airfields where GPWS inhibition is specifically required.

8.4.3 GPWS Modes

The GPWS modes available (depending on type of equipment) are:

- MODE 1 Excessive descent rate
- MODE 2 Excessive Terrain Closure
- MODE 3 Height loss after take-off or missed approach
- MODE 4A Unsafe terrain clearance when gear not down and locked
- MODE 4B Unsafe terrain clearance when flaps not in landing position
- MODE 5 Descent below glideslope
- MODE 6 Descent below "minimums" (i.e. decision height bug on radio altimeter)

Note:- Mode 6 may only be available with advanced equipment.

In addition to the inputs from the ADC and the radio altimeter, information is also fed into the GPWS computer from the following:

- Main Landing Gear Selector Assembly - The position of the landing gear will govern whether or not MODE 3 is activated, and will also determine the height/barometric rate of descent conditions that would activate a MODE 4 warning.
- Flap Selector Assembly - The position of the flap again governs whether or not MODE 3 is activated and will also determine the height/terrain closure rate, which would activate a MODE 2 warning, and the height/barometric rate conditions, which would activate a MODE 4 warning.
- ILS Receiver - The degree of deviation from the glide path, together with glide path validity signals, are used in MODE 5.
- Stall Prevention - Whatever stall prevention devices are fitted to the aircraft, e.g.: stall warners, stick shakers and stick pushers, will normally feed a signal to the GPWS computer to inhibit the GPWS warnings during the incipient stall and/or stalled condition.

8.4.3.1 Testing

The GPWS system has a fully integrated self-test function (Built-in Test Equipment), which is capable of checking the signal path from all of the inputs described above. It is activated by a press to test switch and if the system checks out satisfactorily when the test switch is depressed, the normal indication to the pilot is that both of the visual and both of the aural warnings are activated simultaneously. System testing by this means is normally prohibited when airborne

8.4.4 System Operation

8.4.4.1 MODE 1

MODE 1 is activated when the barometric descent rate is excessive with respect to the aircraft height above the terrain, as determined by the radio altimeter. The barometric rate signal is obtained from the ADC. The warning envelope for MODE 1 has an upper limit of 2 450' above the ground, and at this height a warning will be given if the barometric rate of descent exceeds 7 350 fpm. At the lower limit of the envelope, which is

50' above the ground, a barometric descent rate of 1 500 fpm or more will cause MODE 1 activation. The full operating parameters for MODE 1 are shown below.

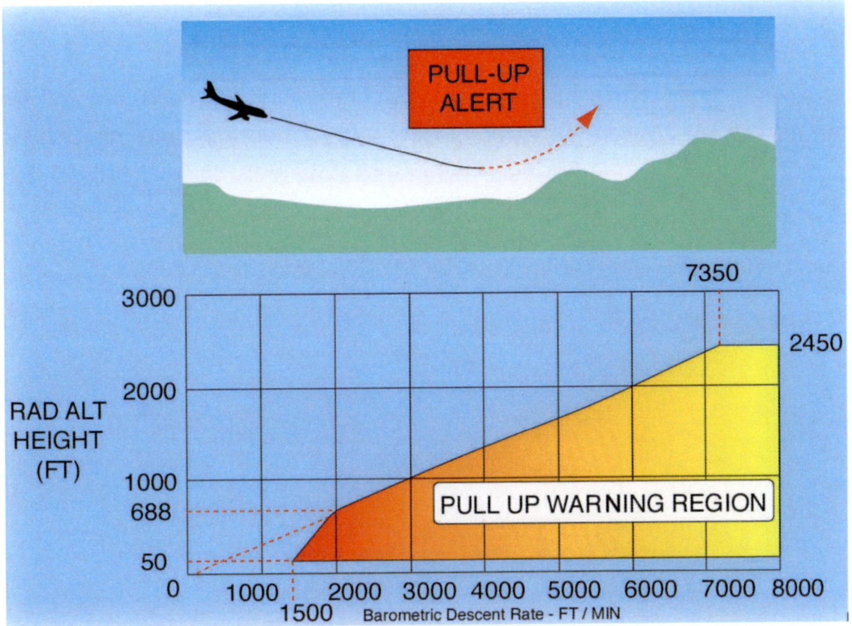

Figure 8.2 MODE 1

8.4.4.2 MODE 2

MODE 2 activation occurs when the aircraft is flying into rising terrain. This is achieved by measuring the terrain closure rate as determined by the radio altimeter. With the aircraft at 1800' above the terrain, and with the flaps NOT in landing configuration, MODE 2 will be activated if the terrain closure rate is equal to or in excess of 6000 fpm. Again, the lower limit of MODE 2 operation is 50' above the ground, and at this height a warning will be given if the terrain closure rate exceeds 2063 fpm with the flaps NOT in the landing configuration. With the flaps in the landing configuration, MODE 2 will be activated at the upper parameter of 790' AGL if the terrain closure rate is equal to, or exceeds, 3000 fpm, or at the lower parameter of 220' AGL if the terrain closure rate is equal to, or exceeds 2250 fpm. The full operating parameters for MODE 2 are shown below.

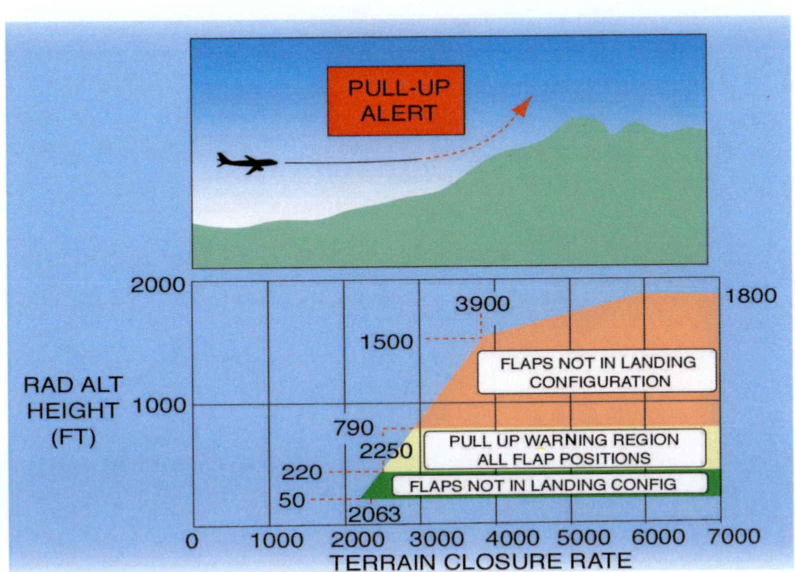

Figure 8.3 MODE 2

8.4.4.3 MODE 3

MODE 3 is activated if an excessive height loss is experienced after take-off or during a go-around procedure, when the aircraft is between 50' and 700' above the ground as determined by the radio altimeter. With the aircraft at 700'. AGL, MODE 3 will be activated if an accumulated barometric height loss of 70' or more is sensed by the ADC. With the aircraft at 50'. AGL, MODE 3 will be activated if the accumulated barometric height loss exceeds 40'. MODE 3 is inactive when the landing gear and flaps are both in the full landing configuration. The full operating parameters for MODE 3 are shown below.

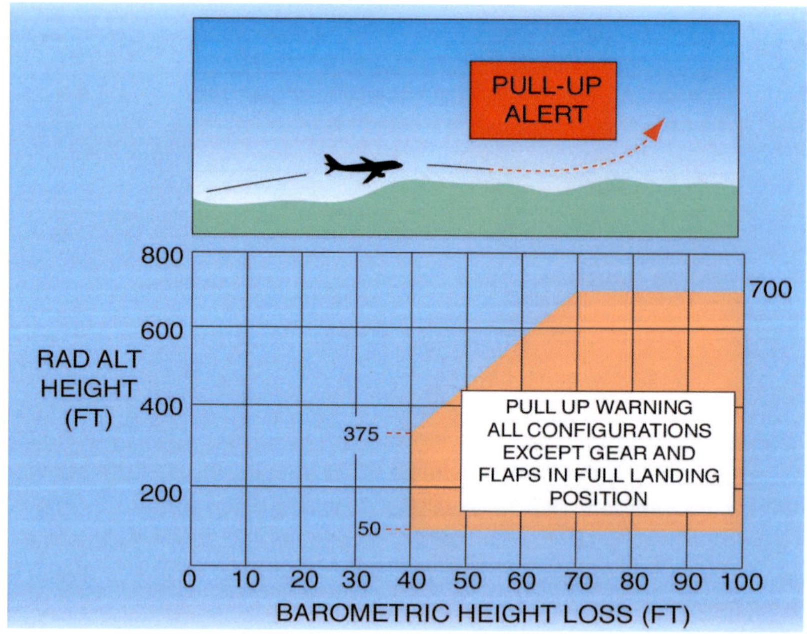

Figure 8.4 MODE 3

8.4.4.4 MODE 4

MODE 4 is activated when an unsafe terrain clearance situation is experienced, with the aircraft NOT in the landing configuration. Regardless of the barometric rate, the MODE 4 will be activated when the terrain clearance reduces to 500' AGL, UNLESS the landing gear is fully down. At 500' AGL, as determined by the radio altimeter, AND a barometric rate of descent of 2 000 fpm or more, MODE 4 will be activated UNLESS the flaps are also in the landing position. The lower operating parameter for MODE 4 is, as always 50' AGL and the full operating parameters are shown below.

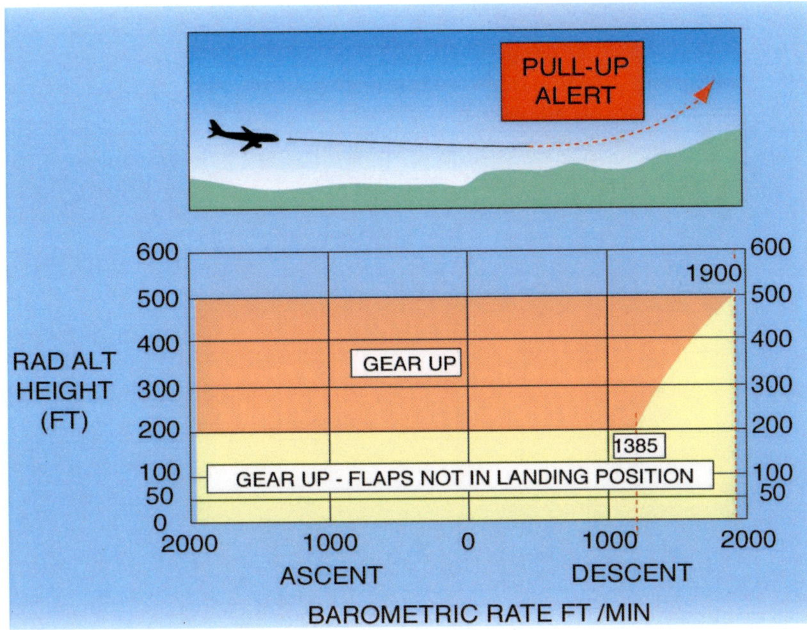

Figure 8.5 MODE 4

8.4.4.5 MODE 5

MODE 5 is activated when the aircraft is significantly below the ILS glide path with the aircraft between 500' and 50' AGL, as determined by the radio altimeter, and with the landing gear down. The glideslope warnings may occur at the same time as pull-up warnings on the occasions when the pull-up alert is due to an active MODE 1, 2, or 4, but NOT MODE 3. If MODE 3 is activated, MODE 5 is automatically inhibited. The full operating parameters for MODE 5 are shown below.

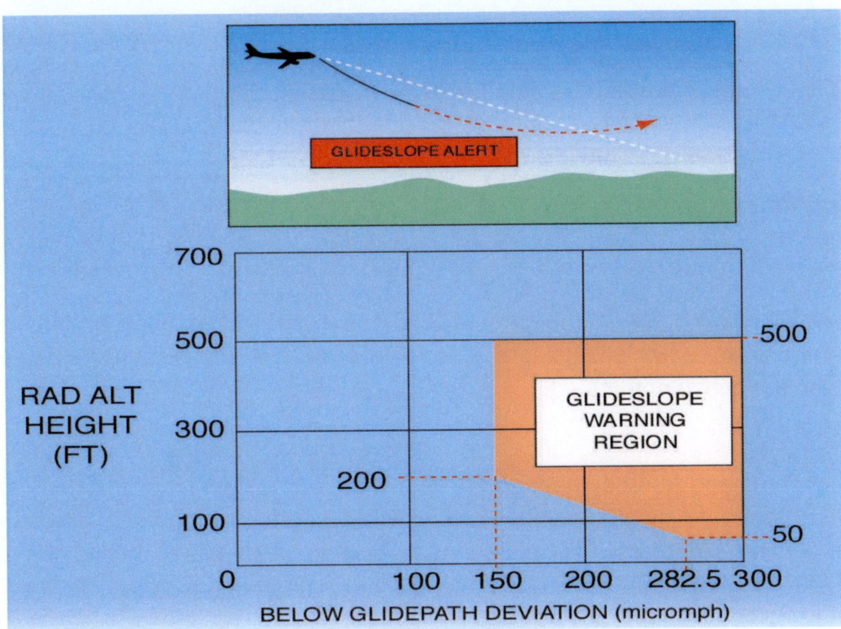

Figure 8.6 MODE 5

A summary of the modes is given in the following table.

<table>
<tr><th>Mode</th><th colspan="2">Radio Altimeter</th><th>Accum. Baro. Ht. Loss</th><th>Descent Rate</th><th colspan="2">Ground Closure Rate</th><th>Inhibit Mode</th></tr>
<tr><td>Mode One
(Descent Rate)</td><td colspan="2">2 450
↕
50</td><td></td><td>7 350 fpm
↕
1 500 fpm</td><td colspan="2"></td><td></td></tr>
<tr><td>Mode Two
(Terrain closure rate)</td><td>Flaps not Ldg
1 800
↕
50</td><td>Flaps are in Ldg
790
↕
220</td><td></td><td></td><td>6 000 fpm
exceeds
2 063 fpm</td><td>3 000 fpm
exceeds
2 250 fpm</td><td></td></tr>
<tr><td>Mode Three
(Height Loss)</td><td colspan="2">700
↕
50</td><td>70’
40’</td><td></td><td colspan="2"></td><td>Gear and flaps in full ldg. configuration</td></tr>
<tr><td>Mode four
(Unsafe terrain clearance)</td><td>Gear Down
500
↕
50</td><td>G & F down</td><td></td><td>exceeds
2 000 fpm</td><td colspan="2"></td><td></td></tr>
<tr><td>Mode Five
(Glidepath)</td><td colspan="2">Gear down
500
↕
50</td><td colspan="4">Significantly below glide path</td><td>When Mode 3 is activated</td></tr>
</table>

Mode 1 Excessive descent rate
Mode 2 Excessive terrain closure rate
Mode 3 Excessive height loss after take-off or missed approach
Mode 4 Unsafe terrain clearance when not in landing configuration
Mode 5 Excessive deviation beneath glide path

8.4.5 Alerts and Warnings

8.4.5.1 Alerts

An alert is a caution. For GPWS operations, only MODE 5, excessive deviation beneath glidepath, gives an alert. This is in the form of an audio "glide slope". The required action is to recover to the glideslope and also to attempt to establish the cause of the alert.

8.4.5.2 Warnings

A warning is a direct command to do something about a situation. In GPWS operations, warnings are given for MODES 1 - 4 and the crew must immediately level the wings, unless a curved flight path is essential, and initiate a maximum gradient climb until the minimum safe altitude is reached. Where an advanced GPWS is fitted, the cause of the warning should be verified after the climb has been initiated.

8.4.5.3 Discretionary Response

Regardless of the type of GPWS, basic or advanced, on receipt of an alert OR a warning, a response must be made. There is a case for a discretionary response to a warning under specific circumstances. When an aircraft is being operated in meteorological conditions of:

- 1 NM horizontally clear of cloud, and
- 1000’ vertically clear of cloud, and

- Visibility of 5 NM or greater, and
- Where it is obvious to the captain that the aircraft is NOT in a dangerous situation with regard to terrain, configuration or present manoeuvre, the response may then be limited to that of an alert.

The alerts and warnings of basic and advanced equipment are summarised in the following tables.

GPWS Mode		Basic Equipment	
		Alert	Warning
1. Excessive descent rate		-	"Whoop Whoop Pull Up"
2. Excessive terrain closure rate		-	"Whoop Whoop Pull Up"
3. Altitude loss after take-off or go-around		-	"Whoop Whoop Pull Up"
4. Unsafe terrain clearance while not in the landing configuration	4A Proximity to terrain - Gear not locked down	-	"Whoop Whoop Pull Up"
	4B Proximity to terrain - flaps not in a landing position	-	"Whoop Whoop Pull Up"
5. Descent below glide-slope		"Glide-slope"	-

Figure 8.7 Basic Equipment GPWS Alerts and Warnings

GPWS Mode		Advanced Equipment	
		Alert	Warning
1. Excessive descent rate		"Sink rate"	"Whoop Whoop Pull Up" plus flashing lamp
2. Excessive terrain closure rate		"Terrain Terrain"	"Whoop Whoop Pull Up" plus flashing lamp
3. Altitude loss after take-off or go-around		"Don't sink"	-
4. Unsafe terrain clearance while not in the landing configuration	4A Proximity to terrain - Gear not locked down	"Too Low Gear"	"Whoop Whoop Pull Up" plus flashing lamp
	4B Proximity to terrain - flaps not in a landing position	"Too Low Flaps"	"Too Low – Terrain"
5. Descent below glide-slope		"Glide Slope"	-
6. Descent below "minimums"		"Minimums"	-

Figure 8.8 Advanced Equipment GPWS Alerts and Warnings

Note:- Although some manufacturers of GPWS equipment may show in their literature "Too Low Terrain" to be an alert, the view of the Authority is that the response to this should be as for a warning.

8.5 Traffic Collision Avoidance System (TCAS)

With intensifying traffic flow the risk of airborne collision has increased and, in order to preserve the safety element, aircraft are being fitted with equipment that endeavours to provide collision avoidance assistance. As originally introduced TCAS I provided a traffic advisory (TA) i.e. information that would advise the pilot of a potential traffic hazard as an aid to visually acquiring the target and avoiding.

Advances in technology have led to the wide implementation of TCAS II. Indeed, as of the year 2000, all commercial aircraft over 15 000 kg and with seating for 30 or more passengers operating in European airspace will be required to carry TCAS II. This shall provide:

- Generation of Traffic Advisories (TA)
- Threat detection
- Generation of Resolution Advisories (RA)
- Co-ordination
- Surveillance
- Communication with ground stations

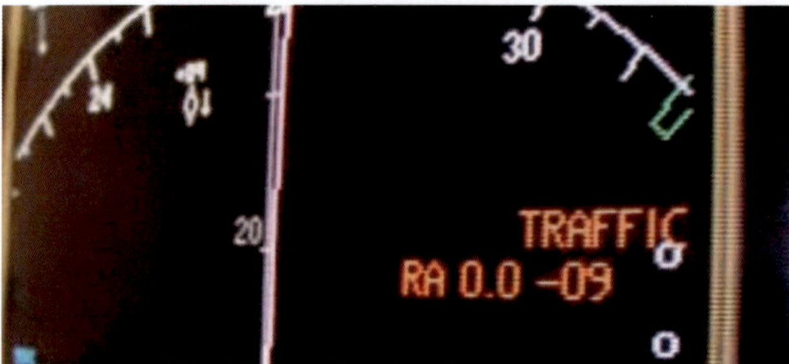

The first four of these items must be processed on each cycle of operation, the cycle taking 1.2 s to complete.

8.5.1 TCAS II

This equipment includes a Mode S data link transponder, two directional aerials (one above and one below the fuselage) a receiver, a computer processor and a flight deck display. Signals from other transponders are detected and processed. The processing of Mode A/C transponders will provide TA/RA outputs. Where a Mode S signal is received and processed, if a collision risk is established, the computer will establish a link with the TCAS II computer on the other aeroplane. The computers will “agree” and co-ordinate “Resolution Advisories” and each will present an RA message on the display. This will advise “climb” or “descend” or “don’t climb/descend”. The display may be a dedicated TCAS display or may be integrated on the EFIS Navigation Display. In either case the symbology used will be the same.

- Hollow White or cyan diamond – other traffic not offering a threat
- Solid White or cyan diamond – traffic within 6NM and 1 200' vertically (proximate traffic)
- Solid Yellow Circle – traffic advisory
- Solid Red Square – resolution advisory

Each symbol will have a tag attached. This will contain data concerning the altitude of the target in reference to your own altitude, (+ 06 indicates 600' above). An arrow will indicate whether the "target" is climbing or descending. Where the target is a Mode A transponder with no height transmissions no data tag will appear and, of course, no RA will be given. If the target does not have a functioning transponder the TCAS system will not be able to detect its presence. The nominal maximum tracking range of TCAS is 14NM. However, in high density traffic areas, the system range could be reduced to 5NM. A RA will be generated between 15 to 35 s before the point of closest approach of the intruder. TAs are generated 5 to 20 s in advance of RAs. The TCAS equipment will be capable of handling a maximum surveillance capacity of 30 aircraft but is nominally capable of surveillance of approximately 27 "high closing speed" targets within 14NM.

TCAS CLIMB RESOLUTION ADVISORY

8.6 Central Warning System

As aeroplanes have become more complex and the number of systems requiring monitoring increases, there has been a corresponding increase in the number of warning devices, both visual and aural. This plethora of flashing lights, horns and bells could lead to immense confusion and 'scan' problems that could cause unnecessary distraction. In order to reduce this probability, aeroplanes are equipped with a Central Warning System (CWS).

8.6.1 System Layout

In its basic form, a system comprises a group of warning and indicator lights connected to signal circuits actuated by the appropriate systems of the aircraft, each light displaying a legend denoting the system and a malfunction or advisory message. All the lights are contained on an annunciator panel installed within a pilot's visual range. In aircraft carrying a flight engineer, a panel is also installed at his station and is functionally integrated with the pilot's panel. An example of such a panel is illustrated in Figure 8.9. In this case, the panel is made up of a number of blue lights which are advisory or normal operating conditions, a number of amber lights, a red "master warning" light and an amber "master caution" light.

8.6.2 Operation

When a fault occurs in a system, a fault-sensing device transmits a signal, which illuminates the appropriate amber light. The signal is also transmitted to an electronic device known as a logic controller, the function of which is to determine whether the fault is of a hazardous nature or is one requiring caution. If the fault is hazardous, then the controller output signal illuminates the red "master warning" light; if caution is required, then the signal will illuminate only the amber "master caution" light.

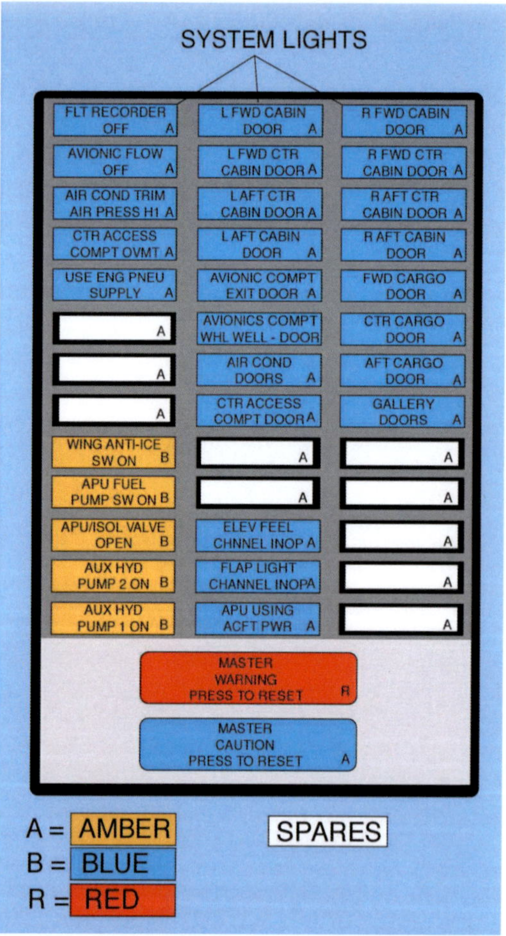

Figure 8.9 Warning layout

8.6.3 Master Caution Lights

Each master light incorporates a switch unit so that when the caps are pressed in, the active signal circuits are disconnected to extinguish the lights and, at the same time, they are reset to accept signals from faults, which might subsequently occur in any other of the systems in the aircraft. The system lights do not reset and remain illuminated until the system fault is corrected. Dimming of lights and testing of bulb filaments is carried out by means of switches mounted adjacent to the annunciator panel. On aeroplanes fitted with EICAS / ECAM the warnings are presented on the upper screen.

8.7 Recording Devices

Recording devices are installed in aeroplanes as part of the never-ending quest to prevent accidents. There are two root causes of all incidents and accidents:

- mechanical failure
- human error

In an aeroplane incident or accident the investigators will endeavour to establish whether the cause is mechanical or human or a combination. Once having established that the investigation will focus on the factors that led up to the occurrence. In the investigation of the mechanical aspects they will be considerably assisted if a complete record of the behaviour of every mechanical/ structural component is available right up to the instant of the occurrence. In the same way, a complete record of the functioning of the human element will provide valuable information. For these reasons extensive pre-flight documentation is retained for both aeroplane and crew. Both crew and ATC keep in-flight records but, in the event of an accident, the on-board documentary records could be destroyed. To enhance the recording system certain aeroplanes are required to carry flight data recording devices (FDR) and cockpit voice recorders (CVR). The FDR is designed to record mechanical features. The CVR records all voice communications in the flight deck.

8.7.1 Flight Data Recorder (FDR)

8.7.1.1 Carriage of an FDR

In accordance with OPS 1 a commercial transport aeroplane that is either:

- multi-engine turbine with more than 9 passenger seats, or
- has a maximum certificated take-off mass over 5700 kg

must carry a FDR that uses a digital method of recording and storing data in respect of certain parameters

A method of retrieving the data (from the storage) must be available.

8.7.1.1.1 Parameters

The parameters to be recorded vary according to the maximum certificated TOM and also, to a degree, with the age of the aeroplane. The data listed here is for an aeroplane with a C of A first issued on or after 1st April 1998. For other variations you should consult OPS 1 Section K.

For all aeroplanes required to carry an FDR

- altitude
- airspeed
- heading
- acceleration
- attitude (pitch /roll)
- radio transmission
- thrust or power on each engine
- configuration of lift and drag devices
- use of AFCS
- angle of attack

Additionally, for aeroplanes over 27000 kg

- positions of primary controls
- pitch trim
- radio altitude
- primary navigation information
- cockpit warnings
- landing gear positions

For aeroplanes that are required to carry an FDR and have a novel or unique design feature, any parameters dedicated to that design feature must also be recorded. All these parameters must be recorded against a common reference time scale. The data must be obtained from aeroplane sources that will enable accurate correlation (matching) with information displayed or presented to the flight crew. It should be noted that on some FDR models a sophisticated design function allows certain parameters to be transmitted at regular intervals through a data link with a ground station.

8.7.1.2 Operation of the FDR

The FDR will be powered from the aeroplane's 24V DC bus.

It must commence operating automatically, before the aeroplane is capable to move under its own power and must automatically cease recording after the aeroplane is incapable of moving under its own power

The crew cannot switch the FDR off. If the FDR is unserviceable the flight may be conducted under certain circumstances. These are given in full in OPS 1 but briefly are as follows:

- It is not reasonably practicable to repair/replace the unit before departure
- Not more than 72 h have elapsed since FDR was first reported u/s
- Not more than 7 previous flights have taken place with the unit in a failed condition

8.7.1.3 Retention of Data

The FDR must be capable of storing up to 25 h of data. (10 h for aeroplanes of 5700 kg or less)

8.7.1.4 Design of the FDR

The FDR is contained in a shockproof box (mounted as far aft as possible) capable of sustaining extremely high impact forces and high temperatures. It is also completely waterproof and is fitted with a device that will aid location in deep water. In order to record the necessary parameters, the sources will vary according to the sophistication of the aeroplane. On earlier generation jets, the sources are the individual sensors. On modern aeroplanes a large number of the parameters are taken from the aeroplane's integrated data source.

8.7.2 Cockpit Voice Recorder

8.7.2.1 Carriage of a CVR

In accordance with the requirements of OPS 1 a commercial transport aeroplane that is either:

- multi-engine turbine with more than 9 passenger seats, or
- has a maximum certificated take-off mass in excess of 5700 kg

must carry a CVR

8.7.2.2 Parameters to be Recorded

The CVR must be capable of recording:

- All radio voice communications transmitted from or received in the flight deck
- The aural (audio) environment of the flight deck including, without interruption, audio signals from each boom or mask microphone in use
- Voice communications of flight crew members using the aeroplane's interphone system and PA system
- All voice or other audio signals related to the identification of navigation or approach aids

8.7.2.3 Operation of the CVR

The CVR should be powered from the aeroplane's 24V DC bus.

The CVR must commence operating automatically, before the aeroplane is capable to move under its own power and must automatically cease recording after the aeroplane is incapable of moving under its own power

8.7.2.4 Retention of Recording

The CVR must be capable of retaining the information recorded in such a way that, at any instant, the previous two hours of recorded information could be recalled. This period is reduced to 30 min for aeroplanes of MTOM 5700 kg or less.

8.7.2.5 Design of the CVR

In aeroplanes over 5700 kg, the CVR must be a separate unit from the FDR. The container, in which the unit is located, should be mounted as far aft as possible and must be impact resistant, shockproof, fireproof and waterproof. It will be fitted with a device to assist location in deep water.

Self-Assessment Test 08

1. Stall warning systems are:
A) Never modified by flap and/or slat position
B) Inhibited on the ground by an airspeed switch
C) Operative at all times
D) Inhibited on the ground by a squat switch

2. On large aircraft, the approach to a stall is detected by an alpha vane:
A) Which operates at the same AoA regardless of aircraft weight
B) Which operates at a varying angle of attack depending upon aircraft weight
C) Which operates at the same IAS regardless of aircraft weight
D) Which operates at the same IAS regardless of flap or slat position

3. When an alpha vane reaches the stall angle, an electrical circuit is energized which:
A) Activates a warning light only
B) Operates a stick shaker motor only
C) Sounds a warning horn only
D) Usually operates all three of the above warning systems

4. An overspeed warning is activated usually if the IAS:
A) Exceeds the normal cruise speed by a specified amount
B) Were to exceed V_{MO}/M_{MO} by a specified amount and a 'clacker' or speed horn operates
C) Exceeds the selected speed or Mach No by a specified amount
D) Approaches the stall warning angle

5. Yellow and black striped overspeed bugs are fitted to the:
A) Airspeed indicators together with a duplicated warning on the ADI
B) Airspeed indicators together with a duplicated warning on the HSI
C) The main airspeed indicators
D) Airspeed indicators together with a duplicated warning on the FMS CDU

6. An altitude warning system operates when the altitude is above or below the selected datum height of:
A) Plus or minus 100'
B) Plus or minus 200'
C) Plus or minus 300'
D) Plus or minus 400'

7. A GPWS provides the following warnings usually at a specified height as follows:
A) A red alert PULL-UP light, an audible whoop and the words PULL-UP, PULL-UP when between 50' and 2 450' above the ground
B) A red alert PULL-UP light when between 50' and 4 000' above the ground, together with an audible whoop whoop and the words PULL UP, PULL UP
C) An amber flashing warning light and the words CAUTION, CAUTION only
D) A red alert light, a clacker and the words PULL UP, PULL UP

8. The following modes relate to the function of the GPWS as follows; which statement is correct:
A) Mode 2 – ILS – Significant deviation below the glideslope
B) Mode 1 – Excess descent rate, excessive terrain closure, height loss after take-off or missed approach
C) Mode 5 – Height loss after take-off or missed approach
D) Mode 3 – Unsafe terrain clearance when not in the landing configuration

9. The flap selection function is associated with:
A) Mode 1 only
B) Mode 2 only
C) Mode 3 only
D) Mode 3, Mode 2, Mode 4

10. ILS receiver functions are to do with:
A) Mode 1
B) Mode 3
C) Mode 5
D) Mode 4

11. The GPWS is inhibited when the:
A) Whenever corrective action is not taken within 10 s
B) Flap and undercarriage selector supplies are inoperative
C) Stall warning system operates
D) When the stall warning system in inoperative

12. In the TCAS II system a TA warning is:
A) Generated 5 to 20 s in advance of a RA
B) Generated 5 to 20 s after a RA
C) Not generated until the target is within 20 NM
D) Is inhibited when the stall warning system operates

13. A TCAS indicator displays a solid white or blue diamond; this means that:
A) Traffic is not transponding
B) Traffic is within 6NM and 1 200' vertically
C) A RA has been generated
D) Traffic is not a threat

14. If a mode S signal is received and processed the:
A) System will operate the TCAS and GPWS on both aircraft
B) Computers on both aircraft will generate TA instructions only
C) Computer will establish a link with the TCAS computer on the other aircraft and generate RA instructions on both aircraft displays
D) Mode C on the transponders of both aircraft are momentarily suppressed so that false height information is not processed by the computers

15. The lights and captions of a central warning system (CWS) are grouped as follows:
A) Lights and captions are white but master caution lights are amber for caution and red for warning
B) Red for advisory, blue for caution and amber for normal operating conditions
C) Amber for advisory situations, red for caution and blue for normal operating situations
D) Blue for normal operating conditions or advisory, amber for caution situations and red for hazardous or warning situations

16. A CVR must, in accordance with the requirements of OPS 1, be fitted to a commercial transport aircraft that is:
A) A multi engined turbine aircraft with more than 9 passenger seats or has a maximum certificated TOM in excess of 5700 kg
B) A commercial transport aircraft which has more than 21 seats or has a TOM in excess of 66000 kg
C) A freighter aircraft which has a TOM greater than 5700 kg
D) A multi engines piston aircraft with more than 5 seats and a TOM in excess of 5700 kg

17. In general terms:
A) A FDR is mandatory and a CVR is not mandatory
B) A FDR is not mandatory; a CVR is mandatory
C) A FDR samples mechanical features and a CVR records voice communications on the flight deck
D) A CVR samples mechanical features and a FDR records voice communications on the flight deck

Self-Assessment Test 08 Answers

1	D
2	A
3	D
4	B
5	C
6	C
7	A
8	B
9	D
10	C
11	C
12	A
13	B
14	C
15	D
16	A
17	C

CHAPTER 9
Powerplant and System Monitoring Instruments

9.1 Sensors

In this chapter we will take a look at some of the devices which sense or measure a particular parameter and create a signal proportional to the measurement.

9.1.1 Pressures

Pressure measurements are required for various applications ranging through:

- Static air pressure
- Fluid pressure
- Manifold pressure
- Differential pressure
- Pressure ratios

These pressures may be measured directly or remotely.

9.1.1.1 Direct Pressure Measurement

Direct pressure measurement may be carried out using bourdon tube, bellows or capsule sensors. The sensors are located within the indicator.

9.1.1.1.1 Bourdon Tube

The tube is in the form of a coil and is manufactured from a metal compound such as phosphor bronze or beryllium-copper. The pressure to be measured is piped directly into the instrument and the deflection of the coiled tube is proportional to the pressure being measured.

A Bourdon tube is used to measure high pressures (e.g. oil pressure, oxygen pressure, hydraulic pressure)

9.1.1.1.2 Bellows

The bellows is more sensitive than the Bourdon tube and may be used to measure lower pressures (e.g. fuel booster pump output pressure).

9.1.1.1.3 Capsule

Used to measure low pressure.

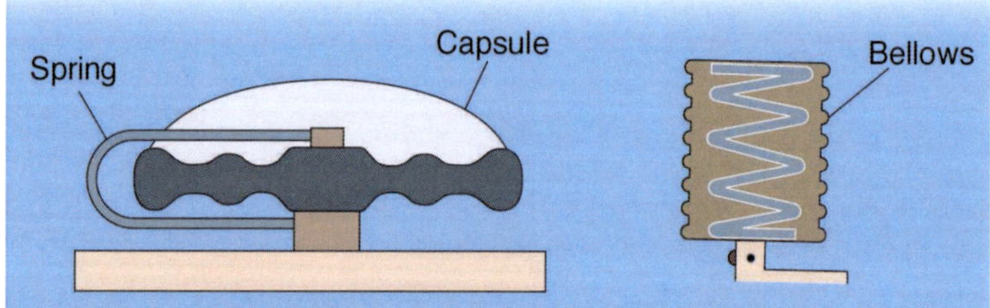

Figure 9.1 Aneroid Capsule and Bellows

When the pressure acting on the external face of the capsule is reduced, the spring causes the capsule to open. If the external pressure increases the effectiveness of the spring is reduced and the capsule collapses.

In some cases it is necessary to measure the difference between two sensed pressures. In this case a modification of the flexible metal capsule is used. In this the capsule is contained in an airtight case. The case is fed from one pressure source while the capsule is fed internally from the second pressure source. Expansion and contraction of the capsule will now be controlled by the effect of both pressures and will reflect the algebraic some of those pressures.

9.1.1.2 Remote Pressure Measurement

In aircraft, the majority of applications in which pressures are measured use remote indicating systems, i.e. the pressure sensor (or transmitter) is connected to a pressure source at a remote point on the aircraft and data is then transmitted electrically through a transmission circuit to a flight deck indicator; the indicator then converts the electrical signal into a mechanical or electronic display.

Depending on design and the range of pressures to be measured the sensor units may be in the form of metal capsules, diaphragms or bellows.

9.1.1.2.1 Bellows pressure sensor

These may be used in an engine oil pressure indicating system. The rotor of the transmitter is connected mechanically to 2 bellows, one which is sensitive to oil pressure and the other sensitive to ambient engine cowl pressure; the rotor position therefore depends on the difference between the 2 pressures (i.e. gauge pressure). The transmitter rotor sends an electrical signal to the indicator rotor which then moves a pointer (via a gear train) on the flight deck instrument by an amount proportional to the pressure sensed. If the electrical power supply fails the indicator pointer will “freeze” at the value being indicated at the time of failure

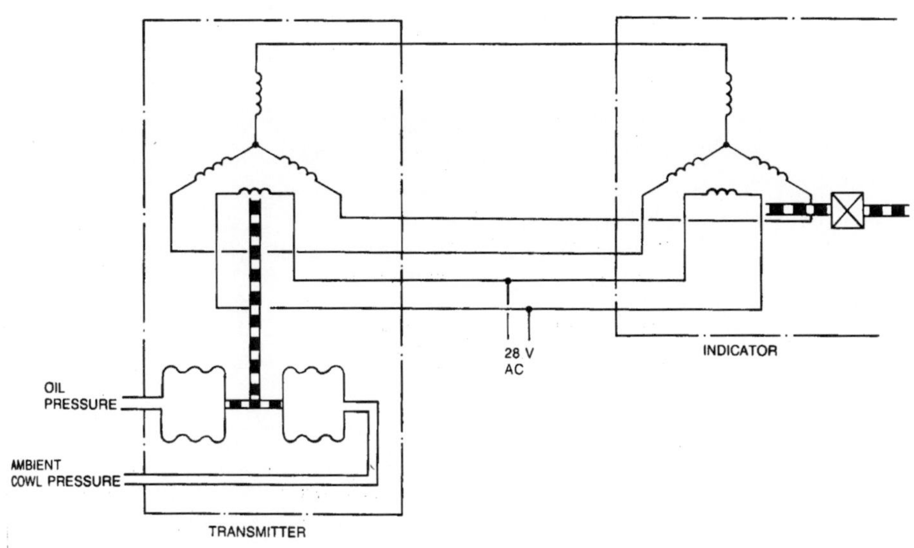

Figure 9.2 Bellows type pressure sensor

9.1.1.2.2 Capsule pressure sensor

These may be used to measure engine oil and oil filter inlet pressures, fuel pump inlet and outlet pressures, engine breather pressure, etc. The typical system employs a capsule, a moving core type inductive sensor and a servo-operated indicator. Pressure applied to the capsule varies the position of the inductor core and results in an output signal, which is proportional to the pressure, the output signals are amplified and used to drive an indicator pointer.

Typically uses 26 V AC supply and a solenoid operated flag in the indicator comes into view when there is a power supply failure.

9.1.1.2.3 Other Systems

In another form of inductor type pressure transmitter a capsule is used to position an armature core which

varies the reluctance of 2 inductor coils and therefore the current flowing in the coils. Output signals are supplied to a moving coil type indicator which operates on the DC ratiometer principle.
Modern aircraft now use piezoelectric pressure sensors (e.g. in air data computers).

9.1.1.3 Pressure switches

Pressure switches are usually connected to cockpit indicator and warning lights and give an indication of pressure variations which may be potentially dangerous (e.g. low oil pressure). The most common types are diaphragm or capsule type sensors exposed to different pressure on either side (e.g. oil pressure on one side of the diaphragm and local ambient pressure on the other). The displacement of the sensor activates a switch at a preset value and can be used to indicate a high or low value of pressure, activation of the switch may also cause an annunciator light to illuminate.
May be used in oil pressure, fuel pressure (to indicate low oil or fuel pressure) or oil filter by-pass systems (to indicate that oil is by-passing the filter).

9.1.1.4 Hysterisis

On all of these pressure sensors, the change of pressure acting upon them is converted into a mechanical motion by the change in shape of the sensor. However, the sensors have an initial resistance to change in shape that results in a time lag between the time of change in pressure and the resultant change in shape. Figure 9.3 is a graphical representation of the change of capsule shape with change of pressure acting on an aneroid capsule. This illustrates the time lag, (known as "Hysterisis") as a hysterisis curve.

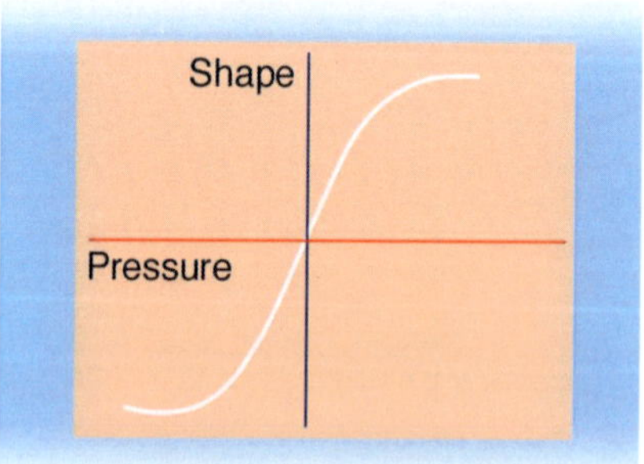

Figure 9.3 Hysterisis

9.1.2 Temperature Measurement

The temperatures that require to be measured vary over the range of:

- Air temperatures
- Gas temperatures
- Component temperatures
- Fluid temperatures

Devices used to measure temperature are called thermometers. In most forms of measurement of temperature we make use of some variation of the physical properties of a substance. These property variations are as follows:

- Expansion – most substances expand as temperature rises, this expansion may be used to indicate temperature
- Vapour pressure – when heated many liquids change state from liquid to vapour, pressure of the vapour may be used to give an indication of temperature, seldom used in aircraft
- Variable resistance – substances change their electrical resistance when exposed to varying temperature
- Electromotive force (emf) – dissimilar metals joined at their ends produce an emf which is dependent on the temperature between the 2 junctions

- Radiation – radiation emitted by a body at any wavelength is related to the temperature of the body (emissivity); this method is called radiation pyrometry and is used in some jet engines to measure turbine blade temperature

9.1.2.1 Liquid Thermometers

The most common example of such a sensor is the mercury or alcohol thermometer. In this, a tube is constructed with a narrow bore and a bulb or reservoir at one end. The tube is partially filled with the liquid medium and is then sealed. When the bulb is exposed to heat the fluid expands and the length of the column of fluid, visible in the tube, becomes greater. The tube can be calibrated in degrees. This type of thermometer is ideal for some purposes but is seldom (if ever) found on an aeroplane except in the medical kit.

9.1.2.2 Bi-Metallic Strips

In many cases, the property of expansion is used in a slightly different way. Different materials expand and contract at different rates when subjected to the same change in temperature. If two thermally dissimilar metals are strapped together and heat is applied, one will expand more than the other will and the bi-metallic strip will distort.

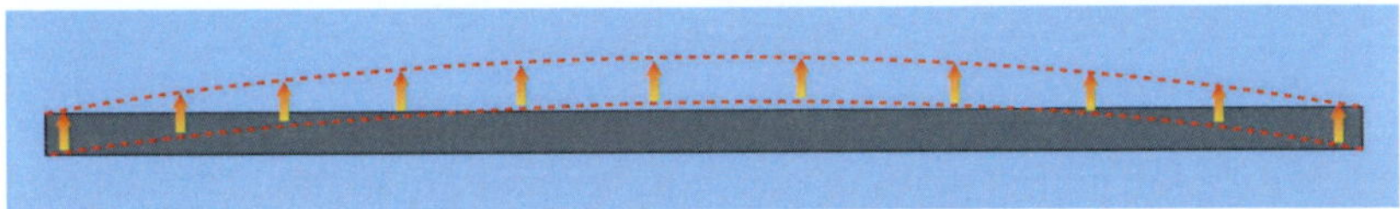

Figure 9.4 Bi-metallic strip

It is normal to form the bi-metallic strip into a coil so that changes in the temperature will cause the coil to wind or unwind and will therefore produce a rotational movement.

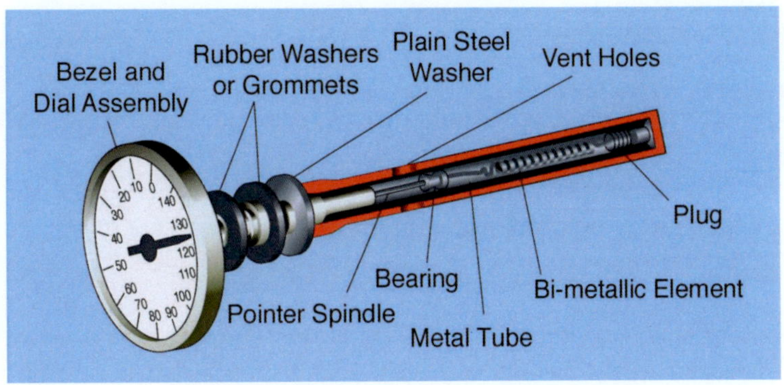

Figure 9.5 Temperature measurement

9.1.2.3 Variable Resistance

This is by far the most widely used sensor in the modern large civil aircraft. It consists of a temperature sensor (called a bulb) and an indicator connected in series to a DC power supply (sometimes rectified AC may be used). Indicator units are the moving coil type with the internal circuits being a Wheatstone bridge configuration or the more common ratiometer.

9.1.2.3.1 Wheatstone Bridge

The Wheatstone bridge circuit consists of 4 resistances as shown in Figure 9.6. The temperature sensor forms the unknown resistance R_X of the bridge circuit and the other 3 resistances (R_1, R_2 and R_3) are of known value and are contained within the indicator. When the sensor is subjected to temperature variations its resistance will change and cause an out of balance bridge circuit with the value of R_X at a particular temperature governing the current flowing through the moving coil, the out of balance current being a measure of temperature sensed. The moving coil then rotates and positions the pointer against a scale to indicate temperature.

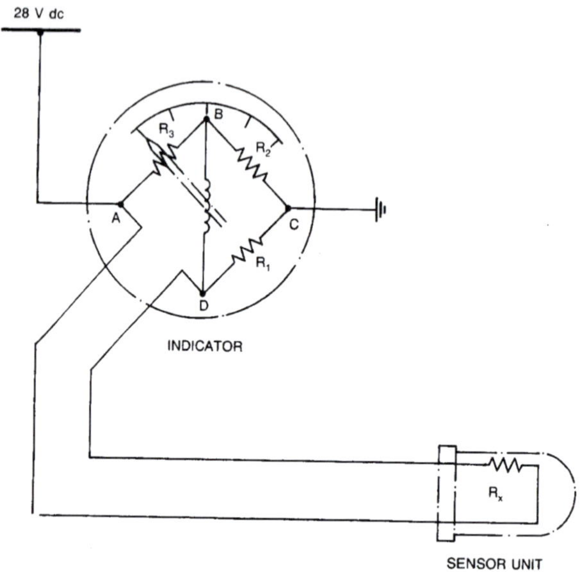

Figure 9.6 Wheatstone Bridge circuit

There is only one point where the circuit is balanced and at which no current flows in the moving coil, this is called the null point. It is denoted on the indicator scale by a datum mark that the pointer rests against when power is switched off.

Disadvantage of the Wheatstone bridge: the out of balance current depends on the voltage of the power supply, errors in instrument reading will occur if aircraft voltage is different to that the instrument was calibrated for

9.1.2.3.2 Ratiometer

The ratiometer also consists of a resistive temperature sensor and moving coil indicator, however, the indicator has 2 coils moving together in a permanent magnetic field of non-uniform strength. The force which moves the coils is caused by the difference in current ratio in the 2 coils.

Advantage of the ratiometer:- as the system works on the ratio of currents it is unaffected by variations of aircraft voltage supply

A typical example variable resistance principle is the air temperature sensor is shown below. The sensing element consists of a platinum wire. This is fed with a DC supply and a device for sensing the output current. If the temperature of the platinum wire changes the resistance changes and the current flow will be altered.

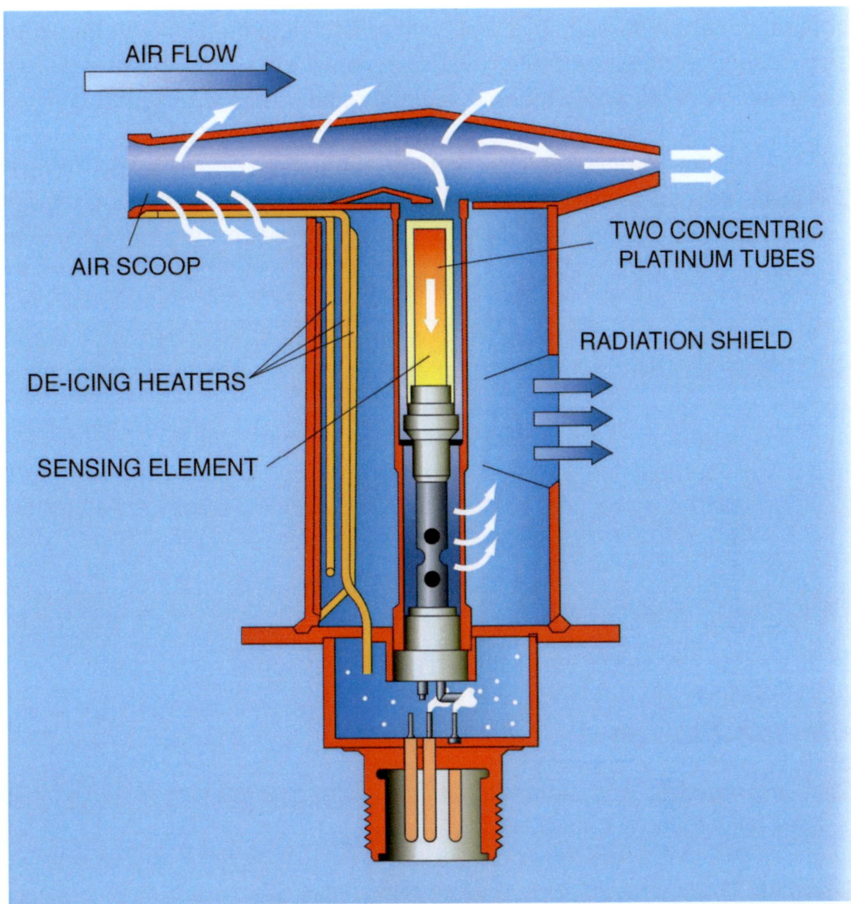

Figure 9.7 Temperature Sensor

Such variable resistance devices may be used as open elements for measuring air temperature or may be sealed in a container for use in measuring temperatures of fluids or relatively hot gases.

9.1.2.4 Thermocouples

This is another application of the variation in electrical properties of substances affected by heat changes. In this arrangement, two wires, made from different metals, are joined at their ends as shown in Figure 9.8.

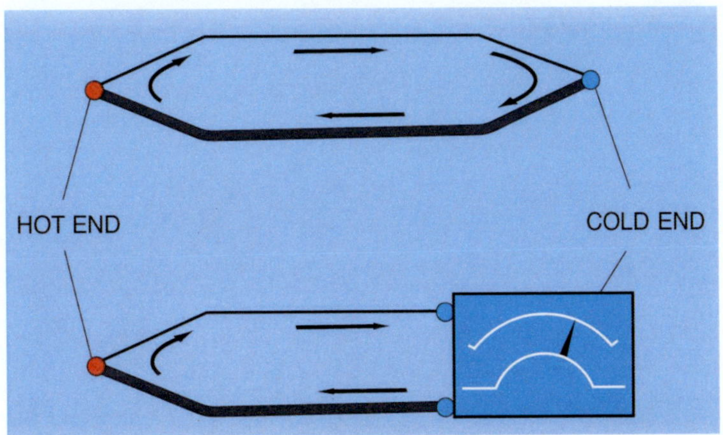

Figure 9.8 Thermocouples

When one end of this arrangement, the hot end, is exposed to heat an electromotive force (emf) is produced by the thermal gradient between the hot end and the cold end. This is called the "Seebeck Effect". The resultant emf can be measured at the "cold" end by a sensitive voltmeter (milli voltmeter) calibrated in degrees. The advantage of the thermocouple is that, with suitable elements, it can be used at extremely high temperatures (e.g. cylinder head temperature (CHT), exhaust gas temperature (EGT)). The maximum temperature measurement in aircraft applications is approximately 1100°C.

Thermocouples may be of the surface contact sensor type used to measure temperature of a solid component (e.g. CHT) or the immersion sensor type used to measure gas temperature (e.g. EGT). A thermocouple generates its own voltage and therefore does not need an input from the aircraft electrical system. For CHT applications the temperature of the hottest cylinder in a piston engine is measured.

For EGT applications several probes are arranged in parallel so that the value given is an average of all the probes (i.e. if one fails the system is more or less unaffected)

EGT probes may be the stagnation type (used in pure jet engines due to high gas velocities) or rapid response type (used in turboprops due to lower exhaust gas velocities). Probes may be located in the exhaust unit, between high and low-pressure turbines or at the leading edge of stator guide vanes between turbine stages.

The cold junction is temperature compensated so that changes in ambient temperature do not affect the indicator reading (i.e. the cold junction is effectively kept at a constant temperature)

9.2 Transmission Systems

Transmission systems are used to relay information from a remote sensor to an indicator which can be viewed by the pilot. They fall into three categories:

- Mechanical
- Electro-mechanical
- Digital

9.2.1 Mechanical Transmission

Figure 9.9 illustrates a typical mechanical system, which consists of gears and shafts that are designed to magnify the movement of the sensor and transmit it to the indicator.

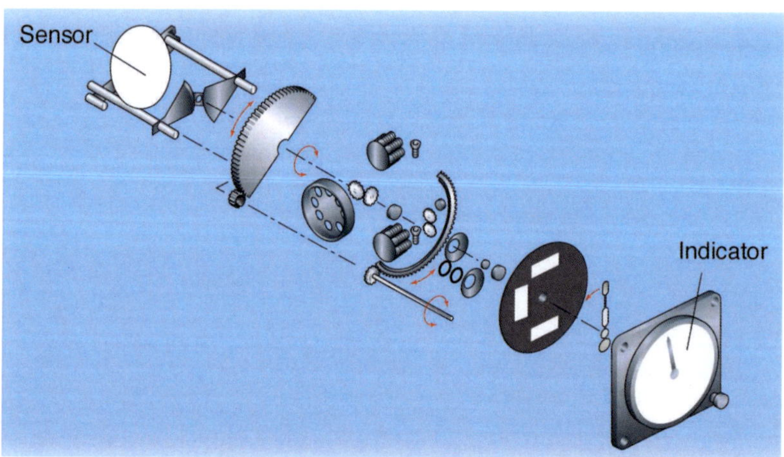

Figure 9.9 Basic Mechanical Instrument Drive System

Although such systems are simple and reliable, they do suffer from some major problems as follows:

- The sensor and the indicator must be located close together
- Friction in the bearings will cause wear and this will reduce the time between overhauls

- Friction in the bearings will cause mechanical (torque) forces that will result in a time lag in transferring the sensor information to the indicator.

These are major problems and steps were taken to at least minimise the latter two using jewelled bearings reduced the rate of wear. Attempts were made to reduce the torque forces by vibrating the mechanism at a fairly high frequency. This caused the bearings to "float" and did result in some reduction of mechanical lag as well as allowing more of the displacing power to be used to drive an improved indicator.
Mechanical linkages are still common and are found in the instrumentation of most small aeroplanes. They may also be found in the stand-by instruments fitted to many large aeroplanes.

9.2.2 Electro-Mechanical Transmission

These systems overcome some of the problems of the direct indicating mechanical system. The systems are known generically as "Remote Indicating Synchronous Data Transmission Systems" but are most commonly referred to simply as "Synchro Systems".

There are four distinct types of synchro systems in general use:

- Torque
- Control
- Resolver
- Differential

9.2.2.1 The Torque Synchro

This is a low power, non-amplified system. It is suitable for use in the transmission of position data, such as the position of flaps.

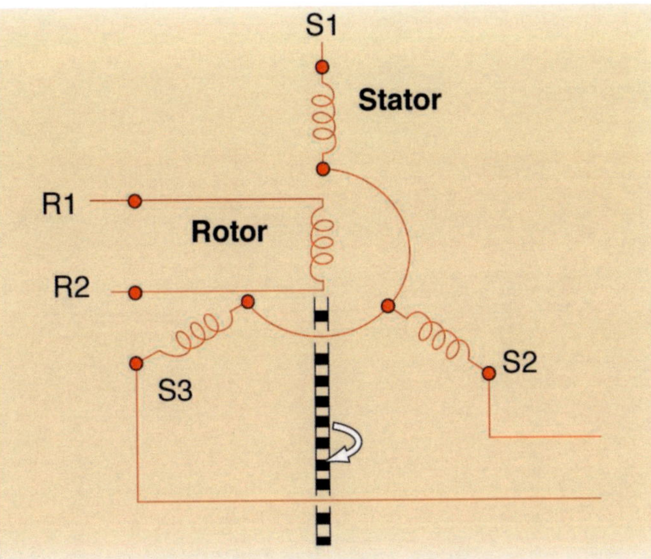

Figure 9.10 Torque synchro

Consider an arrangement such as illustrated in Figure 9.10. In this a shaft passes through the centre of an arrangement known as the stator. The stator consists of three fixed coils, 120° apart and made up of electrically conducting material (S1, S2, S3) Carried on, and fixed to, the shaft is another coil, known as the rotor (R) which rotates with the shaft at the centre of the stator arrangement. The rotor coil is fed with an AC supply and creates in the stator coils alternating voltages. The voltage in each stator coil is governed by the relative position of the rotor coil.

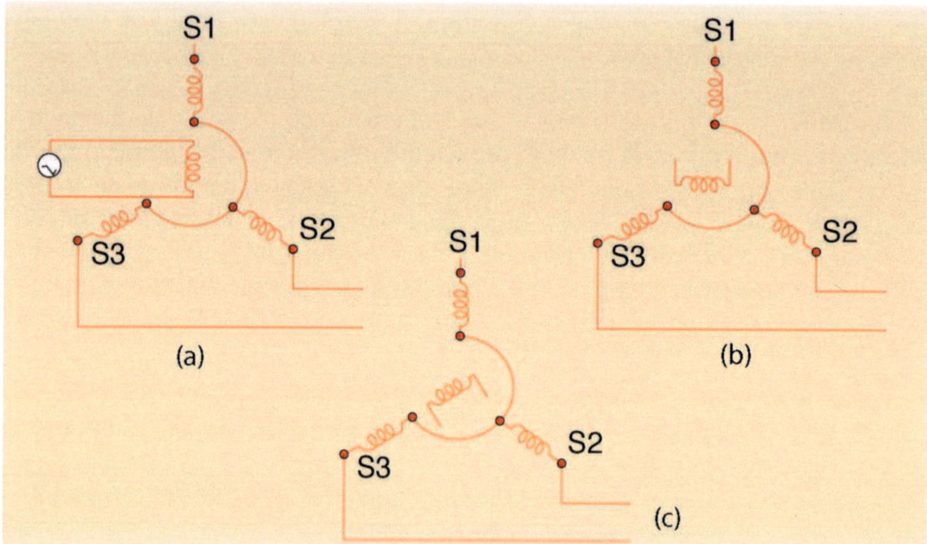

Figure 9.11 Torque synchros

In Figure 9.11(a), coil S1 will have maximum voltage while S2 and S3 will have 0.866 maximum voltage. In Figure 9.11(b), S1 will have zero voltage while S2 and S3 will each have about 0.5 of maximum voltage. In Figure 9.11(c), S3 will experience maximum voltage while S1 and S2 will experience 0.866 of maximum. Clearly, the voltages induced in the stator coils and the relative phase of those voltages is dictated by the position of the rotor.

If now this arrangement (A) is connected to another similar arrangement of coils (B) as shown in Figure 9.12, the stator coils in the second arrangement will reproduce the electro-magnetic field created in stator "A".

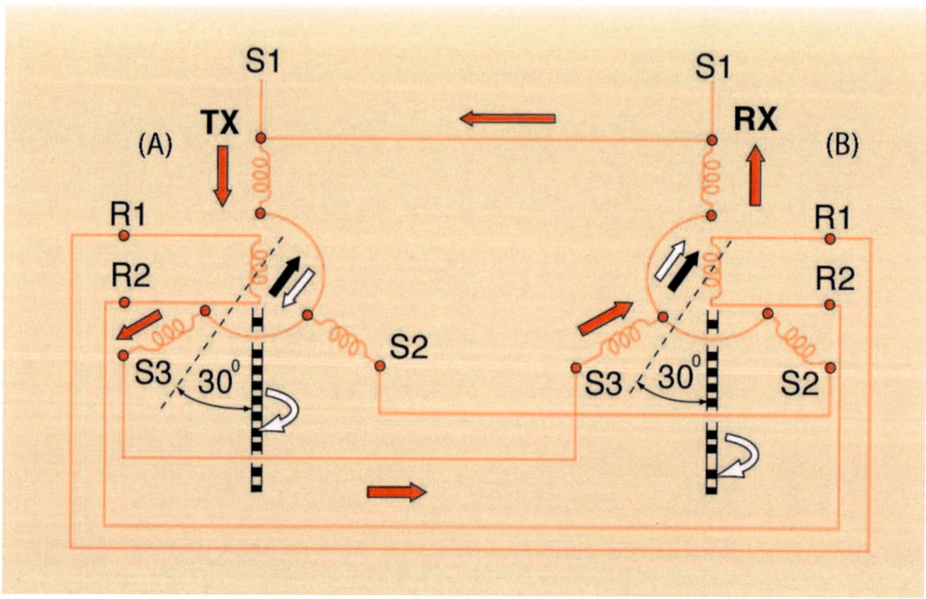

Figure 9.12 Synchros in an AC supply

The rotors in each system are fed from a common AC supply.

As long as rotor A and rotor B occupy the same relative position the magnetic fields at stator B will be equal and opposite to the field created by rotor B so that a net field of zero will result. If rotor A, mounted on the shaft of a sensor, is rotated the field in stator A and B will change. The field in stator B will no longer equal and oppose the field from rotor B and a magnetic torque will be set up. This will drive rotor B and rotate the shaft on which it is mounted until the fields again cancel out.

9.2.2.2 Control Synchro

This system uses the same principles but, instead of creating a torque at the receiver, is used to produce an error signal. Consider the electrical arrangement in Figure 9.13. The first thing to note is that the transmitter rotor is fed with an AC supply but the receiver rotor is not fed with any supply. The field in the receiver stator coils induces its electrical field. In Figure 9.13 the transmitter rotor is aligned with S1 and the alternating fields are shown diagrammatically. This field is reproduced in the receiver but 180° out.

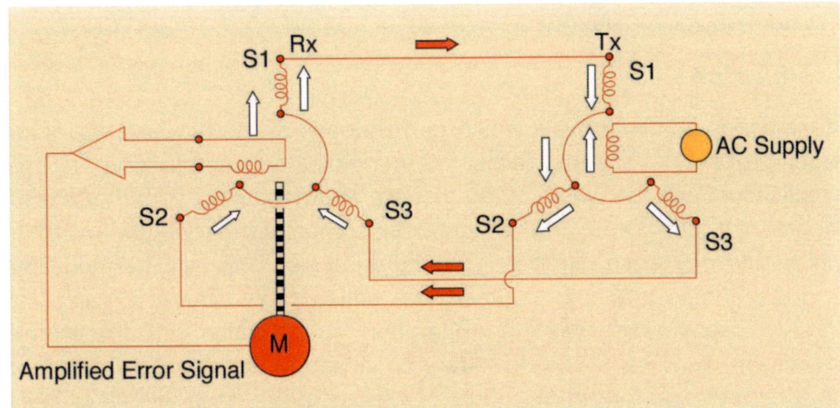

Figure 9.13 Control Synchro

If the receiver rotor is at 90° to the stator field it is at the electrical zero point. If now the transmitter rotor alignment is changed, the stator fields will be displaced and the receiver rotor will be out of the electrical zero. An error voltage will be induced in that coil. The output from the receiver coil is fed to an amplifier from where it can be applied to a torque rotor. This will turn the shaft, on which the receiver rotor is mounted, until the rotor is once more at 90° to the stator field and the error signal reduces to zero. Control synchros are used to transmit data when the power from a torque synchro would be insufficient and would result in large lag errors.

9.2.2.3 Differential Synchro

This system is designed to detect and transmit a misaligned error signal wherever there is a need to combine two inputs into a single output.

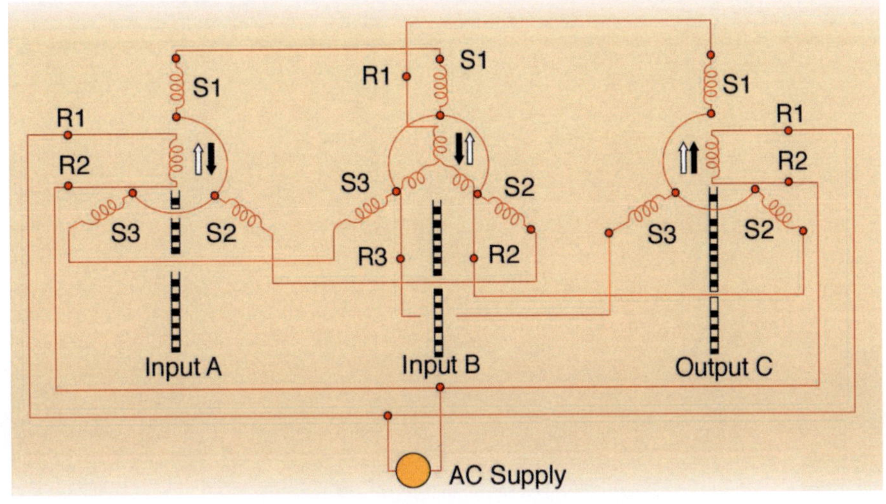

Figure 9.14 Differential synchro

A torque differential synchro system is shown schematically in Figure 9.14. The stator coils of input A are connected to the stator coils of input B. The rotor coils attached to the second input shaft, shaft B, is a three-coil "star" arrangement similar to the stator coils. These are connected to the stator coils at the output "C". The rotor at input A is fed from the same AC supply as the rotor on output shaft C. The three-coil rotor, on the second input shaft B will have an electrical field induced which will depend on the field from stator A and its own orientation with respect to stator B. This field is relayed to stator C where it will interact with the field from rotor C. Any difference between the rotor field and the stator field at the output C will cause a torque to be applied. This will rotate the output shaft until the fields reach electrical zero. Differential Synchros may also be used in a control synchro system so that, rather than a torque being created, an error signal is fed to an amplifier where its power is increased. It is then passed to a torque motor, mounted on the output shaft, where it brings the system back into alignment.

9.2.3 Data Transmission

Recent enormous technology advance owes much to the power of the modern digital computer. With the development of faster processing speeds, larger memories being combined with lighter more compact construction, their application over the whole of the modern air transport environment has developed to such an extent that it is apparent in every area. In the flight deck computers carry out many of the tasks previously carried out by a human and the pilot's role has been changed significantly. The modern digital computer is effectively a super quick adding machine in which the computing function is carried out in the Central Processor Unit (CPU) in accordance with the operation code, which are the instructions held in its programme. These software instructions are in binary code and all data to be worked on – the operand – must be supplied in a binary code format, the style of which can be 'recognised' or is compatible with the programme being used. A binary coding convention, for use in aircraft data systems, has been created by an organisation known as "Aeronautical Radio Incorporated" or ARINC for short. This code, which is identified as ARINC 429, is accepted as a commercial aviation industry standard. There are other additional ARINC codes used where the ARINC 429 does not meet the needs of the requirement.

9.2.3.1 Conversion of Data

By far the greatest proportion of the information that needs to be processed, in the aeroplane's computer, starts life in an analogue form. It must be converted to a digital 'binary code' format before being transmitted. There is also a requirement to convert the data output (D) from the computer into an analogue format (A). The device used to conduct these activities is referred to as a D/A converter. In effect, it takes an analogue input and "samples" it at frequent and regular time intervals. If we imagine an analogue input that is increasing in value, these samples will show increasing values. Each value of each sample can be converted into a unique binary code number. Figure 9.15 illustrates this conversion.

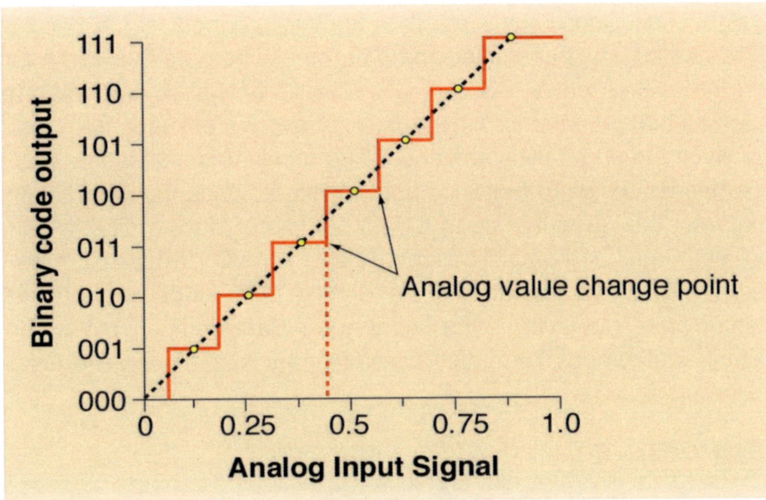

Figure 9.15

9.2.3.2 Data Transfer

Data is transferred as a series of binary code "words". Each "word" consists of 32 binary code "bits", each bit being either Binary 0 or Binary 1.

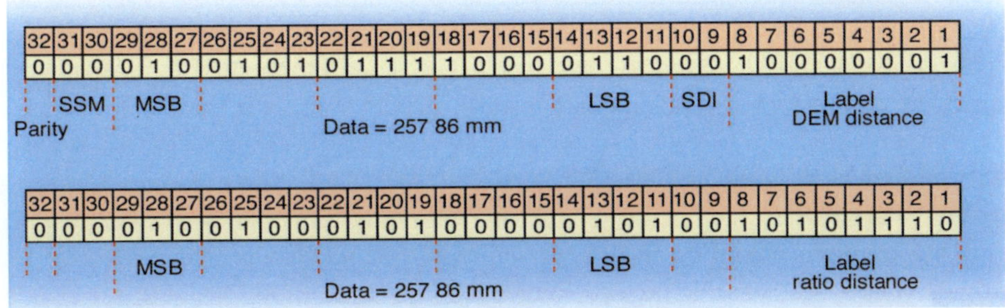

Figure 9.16 Data transfer

Bits 9 and 10 are used as a Series Destination Identifier (SDI) which indicates when a word is to be directed to a specific system in a multi-system fit.

Bits 11 to 29 are allocated to the actual data to be transmitted.

Bits 30 and 31 are used to indicate a positive/negative sense to the value of the data. These could be used to indicate direction (left/right) co-ordinates (X +/- or Y +/-) or geographical co-ordinates (Latitude N/S or Longitude E/W).

Bit 32 is used as a verification check so that the receiver computer can test whether any binary digits have been accidentally changed during the transmission. It is used, as the transmitter, to make the number of 1s transmitted an odd number (in ARINC 429). The receiver counts the total number of 1s in the word and, as long as it is an odd number, the data has probably not been contaminated. This is known as "odd parity".

Transfer once the "word" has been made up it must be sent to the computer. This could be done along a simple conductor. However, with the amount of systems originating data and transferring it to a number of "user units" the electrical wiring involved would be a nightmare of complexity and would carry an enormous weight penalty. To overcome that, a system of data busses is used. A data bus consists of a pair of wires shielded and twisted together and carried in a shielded outer casing. One wire carries nothing but binary O code and the other binary 1 code.

In the ARINC 429 system, each individual aircraft system is grouped into a class (e.g. radio navigation systems) and each class has its own transmitter and data bus. The data bus can be connected to as many as 20 receivers. At the transmitter, each coded binary word to be transmitted is sorted and the words are then transmitted in series so that a sequence of words will provide messages from a sequence of sources in that class of system to which the data bus is assigned. The receiver identifies the source, from the first eight digits of the "word", and passes the word to the computer's input. Once the information has been processed it is then transmitted out from the computer along a data bus directed towards the "user" systems. In ARINC 429 these are therefore both input and output busses. A later ARINC (ARINC 629) allows a single bus to be used for two-way traffic. This technique is used in the Boeing 777. Its obvious advantage is that it requires even fewer wires. Less obvious, however, is the fact that the data transfer rate is considerably faster. This system is known as Digital Autonomous Terminal Access Communication or DATAC for short.

9.3 Engine Parameters

The powerplant (engine) and associated systems instrumentation required in order to achieve safe and efficient handling varies according to the type of engine (piston, turboprop or gas turbine). In many cases individual instruments are identical so we will look first at what combinations of instruments are likely to be found, then will look at the individual instruments.

9.3.1 Piston Engines

The level of instrumentation required for an aeroplane fitted with piston engines is largely governed by the complexity of the engine. We will look at the most complex case and, in so doing, will cover all likely combinations. The pilot of a supercharged piston aeroplane will need to monitor the following parameters:

- The engine speed in terms of revolutions per minute (RPM). This is a measure of how much work is being done by the engine.
- The induction manifold pressure or Boost Pressure. (MAP). This is a measure of engine power of a supercharged engine. MAP is given usually in inches of mercury (In Hg)
- Torque or turning moment acting on the output shaft of the engine is proportional to the horsepower being developed. Sometimes used to provide information for power control.
- Cylinder Head Temperature. Excessive temperatures can cause engine damage (°C)
- Lubricating oil pressure and temperature, in order to ensure that the engine is adequately lubricated.(given in pressure terms or maybe even as 'HIGH' 'LOW'. Temperature is usually in (°C)
- Fuel flow is a measure of the economy of the engine.(Fuel units/h)
- Fuel quantity is necessary in order to ensure that there is sufficient fuel to complete the flight.(Fuel Mass or Volume).
- A fuel pressure gauge may be fitted. A drop in the value of fuel pressure may indicate a fuel filter partial blockage

9.3.2 Turbo Propeller Engines

For a turbo propeller the parameters to be monitored are as follows:

- RPM
- Torque
- Gas Temperatures at the Exhaust of the engine. (EGT) (°C)
- Lubricating oil pressure
- Lubricating oil temperature
- Fuel flow
- Fuel quantity
- Fuel Pressure

9.3.3 Gas Turbine Engines

For the gas turbine engine aeroplane the pilot must monitor: -

- Engine Pressure Ratio (EPR). The amount of useful thrust developed is the product of the mass of air passing through the engine and the velocity at the exhaust nozzle minus the drag due to the air passing through the engine. By comparing the air pressures across the engine, that is compressor inlet to that at the exhaust, we obtain an Engine Pressure Ratio (EPR) that is an indication of the thrust output.
- EPR is usually given as a percentage thrust value.
- RPM. This is normally identified as being given for N1 or N2. Rather than being given in revolutions per minute they are normally calibrated in % of maximum.
- EGT. As for the turbo propeller engine, the exhaust gas temperature must be monitored in order to prevent excessive heat damaging the turbine.
- Oil temperature and pressure monitoring is necessary for safe operation.
- Fuel pressure and temperature are both monitored in order to ensure that a supply of non-cavitated fuel is supplied at an acceptable temperature. A "low fuel pressure" warning light may back this up.

9.4 Engine Instrumentation

9.4.1 RPM Indicator

Engine RPM is an indicator of power for an unsupercharged piston engine; some old mechanical RPM gauges are driven by rotating cables but modern systems are of the electrical transmission type. These instruments, sometimes referred to as tachometers, are of two main types:

- Generator and Indicator
- Tachometer Probe Indicator

9.4.1.1 Generator and Indicator System

The generator (i.e. speed sensor) is a 3-phase AC generator with a permanent magnet rotor (2 or 4 pole) rotating within a slotted stator. This is bolted directly to engine gearbox so that rotation speed is directly related to engine speed

A splined shaft coupling drives the rotor. In order to limit the mechanical loads on generators, ratio gears are used to reduce the operating speeds of rotors in the engine drive system. The signal from the generator unit is passed through a synchro system to the indicator unit.

The indicator consists of a 3-phase synchronous motor with its stator connected to the generator stator the indicator rotor rotates at the same speed as the generator rotor and has the torque characteristics of a squirrel-cage motor

For operation of servo-operated indicators and CRTs, 12 pole generator rotors are used; these produce a single-phase output at much higher frequency and sensitivity.

9.4.1.1.1 Construction

The speed-indicating element consists of a permanent magnet device as illustrated in Figure 9.17. A calibrated hairspring is attached to one end of the shaft, and at the other end to the mechanism frame. At the front end of the shaft, a gear train is coupled to two concentrically mounted pointers; a large one indicating hundreds and a small one indicating thousands of rpm.

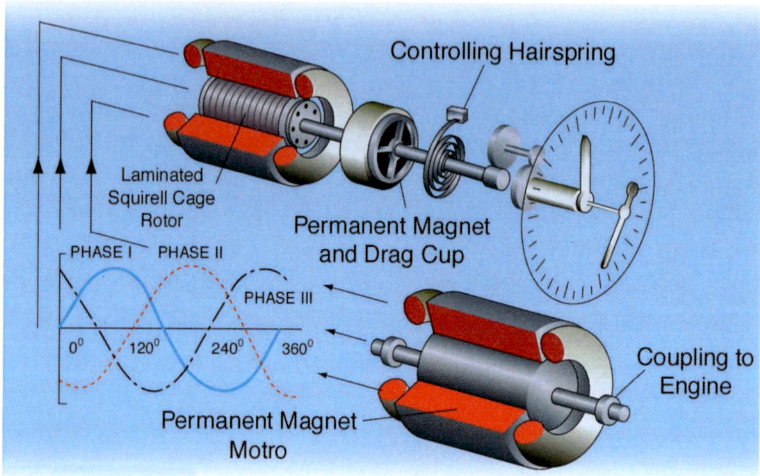

Figure 9.17 Generator indicator

9.4.1.1.2 System operation

As the generator rotor is driven round inside its stator, the poles sweep past each stator winding in succession so that three waves or phases of alternating emf are generated, the waves being 120° apart. Furthermore, as a pair of rotor poles passes each coil, the induced EMF completes one cycle at a frequency determined by the rotational speed of the rotor. Therefore, rotor speed and frequency are directly proportional, and, since the engine drives the rotor at some fixed ratio, then the frequency is a measure of the engine speed. Generator output is referred to an indicator which moves to a position corresponding to that related to output torque from the generator against indicator spring loading. Indicators are compensated for the effects of temperature on the various components of the speed-indicating element.

9.4.1.2 Indicators

The dial presentation of a representative indicator is shown in Figure 9.18.

These may show values of RPM or as a percentage of maximum permitted value, the latter being the favoured option for gas turbines as it allows various types of engine to be operated on the same basis of comparison. The main scales are calibrated from 0 to 100 per cent in 10 per cent increments, with 100% corresponding to the optimum turbine speed. A digital counter (or second pointer) displays speed in one per cent increments.

Figure 9.18 Cockpit indicator

9.4.1.3 Tachometer Probe and Indicator System

This system has the advantage of providing a number of separate electrical outputs additional to those required for speed indication, e.g. automatic power control and flight data acquisition systems. Furthermore, and as will be noted from Figure 9.19, it has the advantage of not being connected to the rotating shaft and there are no moving parts for subjection to high rotational loads.

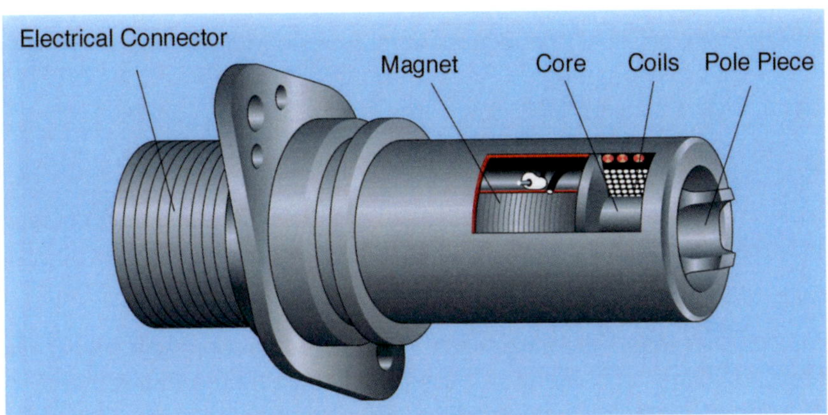

Figure 9.19 Tacho probe

The stainless steel, hermetically sealed probe comprises a permanent magnet, a pole piece, and a number of coils around a ferromagnetic core. Separate windings (from five to seven depending on the type and application of a probe) provide outputs to the indicator and other processing units requiring engine speed data. The probe is mounted on an engine at a station in the high-pressure compressor section so that it extends into this section. In some turbofan engines, a probe may also be mounted at the fan section for measuring fan speed. The fan speed indicating system is, in effect, a fan blade counting device. The sensor heads mounted flush in the fan shroud panel contain permanent magnets. The passage of each fan blade disrupts the magnetic field set up by the sensor magnets, causing an electrical signal pulse. The frequency of the pulses is equal to the number of blades times the RPM, thus giving a signal frequency proportional to fan speed.

In some systems, the probe is mounted in close proximity to a rotating gear wheel (called a phonic wheel)

The signal is amplified, conditioned and transmitted to the cockpit indicator to provide a N_1 readout in percent RPM. To ensure correct orientation of the probe, a locating plug is provided in the mounting flange. The permanent magnet produces a magnetic field around the sensing coils, and as the fan blades pass the pole pieces, the intensity of flux through each pole varies inversely with the width of the air gap between poles and the blades. As the blades move the air gap will vary and an emf will be induced in the sensing coils, the amplitude of the emf varying with the rate of flux density change. Indication of power failure is by a flag which is energised to obscure the counter display.

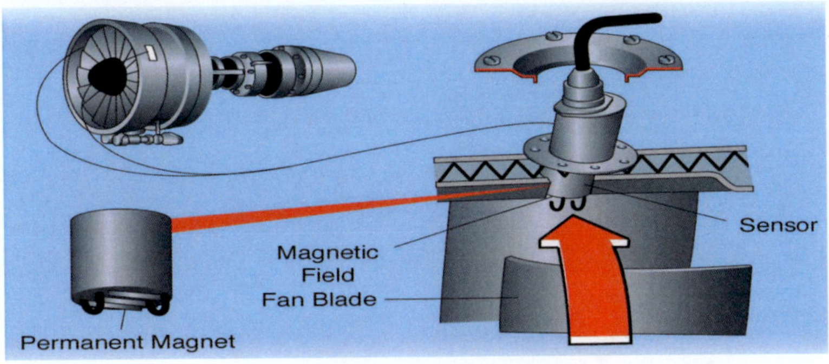

Figure 9.20 Fan speed indicator

9.4.1.4 Synchroscope

The synchroscope allows RPM on multi-engine aircraft to be synchronised to a particular "master" engine; it indicates the RPM difference between engine RPM of a particular engine and that of the master engine. It may also used to synchronise propeller RPM

9.4.2 Pressures

A number of pressures have to be sensed. These include gas pressures and fluid pressures but all will work on the same basic principles.

9.4.2.1 Manifold Pressure (MAP)

These indicators, colloquially termed "boost gauges", are of the direct-reading type and are calibrated to measure absolute pressure in inches of mercury, such pressure being representative of that produced at the induction manifold of a supercharged piston engine.

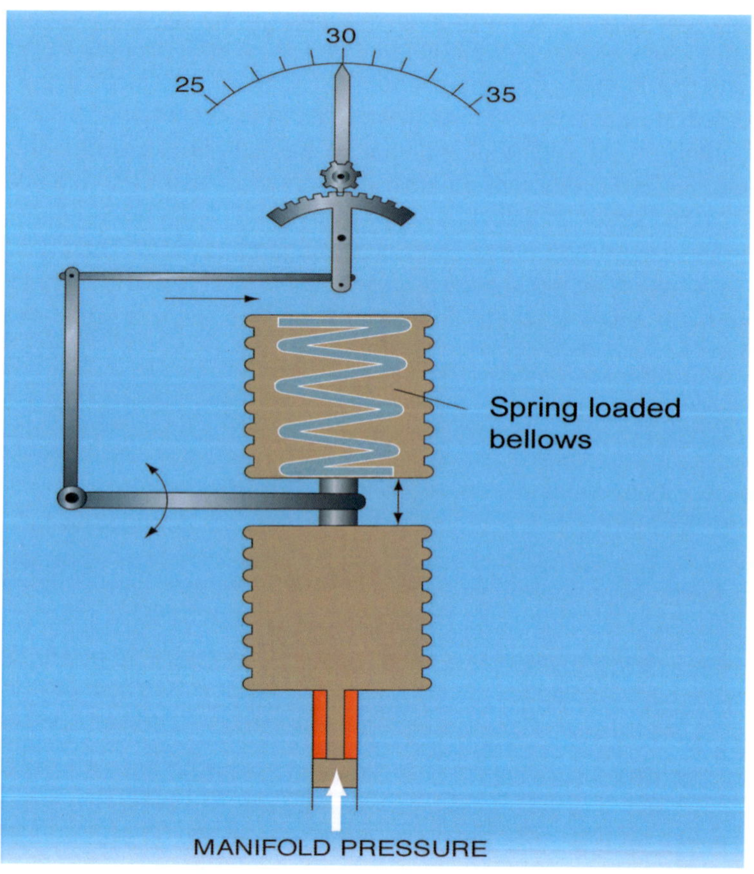

Figure 9.21 Measuring element

The measuring element is made up of two bellows, (see Figure 9.21), one open to the induction manifold and the other evacuated and sealed. A controlling spring is fitted inside the sealed bellows and distension of both bellows is transmitted to the pointer via a lever, quadrant and pinion mechanism. A filter is located at the inlet to open the bellows, where there is also a restriction to smooth out any pressure surges.

When pressure is admitted to the open bellows the latter expands causing the pointer to move over the scale (calibrated in inches of mercury) and so indicate a change in pressure from the standard sea level value of 29.92 (zero "boost"). With increasing altitude, there is a tendency for the bellows to expand a little too far because the decrease in atmospheric pressure acting on the outside of the bellows offers less opposition. However, this tendency is counteracted by the sealed bellows, which also senses the change in atmospheric pressure but expands in the opposite direction. Thus a condition is reached at which the forces acting on each bellows are equal, cancelling out the effects of atmospheric pressure so that manifold pressure is measured directly against the spring.

9.4.2.2 Engine Pressure Ratio (EPR)

In general, a measuring system consists of an engine inlet (compressor intake) pressure probe, a number of pressure-sensing probes projected into the exhaust unit (or turbine outlet) of an engine, a pressure ratio transmitter, and an indicator. The interconnection of these components based on a typical system is schematically shown in Figure 9.22.

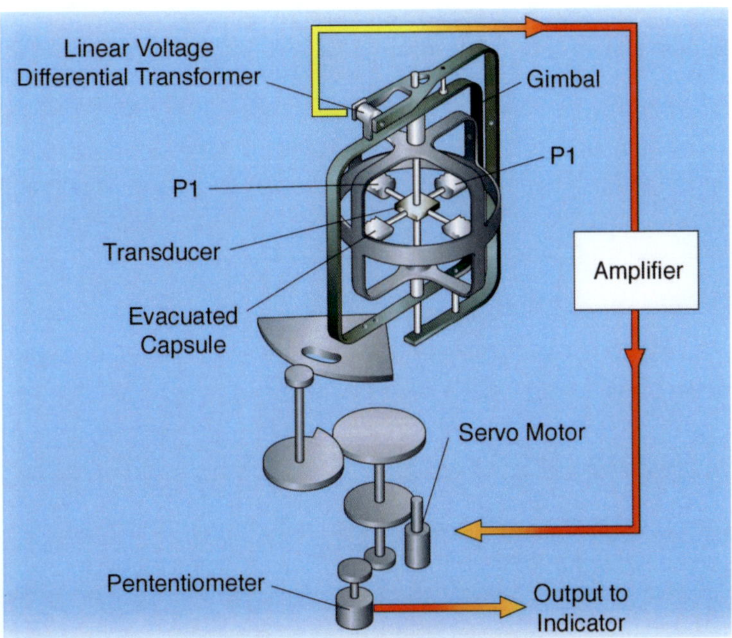

Figure 9.22 EPR measurement

The inlet pressure (P1) sensing probe is similar to a pitot probe, and is mounted so that it faces into the airstream in the engine intake or, as in some power plant installations, on the pylon and in the vicinity of the air intake. The probe is protected against icing by a supply of warm air from the engine anti-ice system.

Pipelines terminating at a manifold interconnect the exhaust pressure-sensing probes in order to average the pressures. In some engine systems, pressure sensing is done from chambers contained within the EGT sensing probes. A pipeline from the manifold, and another from the inlet pressure probe, are each connected to the pressure ratio transmitter which comprises a bellows type of pressure sensing transducer, a linear voltage differential transformer (LVDT), a servomotor, an amplifier and a potentiometer. The bellows are arranged in two pairs at right angles and supported in a frame which, in turn, is supported in a gimbal and yoke assembly. The gimbal is mechanically coupled to the servomotor via a gear train, while the yoke is coupled to the core of the LVDT. The servomotor also drives the potentiometer, which adjusts the output voltage signals to the indicator in terms of changes in pressure ratio.
Indicators may be of the servo-operated type but, in electronic display systems, the transmitter output signals are supplied direct to the appropriate system computer.

When the engine is not running the intake and exhaust pressures are the same and the EPR is therefore 1

9.4.2.2.1 Operation

The intake pressure is admitted to two of the bellows in the transducer, exhaust gas pressure is admitted to the third bellows, while the fourth is evacuated and sealed. When a pressure change occurs, it causes an unbalance in the bellows system, and the resultant of the forces acting on the transducer frame acts on the yoke and causes it to pivot about its axis. The deflection displaces the LVDT and induces an ac signal. This is amplified and applied to the servomotor. The motor, via a gear train, alters the potentiometer output signal

to the indicator so that its pointer and digital counter are servo-driven to indicate the new pressure ratio. Simultaneously, the motor drives the transducer gimbal and LVDT to provide a 'follow up' and to stabilise the system at the new ratio.
If a circuit malfunction occurs, an integrity monitoring circuit within the indicator activates a warning flag circuit, causing the flag to obscure the digital counter display.

9.4.2.2.2 Limiters

In some types of aircraft, a maximum allowable EPR limit indicator is also provided. It is integrated with a TAT indicator and also with an ADC; its purpose being to indicate limits related to air density and altitude values from which thrust settings have been predetermined for specific operating conditions. The conditions are climb, cruise, continuous and go-around, and are selected as appropriate by means of a mode selector switch connected to a computing and switching circuit which generates a datum signal corresponding to each selected condition. The signal is then supplied to a comparator, which also receives temperature signals from the TAT sensor and altitude signals from the ADC. These signals are compared with the datum signal and the lower value of the two is automatically selected as the signal representing the maximum EPR limit for the selected operating condition. The comparator transmits this signal to an amplifier and then to a servomotor driving a digital counter to display the limiting values.

9.4.3 Engine Torque Measurement

A hydro-mechanical torque meter system is illustrated in Figure 9.23. In this the helical gears, driven by the engine shaft, create an axial thrust.

The helical gears are located in the reduction gearbox of the engine

Oil pressure, acting on a number of pistons, resists this axial thrust. The amount of pressure required to resist the axial thrust is directly proportional to the torque. This is transmitted to suitably calibrated indicator dial.

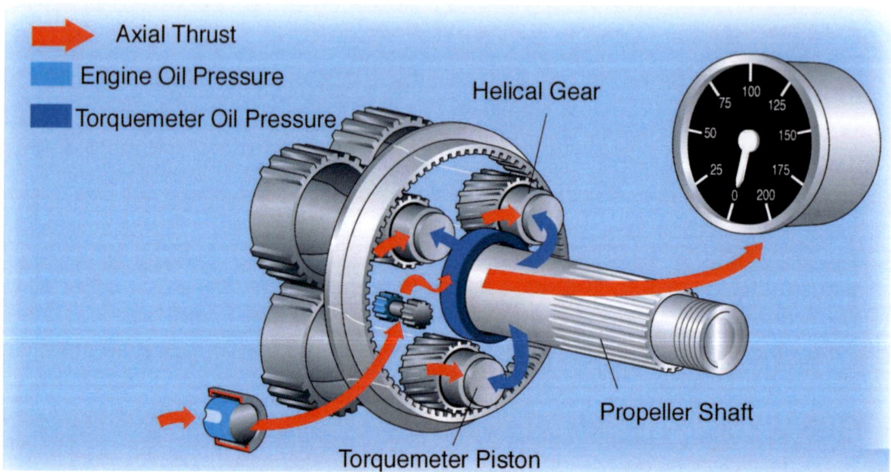

Figure 9.23 Torque meter

An advantage of this type of torque measuring device, on a turboprop aeroplane, is that the system can also be used to operate the propeller feathering device if the torque meter oil pressure falls due to a power failure. On some aeroplanes it is used to automatically operate the water injection system that boosts the take off power at high altitude/ high temperature airfields.

The electrical torque meter measures torsion in the main power shaft by a probe which is similar in operation to the phonic wheel speed sensor. The gap between 2 parts of the shaft is measured and gives an indication of engine torque.

9.4.4 Vibration Monitoring

A turbo jet engine has a very low vibration level and a change in vibration, which could be the first indication of an impending problem, could easily go unnoticed. As examples of the kind of problem we are looking at consider some of these: -

- A damaged compressor blade
- A turbine blade that has a crack or suffers from "creep",
- An uneven temperature distribution around turbine blades and rotor discs may be set up.
- Any part of the rotating assembly which is out of balance

It is therefore imperative that vibration-monitoring equipment is fitted to each engine. They are designed to indicate when the maximum amplitude of vibration of the engine exceeds a pre-set level. Their indicators are located within the control group of instrumentation. The monitor is mounted on the engine casing. It consists of a vibration pick-off, or sensor, mounted at right angles to the engine axis, an amplifier-monitoring unit, and an indicator calibrated to show vibration amplitude in thousandths of an inch (mils).

Vibration may also be displayed as relative amplitude in the form of a non-dimensional number

9.4.4.1 Construction

The sensor (Figure 9.24) is a spring-supported permanent magnet suspended in a coil attached to the interior of the case. As the engine vibrates, the sensor unit and core move with it, the magnet, however, tends to remain fixed in space because of inertia.

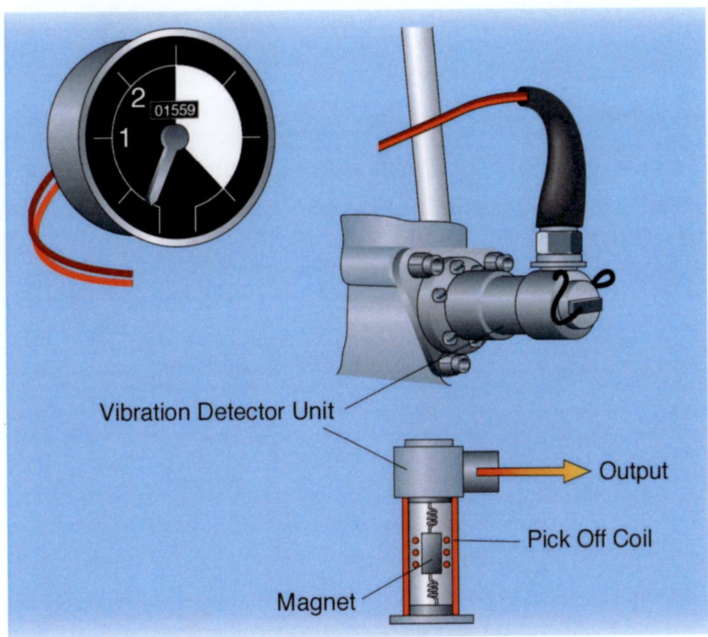

Figure 9.24 Vibration Monitor

The motion of the coil causes the turns to cut the field of the magnet, thus inducing a voltage in the coil and providing a signal to the amplifier unit. The signal, after amplification and integration by an electrical transmission system, is fed to the indicator via a rectifying section.

9.4.4.2 Warning Indications and Systems

An amber indicator light also forms part of the system, together with a test switch. The light is supplied with dc from the amplifier rectifying section and it comes on when the maximum amplitude of vibration exceeds the pre-set value. The test switch permits functional checking of the system's electrical circuit. In some engine installations, two sensors may be fitted to an engine: for example, in a typical turbofan engine, one monitors vibration levels around the fan section, and the other around the engine core section. In systems developed for use in conjunction with LCD and CRT display indicators, the vibration sensors are of the type whereby vibration causes signals to be induced in a piezoelectric sensor stack.

9.5 Fuel Gauging

Fuel quantity is obviously of great interest to the pilot since he/she must know that sufficient fuel remains to complete the flight with adequate reserves. A check on fuel remaining against the planned quantity at significant route points will reveal any divergence or excess of fuel burn. Fuel quantity may be given in volume or mass and indicating systems may be the float or capacitance type.

9.5.1 Float system

In simple systems, the volume of the fluid is measured by the action of a float linked to a suitable indicator. As fluid is put into the tank or reservoir the float rises and through the action of a variable resistance which is positioned by movement of the float, the indicator reflects the new position and therefore the increased quantity.

The float system is normally used in small aircraft and measures the volume of fuel. It uses a DC power supply.

The disadvantages of this system are:

- inaccurate and coarse indications
- susceptible to manoeuvre errors (fluid surges)
- indication is not linear

9.5.2 Capacitance system

On more sophisticated systems, fuel level is measured using capacitance probes, the capacitance of these units varies with:

- The dielectric constant of the fuel
- The amount of wetted area of the probe

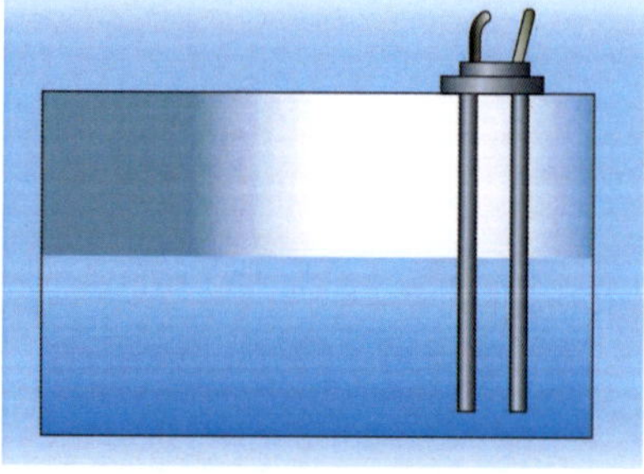

Figure 9.25 Fluid measurement

The capacitor consists of two plates separated by a non-conducting medium known as a dielectric. Various fluids have different dielectric values as shown in the table below.

Fluid	Dielectric value
Air	1.0
Gasoline	1.95
Kerosene	2.1

The ability of a given capacitor to “hold” a charge (its capacitance) is dependent upon the properties of the dielectric. In a volume measuring device the probe consists of two capacitor plates (Figure 9.25) immersed in a container. As the container fills up, the air between the plates is progressively replaced by the fluid and the nature of the dielectric changes.

This causes a progressive change in capacitance that can be measured by a suitable electrical pick-off

A number of probes, depending on the size of the tank, are used in each tank and the sum of their capacitance is a measure of the quantity of fuel in the tank. Since the tanks are fitted into wings and bellies in aeroplanes, they are of irregular shape. To account for this the capacitors must be matched or characterised to their specific locations and degrees of structural flex and attitude change.

As the probes are connected in parallel, manoeuvring errors are eliminated

9.5.3 Temperature and Density

Since temperature affects the density of fuel, the volume occupied by a given quantity of fuel increases if temperature increases and density falls. To compensate for this error, a balancing (short) capacitance unit is installed at the lowest part of the tank where it will be totally immersed whenever there is a useable quantity of fuel in the tank. Since this is totally immersed, the only variation in the capacitance it measures will be due to changes in the fluid density. This variation is used to adjust the calibration of the fuel quantity probes. However water suspended in the fuel can cause erroneous readings. Water drains checks must be carried out at the stated frequencies.

9.5.4 Fuel Mass

A measurement of fuel mass is obtained by converting the measured volume into a mass on the basis of an assumed density. Although the balancing probe corrects for some of the density variations that may occur, it is unlikely to give compensation to a sufficiently accurate degree to provide an exact fuel mass. In some sophisticated aeroplanes a densitometer is fitted. This uses the phenomena that if gamma rays are passed through fuel the detected radiation will vary in proportion to the density of the fuel. The output of the densitometer is fed to the fuel quantity processor unit where it is used to derive density.

In the event of a failure of the signal flow from the capacitors the indicator pointer is driven to the "empty" position

9.5.5 Fuel Totaliser

Fuel quantities are sometimes additionally displayed as a total fuel on board indication together with aircraft all up weight. An upper scale showing the aircraft weight (mass) is manually set at completion of loading. As fuel is burned, both the fuel remaining and the weight scales reduce.

9.5.6 Fuel Flow

Fuel flow measuring systems consist of a transmitter and indicator. Transmitters produce output signals which are proportional to flow rate which can be indicated in volumetric units (e.g. gal/h) or mass units (e.g. kg/h). Transmitter output may also be integrated to give the amount of fuel consumed. The transmitter is fitted in the delivery lines of the engine fuel system and can be a rotating vane or integrated flowmeter (impeller/turbine) type.

9.5.6.1 Rotating vane fuel flowmeter

In this system, the shaft carrying the vane forms the transmitter of a synchro transmission system. The receiver rotor is attached to and drives a needle moving against a scale calibrated in fuel used per unit time, which can be either volume or weight related.

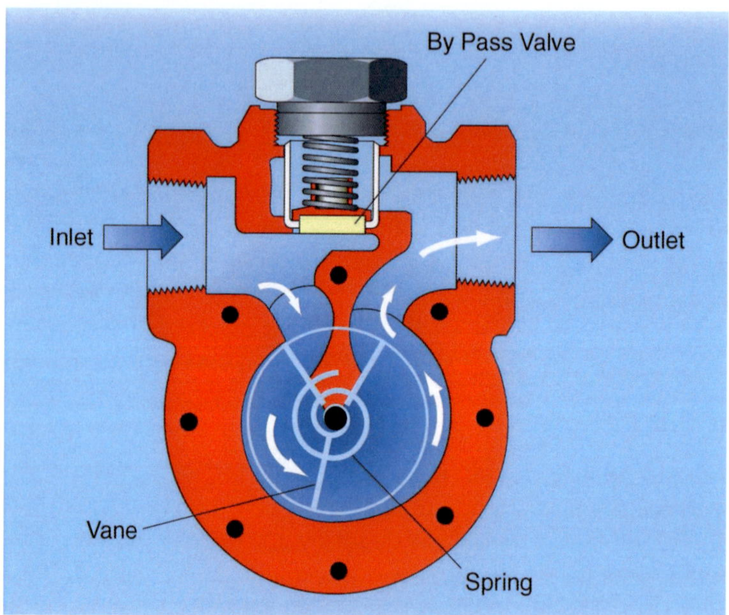

Figure 9.26 Rotating vane fuel flowmeter

The metering vane in the chamber is pivoted so that it can rotate under the influence of fuel passing through the chamber. The vane is restrained by a calibrated spring so that vane deflection is proportional to fuel flow. The position assumed by the valve is therefore a direct measure of fluid flow and this is transmitted to the indicator.

9.5.6.2 Integrated Flowmeter

A more complex system, in common use in large aeroplanes, is the integrated flow meter system.

The fuel flow is measured and is not only presented on a suitable scale but is also passed to an integrator where it is processed (integrated) with respect to time to obtain fuel used

The transmitter/sensor unit consists of a tube, narrowed at the ends and fitted into the appropriate engine fuel supply line. Within the tube (Figure 9.27) there is an impeller (driven by a 2 phase AC motor) through which the fuel passes. The impeller makes the fuel swirl at a rotation rate that varies with the flow rate. On leaving the impeller, the swirling fuel impacts a receiver turbine and induces a rate of rotation of that turbine that is directly proportional to the swirl rate. This rotation is electronically detected and transmitted to the fuel flow indicator and, via the integrator, to the fuel-consumed indicator.

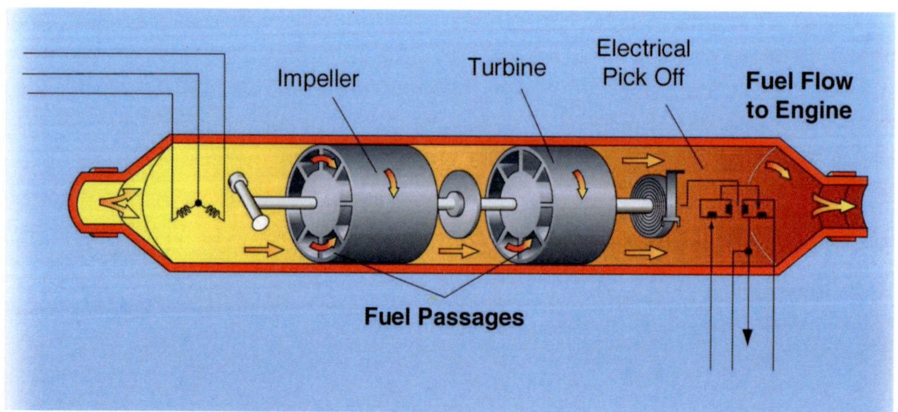

Figure 9.27 Integrated flowmeter

Fuel flow is measured at the fuel intake of each engine (LP fuel supply line on a gas turbine). If fuel flows increase, for a particular engine power, it will indicate a reduction in efficiency and probably an impending mechanical problem.

9.5.7 Flight Hour Meter

The flight hour meter monitors engine running time and is a basic electro-mechanical device with a digital presentation. The meter is usually activated by an airspeed switch, operative at a specific IAS.

9.6 EICAS / ECAM

The Engine Indication and Crew Alerting System (EICAS) or Electronic Centralised Aircraft Monitoring (ECAM) primarily displays engine indications and provides a centrally located crew alerting system for non-normal situations. EICAS also shows system status not otherwise displayed in the cockpit and provides maintenance personnel with a variety of system data.

9.6.1 System and Display Layout

Two EICAS computers receive inputs from engine and system sensors. The computers display information from the sensors on two CRTs.

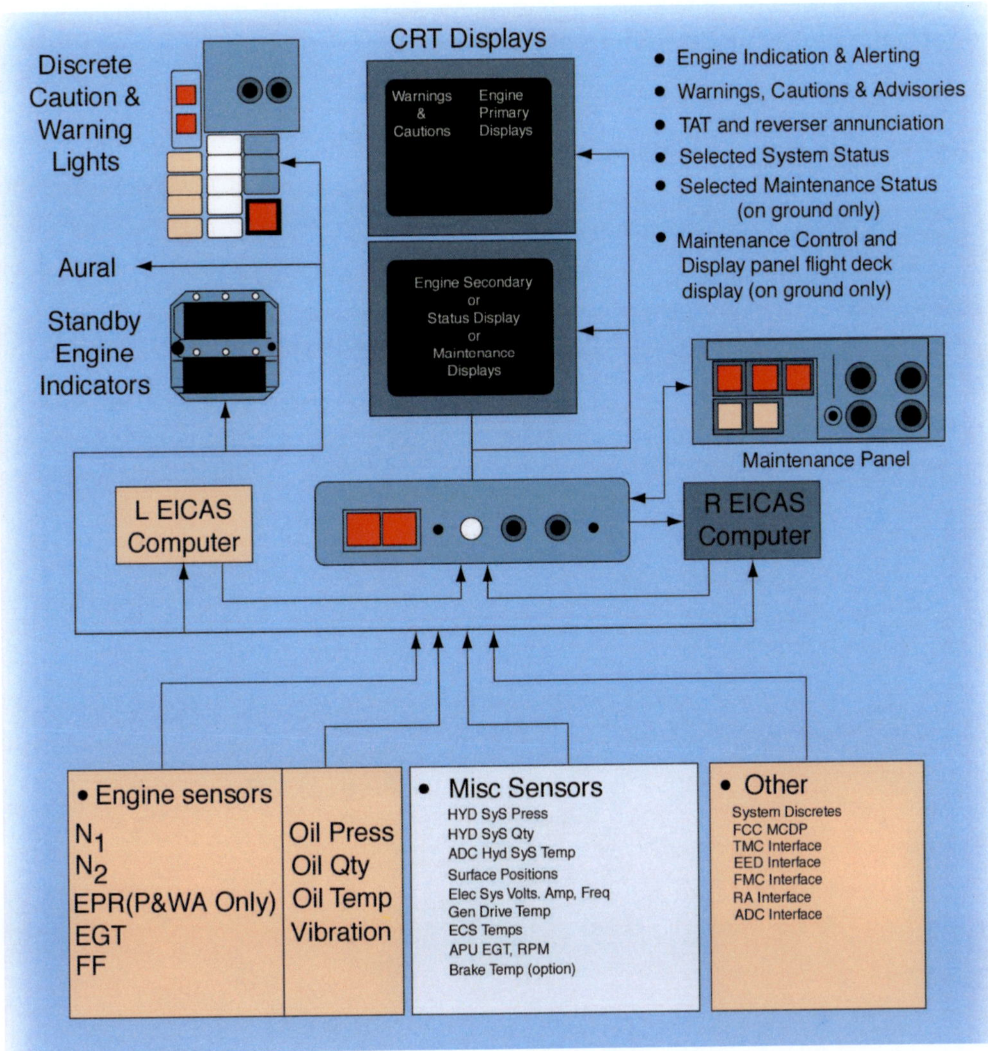

Figure 9.28 EICAS / ECAM

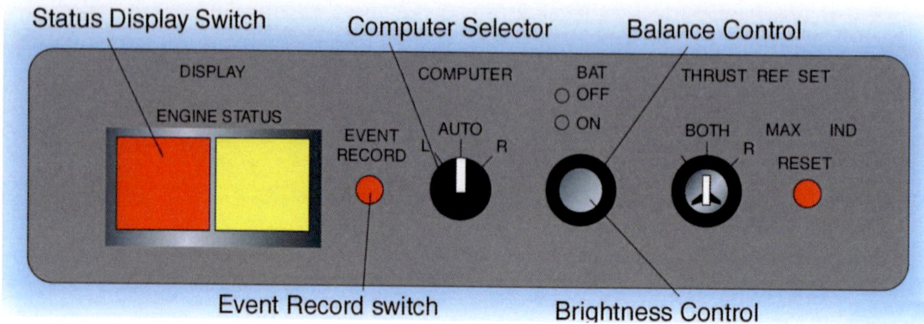

Figure 9.29 Cockpit selector

A Computer Selector, illustrated in Figure 9.29, determines which computer controls EICAS. When the selector is in the AUTO position the left computer is used. If the left computer fails, control switches to the right computer. When the L position is selected only the left computer can control EICAS. When the selector is in the R position only the right computer can control the system. The Brightness and Balance Controls are used to adjust the brightness level of the CRTs. Rotating the Brightness Control adjusts the brightness level of both CRTs. Rotating the Balance Control varies the relative brightness level between the two displays. The Event Record Switch is used to store systems data in an EICAS memory for later use by maintenance personnel. When the switch is pushed, current data from the engine and system sensors is recorded, and any previously recorded data is erased from the memory. System lights and a Standby Engine Indicator (SEI) provide backup indication for the CRT displays.

9.6.2 Engine Display

The CRT screens are located in the centre of the instrument panel above the throttle pedestal and are illustrated in Figure 9.30. Primary engine monitoring display appears on the upper screen. Secondary Engine Indications appear on the lower screen.

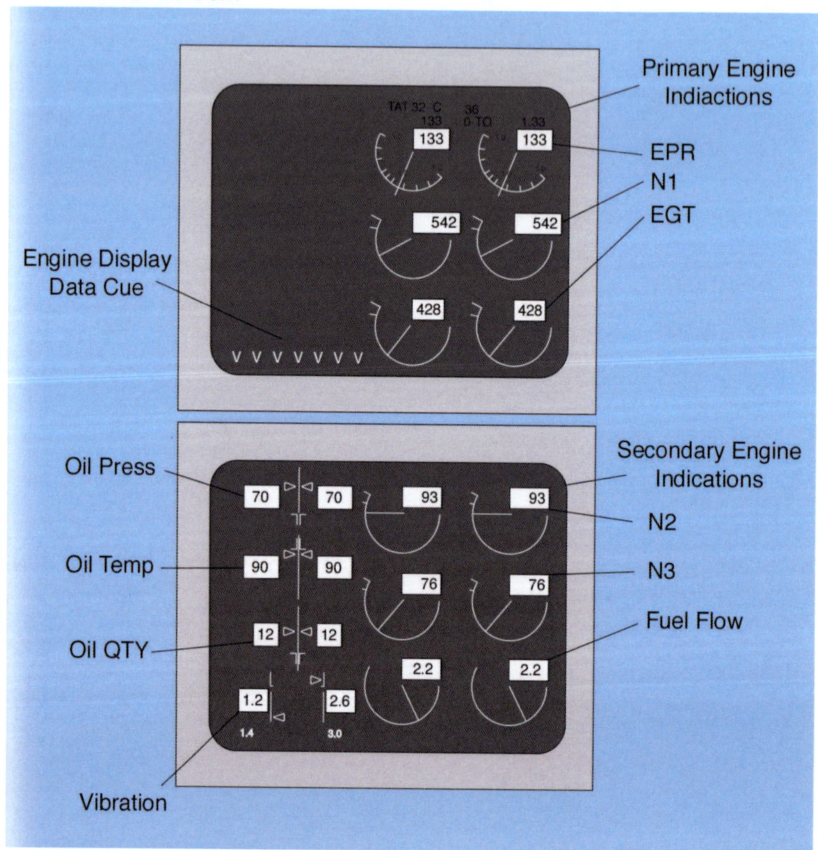

Figure 9.30

In the event of failure of the upper screen the primary engine indications will be automatically transferred to the lower screen and the Engine Display Data Cue will be displayed on the upper screen.

9.6.3 Crew Alerting

The crew alerting portion of EICAS continually monitors aircraft systems. If a fault occurs or any system fault light illuminates in the cockpit, EICAS displays a crew alerting message on the upper CRT. In addition to the display messages, some crew alerts are also indicated by aural tones and Master Warning/Caution lights.
All 'crew alert' messages are divided into one of three categories:- Level A - Warnings, Level B - Cautions or Level C - Advisories as follows:

Warnings - indicate, in RED, operational or aircraft system conditions that require prompt corrective action. They are the most urgent types of crew alert. Master warning lights illuminate and aural warnings are given. An engine fire is a typical warning.

Cautions - indicate, in AMBER, operational or aircraft system conditions that require timely corrective action. They are less urgent than warnings. Message caution lights illuminate and an aural tone is repeated twice. A hydraulic system overheat is a typical caution.

Advisories – also indicate in AMBER, operational or aircraft system conditions that require corrective action on a time available basis. Advisories are the least urgent type of crew alert. No caution lights illuminate and no aural tones are given. A yaw damper fault is a typical advisory.

9.6.4 Master Warning/Caution Light

Two Master Warning Lights illuminate when any warning occurs. The lights remain on as long as the warning exists, or until either Master Warning/Caution reset switch is pressed:

- Pushing the reset switch silences the fire bell and cabin altitude siren
- Pushing the reset switch may also silence the landing configuration siren, depending on the reason for activation.
- Two Master Caution Lights illuminate when any caution occurs. The lights remain on as long as the caution exists, or until either Master Warning/Caution reset switch is pressed.

9.6.5 Display Messages

Crew alerting messages appear on the upper CRT to indicate all non-normal conditions detected by EICAS. Figure 9.31 illustrates some examples. Messages are arranged by their urgency and order of occurrence as follows:

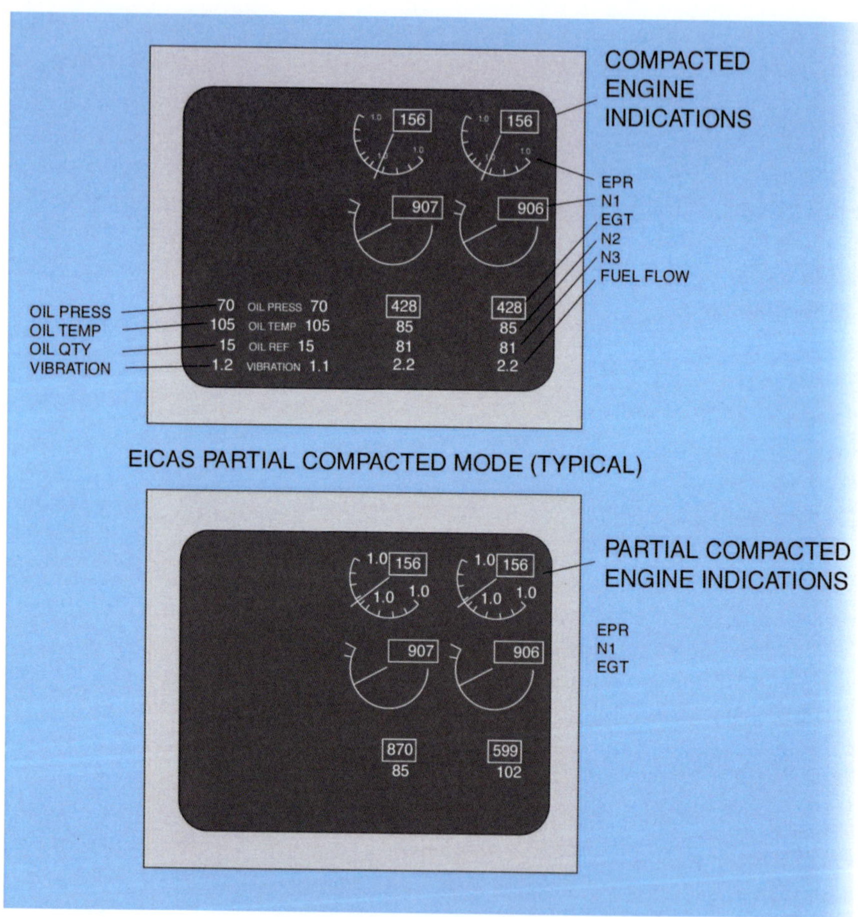

Figure 9.31 Engine display

- Warnings are indicated by red messages at the top of the message list.
- Cautions appear as amber messages below the lowest warning.
- Advisories appear below the lowest caution and are also indicated by amber messages. They are indented one space so that they can be distinguished from cautions.

The most recent warning, caution and advisory message appear at the top of its respective group of messages. A message is automatically removed from the display when the associated condition no longer exists. In this case, all messages that appeared below the deleted message move up one line.

When a new fault occurs, its associated message is inserted on the appropriate line of the display. This may cause older messages to move down one line. For example, a new caution message would cause all existing caution and advisory messages to move down a line. If there are more messages than can be displayed at one time, the lowest message is removed and a white page number appears on the lower right side of the message list. Messages 'bumped' from the bottom of one page appear on the next page.

The Cancel and Recall switches are used to manipulate the message lists. Pushing the Cancel Switch removes the caution and advisory messages from the display but warning messages cannot be cancelled.

9.6.5.1 Display Message Switching

If there is an additional page of messages, pushing the Cancel Switch displays the next page. Warning messages are carried over from the pervious page. When the last page of messages is displayed, pushing the switch once more removes the last caution and advisory messages and the page number.

- Pushing the Recall Switch displays the caution and advisory messages that were removed with the Cancel Switch, if the associated faults still exist. If there is more than one page of messages, page one is displayed. A white RECALL message appears for about one second on the lower left side of the message list to indicate the Recall Switch was pushed.

- New display messages appear on the page being viewed. For example, if page three is selected and a new caution occurs, the caution message appears on page three below any warning messages. If the Recall Switch is subsequently pushed, the new caution message appears as the top caution message on page one.

9.6.6 Inhibits

Portions of the crew alerting system are inhibited or deactivated to prevent distractions during certain phases of flight. Multiple display messages of a similar nature are sometimes replaced by a single, more general display message. For example, if only the forward or aft entry door is open on the left side, an L FWD ENT DOOR or L AFT ENT DOOR message appears. If both doors are open, only an L ENTRY DOORS message appears. Some display messages are also inhibited for a brief time period even though system lights are illuminated. This inhibit prevents normal in transit indications from appearing on the display. For example, the GEAR Light illuminates as soon as landing gear retraction begins. However, the associated GEAR DISAGREE display message is inhibited for 25 s, allowing sufficient time for normal landing gear retraction to occur.

9.6.7 Status

The status portion of EICAS is used to determine the aircraft readiness for dispatch. When the Status Switch is pushed, the status display appears on the lower CRT. The status display includes system indicators, flight control position indicators, status messages and brake temperature indicators.

- System indicators appear in the top left corner of the display. The indicators show hydraulic quantity and pressure, APU EGT, RPM and oil quantity; and oxygen pressure.
- Flight control positions for the rudder, ailerons and elevators appear in the bottom left corner of the status display.
- White, status messages appear on the right side of the status display. These messages indicate equipment faults that require awareness at dispatch and that are not otherwise shown in the flight deck.
- Status messages are arranged by order of occurrence. The most recent status message appears at the top of the list.
- A message is automatically removed from the display when the associated condition no longer exists. Messages, which appear below the deleted message, each move up one line.
- When a new status fault occurs, its associated message is inserted at the top of the list and all other messages move down one line.
- If there are more messages than can be displayed at one time, the lowest message is removed and a white page number appears on the lower right side of the message list. Messages bumped from the bottom on one page appear on the next page.
- If there is an additional page of status messages, pushing the Status Switch displays the next page. When the last page of messages is displayed, pushing the switch removes the status display from the lower CRT and blanks the screen.
- New status messages appear at the top of the page being viewed. If the status display is deselected and subsequently reselected the message list is reordered, with the newest status message now appearing at thc top of the first page.
- A Status Cue appears in the left upper corner of the lower CRT if a new status message occurs, the status display is not currently selected and the airplane is in the air. The cue disappears when the status page is displayed. Status messages do not need to be checked in flight; however, they can be useful in anticipating possible ground maintenance actions.
- Brake temperature indications appear on the lower right side of the status display

9.6.8 Maintenance

The maintenance portion of EICAS provides a cockpit display of system data for use by maintenance personnel. Maintenance displays can only be used on the ground.

9.6.9 Non-Normal Indications

If a fault is detected in one of the CRTs, the faulty display is blanked. Engine indications and crew alerting messages appear on the operable display as 'compacted' displays. An EICAS CRT and advisory message displays when one of the CRT fails. To ensure that all engine indications can be displayed with a CRT failure, an EICAS compacted display mode is available. However, a partial computed mode is available to display secondary indications if a red band or amber band indication was reached. In addition if a CRT fails, status can only be displayed on the ground.
When the partial compacted mode is used, secondary indications would only be displayed if an amber band or red band limit were reached.
When a CRT fails, status can only be displayed on the ground.

9.6.9.1 Control Panel Failures

If the EICAS Control Panel fails an EICAS CONT PNL advisory message displays and the EICAS full up engine mode automatically displays. The cancel and Recall Switches will not operate when the EICAS Control Panel fails. In the event of the failure of either both EICAS computers or both CRTs, a Standby Engine Indicator (SEI) is automatically activated. The SEI system lights and system indicators are used to monitor the engines and system operation when a total EICAS failure occurs.

9.7 Power Computation and Thrust Control

Modern aircraft are equipped with systems to control and compute engine thrust. The following section will discuss how engine thrust is computed, controlled and how engine inputs are collected. Basic engine indications and controls will be covered first.

9.7.1 Engine Instrumentation and Controls

We have already looked at the various instruments, controls, indicating and warning devices that are necessary for normal control and operation of a modern gas turbine engine. Instrumentation, controls, and fuel system arrangement may vary among engine series and models, but there will be a basic similarity.
The airframe manufacturer, with some input from the operator, will determine and be responsible for many of the items required in the final installation configuration.

9.7.1.1 Tachometers

A single compressor turbofan engine is normally equipped with a tachometer indicating N_2, the rotational speed of the high-pressure compressor. On modern turbofan engines an additional tachometer is provided, indicating fan (low-pressure compressor) speed (N_1) in percent of RPM. These instruments are 'pressure compressor' calibrated in percent of RPM rather than actual RPM. The compressor speed at which the tachometer indicates 100% is determined by the instrument drive gear ratio to the particular series engine. The 100% RPM values of any series or model engine will be found in the aircraft flight manual. The 100% RPM value depends on the instrumentation-to-engine relationship. You should note that indications of 100% N_1 or N_2 do not denote any fixed thrust levels, such as takeoff thrust, that are applicable to all aircraft. Under similar environmental conditions, each series or model engine will require different speeds to attain comparable thrust levels. The high-pressure compressor (N_2) tachometer is referred to primarily during starting, in order to determine the point at which fuel and ignition is to be applied, and to indicate start acceleration and overspeed conditions if one should occur. On the modern 'high bypass' turbofan engines it has been found that fan speed (N_1) provides an accurate indication for setting thrust.

9.7.1.2 Engine Pressure Ratio (EPR) Indicator

When used in conjunction with the basic turbojet and the aft fan turbofan engine, the Engine Pressure Ratio Indicator is considered the primary indicator for equivalent thrust measurement. The EPR instrument provides a readout of the ratio of the turbine discharge total pressure to the compressor inlet total pressure. The new high bypass turbofan engine has some what obscured the original concept of engine pressure ratio as a primary thrust measuring parameter.

9.7.2 Fuel Control

The fuel control also referred to, as the main engine control (MEC), is a hydro-mechanical fuel-metering device. The unit is an engine-driven accessory that regulates fuel flow to govern engine speed, control acceleration and deceleration rates, and compensate for altitude, temperature and compressor discharge pressure variations. The fuel control functions in response to:

- Compressor inlet temperature (CIT)
- Compressor discharge pressure (CDP)
- Core engine speed (N2)
- Power demand input (throttle position)

This control provides and schedules control fuel pressure, as a function of compressor inlet temperature (CIT) and core engine speed (N2), to actuating cylinders for positioning of the variable inlet guide vanes, stators and variable area bypass valves.
Some engines are fitted with an electronic system of control and this generally involves the use of electronic circuits to measure and translate changing engine conditions to automatically adjust the fuel pump output.

9.7.2.1 Fuel Control Systems

The usual method of varying the fuel flow to the engine is by adjusting the output of the high-pressure fuel pump. This is effected through a servo system in response to some or all of the following:

- Throttle movement.
- Air temperature and pressure.
- Rapid acceleration and deceleration.
- Signals of engine speed, engine gas temperature and compressor delivery pressure.

9.7.3 Setting the Power

9.7.3.1 Throttle

By placing the throttle in the cockpit to any position above IDLE, the main fuel control power lever moves accordingly to introduce the desired engine speed request. The fuel control meters the required fuel flow to maintain the core engine at selected speed, automatically compensating for variations in the high pressure compressor speed (N2), compressor discharge pressure (CDP), and compressor inlet temperature.

9.7.3.2 Determining Required Thrust

Thrust curves and charts published in the aircraft manual and in the performance manuals, are used to determine the required engine pressure ratio (EPR) and/or fan speed (N1) for any desired engine rating at prevailing ambient temperature and barometric pressure. Takeoff rated thrust is limited by time, engine speed, and exhaust gas temperature (EGT). Maximum continuous, maximum climb and maximum cruise thrust ratings are limited by EGT for a given length of time or continuously, as the case may be.

9.7.3.2.1 Rated Maximum Continuous Thrust

According to EASA, the maximum continuous thrust rating is defined in the flight manual. It is the thrust that is approved for unrestricted periods of use.

9.7.3.2.2 Maximum Continuous Thrust (MCT)

MCT is authorised for emergency use at the discretion of the pilot, for aircraft certification requirements and for climb operations as determined by the airframe manufacturer.

9.7.3.2.3 Maximum Climb Thrust

This thrust rating is the maximum thrust approved for climb. On some engines maximum climb and maximum continuous thrust levels are the same. To select the rating, the throttle is positioned to obtain the appropriate thrust setting value of engine pressure ratio (EPR) or fan speed (N1), for the prevailing climb profile and engine inlet temperature. The climb thrust curves or charts are contained in the aircraft performance manual.

9.7.3.2.4 Maximum Cruise Thrust

This rating is the maximum approved thrust for cruise operation. These ratings are warranty limitations established by the engine manufacturer to ensure optimum operation and engine life.

9.7.3.2.5 Thrust versus Inlet Air Density

The amount of thrust a turbofan engine is able to produce will vary greatly with the density of the air in the engine inlet. Air density is a resultant of barometric pressure (altitude) and ambient air temperature (OAT). In flight, thrust is also affected by airspeed. During flight, both the air temperature and pressure in the engine inlet will rise above ambient conditions due to ram effect. An engine can produce more thrust on a cold day than on a hot day. In response to a throttle setting, the main fuel control automatically compensates for variations in air density and engine inlet temperature and meters fuel flow to the engine accordingly to meet the engine speed demand input.

Considering the number of variables involved, it is obvious that when selecting a thrust rating, it is necessary to use the appropriate thrust curves or charts.

The required curves or charts for takeoff, climb, and cruise operations are provided in the aircraft performance manual.

9.7.4 Setting Thrust by Fan Speed (N_1)

With the development of the advanced technology high bypass turbofan engine, the use of an equivalent EPR system would necessitate an integrated version using pressures and areas of both the fan discharge and core jet nozzles.

Considering the close similarity of the high bypass turbofan engine to the fixed pitch propeller, and the fact that the fan generates the major part of the total thrust, the fan speed (N1) became a logical parameter for setting power.

Evaluation of analytical and experimental data has established that N1 provides minimum thrust spread and is insensitive to deterioration encountered during engine operation.

Various inter stage and compressor discharge bleed tests have also shown that 'thrust to N1' relationship is unaffected by bleed air extraction.

9.7.5 Determining Takeoff Thrust

Takeoff thrust values, expressed in the appropriate parameters Fan Speed - % N1 and/or engine pressure, operating at the high thrust levels for the shortest possible time and maintaining the lowest possible EGT conditions both have a very important bearing on the ultimate service life of the engine. Prolonged operation at takeoff thrust, particularly with abnormally high EGTs, must be avoided. The combined effects of high temperatures and high engine speeds are conducive to stress rupture and progressive oxidation in the turbine blades. When power changes are required, resulting in large EGT excursions, the changes should be made as slowly as practical to reduce thermal strain in the turbine nozzle and blade metals.

9.7.6 Reduced Thrust Takeoffs

Takeoffs made from today's long runways generally require considerably less thrust than all the available takeoff thrust developed by current and advanced technology commercial engines. In an effort to increase engine life, reduced thrust takeoff procedures have created considerable interest among operators.

Thrust reduction procedures are authorised by supplements to the JAA-approved manuals and do, within limitations, contribute toward increased engine life.

9.7.7 Calculation of Climb and Cruise Thrust

To determine the necessary thrust to obtain the desired climb and cruise performance, the pilot must consult the charts in the aircraft performance manual.

A simplified method to calculate reduced thrust is the assumed temperature method. This is based on using takeoff thrust and aircraft speeds for an assumed temperature higher than the actual ambient temperature (OAT). The assumed temperature procedure enables pilots to make thrust reductions to any extent permitted by prevailing conditions and within practical limits.

9.7.7.1 Climb

Climb thrust is established by adjusting the throttle to obtain the appropriate parameter indication (N1 or EPR) in accordance with the published climb thrust setting charts or curves. On some engines, the maximum continuous and maximum climb thrust levels may be the same.
During the climb, at fixed throttle, as altitude is gained and total air temperature decreases, fan speed (N1) and engine pressure ratio (EPR) increase progressively in accordance with the thrust curves. Normally only one or two throttle adjustments should be required throughout the climb, depending on whether a high speed or long range climb is being performed. Significant temperature and speed deviations may require slight throttle adjustments to avoid exceeding thrust curve values. Typical changes in ambient temperature and Mach number will not require any such adjustments.
Exhaust gas temperatures must be monitored throughout the climb to prevent exceeding the established maximum climb EGT.

9.7.7.2 Cruise

Upon reaching the selected flight level, climb thrust may be maintained long enough to expedite acceleration to cruising speed. To maintain the desired speed, the required N1 or EPR is set in accordance with cruise charts or curves applicable to the prevailing cruise conditions.
Cruise thrust values are based on cruising speeds, in knots of indicated airspeed (KIAS) and Mach number, aircraft gross weights, total air temperatures (TAT), and pressure altitudes. The charts and curves cover all realistic combinations of these factors, within the operational scope of the engine and aircraft up to and including maximum cruise thrust.
Exceeding maximum cruise thrust, to maintain altitudes and speed which are not compatible with aircraft gross weights, must be avoided. Maximum cruise thrust is an engine warranty limitation.

9.7.8 Fuel Flow Indications

In conjunction with N1 or EPR, fuel flow (normally Kg/h) is a reliable thrust setting parameter aiding in establishing balanced power. Fuel flow indication also provides a good check on proper engine operation. One of the first signs of engine malfunctions or fuel control troubles will be abnormal or erratic fuel flow.
The cruise thrust tables and curves in the performance manual, provided by the aircraft manufacturer, generally include the computed fuel flows associated with N, or EPR values.

9.7.9 Cruising Methods

Procedures used for cruising depend primarily on the length of time at cruise during a flight. For short flights, within given periods of time, depending on aircraft-engine type and cruising environments, the fixed throttle cruise will provide a favourable or acceptable balance of fuel consumed versus time saved. Once the thrust has been set to obtain the desired cruising speed, the throttle position may remain fixed throughout the cruising portion of the flight.

9.7.10 Electronic Engine Control (EEC)

Modern engines utilise a system of electronic control to monitor engine performance and make necessary control inputs to maintain certain engine parameters within pre-determined limits.
The main areas of control are engine shaft speeds and exhaust gas temperature (EGT) which are continuously monitored during engine operation. Some types of electronic control function as a limiter only, that is, should engine shaft speed or EGT approach the limits of safe operation, then an input is made to a fuel flow regulator to reduce the fuel flow thus maintaining shaft speed or EGT at a safe level.
Supervisory control systems may contain a limiter function but, basically, by using aircraft generated data, the system enables a more appropriate thrust setting to be selected quickly and accurately by the pilot. The control system then makes small control adjustments to maintain engine thrust consistent with that pre-set by the pilot, regardless of changing atmospheric conditions.

9.7.11 Full Authority Digital Engine Control (FADEC)

FADEC is a digital electronic fuel control for a gas turbine engine that functions during all engine operations, hence "full-authority." It includes the electronic engine control, functions with the flight management computer, and schedules the fuel to the engine in such a way that prevents overshooting of power changes and over-temperature conditions.

FADEC takes over virtually all of the steady state and transient control intelligence and replaces most of the hydro mechanical and pneumatic elements of the fuel system. The fuel system is thus reduced to a pump and control valve, an independent shut-off cock and a minimum of additional features necessary to keep the engine safe in the event of extensive electronic failure.

FADEC also furnishes information to the engine instrument and crew alerting system.

FADEC advantages include:

- Better performance - lower fuel burn
- Better operability - interaction with FMC data
- Increased engine life - better thrust overshoot protection

9.7.12 Thrust Management Computer (TMC)

The TMC is a component in the flight management system that senses the engine parameters and power requests and controls the thrust produced by the engines.

The TMC performs 'thrust limit' calculations and controls the autothrottle operation. Limits are based on selected mode and operating conditions and functions in all modes to maintain thrust within engine design parameters and prevent overboost or overspeed.

Throttle position for each engine is controlled to maintain a specific engine thrust e.g. N1, or target airspeed / MACH. Modern systems are designed to operate in conjunction with automatic flight control systems (AFCS) and flight management computer systems (FMCS). Thrust computation may also interface with IRS, EFIS and other systems. The thrust computations are conducted for various flight regimes (modes), from takeoff through to landing.

9.7.13 Autothrottle (A/T)

The autothrottle (A/T) system is a computer controlled electromechanical system that controls engine thrust within engine design parameters.

Throttle position for each engine is controlled to maintain a specific engine thrust (N1 or EPR) or target airspeed, for all flight regimes as directed by the TMC

The A/T and AFCS work together to maintain aircraft airspeed and vertical path. With the A/T 'ON', and either the autopilot or the flight director 'ON', airspeed is maintained by one system or the other. When the AFCS mode is controlling airspeed, the A/T controls engine thrust to a specific value. When the AFCS mode is controlling the vertical flight path, the A/T maintains airspeed through thrust control.

On some aircraft (Airbus) the FADEC driven engine's electrical signals for thrust control has been utilised in order to eliminate the weak points of the conventional autothrottle that moves mechanically. On the Airbus series of aeroplanes, the actual throttles (thrust levers) position does not move automatically. This is unlike the early autothrottles. When these were introduced they suffered from several weak points such as GO-levers, backdrives, clutches with spurious engine retards on take-off, jams and runaways.

The Airbus system can be operated with manual or autothrust. In manual thrust the pilot moves the thrust levers between idle and full thrust as usual. In autothrust, the thrust levers are set to a fixed position, which defines the maximum thrust available.

Whether in manual or auto-thrust, speed and power changes are monitored via N1, indicated speed and speed trend as on any aircraft.

Compared to the old system, this new system has a reliability, which according to Airbus, is increased by an order of magnitude. It may take a few minutes to get used to the thrust levers. It is a training issue and experience shows that pilots master the fully automated thrust levers after some practice in the simulator.

9.7.13.1 Thrust Management

The autothrottle operates in response to flight crew mode control panel inputs or to automatic FMC commands.

The autothrottle system:

- Uses reference thrust limits calculated by the FMC
- Commands the thrust levers
- Commands thrust equalisation through the electronic engine controls

The FMC calculates a reference thrust for the following modes (typical):

- Takeoff
- Reduced thrust takeoff (also called de-rated takeoff)
- Assumed temperature takeoff
- Climb
- Reduced climb
- Cruise
- Go-around

The mode used for thrust reference, automatically transitions for the respective phase of flight. These modes can be selected through the FMCS. The selected thrust reference mode is displayed on the thrust mode display.

9.7.13.2 Autothrottle Operating Modes

Autothrottle system operation is controlled primarily through the mode control panel (MCP) of the AFCS. There are basically two modes of operation: take-off and speed control mode.

Self-Assessment Test 09

1. The essential piston engine power measuring instruments are:
A) Fuel flowmeter and RPM indicator
B) RPM indicator, Boost or MAP gauge and torquemeter
C) Fuel flow, MAP and RPM indicators
D) RPM, torque, oil pressure and oil temperature

2. The essential turbo-prop power measuring instruments are:
A) RPM, torque and fuel flow
B) RPM, exhaust gas temperature and fuel flow
C) RPM and torque
D) RPM, torque and exhaust gas temperature

3. The essential turbo-jet thrust measuring instruments are:
A) JPT and RPM
B) EPR or RPM or EPR only if no RPM system fitted
C) RPM, fuel flow and oil temperature
D) RPM and EPR or RPM only if no EPR system fitted

4. TAT is the:
A) Total outside air temperature (TAT) and is sometimes called ram rise
B) Temperature derived from adding ram rise to SAT
C) Temperature derived for use by the digital engine control unit
D) Temperature derived for use by an ADC

5. A cylinder head temperature gauge would be typically of the:
A) Thermo-couple type
B) Mercury bulb type
C) Alcohol bulb type
D) Bourdon tube type

6. Manifold air pressure (MAP) is measures in units of:
A) Cms of mercury
B) PSI
C) Inches of mercury
D) Inches of water gauge

7. Fuel and oil pressures are usually measured by the operation of:
A) Spring balances and torsional rods
B) Metal capsules and/or diaphragms, and piezo electrical sensors on the latest aircraft
C) Bourdon tubes
D) Capillary tubes filled with mercury

8. Fuel flowmeters are usually of the:
A) Rotating turbine type
B) Rotating impeller type
C) Straight through tube type
D) Rotating vane or impeller/turbine types

9. Capacitors are incorporated into aircraft fuel tanks to:
A) Measure the quantity of fuel in the tanks, taking into account their shape, and correct for changes in fuel density
B) Balance out fuel tank levels when the aircraft is subjected to positive G conditions
C) Correct fuel content measurement when the fuel is contaminated with water
D) Improve the power factor of highly inductive AC motor driven fuel pumps

10. Two vibration sensors are fitted to turbo-fan engines and are located:
A) One in the combustion area and one on the exhaust unit
B) On the fan casing
C) One on the fan case and one on the engine core section
D) On the engine core section

11. The purpose of the EICAS/ECAM systems is to provide:
A) An analogue system of instruments which will indicate engine status
B) A comprehensive display of engine thrust management status and parameter stability
C) Engine indication displays and a centrally located crew alerting system
D) A centrally located control system which will respond to FMS as well as manual inputs

12. When the computer selector is set to AUTO, the:
A) Controlling element of the system is arranged so that automatic reversion to analogue instrumentation occurs in the event of a single computer failure
B) System is set so that both computers work in duplex
C) Right computer is in use; if this computer fails the left computer automatically takes over
D) Left computer is in use normally; if this computer fails the right computer automatically takes over

13. Typical engine parameters displayed on the upper screen are:
A) EPR, N1, EGT
B) EPR, N1, N2, N3, EGT
C) EPR, oil pressure, oil temperature, vibration level indicators, N3
D) N2, EGT, fuel flow, vibration levels

14. When the EVENT button is pushed in:
A) Current engine data is recorded and previous data is retained
B) Current data is recorded and previous data is erased
C) Only upper screen engine data is recorded
D) Only lower screen engine data is recorded

15. Typical engine parameters displayed on the lower screen are:
A) EGT, N1, EPR
B) EGT, N2, N3, vibration, oil press, oil temp, oil quantity, fuel flow
C) EPR, N1, oil press, oil temp, oil quantity, vibration, fuel flow, N2, N3
D) Oil press, oil temp, oil quantity, vibration, N2, N3, fuel flow

16. If the upper screen fails the:
A) Secondary engine indications are transferred to the lower screen
B) Primary engine indications are no longer available
C) Primary engine indications are transferred to the lower screen
D) Primary engine indications are transferred to standby engine instruments

17. Crew alerting is provided by:
A) Aural tones, master caution warning lights and three stages of alert messages
B) Master caution warning lights only
C) Aural tones only
D) Master caution warning lights and three stages of alert messages

18. Messages are removed from the displays when the:
A) Appropriate drill has been carried out whether or not the condition still exists
B) Associated condition no longer exists and pushing the CANCEL switch removes caution and advisory messages from the display
C) Associated condition no longer exists and pushing the CANCEL switch removes all messages from the display
D) CANCEL switch is pressed

19. When the RECALL switch is operated:
A) Warning messages, removed by operation of the CANCEL switch are reinstated
B) Warning, caution and advisory messages, removed by operation of the CANCEL switch, are reinstated
C) All warning messages are reinstated whether or not the CANCEL switch has been previously operated
D) Caution and advisory messages, which were removed by operation of the CANCEL switch, are reinstated provided the associated fault still exists

20. The status portion of EICAS is used to:
A) Check FMS readiness for the flight
B) Display maintenance data only
C) Determine aircraft readiness for dispatch and is activated by pressing STATUS on the control panel
D) Show upper screen primary engine indications status

21. An engine EPR indicator provides a readout of the ratio of the:
A) Turbine discharge total pressure to the compressor inlet total pressure
B) Turbine inlet pressure to outlet pressure
C) Compressor inlet to outlet pressure
D) Exhaust unit inlet pressure to outlet pressure

22. In the main, N2 and N1 are used to:
A) Set power and determine HP cock open point respectively
B) Set power only
C) Determine HP cock open point and to set power respectively
D) Set power and determine vibration monitoring point respectively

23. The usual method of varying fuel flow to the engine is by adjusting the output of the HP fuel pump. This is effected by a response to the following basic inputs to the fuel flow control system:
A) Air temperature and pressure
Acceleration and deceleration
RPM, EGT, compressor delivery pressure (P3)
Throttle position, exhaust unit pressure, jet pipe temperature difference
B) Throttle movement
Air temperature and pressure
Acceleration and deceleration
RPM, EGT and P3
C) Air temperature
RPM, EGT and P3
D) Throttle movement
Air temperature and pressure and EGT

24. Take-off rated thrust is limited in use by:
A) Time, RPM and EGT
B) Time only
C) RPM only
D) RPM and EGT only

25. Maximum Continuous Thrust (MCT) is:
A) Specified only for use in turbo-prop engines
B) Limited to RPM and EGT parameters for the power setting
C) Used at any time at the discretion of the aircraft Captain
D) Only authorized for specific reasons, for example, emergency use (one engine out) or climb power (for air traffic purposes) as stated in the flight manual; there is sometimes a specific and cumulative time limit per flight

26. Reduced thrust take-offs are used where authorized and:
A) May be carried out in accordance with the instructions set out in the flight manual. Typically, take-off mass will be at a set value below the maximum all up mass for the runway and much conservation in engine life is achieved
B) May be carried out at any time at the discretion of the Captain irrespective of all up mass and much quieter operations result
C) Is a requirement of most international airports; the power setting is the same as MCT
D) Is the same as noise abate power; therefore, when used, noise regulations are not infringed irrespective of the selected noise abate option

27. When Cruise altitude is reached:
A) Power is reduced to the selected cruise thrust immediately and speed will increase to cruising speed eventually
B) As in A above but MCT is set if cruising speed is not achieved within 15 min
C) The aircraft is leveled out, the speed is allowed to rise to the selected cruise Mach number or IAS, and cruise power is then set
D) The limiting EGT for the condition is selected and the electronics limiters control the engine thereafter

28. An Electronic Engine Control System provides:
A) Full fuel flow control and throttle setting functions regardless of engine thrust lever position
B) Full fuel flow control which operate once the trust lever is put into the required thrust range
C) A limiter function for engine RPM and EGT and fine adjustment to engine fuel flow, to take account of changing atmospheric conditions, once the thrust lever is set to the power required. Engine fuel control system hydro-mechanical components are utilised for main fuel control operation
D) Control of RPM only and relies on the thrust lever setting to select the RPM mode depending on the thrust range required

29. A Full Authority Digital Engine Control System (FADEC) provides:
A) Fuel pump and HP cock position requirements
B) Positive control of bleed air requirements for air conditioning and ice protection systems
C) Partial control of fuel flow requirements but a mechanical/fuel control unit provides positive control of thrust lever settings
D) Complete electronic control of fuel flow scheduling to take account of thrust lever settings and ambient conditions, and replaces virtually all of the traditional hydro-mechanical components except for the fuel pump and the HP (shut-off) cock

30. The thrust management system computer:
A) Is controlled by the auto-throttle system and directly schedules power requirements to the FADEC system
B) Senses engine parameters and power requests, controls the thrust produced by the engine via the auto-throttle system and interfaces with the requirement of the AFCS and FMS for automatic operation
C) Interfaces with the mode selector panel only
D) Has replaced the auto-throttle as an engine thrust control system

31. Auto-throttle operation is controlled primarily by the:
A) Mode control panel (MCP) of the AFCS and there are two modes of operation
B) Pitch attitude of the aircraft as selected by the AFCS to control the IAS
C) Operation of the speed control input selector which is operated in conjunction with the IAS speed control selector
D) Deflection of the glide slope only after acquisition of the ILS

Self-Assessment Test 09 Answers

1	B
2	C
3	D
4	B
5	A
6	C
7	B
8	D
9	A
10	C
11	C
12	D
13	A
14	B
15	D
16	C
17	A
18	B
19	D
20	C
21	A
22	C
23	B
24	A
25	D
26	A
27	C
28	C
29	D
30	B
31	A